STUDIES IN IMPERIALISM

general editor John M. MacKenzie

Established in the belief that imperialism as a cultural phenomenon had as significant an effect on the dominant as on the subordinate societies, Studies in Imperialism seeks to develop the new socio-cultural approach which has emerged through cross-disciplinary work on popular culture, media studies, art history, the study of education and religion, sports history and children's literature. The cultural emphasis embraces studies of migration and race, while the older political, and constitutional, economic and military concerns will never be far away. It incorporates comparative work on European and American empire-building, with the chronological fr primarily, though not exclusively, on th twentieth centuries, when these cultur most powerfully at w

MANCHESTER
UNIVERSITY PRESS

Propaganda and Empire

THE MANIPULATION
OF BRITISH PUBLIC OPINION
1880–1960

John M. MacKenzie

MANCHESTER UNIVERSITY PRESS
Manchester and New York

Distributed exclusively in the USA by
ST. MARTIN'S PRESS

Published by **MANCHESTER UNIVERSITY PRESS**
OXFORD ROAD, MANCHESTER M13 9NR
and ROOM 400, 175 FIFTH AVENUE, NEW YORK, NY 10010, USA

Distributed exclusively in the USA
by **ST. MARTIN'S PRESS, INC.**
175 FIFTH AVENUE, NEW YORK, NY 10010, USA

British Library cataloguing-in-publication data
MacKenzie, John M.
  Propaganda and empire: the manipulation of
  British public opinion, 1880–1960.
  1. Public opinion — Great Britain. 2. Mass
  media — Great Britain. 3. Commonwealth of Nations
  — History. 4. Great Britain — Colonies —
  Public opinion.
  I. Title.
  909´.0971241081   DA18

                              ISBN 0-7190-1869-2

Library of Congress cataloging in publication data
MacKenzie, John M.
  Propaganda and empire
  Bibliography: p.259
  Includes index.
  1. Great Britain — Colonies — Public opinion.
  2. Public opinion — Great Britain. 3. Propaganda,
  British — History — 19th century. 4. Propaganda,
  British — History — 20th century. I. Title.
  JV1011.M34 1984   325´.341   83-25325
  ISBN 0-7190-1869-2

ISBN 0 7190 1869 2 *paperback*

Reprinted in paperback 1985, 1988, 1990, 1994, 1997

Printed in Great Britain
by Redwood Books, Trowbridge

CONTENTS

ILLUSTRATIONS

ACKNOWLEDGEMENTS

A work of synthesis of this sort owes extensive debts to many people. A number of scholars may, if they ever read this book, recognise the obligations I bear to their work. I trust that all have been adequately acknowledged in the footnotes, and that paraphrase has never slipped into plagiarism.

More personally, I should like to thank a number of friends and colleagues who have lent books and advice, donated ideas and offprints, or risked letting me loose in their private collections: Frank and Gladys Bell, Patrick Dunae, Philip French, Simon Holt, John Heeley, Lawrence James, John Lynton, Tony Mangan, Norman McGilvray, Maurice Rickards, Alec Ross, Penny Scales, John Springhall, Penny Summerfield, and John Walton. Donald Simpson and his staff at the Royal Commonwealth Society Library have been unstinting in finding materials and sharing information. Peter Glenn opened up some of the fascinating Bethnal Green Museum of Childhood collections for me. Judith Knight, at the Grange Museum of Local History, gave me an enthralling day exploring that museum's remarkable collections of material on the Wembley Exhibition. Rachel Hasted of the Lancashire County Museums Service not only demonstrated to me the riches of childhood memorabilia, but also shared with me her knowledge of school archives and log books in Lancashire, some of which she has herself rescued. James Porter, the Director of the Commonwealth Institute, kindly arranged for me to use the Imperial Institute records at the Public Record Office released from the thirty-year rule.

My colleagues at the University of Lancaster have proved forbearing, receptive even, in the face of my Celtic loquacity, while the Senate Research Grants committee of the same university won relief by providing me with a grant for part of the research. Terence Ranger and Paul Hair have encouraged me in all my work. I owe a particular debt to Stephen Constantine and Jeffrey Richards, who permitted me to read unpublished work, lent me innumerable materials, and provided friendship, advice, and conversation far beyond the call of professional duty. The Calvinist work ethic of my parents, the dedicatees of this book, played no small part in its completion. Nigel Dalziel helped in more ways than he even realises. Amanda MacKenzie lightened the labour of indexing.

J.M.M.

Defenders of the Empire

AFRICA

CANADA

INDIA

1924

AUSTRALASIA

FROM THE PICTURE PRODUCED BY RAPHAEL TUCK & SONS L^TD

FOR

MACDONALD, GREENLEES & WILLIAMS (DISTILLERS) L^TD

LEITH LONDON ABERDEEN & GLASGOW

SOLE PROPRIETORS OF

CLAYMORE, OLD PARR AND SANDY MACDONALD

SCOTCH WHISKIES

INTRODUCTION

The British, it has often been said, were indifferent to imperialism. Apart from a brief, aberrant (and indeed disputed) burst of jingoism in the last quarter of the nineteenth century, they concentrated on more hard-headed domestic affairs. By the 1920s all residual imperial sentiment had been destroyed by the First World War. Imperialism as a sophisticated concept had been, and remained, the preserve of an elite, and a fractured elite at that. The public's lack of ideological commitment was matched by almost complete ignorance of the territories of Empire, the principles of its government, or the economic dimensions of the imperial connection. It was this combination of indifference and ignorance which ensured that the Empire was never a significant electoral issue and that decolonisation was accomplished without any of the national trauma experienced by France.[1] Indeed, by the time decolonisation had been achieved, Empire was already forgotten, surviving in the national consciousness as little more than a source of nostalgic philately.

Imperialism failed to make an impact, the argument continues, because of the diffuse nature of the British imperial experience, and because the Empire was never given a powerful constitutional or cultural expression. The Empire was at least four separate entities. It was the territories of settlement, which by the era of 'popular imperialism' were beginning to emerge as semi-independent political units. It was India, its central economic significance masked by the romantic aura Disraeli created round it in the 1870s on the eve of the 'new imperialism'. It was a string of islands and staging posts, a combination of seventeenth-century sugar colonies and the spoils of wars with European rivals, China and other non-European cultures. And finally, Empire was the 'dependent' territories acquired largely in the last decades of the nineteenth century. The Empire's diverse character ensured that imperialism meant different things to different people at different times. Such attempts as there were to develop a grander design were bedevilled by this problem of definition. And so was any effort at national comprehension.

Such is, perhaps, conventional historical wisdom. The purpose of this book is not to assault the essentials of this view. In some respects, indeed, they are unassailable. But that is not to suggest that imperialism was thereby an insignificant element in British domestic social

[1]

history in the late nineteenth and early twentieth centuries. The idea that Empire was unimportant to the public has arisen from an excessive concentration on the effects of Britain on the Empire. Imperial history and the imperial idea have been examined almost entirely in a centrifugal manner, as the radiation of influences from Britain into its wider hinterland. Imperialism on the domestic scene has been discussed largely as the debate of an elite, while 'popular imperialism' has been approached by those more interested in elements of popular culture than in imperialism itself. This study seeks to explore the centripetal effects of Empire, in creating for the British a world view which was central to their perceptions of themselves. Even if they knew little and cared less about imperial philosophies or colonial territories, nonetheless imperial status set them apart, and united a set of national ideas which coalesced in the last three decades of the nineteenth century. As Field has put it, imperialism should be studied as an essential part of British social history.[2]

It is possible to identify an ideological cluster which formed out of the intellectual, national, and world-wide conditions of the later Victorian era, and which came to infuse and be propagated by every organ of British life in the period. It was made up of a renewed militarism, a devotion to royalty, an identification and worship of national heroes, together with a contemporary cult of personality, and racial ideas associated with Social Darwinism. Together these constituted a new type of patriotism, which derived a special significance from Britain's unique imperial mission. That the mission was unique in scale was apparent to all. That it was also unique in its moral content was one of the principal propagandist points of the age. Empire had the power to regenerate not only the 'backward' world, but also the British themselves, to raise them from the gloom and apprehension of the later nineteenth century, and by creating a national purpose with a high moral content lead to class conciliation.

It has often been said that propaganda does not come easily to the British, that official propaganda was contemplated only in the conditions of the First and Second World Wars, and then only reluctantly, and principally for the consumption of foreigners, allies and neutrals.[3] Home government propaganda was virtually unknown. As the following pages will demonstrate, this was not true in the case of imperialism. Indeed, imperial propaganda was the one area of official propagandist activity which seemed to be generally acceptable, for reasons which will be discussed. But the government effort was never very considerable, largely because it was unnecessary. A large number of imperial propagandist agencies were founded in the later nineteenth century, and their ideas and influence extended deeply into the educational system, the armed forces, uniformed youth movements, the Churches and missionary societies, and forms of public entertainment like the music hall and exhibitions. Many of the most important companies of the day issued imperial propaganda through advertising and other marketing techniques. Sources of popular entertainment like the music hall and later the cinema embraced the new imperial nationalism, while juvenile literature and publishers' lists generally found the imperial adventure tradition socially and politically acceptable, as well as immensely popular. In other words, a wide variety of non-governmental agencies discovered that imperial patriotism was also profitable.

There can be no doubt that much of this activity was overtly propagandist. Propaganda can be defined as the transmission of ideas and values from one person, or groups of persons, to another, with the specific intention of influencing the recipients' attitudes in such a way that the interests of its authors will be enhanced.[4] Although it may be veiled, seeking to influence thoughts, beliefs and actions by suggestion, it must be conscious and deliberate. The study of censorship will always be an important part of the consideration of propaganda, for, as Philip Taylor has put it, 'censorship and propaganda are Siamese twins, inseparable and inextricable'.[5] Much 'conscious and deliberate' propaganda was conveyed through all the agencies cited above by means of the various media examined in the chapters that follow. Many of them wished to propagate a view of the world which was essential to their own successful operation, and most of them made knowing and intentional efforts to control individual thought. Particular attention will be paid to theatrical and cinema censorship, which go far to illustrate official attempts to influence popular culture.

One of the central concerns of this book must be an examination of the extent to which all this constituted self-generating ethos reinforcement, a constant repetition of the central ideas and concerns of the age, and how far it represented conscious manipulation on the part of those who controlled the powerful religious, commercial, military, and official agencies. To what extent was an essentially middle-class ethos transferred to the other social classes through the potent media of printing, photography, spectacle, and pageant? The rapidly expanding paper, printing, photographic, display, and advertising industries (surveyed in chapter 1) were well placed to serve the ideological convergence of the day by creating for the Establishment what were in effect the first embryonic mass media.

Reverence for the monarchy developed only from the late 1870s, and when it did it was closely bound up with the monarch's imperial role. Republican associations proliferated in the early '70s during the period of the Queen's seclusion in her widowhood at Windsor.[6] Between 1861, the year of Albert's death, and 1876 she made few public appearances and refused to participate in national ceremonies. When she re-emerged to open Parliament in 1876, it was to announce a change in her royal style and titles. She was to be proclaimed Empress of India, and thereby legitimate her imperial status in the relationship between the Crown and the princely rulers of the subcontinent.[7] The Indian rulers were now to be integrated into British aristocratic principles, provided with armorial devices, a variety of symbols of status, and a strict order of precedence, a process which was begun in the Prince of Wales's visit to India in 1875-76. As the Queen transformed herself in the public mind from petulant widow to imperial matriarch, it was her world-wide role which at one and the same time provided her with excitements and concerns in her old age and a new significance to the ceremonial surrounding her. That she was a Tory imperialist herself is beyond doubt (even if tempered by many of the philanthropic and humanitarian concerns of the age), and the public was more than dimly aware of where her preferences lay.[8]

As her power declined, her ceremonial role grew.[9] In the 1880s she opened the Exhibition of Shipping, Commerce, and Industry at Liverpool, the Indian and Colonial Exhibition in London, and laid the foundation stone for the Imperial Institute. All were enacted with considerable pageantry, replete with imperial trappings, poetry by Tennyson and music by the composers of the contemporary renaissance of English music. If there were still some rumblings of anti-monarchical feeling in the Jubilee celebrations of 1887, they had largely disappeared by 1897. *Lloyd's Weekly* (with a million sales) was critical of the 1887 jubilee, but had become unswervingly loyal by 1897. By the latter date there was much press comment on the role of the monarchy in uniting the classes, and on the beneficial propagandist effects of the jubilees on schoolchildren. A local study of the 1897 jubilee in Cambridge has revealed that if there were class disputes about the actual organisation of the jubilee there were none on the principle of the jubilee itself.[10] Both the 1887 and 1897 celebrations brought to London colonial Premiers and Indian princes, together with troops and retainers as exotic in their race, colour, and creed as they were colourful in their uniforms. From then until the accession and coronation of Elizabeth II all great royal occasions would be imperial, drawing to the capital apparently loyal denizens from the furthest corners of the Empire.[11] Edward VII, George V and George VI wholeheartedly accepted their imperial role, and shared, in suitably

[4]

modified form, Victoria's politics. Even if Edward VIII did not share his father's or his brother's personal morality or acceptance of the ceremonial role, he nonetheless contributed to the imperial image of the monarchy through his extensive Empire tours. Coronations, funerals, weddings, and jubilees all followed and elaborated the late Victorian precedents, and the wave of programmes, ephemera, publications, films, and later broadcasts which accompanied each of them all invested the monarchy with a global imperial mystique. Until the 1870s royalty was seen to contain little in the way of opportunities for commercial exploitation. From that date, advertising, bric-a-brac, and packaging all exploited royalty and imperialism, taking symbols of colonial adventures into every home. For imperialism made spectacular theatre, with the monarchy its gorgeously opulent centerpiece (though Victoria herself often resisted display).

The growing popularity of the armed forces antedated the enhanced reputation of the monarchy by several decades. Military subjects had long been popular in spectacular theatrical presentations and in melodrama.[12] But it was not until the second half of the nineteenth century that the army and its personnel rose in the public's esteem. Regiments became a source of local and civic pride, a vital part of national and local ceremonial and pageantry, particularly after the great expansion in the number of army bands took place. The new respect for the army was a product of the fear of militarist European nationalisms and the recurrent invasion scares of the nineteenth century and the years before the First World War. Military sentiments and rhetoric spread into civilian life. The cult of the Christian military hero developed out of the Indian Mutiny and reached its apotheosis in General Gordon.[13] Through army chaplaincies and missions the Churches began to take a more active part in army life, and in return the Churches took on a more militant and militarist tone which infused the missionary evangelicalism and revivalism of the period. The language of war entered into hymns, tracts, and sermons. The paramilitary organisation and ranking of William Booth's Christian mission, the Salvation Army, founded in 1878, were specifically designed to exploit the popular militarism of the contemporary Russo-Turkish war. It was followed by the Church Army and uniformed youth organisations which began to drill and to process in church. As a result, many of the Churches were swept up into 'the tidal wave of race patriotism' of the late 1890s and Edwardian years.[14]

It was a short step to the dissemination of militarism in the schools. The public schools became wholehearted exponents of the new militarism, closely intertwining it with patriotic and imperialist endeavour.[15] The games field came to be seen as a preparation for war, and some schools specifically devoted themselves to the education of the officer corps.[16] State schools were now urged to take the public schools as their model, and the successful aping of militarist ideology and training became the leading imitative norm. Cadet corps proliferated in both types of school from the 1880s. Drilling was adopted as a crucial source of discipline in working-class State schools. Military activities became an important source of recreation for the working classes, through the highly successful Volunteer forces, rifle clubs, ceremonial and drill units in factories, and brigades of shoeblacks and other youthful street arabs and industrial apprentices. In all these ways a very large proportion of the population came to have some connection with military and paramilitary organisations.[17] Popular recruitment was enhanced and the scene was set for the dramatic waves of volunteering for the armed services in the Boer War and in 1914.

Not surprisingly, this popular military activity was matched by an appropriate ideology. War came to be seen as a 'theatrical event of sombre magnificence', while theories of the inevitability of warfare emerged from the social application of Darwinism.[18] Warfare was endemic to civilisation, it was argued, both in the competition of rising States and in the conflict between them and their decaying counterparts. In naval building, the manufacture of armaments, and the soaking up of excess labour, it was crucial to the modern industrial economy. It was, moreover, a source of personal and national moral regeneration. There have been efforts to absolve the working class from jingoist militarism, but they do not convince. Richard Price's attempt to demonstrate a low working-class involvement in the Boer War[19] has been effectively countered by Michael Blanch.[20] In any case, by the end of the century, the working men's clubs from which Price derives so much of his evidence had adopted the patriotic music hall as their principal attraction, and rifle clubs and service associations had become an important part of their range of 'interest groups'.[21]

Juvenile literature of all sorts exploited this interest in warfare and militarism and wedded it to an overseas adventure tradition which became the leading popular literary genre of the period. The locus of hero-worship moved from Europe to the Empire; colonial exploits were enthusiastically followed by the public; war became a remote adventure in which heroism was enhanced by both distance and exotic locales. Modern armament technology ensured that the risks to European troops were relatively slight. The popular press exploited this spectatorial fascination with colonial warfare, and its power was such that not only the jingoist *Daily Mail* but also labour papers like

Reynold's News were swept up into it. In 1898 the *Labour Leader* complained that the working class were more interested in celebrating Omdurman than in supporting the Welsh coal strike.[22]

It was perhaps, principally through warfare that the racial ideas of the day were diffused to the public at large. Concepts of race were closely related in popular literature to the imperative of conflict between cultures, and the evidence of superiority it provided. Colonial heroes became the prime exemplars of a master people, and this enhanced their position in the military cult of personality. Their fame enabled them to exert great influence in leading service and conscription associations and youth organisations, in travelling extensively on speaking visits to schools or in public lectures in civic halls, as well as participating in ceremonial throughout the country.

The assembling of this ideological cluster of monarchism, militarism, and Social Darwinism led to a dramatic shift in the class and intellectual context of the 'language of patriotism'. Whereas in the early nineteenth century patriotic rhetoric had been seized by political radicals, it was progressively reclaimed by government in the succeeding decades, particularly in time of war. Hugh Cunningham sees the 1870s as the vital decade in the wedding of patriotism to the new nationalist, imperialist, and royalist ideology, in the new romantic treatment of the Indian Empire, and the famous outburst of jingoism of 1878.[23] Patriotism became the 'key component of the ideological apparatus of the imperialist state'. It also became a vital counterweight to class consciousness, 'a half-accepted false consciousness' for the working classes. A very considerable debate has indeed raged around the class dimensions of the late nineteenth-century fervour. The attempt to acquit the working class of contamination can be discounted, but the accusation that the lower middle class and the aristocracy of labour were the prime mediators of the popular imperial ideology between the upper classes and the rest of society is more difficult to dispose of.[24]

The diversion of working-class consciousness into patriotic imperialism and 'social chauvinism' was of course postulated by Lenin. He attributed the 'temporary decay in the working-class movement' to 'the tendency of imperialism to split the workers'.[25] The natural leadership of the labour movement was 'bribed' by the economic benefits of imperialism, and in consequence trade union and other labour organisations in Britain permitted socialist internationalism to be subverted by a dominant imperial nationalism. Hobsbawm eleborated this thesis and found in it the source of the developing social stability of the mid-nineteenth century.[26] In this period the semi-skilled lost ground to the skilled, and the aristocracy of labour, which constituted 15% of the working class by 1890, were assimilated to the conservatism and respectability of the middle-classes, apparently confirming the process of bourgeoisification of the proletariat which Engels had identified and which Orwell noted anew in the 1930s.[27] In Birmingham the dominance of skilled trades ensured that past radicalism was forgotten, and the city largely followed Chamberlain into Conservative imperialism. Queen Victoria expressed a gratified surprise at the unexpected adulation she received there in 1887.[28] An onlooker at the 1887 jubilee celebrations was reported to have said that years of socialist activity had been destroyed on that day.[29] The labour aristocracy thesis has been carried forward into the 1920s, and has been used to explain the failure of the General Strike and the increasing 'respectability' (including imperial respectability) of the Labour Party in that decade[30] Non-Marxists have suggested that the aristocracy of labour was a much more heterogeneous group than the Marxists would allow, prepared to pursue their own independent economic and social ends by whatever means lay open to them.[31]

This debate has intersected with the discussion between the revisionist optimists and the traditional radical pessimists on leisure, a discussion which has centred on the problem of whether popular culture was the 'locus of struggle or of control',[32] whether class consciousness was diverted into 'controlled decorum', 'obedient recreation',[33] whether leisure was class-conciliatory or created means of class expression.[34] Opportunities for recreation were widened by shorter hours of work and an increased surplus income available for leisure pursuits. Together these stimulated a mass leisure market, which was soon taken over by capitalist operations like the music hall.[35] Some recent studies have revived the hegemonic theory of Gramsci, that power lay with those who 'controlled the means of mental production', whether in education or in mass entertainment like the music hall or later the cinema.[36] The question resolves then into the extent to which the diffusion of the core patriotic ideology was supply- or demand-orientated.

It has, moreover, become customary to stress the stability and conservatism of British society in the late nineteenth and twentieth centuries. Brian Harrison, writing of the 1880s, has suggested that the forces for stability in that decade were able to counterbalance the forces for social disruption.[37] Martin Wiener has surveyed the mental and cultural 'gentrification' of the industrial bourgeoisie, such that the aristocracy succeeded in 'educating its successors to its world-view'.[38] And by the 1880s and '90s part of that world view was the greater social acceptability of occupations in the army and the Empire than in the demeaning world of business. In the same period, as Noel Annan has put it, the 'propaganda of the intelligentsia' became 'the accepted gospel of the country'.[39] Each of these debates will necessarily be touched upon in this book.

Yet despite these controversies there has been little attempt at a synthesis of studies of education, juvenile literature, the theatre, youth organisations, and propagandist movements, which have a significant bearing upon these problems of leisure, ideology, and social discipline. Moreover, there has been little attempt to take the debate beyond the First World War. The war has acted as a convenient climax to most studies, and the inter-war years have not been blessed with the close examination the earlier period has enjoyed. Many historians have merely argued from silence. Those dealing with some aspect of popular imperialism or militarism have usually concentrated on the late Victorian and Edwardian periods, when such manifestations are most apparent. They have invariably seized upon the all too convenient means of winding up with the bald suggestion that after the First World War imperialism was discredited and lost much of its popular edge. Historians who have dominated the inter-war period, themselves often intellectually influenced by the ideas of the 1920s and '30s, have discounted imperialism as having any significance for the public at large. Indeed, the public are alleged to have viewed Empire with the greatest indifference. By the 1930s emigrants were returning, disillusioned, with unhappy tales of an Empire failing to live up to its propagandist promise.[40]

Some have seen the Boer War as cracking the imperial spirit.[41] More conventionally, the Great War has been regarded as the critical turning point. The war, it is alleged, was followed by a period of pacifism, and militarism and imperialism were so intertwined in the late Victorian and Edwardian periods that revulsion from the one led to rejection of the other. After 1918 imperial propaganda had lost its power. Imperial studies fell on hard times.[42] The membership of the Royal Colonial Institute, which had burgeoned, went into steep decline.[43] The Empire Exhibition at Wembley in 1924-25 was treated with contempt by the intelligentsia and as a mere funfair by the populace.[44] The most successful of the youth movements adapted to the new creed of internationalism in order to protect and develop their membership.[45] Moreover, one of the most important vehicles of the popular imperialism of the nineteenth century, the music hall, was rapidly becoming moribund,[46] and the people turned from a jingoistic topicality to a romantic escapism.

There are, perhaps, two problems to an over-eager acceptance of this view. The first is that the intelligentsia have too often been allowed to speak for everyone. The classic expressions of alienation from the imperial ethos by Robert Graves, H. G. Wells, E. M. Forster, and George Orwell, among many others, have been seen as representative of a general spirit in the inter-war years. Yet Orwell himself pointed out that the intelligentsia had become cut of from the common culture of the people and went on to argue for a new alliance between intelligence and patriotism.[47] The second problem is the continuing one of definition. Imperialism is of course open to many different definitions, but in its popular context it has usually been seen as synonymous with jingoism — aggressive, offensive, and xenophobic. But there is no reason why a popular imperialism should be so narrowly defined. Those who deplored jingoism were often the most fervent exponents of a 'moral' imperialism, and it was just such people who controlled the levers of propaganda between the two wars, a time indeed when the professions of marketing, public relations, and propaganda (including censorship) all came of age. At the end of the First World War a greatly extended Empire no longer seemed to be under serious threat. Much of the landscape of a defensive, nationalist popular imperialism had become so familiar as to be barely noticed. A Britain without an Empire seemed almost a contradiction in terms. If it was, quite simply, there, a source of pride, not lightly to be put aside, it was also to gain a new economic significance. The crucial thing now was to exploit it more effectively in a period of increasing world economic difficulty. As in the late nineteenth century, Empire could be portrayed as a means of arresting national decline.

It was in such an atmosphere that popular imperialism seemed to secure dramatic new cultural and institutional expressions. Music hall was replaced by even more powerful media in the cinema and broadcasting. Although the need for official propaganda, directed towards 'selling' Britain in the rest of the world, was slow to gain acceptance in Whitehall, nonetheless much propaganda was directed at the public at home. Imperial exhibitions, school texts, popular juvenile literature, the ephemera issued by commercial companies and mission societies remained little changed from their pre-war guise, and all continued to convey an imperial message. The cinema found the adventure tradition of imperial literature congenial to treatment on celluloid. The British documentary film movement, for all its alleged left-wing commitment, in fact had its origins in an imperial propagandist body, the Empire Marketing Board, and treated Empire as an existing commitment, open to reform perhaps, but offering the British public excitement (imperial air routes and the like) and valuable products (Ceylon tea, etc.). Reithian broadcasting sought to educate the public to a national consensus which included a royal and imperial ethos as part of an immutable order. In short, an implicit imperialism, partly economic, partly moral, underlay most propagandist and entertainment output in the 1920s and 1930s. In 1940 George Orwell was able to write that he felt a positive surge of patriotism, for 'that long drilling which the middle class go through had done its work'.[48] Orwell went on to consider the extent to which the middle class had also successfully drilled the rest of the population.[49]

This book aims to use popular imperialism as a focus for the examination of the theatre, the cinema, education, juvenile literature, imperial exhibitions, youth movements, and a variety of imperial propaganda bodies between the mid-nineteenth and mid-twentieth centuries in an attempt to underline the strengths and durability of imperial propaganda. Some of the material constitutes a synthesis of work not previously brought together; the rest emerges from research in little-noticed areas of imperial propaganda. These are of widely varying significance, some relatively obscure, others in central, yet ignored, fields like the teaching of imperialism in schools. But each derives its true importance from its position within a strikingly consistent overall picture. At the end an attempt will be made to establish imperialism and its related reverence for royalty and other elements of established authority, its racial ideas, its national complacency and conceit, as a core ideology in British society between the 1880s and the 1950s.

The mid-1980s seems an appropriate time to undertake such a study. A generation of scholars has emerged largely uncontaminated by intellectual influences of the 1920s and '30s which so often misled their predecessors. Moreover, the Falklands war of 1982 aroused many echoes of the earlier period of popular imperialism — the jingoistic press, the wildly enthusiastic reception of returning troops and ships, victory parades, repeated medal distributions, the stealing of the clothes of patriotism by an established government, and the apparent lulling of domestic economic and social discontents. Increased newspaper circulations, higher viewing figures for television, and the major publishing event which the war constituted seemed once more to confirm Hobson's 'spectatorial passion' induced by warfare.[50] Once again the Church seemed to be overwhelmed by the combination of government propaganda and popular enthusiasm. The Bishop to the Armed forces spoke of the campaign as acting upon the nation 'like a purifying fire', an argument for the moral effects of warfare strikingly akin to those of the late nineteenth century, while some historians and politicians began to call for the teaching of a new nationalist and patriotic history in schools.[51]

[11]

J. H. Plumb has remarked that 'the old past is dying, its force weakening, and so it should. Indeed, the historian should speed it on its way, for it was compounded of bigotry, of national vanity, of class domination.'[52] Maybe that past lingers on. This book seeks to expose the extraordinary durability of the late nineteenth-century ideological conjunction, the striking congruence of which carried it forward to the mid-twentieth century, and contributed to the national conceit and complacency which have, perhaps, proved such a barrier to Britain's economic progress.

NOTES

1 Henry Pelling, 'British labour and British imperialism', in *Popular Politics and Society in Late Victorian Britain*, London, 1979, 82-100. James Morris has written that few people in Britain found the Empire interesting, and its dissolution was met with indifference. James Morris, 'The popularisation of imperial history', *Journal of Imperial and Commonwealth History*, 1 (1973), 113-18.

2 H. John Field, *Toward a Programme of Imperial Life*, Oxford, 1982, 20.

3 Philip M. Taylor, *The Projection of Britain: British Overseas Publicity and Propaganda, 1919-1939*, Cambridge, 1981. M. L. Sanders and Philip M. Taylor, *British Propaganda during the First World War*, London, 1982. See also Cate Haste, *Keep the Home Fires Burning*, London, 1977, which does emphasise the role of home propaganda.

4 For good definitions of propaganda, see Richard Taylor, *Film Propaganda*, London, 1979, 19-20, and Taylor, *Projection*, 4-5.

5 Taylor, *Projection*, 4.

6 For an excellent discussion of the rolling back of republicanism by pageantry and ritual, see P. S. Baker, 'The Social and Ideological Role of the Monarchy in Late Victorian Britain', unpublished M.A. dissertation, Lancaster, 1978. See also Jeffrey L. Lant, *Insubstantial Pageant*, London, 1979.

7 Bernard S. Cohn, 'Representing authority in Victorian India', in E. J. Hobsbawm and T. O. Ranger (eds.), *The Invention of Tradition*, Cambridge, 1983, 165-209.

8 Richard Faber, *The Vision and the Need*, London, 1966, 90. See also Frank Hardie, *The Political Influence of the British Monarchy*, London, 1970, 11-39.

9 David Cannadine, 'The context, performance and meaning of ritual: the British monarchy and the invention of tradition, 1820-1977', in Hobsbawm and Ranger, *Invention*, 101-64.

10 Elizabeth Hammerton and David Cannadine, 'Conflict and consensus on a ceremonial occasion: the Diamond Jubilee in Cambridge in 1897', *Historical Journal*, 24 (1981) 111-46.

11 The public programmes of both the coronations of George VI in 1937 and Elizabeth II in 1953 were firmly imperial, bearing the arms of all the Dominions and colonies on their covers and listing all the colonial troops present.

12 J. S. Bratton, 'Theatre of war: the Crimea on the London stage, 1854-5', in David Bradby *et al.* (eds.), *Performance and Politics in Popular Drama*, Cambridge, 1980.

13 Olive Anderson, 'The growth of Christian militarism in mid-Victorian Britain', *English Historical Review*, LXXXVI (1971), 46-72.

14 Stephen Koss, 'Wesleyanism and Empire', *Historical Journal*, XVIII (1975), 110.

15 Geoffrey Best, 'Militarism and the Victorian public school' in Brian Simon and Ian Bradley (eds.), *The Victorian Public School*, London, 1975, 129-46.

16 Best, 'Militarism', 131-2. See also J. A. Mangan, *Athleticism in the Victorian and Edwardian Public School*, Cambridge, 1981.

17 Hugh Cunningham, *The Volunteer Force*, London, 1975. M. D. Blanch, 'British society and the war', in Peter Warwick (ed.), *The South African War*, London, 1980.

18 John Gooch, 'Attitudes to war in late Victorian and Edwardian England', in B. Bond and I. Roy (eds.), *War and Society*, London, 1975, 91-3. Anne Summers, 'Militarism in Britain before the Great War', *History Workshop*, 2 (1976), 104-23.
19 Richard Price, *An Imperial War and the British Working Class*, London, 1972.
20 Blanch, 'British society'.
21 John Taylor, 'From self-help to glamour: the working men's club, 1860-1972', History Workshop pamphlet No. 7, 1972, 31. See also Gareth Stedman Jones, 'Working-class culture and working-class politics in London, 1870-1900', *Journal of Social History*, 7 (1973), 460-508.
22 Blanch, 'British society', 216.
23 Hugh Cunningham, 'The language of patriotism, 1750-1914', *History Workshop*, 12 (1981), 8-33.
24 R. N. Price, 'Social status and jingoism: the social roots of lower middle class patriotism, 1870-1900', in Geoffrey Crossick, *The Lower Middle Class in Britain*, London, 1977, 89-112.
25 V. I. Lenin, *Imperialism: the Highest Stage of Capitalism*, London, 1968, 100.
26 E. J. Hobsbawm, 'The aristocracy of labour', in *Labouring Men*, London, 1964, 272-303.
27 Quoted in Lenin, *Imperialism*, 100. Orwell wrote of an enlarged middle class, spreading 'middle-class ideas and habits among the working class'. 'To an increasing extent, the rich and the poor read the same books, and they see the same films and listen to the same radio programmes.' George Orwell, *The Lion and the Unicorn*, London, 1982, 66-7.
28 Colin Ford and Brian Harrison, *A Hundred Years Ago*, London, 1983, 263.
29 Lant, *Insubstantial Pageant*, 13.
30 John Foster, 'British imperialism and the labour aristocracy', in Jeffrey Skelly (ed.), *The General Strike, 1926*, London, 1976.
31 Robert Q. Gray, *The Aristocracy of Labour in Nineteenth Century Britain, 1850-1914*, London, 1981.
32 Robert D. Storch (ed.), *Popular Culture and Custom in Nineteenth Century England*, London, 1982, introduction, 13.
33 Gareth Stedman Jones, 'Class expression versus social control? A critique of recent trends in the social history of leisure', *History Workshop*, 4 (1977), 163.
34 Hugh Cunningham, *Leisure in the Industrial Revolution*, London, 1980, 11. Peter Bailey, *Leisure and Class in Victorian England: Rational Recreation and the Contest for Control, 1830-85*, London, 1978.
35 Peter Bailey, 'Custom, capital, and culture in the Victorian music hall', in Storch (ed.), *Popular Culture*, 180,205.
36 S. Humphries, '"Hurrah for England": schooling and the working class in Bristol, 1870-1914', *Southern History*, 1 (1979), 172. Lawrence Senelick, 'Politics as entertainment: Victorian music hall songs', *Victorian Studies*, XIX (1975), 149-180.
37 Ford and Harrison, *Hundred years*, 199.
38 Martin S. Wiener, *English Culture and the Decline of the Industrial Spirit, 1850-1980*, Cambridge, 1981.
39 Quoted in Wiener, *English Culture*. 131.
40 A. J. P. Taylor, *English History, 1914-1945*, Oxford, 1965, 300-1.
41 James Morris, *Farewell the Trumpets*, London, 1979, 91. Koss, 'Wesleyanism and Empire', 105-18. Pelling, *Popular Politics*, 100.
42 J. G. Greenlee, 'Imperial studies and the unity of the Empire', *Journal of Imperial and Commonwealth History*, VII (1979), 332.
43 Trevor Reese, *History of the Royal Commonwealth Society*, London, 1968, 134. However, membership grew to a record figure in 1930, and after some initial decline in the 1930s reached a new peak in 1939.
44 Morris, *Farewell*, 302.
45 Paul Wilkinson, 'English youth movements, 1908-1930', *Journal of Contemporary History*, 4 (1969), 16. J. O. Springhall, *Youth, Empire, and Society*, London, 1977, 63.
46 Senelick, 'Politics as entertainment', 180. Senelick suggests that music hall declined because imperial sentiment declined. In fact it was merely superseded by other forms

of entertainment, and imperial sentiment migrated into them.

47 George Orwell, *The Lion and the Unicorn*, 63-5

48 George Orwell, 'My country right or left', *Collected Essays, Journalism, and Letters of George Orwell*, London, 1970, 591.

49 For example, George Orwell, 'Boys' weeklies', *Collected Essays*, 505-31.

50 J. A. Hobson, *The Psychology of Jingoism*, London, 1901, 12.

51 *The Guardian*, 21 and 22 June 1983.

52 J. H. Plumb, *The Death of the Past*, London, 1969, 145.

The late nineteenth-century imperial world view was an integral part of the commercial, industrial, and social revolution which took place in Britain between the 1850s and 1914. During that period the population nearly doubled; incomes exhibited a similar growth at a time when prices remained relatively steady; and British society achieved nearly universal literacy.[1] Dramatic changes occurred in patterns of consumption in the last two decades of the century as new sources of supply were opened up, new tastes created, new means of preservation, packaging, and marketing found.[2] There were also unrivalled opportunities for the leisure and entertainment industry, and a voracious new demand for collectible items, which contributed to the taste for bric-a-brac so characteristic of all but the very poorest of homes. All these changes reflected technical developments which lay at the heart of the 'new imperialism', providing its motive power, its justification, and also the instruments through which its propaganda could be disseminated.

It has been customary to see the age of the mass media as arriving with the cinema, the wireless, and television. But before the era of the electrical and electronic media, printed and visual materials became available at prices so low as to place them in almost every home. It is perhaps difficult for us, jaded by the printed word and the omnipresent electronic image, to comprehend fully the impact of these materials. There seems to have been a craving for visual representations of the world, of events, and of the great and famous, which a large number of agencies and commercial companies sought to satisfy in the period from the 1870s to the First World War. New advertising techniques were central to all this activity, and companies creating and supplying the new tastes were concerned to sell not just their own product, but also the world system which produced it. The most aggressive and innovative advertisers of the day were companies dependent on the imperial economic nexus, in tea, chocolate, soaps and oils, tobacco, meat extracts, shipping, and later rubber. They set out not only to illustrate a romantic view of imperial origins, a pride in national possession of what Joseph Chamberlain called the imperial 'estates', but also to identify themselves with royal and military events, and to score from the contemporary cult of personality.

In his classic description of Edwardian Salford, *The Classic Slum*,

Robert Roberts refers to a 'culture of the streets from which the young especially profited'.[3] It consisted of 'information of every kind from posters and advertisements', the 'regular scrutiny of newsagents' windows', which were 'festooned' with hundreds of picture postcards, the new marketing gimmick, cigarette cards crying out to be collected, and a wealth of boys' papers which could be read and swapped. Such ephemera (a term belied by the craze for collecting which they engendered) became a prime source of news, information, and patriotic and militarist propagada. During the First World war this material inevitably became devoted almost entirely to patriotic ends, and, as we shall see, its imperial and colonial content became even more pronounced. The period from the late 1890s to 1918 has often been seen as the golden age of picture postcards, cigarette cards, juvenile journals, and the like, but in fact they continued to be used for propagandist ends until after the Second World War. Moreover, it was between the wars that marketing and advertising emerged as a separate profession, and they helped to sustain a new range of popular journals and literature in that period. The provision of ephemera and popular literature of all sorts will be an underlying theme in what follows, for many of the agencies described in subsequent chapters made assiduous use of the public interest in such material and the collecting activities associated with it.

It was of course nineteenth-century developments in printing that created this new mass medium of the printed word and the visual image. During the century, conservatism in printing was gradually broken down; wood gave way to iron, and steam power was applied from 1810.[4] But more important was the gradual widening of the range of printing processes. Specialised areas of printing appeared, stimulated by and in turn stimulating mechanical innovations. By the last quarter of the century; rotary presses, mechanised typesetting, and a range of machines for different types of printing were available. The treadle and light jobbing platens made possible large runs of posters, leaflets, and the like. Some aspects of mechanisation, including machine binding, aided the collapse in the unit cost of book production, a vast expansion in the publishing trade, and the first appearance of cheap popular editions available for every home. All this was made possible by associated developments in the paper industry. Hand-made rag paper was the rule until the middle of the century. The invention of the wood-pulp and other natural processes, together with the rapid development of machine manufacture, greatly reduced the cost of paper, assisted by the removal of all paper duties in 1861. Annual production in Britain expanded from 11,000 tons in 1800 to 100,000 tons in 1860, and to 652,000 tons in 1900.[5] Recent research indicates that the growth may have been even greater.[6] At the beginning of the century, the printed word had still been the preserve of a small social class, and books were expensive even by today's standards. Printers and binders concentrated on the aesthetics of their trades, and were more interested in short runs of high value than in the wider dissemination of their wares. By the last quarter of the century all that had changed.

The new processes rendered large print runs of popular editions highly profitable. Publishing houses like Nelson grew rapidly after the introduction of the rotary press from the 1850s, and began to cater for a fast-expanding juvenile market, as well as for the new taste in books of illustrations and information.[7] All the literary classics were reissued in cheap editions, at prices as low as 6d, 3d, or even 1d.[8] But even more important than the classics were works which enshrined contemporary hero-worship, the cult of personality which was an inseparable part of imperialism. Stories of travel and exploration, missionary writings and biographies, the endless stream of popular lives of General Gordon and other heroes, books celebrating military and naval exploits, the 'romance' of transport, communications and engineering, the excitements of migration and pioneering life, the quaint and exotic among indigenous peoples of the Empire, all these became Christmas and birthday present staples, and above all prizes for school and Sunday school. To them we can add the vast range of children's novels and stories by G. A. Henty, F. S. Brereton and others, surveyed in chapter 8. In some working-class homes a little library of such books would be composed entirely of prizes for regular attendance at the Band of Hope or Sunday school.[9] Publishers provided both propaganda and bribes, dressed up in dust jackets (invented in this marketing age) and board covers which vividly conveyed the message carried within. Even if books were not read, their owners could scarcely miss the stirring titles and equally exciting cover illustrations which depicted an heroic and expansionist age, in which fellow countrymen generally overwhelmed or converted people of 'lesser' cultures.

Even more influential was the burgeoning popularity of journals for boys and, later, girls. A tremendous expansion in the publication of juvenile literature occurred in the 1870s and 1880s. At first, adult middle-class opinion saw this growth as untrained, rank with murder, crime, and sensation. A considerable controversy raged about the nature and quality of the material, and the provision of satisfactory periodicals for adolescents became part of the search for 'rational recreation', so much a feature of the age. Journals acceptable to adults' conception of appropriate juvenile interests, mainly enshrining adventurous and militaristic patriotism, began to appear from the late 1870s.

Dozens of different titles appeared, many sold for only a penny, and some of them reached enormous sales. They were exceptionally sensitive to developments in national concerns and contemporary events, as is illustrated by the new range of journals which mushroomed in the jingoistically dank conditions of the Boer War.[10]

The growth of 'jobbing' printing led to a great increase in the publication of leaflets, pamphlets, booklets, programmes, and other small ephemeral items which could be distributed free as advertising and propaganda or sold for a few pence each. Such material was used by all forms of entertainment, by the exhibitions, the armed forces, and missionary societies. Much of it must indeed have been ephemeral, but some was sufficiently attractive to be collected, and contemporary agencies and advertisers certainly saw these cheap pieces of printed paper as an effective way of purveying their ideas or their wares. Posters could be run off at the rate of 10,000 an hour at extraordinarily low cost from the 1860s, and 'poster art' emerged as a new art form which was to reach a great peak in production and quality in the inter-war years of the twentieth century.[11]

As this 'veritable revolution' in printing was taking place, another, visual, revolution was under way.[12] Whereas printing advances represented dramatic change in an old technology, photography represented an entirely new one. Photography perfectly demonstrated the rapidity of technical and scientific discovery of the period, and at the same time literally captured the world on glass and paper. It has been described as offering a new lining to the human brain;[13] it captivated contemporaries, not just by transmitting and revealing the 'realities' of a newly opened world (like Felice Beato's photographs of Japan in the 1860s), but by offering them the opportunity to illustrate their achievements to their successors.[14] Through photography Europe could provide itself with a visual representation of the remodelling of the world through economic and political control. From the 1850s travelling photographers set out for North Africa, Egypt, India, Burma, and China to create and satisfy both a new taste for exotica and a fascination with the technology, the ships, railways, post offices, troops and arms, which facilitated Western intrusion in far-flung parts of the globe.[15] As Ian Jeffrey has put it, the camera became a coloniser, a preparer of the route to European expansion in the late nineteenth century.[16]

Above all, the camera was a source of entertainment, creating as much pleasure, as Jane Carlyle asserted, as any other development of the century.[17] But it was to take some time for photography to democratise itself. Until the 1890s it remained largely an aristocratic and upper middle-class preserve. The first books of photographs were all very expensive. By the last quarter of the century, photographers were selling 'shilling' views, and, judging by surviving albums, members of the middle class began to collect the small *cartes de visite* photographs of royalty, famous statesmen, soldiers, and theatrical personalities as part of a developing personality cult, a careful manipulation of publicity by public figures ranging from the royal family (whose photographic popularity was engineered by the Queen herself) to music hall celebrities. Large framed photographs, instead of paintings, appeared on the walls of middle-class homes.

The main photographic craze of the period before the 1890s probably did not penetrate far into the working-class home either. This was the stereoscope, which was invented in time for the Great Exhibition of 1851, and no fewer than one million were sold within three months. It experienced a great growth of popularity from the 1860s, and the leading stereoscope company made 'One in every home' its marketing ambition.[18] The principle of the stereoscope was that two photographic images viewed through lenses in a simple hand-held or table-top device provided a three-dimensional effect. Vast numbers of stereoscope cards in sets were produced, and many of these represented other places, other climes, offering visual imperial propaganda for colonisation and migration. Some remain important photographic sources for the period, but the relative lateness of the popular exposure to photography is reflected in the actual growth rather than decline in wood-block engraving before 1890. Not until the invention of photographic film made possible the appearance of the cheap Eastman Kodak camera from 1888 could the magic circle of practitioners wrestling with complicated equipment and chemicals be extended. But more important than the practice of photography was the printing of the results. Processes for rapid and cheap printing of large runs appeared in the 1890s, and only then could the shilling view become the penny postcard view.

Until that time all but the most expensive books continued to be illustrated by woodcuts, and woodcuts (often themselves copies of photographs) continued to reign supreme in the illustrated journals like the *Illustrated London News*. Although there had been attempts to introduce the photographic half-tone in popular newspapers in the 1880s and 1890s, it was not until 1904 that they began to appear regularly. The photographic journals in existence by 1899 could not be produced cheaply enough to secure a mass circulation. Earlier in the century, Charles Knight's *Penny Magazine* and *Penny Cyclopaedia*, both using woodcuts, had sold as many as 200,000 and 75,000 copies respectively. But they had collapsed when production costs pushed their price up from the original basic penny. The *Illustrated London News*, founded in 1842, became a prime conveyor of the dominant attitudes of the late nineteenth-century, but its circulation was never large enough to be described as truly popular. Its engravings, however, provided some of the most striking imperial and militarist icons of the age, and large numbers of servants (at a time when domestic service remained the largest single employer) must have seen copies when their masters and mistresses were finished with them. The difficulties of producing popular visual journals at the right price were well illustrated by George Newnes's *Ideal Magazine* of 1903. It attempted to use coloured photogravure, but the costs were too high, and only one issue appeared.

The influence of cheap photography, its sharpness of definition, its immediacy, even attempts at colour, were to be conveyed primarily through the sales of photographic ephemera. The democratisation of the visual image was undertaken by the postcard, and it must be seen as a central element in the ephemera boom of the period. The height of the picture postcard's popularity is generally regarded as lying between 1898 and 1918, a period in which it represented something of a mass craze in Europe, the United States, and the British Dominions.[19] The expansion of companies producing them, the millions purchased and posted each year, and the mania for preserving and collecting them, were a phenomenon of the age, meriting much comment at the time. The postcard represented a set of technical achievements — in photography, printing and mass production, not to mention the extension and speed of the postal service — which together symbolised several of the great achievements of the Victorian age. The Queen herself was fascinated by photography all her life, both as a source of entertainment to herself and as a means of influencing her subjects.

The postcard's antecedents reflected the possibilities of visual propaganda. Engravings at the head of notepaper and above all on envelopes did much more than simply offer pretty pictures: they were propagators of news and propagandisers for issues of the day, from Chartism to Sabbath observance, from temperance to imperial policies (for example, the issues associated with the Gordon crisis in the Sudan in 1884-85).[20] By the end of the century the picture postcard, astonishingly cheap to purchase and to post, was becoming the supreme vehicle for these various purposes, the dissemination of news and views in images which heightened the actions of the age, pictures that encapsulated the world, and brought it into even the humblest living room, the supreme expression of control through a particular type of slanted visual understanding. There was nothing objective about photography so used, and, far from tending to 'deflate prevailing romantic rhetoric', it helped to inflate it.[21] Both sentiment and romance were never far from nineteenth-century photography, and it was a short step to propagandist manipulation, as Dr Barnardo's fake photographs of indigent children and the carefully posed 'before' and 'after' transformations illustrated.[22]

The postcard canalised photographic developments, and offered cheap visual reminders of other aspects of popular culture. It took over the role of the stereoscope, visual notepaper and envelopes, and gave wider circulation in yet cheaper form to songs and ballads, music hall turns, and sentimental poetry about emigration and the armed forces. Above all, the postcard contributed massively to the royal, political, military, and missionary personality cult of the period.[23] Issues on regiments, armaments, naval ships and navy life contributed greatly to the militarism of the age and aided recruitment. In the very earliest edition of *Scouting for Boys* Baden-Powell advised Scouts to collect postcards of naval vessels, so that they could understand the important defence issues of the day.[24] Both the Boer War and the First World War gave a massive fillip to the use of the postcard for propaganda purposes. The Dominion governments used them to encourage emigration, while companies like Lever Brothers, Lipton's, Fry's, and Cadbury's issued them not only to advertise their wares, but also to present an imperial economic and social ethos, reflecting a chain of activity from the colonial tropical product to the contented workers of Port Sunlight or Bournville.[25] Even those without an overtly propagandist purpose helped to reinforce contemporary attitudes, illustrating architecture, public occasions, transport, and the whole range of economic enterprises of the age. Indeed, postcard production was one of the most notable areas of commercial expansion. One source lists over three hundred postcard companies which appeared at this time, and there were many more local photographers, printers, stationers, and chemists, all producing cards of both local and national interest.[26]

The postcard was influential as news disseminator and educator. As Robert Roberts put it:

> English traders soon realised that a new craze had arrived.... Clubs sprang up in every town and people collected and exchanged specimens. A family album filled with a varied selection was not the least item of entertainment in an evening spent at home. To a child avid for experience a newsagent's shop with a good display provided pleasure free and delightful. The picture postcard became a new aid to self-education as effective as any of his school lessons. Every great event of the day was reflected in illustration and explained in simple text.[27]

The power of the postcard was recognised early. Sir Evelyn Wrench, later founder of the English-speaking Union, founded a postcard company in 1900 when he was only eighteen, with the twofold intention of matching German success in postcard production, and commemorating contemporary events.[28] Wrench formed a connection with W. T. Stead, editor of the *Review of Reviews*, through Stead's son Henry, and Stead soon became involved in using postcards to further imperial ends, notably tariff reform and imperial preference. Several companies formed close links with the armed forces and issued sets of cards to aid recruitment and secure public favour.[29] The missionary societies all issued large numbers of cards to secure both financial and moral support for their work. Inevitably, they heightened the heroism of missionary endeavour and the 'primitiveness' and 'superstitions' of the peoples of the missionary fields.

Vast numbers of cards were produced of the Empire itself, recording new buildings, transport and engineering achievements, colonial products, visits of governors and royalty, colonial forces and frontier warfare, labour migration, 'ethnics' showing the whole range of indigenous peoples under imperial rule, pioneering farmers, prospectors and miners, together with romantic (and sometimes fictional) deeds of imperial heroism. Not only were these cards sent through the post by people who had emigrated or by members of the armed forces, they were also available – since most of them were produced by British companies – at the corner shop. The important companies, like Tuck's, Valentine's, Rotary Photographic and others, marketed their wares everywhere. Sales of cards were not limited to the areas they represented, as today's garish counterparts tend to be. Shops maintained a full range, and people collected them just like stamps. Picture postcards were a great deal more than a means of communicating a quick message.

Postcards experienced only a slow decline after the First World War. The larger companies were still in business; the armed forces continued to make effective use of them until after the Second World War, as did the missionary societies. The Imperial Institute began to use them extensively in the 1920s and 1930s to convey its propaganda on the economic benefits of empire. The Empire Marketing Board produced several sets during its period of operation between 1926 and 1933. A fresh wave of patriotic, militarist material appeared with the Second World War, and if the imperial content was now rather more muted, it was nonetheless still present.

Cigarette cards, the other most influential form of ephemera, experienced a similar development. Despite their name, cigarette cards were issued not just by tobacco companies, but by a whole range of other concerns, including most notably tea, confectionery, and magazines. One source lists almost two hundred tobacco companies that issued cards, and another catalogues more than three hundred companies of all sorts which used cards as a marketing technique.[30] Cigarette cards seem to have had their origins in the 1880s, but it was not until the end of the following decade that they began to experience a boom, helped along, like so many propagandist and marketing techniques, by the Boer War. Robert Roberts was even more unequivocal about the power of the cigarette card:

> 'Programmed' learning and visual aids, too, came to the child in the shape of cigarette card series. The value of the 'fag' card from 1900 onwards, as a conveyor of up-to-date information was enormous. First used in plain board to stiffen the paper packet holding cigarettes, it developed into offering a panorama of the world at large. The Ogden tobacco company alone, with its original 'Guinea Gold' brand, issued no fewer than eight thousand pictures, from nature series of all kinds through patriotic sets to 'Statues and Monuments'. In the end, all the great tobacco companies took up the gimmick and no field of popular human knowledge seems to have been left unexplored. Before 1914 it would have been hard indeed to have found a boy in the working class without at least a few dog-eared cards about his person, dreaming of making up, by swap and gambling games, that complete set of fifty.[31]

Speaking of the 1930s, a film critic, Philip French, has asserted that he learned as much about the world from cigarette cards as he did from the cinema,[32] while John Julius Norwich has written of the same period that Empire 'was all around us, celebrated on our biscuit tins, chronicled on our cigarette cards, part of the fabric of our lives. We were all imperialists then.'[33]

Analysing cigarette cards is rather easier than analysing postcards, for it is a more restricted and better recorded medium. Almost all the sets issued are known, and all their titles have been listed. But if the subjects of cigarette cards are more circumscribed than those of postcards, their circulation almost certainly was not. It is impossible to secure figures, but the sets of the larger companies, like W. D. & H. O. Wills, John Player, Churchman, and the like must have been distributed in large numbers. Five subjects predominate: sports, music hall performers and later, film stars, the armed forces, the Empire, and transport. Every company, almost without exception, issued sets on the armed forces, and sets of colonial troops and Indian regiments are common. Empire flags and coats of arms, Dominions, builders of Empire, British Empire series and scenes, picturesque peoples of Empire, products and industries of Empire, are all frequently found, as are Boer War sets, deeds of the Great War, and many others. Many featured the Royal Navy, merchant shipping, and railways, all celebrating technological achievements which seemed to lay the world open to British commerce and British people. Boy Scouts and Girl Guides prompted a number of sets soon after their founding, and many more appeared through the First World War and to the 1930s. The cult of personality was developed in cigarette cards even more notably than postcards, for many sets featured royalty, generals, admirals, war heroes, and medal winners.

Because of a shortage of paper, production was suspended between 1917 and 1922, but they soon recovered their popularity and continued to be issued in large numbers up to the Second World War and beyond.[34] Empire and military subjects remained popular throughout. If John Player had a 'British Empire' series in 1904, they also had a 'Military Uniforms of the British Empire Overseas' set in 1938. W. D. & H. O. Wills had 'Builders of the British Empire' in 1898, 'Indian Regiments' in 1907, 'Arms of the British Empire' in 1910, 'Governors General of India' in 1911, several series of 'Overseas Dominions' in 1915, 'Picturesque People of the Empire' in 1926, and 'Flags of the Empire' in 1926 and again in 1929. Gallaher's had a South African series in 1901, their first Boy Scouts set in 1911, and 'Scenes from the Empire' in 1939, while Churchman produced a set of the British Empire in 1934. Lambert & Butler had a set advertising Rhodesia as a destination for emigration in 1938, no doubt because they bought their tobacco from that colony.

These are only a few of the series relating to Empire from the largest companies. Hundreds of similar sets were issued by smaller concerns. Military and naval sets emphasised imperial unity in defence and the benefits to Britain of colonial forces, white and native. Transport series, which continued into the 1960s long after other imperial themes had disappeared, emphasised an alleged British maritime supremacy. Air transport sets, most common in the 1930s, were invariably presented in the context of 'Empire Air Routes'. In 1928 there was even an anonymous Empire shipping series that may have been connected with the Empire Marketing Board. Imperial and military themes, their popularity heightened by the periodic stimulation of warfare, continued to be much in evidence to the Second World War and beyond.

J. A. Hobson commented on the power of advertising to convey dominant ideas of the age in *The Psychology of Jingoism*.[35] In the last two decades of the nineteenth-century the growth of newspapers and popular journals had led to a tremendous growth in the advertising industry.[36] Indeed, an extraordinarily high proportion of such journals was devoted to advertising in the effort to keep unit costs down to achieve a mass circulation. Much of this advertising in newspapers, on hoardings, postcards and cigarette cards sought to convey the romantic and adventurous connotations of the companies' products, to associate them with the leading figures, stirring events, or royal occasions of the age. Liebig's Extract of Meat Company seized upon the Emin Pasha expedition of 1887, issuing posters and adverts of members of the relief party revived by its product.[37] A famous Bovril advertisement during the Boer War purported to demonstrate that Lord Roberts's route had spelt out the word Bovril across the Orange Free State.[38] Bovril produced many other advertisements describing its role as a comforter of the troops. Army and Navy Stores, founded in 1871, inevitably used patriotic images of the two services and their flags as its trade mark. Tobacco companies adopted patriotic names for their products at an early date. Cigarettes were of course particularly identified with the armed forces, with names like 'First Lord', 'Flagship', 'Invader', 'Royal Navy', 'Silent Force', 'Target', 'HMS' 'Soldiers of the Queen', 'Admiral', 'Grand Fleet', 'Fighter', 'Victory', 'Welldone', and 'British Pluck' (the latter a tobacco tin showing Boers being put to the sword).[39] One company issued the 'Havelock' brand, with a picture of Havelock before Lucknow, while another continent's lore was invoked in 'Cape to Cairo'.[40] In the 1920s the Prince of Wales appeared on the cover of the 'Prince Charming' brand.

Tea, biscuit, and tobacco companies were able to package their products in tins and boxes, which could be adorned with pictures of members of the royal family, famous generals and other heroes, and royal or military occasions.[41] Lipton's emphasised their vertical control of the tea industry, 'from the tea gardens to the tea pot', and illustrated their advertisements with elephants bearing tea chests from Ceylon to the home retailer. Horniman's, Mazawattee, the C.W.S., and other tea companies used similar images and sentiments in their advertising. Camp coffee associated itself with the army in India, while Fry's, Cadbury's and Lever Brothers all sought to illustrate their imperial connections together with their social concern for both their domestic labour force and their colonial suppliers. The popular art on imperial, royal, and military subjects by artists like Lady Butler, Harry Payne, George Havant, Fred Evans, Cress Woolett, and R. Caton Woodville appeared on postcards, in advertisements, and as marketing attractions. *Cassell's Magazine* Christmas number in 1900 offered 'Goodbye', the 3rd Battalion Grenadier Guards Leaving Waterloo Station for the Front, by George Havant, exhibited at the Royal Academy in 1900, as a free gift.[42] *Welldon's Illustrated Dressmaker* offered a whole range of souvenirs of the coronation of 1902 which included pictures of the Proclamation at Calcutta, at Ottawa, and at Sydney. 'A Chip of the old

Block' a watercolour by Fred Evans (portraying an old soldier in uniform drilling a young lad) was one of four coloured plates given with *Pears' Annual* of 1907. Harry Payne's 'Defenders of the Empire' was used in the '20s to advertise Claymore Scotch whisky. There is evidence to suggest that these sentimental and patriotic free gifts were framed and hung on school walls by teachers. These examples could be multiplied many times.

Some companies, particularly tea, biscuit, and tobacco concerns, exploited the commemorative market with special packaging at times of jubilees and coronations, and securing contracts from cities and municipalities throughout the country to supply chocolates and biscuits to schoolchildren and others. Less durable items included commemorative table and tea cloths bearing flags and arms of imperial territories as well as royal and military images. Commemorative plates, mugs, and cups have a longer history, from the eighteenth century, but it was in this period that they became readily available to the entire population. The jubilees of Queen Victoria in 1887 and 1897 produced a plethora of such material, and all subsequent coronations and jubilees became significant commercial events. The distribution of mugs, as with chocolate and biscuit tins, became one of the prime means by which school boards encouraged patriotism in schoolchildren. They were given out to commemorate royal visits, the opening of public buildings, and other occasions, as well as the great national royal events.[43] Much of this material was overtly imperial in tone, bearing impressions of the flags of the Dominions and the like. Some of the commemorative plates contained surprising quantities of information. One, issued for the 1887 Jubilee, bore a world map of the Empire, the arms of Australia, Canada, Cape Colony, and India, a scene of Australian troops on march in the Sudan, a clock showing G.M.T. and the time around the Empire, figures of population, total area, imports and exports, as well as images of Britannia flanked by colonial 'types', the Prince of Wales, and of course the Queen herself.[44] The mottoes included 'Ubi virtus, ibi Victoria' and inevitably, 'The Empire on which the Sun never Sets'. The Boer War produced a fresh spate of commemorative pottery and china. One plate was adorned with pictures of 'highlander' and 'Colonial' troops, marines with artillery, flags and flowers, and the legends 'War Declared in South Africa by President Kruger, October 11th, 1899, Lord Roberts, Commander-in-Chief, Cape Colony, General Buller, Commander-in-Chief Natal', 'Ready Aye Ready 1900', and 'England Expects Every Man to Do His Duty'. A baby's plate from the same period contained pictures of Generals Kitchener and French and the legend 'Conquer or Die'.

Politicians and generals, together with heroes like Livingstone and Gordon, were commemorated on plates and in a great range of Staffordshire pottery busts to adorn mantelpiece and dresser. Particular events produced 'novelties' of many sorts. The martyrdom of General Gordon stimulated the production of anti-Gladstone, pro-Gordon materials ranging from medals to bookmarks, jugs to scraps for children's albums.[45] The 1897 Jubilee was celebrated in the 'filoscope', a collection of photographs of the processions, which, when flicked through rapidly, produced an impression of movement. These are but a few examples of the bric-a-brac which, treasured in many homes, continued to radiate imperial and patriotic images long after the events they commemorated. In all these ways the imperial myths were exploited for commercial ends.

The late nineteenth century was a period when board games also became exceptionally popular.[46] There are some excellent geographical and topical examples from earlier in the century, but these were expensive and cannot have had a wide circulation. By the end of the century they were being produced very cheaply, and were used as teaching aids, often reflecting the military and imperial preoccupations of the age. Many used maps as the setting over which the game was played. The Emin Pasha relief expedition inspired such a game, as did some of the wars of the period. There were games on the Russo-Turkish War of 1877-78, several on the Spanish-American War of 1898, the Boer War (like 'The Siege of Ladysmith') and many others. There was an invasion scare game in 1910, a whole range of Scout games ('Scout Tests', 1911, 'Scout Signaller', 1915, and 'Scout's Outfit', 1915), generally depicting the role of Scouts in war. The First World War produced 'Trencho' in 1917, and George Newnes issued the 'Strand' war game for 1s 3d in 1915. There were many aviation games (like 'Sky Raiders') and naval variants ('Dover Patrol', 'Naval Tactics') in the years between the wars. Even jigsaw puzzles had topical and propagandist content.[47] A set of twelve featured 'Stanley in Africa'; Nelson issued in 1900 a set of 'Soldiers of the Queen' (one portrayed 'The Charge of the 21st Lancers at Omdurman'); jigsaws of coronations, jubilees and members of the royal family were commonplace.

Toy soldiers were even more significant as recruiters for the forces than board games or jigsaws.[48] The firm of Britain's dominated the market after they had succeeded in casting hollow soldiers, thereby greatly reducing the cost. By the last decades of the century, these were being produced in massive numbers and with great sophistication, representing all British, Indian, and colonial regiments, as well as allies, enemies, and 'ethnic' fighters. The company's catalogue continued to include much of the same material up to the 1950s. As is well known, Winston Churchill had a large collection of toy soldiers, and seems to have found some emotional satisfaction in drilling them. E. H. Shepard, the illustrator, described in his memoirs his favourite game of lining up black and white soldiers against each other. The biography of a recent Falklands War victim seems to indicate that he was led to the forces by his toy soldier collection.[49] No doubt toy soldiers appealed to children of all ages, but there were also patriotic and military materials, dressed up in educative guise, for very young children. Mr and Mrs Ernest Ames produced an 'A.B.C. for Child Patriots', in which each letter stood for some patriotic or xenophobic slogan, as well as 'The Tremendous Twins' or 'How the Boers were Beaten in Verses and Pictures'.[50]

Commercial companies also attempted to satisfy the craving for information and facts of all sorts which had developed by the end of the century. Local companies produced almanacks and manuals full of the standard images of the age. For example, T. Dawson, a tea dealer, grocer, provision and corn merchant of Bradford published one annually for his customers. The 1898 edition contained over fifty pages of information and advertisements, together with an extended section on the 1897 Jubilee and photographs of processions of colonial troops, including Indian officers, British North Borneo Police and the New South Wales Lancers. There was a feature on the navy, and illustrations of earlier military events like the Crimea and the Napoleonic Wars. The soap firms Pears and Lever Brothers produced famous annuals, which were miniature encyclopaedias, at remarkably low cost. The *Sunlight Annual* began publication in 1894, and over the succeeding years the quantity of imperial, royal, and military information greatly increased. In 1898 a section on the British Empire was included in 'The States of the World'.[51] In 1899 information on the British colonies, dependencies, and possessions consumed no fewer than twenty-three pages, while the States of the world were compressed into nine. From the latter year there were diagrammatic representations of the importance of the Empire to the home population, demonstrating the massive increase in the supply of tea from Ceylon, frozen meat from Australia and New Zealand, cheese from Canada, wool from Australia, and gold from South Africa in the course of the 1890s. Each issue contained a map of the world, showing Port Sunlight's position as an importer of colonial products and as a distribution centre to the Empire and the world. Copies of *Sunlight's Year Book* were sent to all masters and mistresses of the board schools, and other companies soon joined the 'annual' technique of spreading information about themselves dressed up in encyclopaedic form.[52]

Advertising was given a fresh fillip by the enamel advertising signs, which became one of the most striking aspects of street furniture between the 1880s and the 1950s.[53] Again, it was mainly the imperial companies, tea, cocoa, tobacco, and soap firms, which were the principal users of this technique. G. J. Goschen remarked in a budget speech that the demand for cocoa had been created by such signs.[54]

The climax of the sheet music boom in the same period represented the extension of an older tradition. Street ballads and songs had long been issued in words only at very little cost. Developments in colour lithography from the 1840s led to music hall songs being issued in attractive illustrated covers.[55] The grittier ballads were superseded by more prettified and titillating musical commentaries on social *mores*. Topicality had always been a feature of such songs, but from the late 1870s topical content took a new twist. The popular song ceased to be a vehicle for dissent and became an instrument of conformity. Its conformity was nationalist and xenophobic, respectful of authority, glorifying military adventures, and revelling in the defeat of 'inferior' peoples. Such patriotic songs represented only one part of the popular music output, but they became a noisy staple of all music hall performances, and they could of course be bought for use at home. The combination of lithographed cover and engraved music made them expensive to produce, and only the middle classes could afford songs selling at 1s or 2s 6d, but pirated editions, at least of the words, continued to be sold very cheaply until the First World War. The music shops, which had proliferated by this time (by 1888 there were a hundred in central London alone), sold songs and sheet music in large quantities, and, like the newsagents described by Robert Roberts, covered their windows with their wares, the lively illustrated covers of the sheet music. At a later date, postcards provided a wider circulation for patriotic songs and poetry. The Bamforth company produced thousands of cards of songs, ballads, and hymns, many of which had a patriotic or military flavour.[56] By 1909 their numbering had reached 4,650. The use of such songs in the music hall and in workingmen's clubs will be considered in a later chapter.

There can be little doubt that the shift in the emphasis in the content of popular songs later in the century was related to the belief of the middle classes that singing constituted an important part of the search for rational recreation. Tonic sol-fah was invented in 1840, and was soon recognised as a vehicle for religious and moral crusades. Sol-fah had the power to bring music to people who could never read formal notation. It provided the opportunity for the creation of choirs in a period when size was always more important than quality. From the 1870s singing was compulsory in schools, and regarded as an important source of discipline. Choral competitions and choral participation in public ceremonial of all sorts became a characteristic of the period.

The dispersal of music and songs was greatly aided by the very considerable growth in the sale of pianos. By the Edwardian period a piano was the status symbol most eagerly sought after by all classes seeking upward mobility.[57] Between 1870 and 1910 the production and sale of pianos in Britain multiplied fivefold.[58] In the latter year sales probably reached 100,000 per annum. Contemporary popular composers turned their attention to the production of piano fantasias of varying difficulty to satisfy this market of budding pianists. There were fantasies on the Indian Mutiny, the Abyssinian campaign of 1868, the Ashanti War of 1874, and many other topical events. It was a tradition which continued into the inter-war years, when a piano fantasia appeared entitled 'The Aerial Post'. Music was composed for the British efforts to annex the Transvaal in 1877-81 ('The Cape March', dedicated to Sir Bartle Frere), the Egyptian invasion of 1882, the death of Gordon, the 'rescue' of Emin Pasha, and on countless military and naval topics.[59]

The brass band movement was, perhaps, even more significant in encouraging mass musical involvement than choral music. Like singing in schools, bands were seen as capable of burning up the excess energies of the working class, supplying a disciplined form of self-entertainment. There were works' bands, mechanics' institutes' bands, temperance bands, school and club bands, and of course large numbers of military bands. The formation of bands was an important part of the consciously recreational approach to the Volunteer movement.[60] The journal *Brass Band News* was founded in 1881, and band competitions, based on the centre of the movement at Belle Vue in Manchester, became the main stimulus to constant practice for improved quality. There were no fewer than 40,000 brass bands in 1889, the Salvation Army alone fielding 1,000.[61] The band movement has often been seen as primarily a northern phenomenon, but by the Edwardian period bands were an important feature of the southern musical scene too. Annual festivals at the Crystal Palace saw a steady growth in the numbers of bands participating. Twenty-nine bands took part in 1900, 165 in 1908. Even the navy decided that the army was stealing a propagandist march with its profusion of regimental bands (among which there was considerable rivalry). The first naval bands were founded in 1903 and by 1908 there were fifty-three of them. This seems to be remarkable confirmation of the successful part bands played in recruitment.

Bands had also become a central feature of the activities of youth movements by this time. All these bands were vital in the development of the tradition of public music.

By the late Victorian period, choirs and bands had created, in effect, an al-fresco musical boom. Stages were built in public parks to accommodate choirs and travelling 'concert parties'. Attractive wrought iron bandstands sprouted in public spaces and on promenades throughout the country, and indeed the Empire. There were efforts to popularise light classical music (much of it German, of course), but the staple fare of band concerts consisted of military marches (of which a large number were composed at this time), patriotic numbers and selections from musical hits of the London stage. So prominent were bands in British life that they were taken over by the Japanese. When in 1907-08 *The Mikado* was banned by the Lord Chamberlain lest it caused offence to the visiting Japanese Crown Prince, it was found that the bands of the ships accompanying his party were playing selections from it at ports of call.[62] Bands swept up large numbers of participants into the performance of often nationalist music, creating at the same time the disciplines of rhythmic marching and constant practice. They added to the attraction of ceremonial and outdoor display, and could scarcely be missed by any member of the population.

Two other visual techniques were devoted to topical and imperial events at this time. One was very old, the magic lantern; the other was the newest, moving film, which was to be quickly recognised as a powerful propagandist medium. The magic lantern was invented as early as the seventeenth century, when it seems to have been used largely to satisfy a contemporary taste for magical effects, spectres and monsters.[63] It continued to have a religious use until the nineteenth century, when it was taken over by travelling showmen, who turned it to comic and anecdotal, as well as religious, ends. By the later nineteenth century it had achieved a degree of standardisation, projecting 3¼ in. by 3¼ in. glass slides, often with considerable sophistication. Triple-lens projectors were used, providing opportunities for dissolving views and the like. Colouring was introduced by hand-painting, chromolithography, and transfers. Slides were particularly suited to travel and missionary subjects. Church hall presentations became the rage, and slides were also shown by famous explorers and missionaries in large halls and theatres.

Sets of slides were produced for sale. Several were devoted to the life of David Livingstone. Another was produced by H. M. Stanley after the Emin Pasha relief expedition, some of the slides highly coloured. Various sets on missionary activities, available in the 1890s, included

'Celestials and Barbarians', 'Glimpses of India', 'Heroes and Fanatics of the Sudan'. One collection of slides entitled 'Soldiers of Britain' (including shots of troops bayoneting 'fuzzy-wuzzies' in the Sudan campaign of 1898) was donated to a Lancaster museum by the church where they had once been shown in church hall slide shows.[64] An official of the Imperial British East Africa Company took a series of photographs in East Africa between 1889 and 1891, from which slide series were made.[65] Many others were produced to illustrate Africa, India, and the South Sea Islands. A hand-coloured set of Samoa (sixty slides) featured the hurricane of 1889. The South African war prompted the production of sets with titles like 'Soldiers of the Queen', 'India and the Colonies', 'Departure of Yeomanry to South Africa', 'Britons and Boers'. Some were produced from illustrations by artists of the *Illustrated London News* and the *Sphere*. Ingenious moving slides showed armoured trains with searchlights switching on and off, shellbursts appearing and disappearing, and the like. Slides were also produced to pander to the sentiment of the time ('The Poor and Honest Sodger', illustrating the Burns poem), and to illustrate contemporary hit songs.

There can be no doubt that missionaries and religious organisations were adept at using these materials. They had the necessary buildings in church halls and chapels, widely dispersed throughout the land; they had subjects which were highly amenable to such treatment, and they required funds to continue their work. Even if the working class in Victorian England were not notable for their religious observance, they were prepared to be thoroughly eclectic in their search for entertainment and indiscriminating in the Christian denominations that offered it. Famous travellers and missionaries could fill the Albert Hall and theatres and concert halls throughout the country. When the Royal Colonial Institute decided to promote imperial propaganda through the use of a professional lecturer in the years just before the First World War, it found that he could fill the largest halls, particularly when his lectures were supplemented by lantern slides, trumpet fanfares, patriotic songs, and recitations.[66] The American, Lowell Thomas, who more than anyone created the Lawrence of Arabia myth, used the same techniques in London, where he filled, in turn, Covent Garden, the Albert Hall, the Philharmonic Hall, and the Queen's Hall, and travelled throughout Britain and the United States.[67] Lowell Thomas, however, used a film, and although slides continued to be used for educational purposes they were quickly rejected as a means of entertainment once they had been supplanted by the excitement of film. The Colonial Office Visual Instruction Committee, examined in chapter 6, failed in its efforts at imperial propaganda precisely because it took up the technique of the lantern slide when it had already become obsolescent.

Brief films began to be shown by travelling showmen and as short excerpts in music hall and theatre programmes from 1896.[68] Once the early film-makers had got over their initial fascination with railway trains, the most dramatic movers of the day, they settled down to concentrate on actuality films and short dramas. They recognised the propaganda potential of their medium at once. In addition to the films of great occasions like the Jubilee of 1897, the coronation of 1902, the Delhi Durbar of 1903, which were perhaps neutral recordings of imperial events, the Boer War gave the screen a great opportunity, as it did so many of the communication techniques of the period. Large numbers of films were made on military and naval topics, encouraging recruiting and patriotic fervour. Anti-Boer propaganda was produced, and many war scenes were faked. Even more explicit propaganda appeared in 1905 with films attacking Jewish immigration and promoting 'Fair Trade'.[69] Films were available for hire from an early date, and distribution lists include stores, Church mission halls, and the Salvation Army. Just as the Imperial British East Africa Company had produced slides of East Africa, so another chartered company, the British North Borneo Company, financed a series of films about Borneo in 1903.[70]

Up to 1914 films of royal events, always featuring colonial pageantry, expedition films, 'scenics' set almost entirely in India, the South Seas and tropical Africa, military and naval films, as well as films of contemporary imperial events like the Moroccan crisis of 1907 and films specifically devoted to imperial expansion continued to be made. Moreover, the newsreel made its appearance. But the British film industry was already beginning to be overtaken by the American, and 'factual' films were declining as a proportion of the whole. As Rachael Low has put it, film did not develop as a popular form of educational entertainment along the lines of the once fashionable lantern lecture; it became much more a form of story-telling.[71] The stories told in cinematic form, however, reflected just as strongly, and probably more potently, the aggressive militarism of juvenile literature, the easy superiority of Europeans and Americans, the triumphs of 'civilisation' over the rest of the world.

Films lie at the crossroads of so many of the other communications techniques of the period. They were shown in the theatre, music halls, chapels and churches. All the favourite subjects of topical and actuality films are the same as those of postcards and cigarette cards. One of the most notable postcard companies, Bamforth, went into film-making.[72] And films were used to supplement lectures just as slides had been. Film supplanted the lantern slide, and the cinema eventually supplanted the music hall, but the film industry provided new subjects for postcards and cigarette cards, which helped them to survive into a much later period, as well as creating new musical needs. The immense popularity of the cinema damaged many of the reading habits created in the late nineteenth century, but it soon added new dimensions to the continuing popularity of adolescent journals. Moreover, as we shall see in chapter 3, films continued to purvey themes and ideas which were rooted in the late nineteenth century, until the early 1950s.

The period 1870 to 1914 saw the appearance of several new communications techniques and the development of some old ones. All these rapidly became the servants of the dominant ideology of the age, patriotic, militaristic, and imperialistic. They celebrated the excitements of an expansionist age — exploration, colonial campaigns, and missionary endeavour. They allied such activities to entertainment, the mass entertainment of music hall, Band of Hope, and missionary meetings, public lectures, slide and cinema shows, and the new opportunities for home entertainment provided by cheap music, cheap journals, and even cheaper ephemera. Almost all these techniques were also harnessed to the search for improving recreation which was a feature of the later Victorian period. Many exerted their power principally over the young, and it was a power well recognised by the adult world. Even those forms that were rooted in dissent, mass adult entertainment like songs, ballads, and music hall, became respectable in this period.

All these materials lay ready to hand for the great exercise in propaganda which was mounted during the First World War.[73] Music, postcards, cigarette cards, all forms of ephemera and popular texts, lantern slides and film were bent to a war effort which was depicted as righteous moral empire pitted against upstart, undeserved empire. All imperial agencies and all the commercial forces which depended on empire and promoted its extension received a tremendous boost. Although the war was to develop Dominions nationalism, wartime propaganda emphasised that it was a joint imperial effort, sweeping up the white Dominions, India, and the dependent territories into a crusade for freedom.[74] The surprising thing is that the propagandist patterns laid down in this period did not represent the end of nineteenth-century perceptions, as has so often been argued, but the beginning of a propagandist era, utilising all the technical developments described above, which was to last at least until the Second World War. Intellectual and administrative attitudes towards Empire may have changed dramatically in the course of the inter-war period, but the agencies which influenced, and manipulated, popular opinion continued to run largely in old channels. The chapters which follow will examine these various propagandist techniques in the hands of a wide range of official and unofficial agencies.

NOTES

1 Eric Hobsbawm, *Industry and Empire*, London, 1969, 154-71. W. Hamish Fraser, *The Coming of the Mass Market, 1850-1914*, London, 1981, 3-25.
2 Fraser, *Mass Market*.
3 Robert Roberts, *The Classic Slum*, London, 1971, 168.
4 S. H. Steinberg, *Five Hundred Years of Printing*, London, 1955. Colin Clair, *A History of Printing in Britain*, London, 1965.
5 Steinberg, *Printing*, 278.
6 J. Neville Bartlett, 'Alexander Pirie & Sons of Aberdeen and the expansion of the British paper industry', *Business History* XXII (1980), 18-34.
7 J. S. Bratton, *The Impact of Victorian Children's Fiction*, London, 1981, 59.
8 Fraser, *Mass Market*, 227.
9 Roberts, *Classic Slum*, 170.
10 Louis James, 'Tom Brown's imperial sons', *Victorian Studies*, 17 (1973), 89-99. Patrick A. Dunae, 'Boy's literature and the idea of Empire, 1870-1914', *Victorian Studies*, 24 (1980), 105-21.
11 John Barnicoat, *A Concise History of Posters*, London, 1979.
12 Steinberg, *Printing*, 281.
13 Alan Thomas, *The Expanding Eye: Photography and the Nineteenth-Century Mind*, London, 1978, 22.
14 One of the great nineteenth-century photographers put it this way: 'We are now making history, and the sun picture supplies the means of passing down a record of what we are, and what we have achieved in this nineteenth century of our progress.' Gail Buckland, *Reality Recorded: Early Documentary Photography*, Newton Abbot, 1974, 9.
15 G. Macdonald, *Camera*, London, 1979. J. Falconer, 'The photograph collection of the Royal Commonwealth Society', *Photographic Collector*, V (1981), 34-53.
16 Ian Jeffrey, *Photography: a Concise History*, London, 1981, 63-4.
17 Ford and Harrison, *Hundred Years*, 23.
18 Macdonald, *Camera*, 50.
19 Tonie and Valmai Holt, *Picture Postcards of the Golden Age*, London 1978. The Post Office permitted the printing of cards by private companies in 1894. The imperial penny post was introduced in 1898.
20 F. Staff, *The Picture Postcard and its Origins*, London, 1979. Frank Staff, *The Picture Postcard and Travel*, London, 1979.
21 Macdonald, *Camera*, 5.
22 Buckland, *Reality*, 92-3. G. Wagner, *Children of the Empire*, London, 1982.
23 J. M. MacKenzie, 'By jingo', *The Listener*, 6 January, 1983, 12. J. M. MacKenzie, 'Ephemera, reflection or instrument', *The Ephemerist*, 2 (June 1983), 4-7.
24 R. S. S. Baden-Powell, *Scouting for Boys*, London, 1908, 153.
25 The author's own collection contains several thousand propaganda, commercial, and imperial cards. There are no national collections, although postcards can be found in the Royal Commonwealth Society's photographic collections and in the Imperial Institute papers at the Public Record Office.
26 Anthony Byatt, *Picture Postcards and their Publishers*, Malvern, 1978.
27 Roberts, *Classic Slum*, 168.
28 Byatt, *Picture Postcards*, 335-8.
29 MacKenzie, 'Ephemera', 5.

30 London Cigarette Company, Catalogue, 1975, and subsequent issues. Murray Cards Ltd, Catalogue of Cigarette and other Trade Cards, 1977. Dorothy Bagnall, *Collecting Cigarette Cards*, London, 1978. Fraser, *Mass Market*, 146.
31 Roberts, *Classic Slum*, 169.
32 Private communication.
33 3, *The Radio Three Magazine*, November 1982, 42.
34 Frank Doggett, *Cigarette Cards and Novelties*, London 1981, 11. Doggett describes the period between the wars as 'The Golden Age of Cigarette Cards', 12.
35 Hobson, *Psychology*, 10.
36 Ford and Harrison, *Hundred Years*, 55.
37 D. H. Simpson, 'Emin Pasha relief expedition', R.C.S. Library Notes. November/December 1972.
38 Fraser, *Mass Market*, 139 and 142.
39 I am grateful to Mr Hilary Humphries for sharing with me his knowledge of cigarette brand names and the designs of their packets.
40 Kenneth Bradley, *Once a District Officer*, London, 1966, 31. Bradley mentions this brand as an interesting example of the Cape to Cairo myth.
41 M. J. Franklin, *British Biscuit Tins*, London, 1979. David Griffith, *Decorative Printed Tins*, London, 1979. I am grateful to Frank and Gladys Bell for showing me their collection of tins, boxes, and packagings.
42 This and other examples of popular art are in the Judges' Lodgings Collection, Lancaster.
43 One, distributed by the Co-operative Society of Dalton-in-Furness in 1897, bore illustrations of a warship, of a cavalry charge, and of the Prince of Wales riding on an elephant on his visit to India.
44 I am grateful to Professor Paul Smith for providing me with a drawing and description of this plate.
45 Many of these items were illustrated in the Time-Life *British Empire*, 1971. Alistair Allen, *A History of Printed Scraps*, London, 1983.
46 Brian Love, *Play the Game*, London, 1978. Brian Love, *Great Board Games*, London, 1979. I am grateful to Mr. Peter Glenn of the Bethnal Green Museum for showing me that museum's collection of board games.
47 Linda Hannas, *The Jigsaw Book*, New York, 1981.
48 I am grateful to Mr Lawrence James for information about toy soldiers.
49 Hugh Tinker, *A Message From the Falklands*, London, 1982, 72. Lieutenant Tinker had also been intrigued by coins of the British Empire, and 'haunted' by the Great War, 2, 6.
50 These items are in the collection of the Museum of Childhood, Haggs Castle, Glasgow.
51 *Sunlight Year Book*, 1898 and 1899.
52 Fraser, *Mass Market*, 142.
53 Christopher Baglee and Andrew Morley, *Street Jewellery*, London, 1978.
54 Fraser, *Mass Market*, 135.
55 R. Pearsall, *Victorian Sheet Music Covers*, Newton Abbot, 1972.
56 Byatt, *Picture Postcards*, 38.
57 Roberts, *Classic Slum*, 153.
58 Cyril Ehrlich, *The Piano: a History*, London 1976, 157.
59 D. H. Simpson, 'The Imperial Impact on Britain', unpublished paper. I am grateful to Mr Simpson for allowing me to see this paper and for drawing my attention to the collection of music and ephemera in the R.C.S. library. D. H. Simpson, 'Variations on an imperial theme', R.C.S. Library Notes, April, 1965. Patricia Carroll, who gives lecture recitals on these works, supplied further information.
60 Hugh Cunningham, *The Volunteer Force*, London, 1975, 71.
61 Ronald Pearsall, *Edwardian Popular Music*, Newton Abbot, 1975, 11.
62 Richard Findlater, *Banned! A Review of Theatrical Censorship in Britain*, London, 1967, 88.
63 D. H. Simpson, 'The magic lantern and imperialism', R.C.S. Library Notes, May 1973; 'Pictures from the dust', R.C.S. Library Notes, May 1969.
64 Lancaster, Judges' Lodging Collection.

65 Simpson, 'Magic lantern'.
66 J. G. Greenlee, 'Imperial studies and the unity of the Empire', *Journal of Imperial and Commonwealth History*, VII (1979), 324.
67 Lowell Thomas, *With Lawrence in Arabia*, London, 1924. Richard Aldington, *Lawrence of Arabia*, London, 1969, 285-7.
68 Rachael Low and Roger Manvell, *The History of the British Film, 1896-1906*, London, 1948, 36.
69 Low and Manvell, *British Film*, 58-9.
70 Low and Manvell, *British Film*, 60-1.
71 Rachael Low, *The History of the British Film, 1906-1914*, London, 1948, 146.
72 Low and Manvell, *British Film*, 15-6.
73 Maurice Rickards and Michael Moody, *The First World War: Ephemera, Mementoes, Documents*, London, 1975.
74 Cate Haste, *Keep the Home Fires Burning*, London, 1977.

THE THEATRE OF EMPIRE

THE VICTORIA PALACE

OPPOSITE VICTORIA STATION - - - - S.W.

MATINEES DAILY AT 3 P.M.

Managing Director Mr. *ALFRED BUTT*

"SIXTY YEARS A QUEEN"

The World's Greatest Record of our Empire's History

THE LIFE AND REIGN OF VICTORIA
THE GOOD

To many writers and historians there has only been one form of imperial theatre, the music hall. In this they have taken their cue from J. A. Hobson, who saw the music hall as the prime villain in the dissemination of jingoism, 'a more potent educator than the church, the school, the political meeting, or even than the press'.[1] The art of the music hall, he went on,

> is the only 'popular' art of the present day; its words and melodies pass by quick magic from the Empire or the Alhambra over the length and breadth of the land, re-echoed in a thousand provincial halls, clubs, and drinking saloons, until the remotest village is familiar with air and sentiment. By such process of artistic suggestion the fervour of Jingosim has been widely fed . . .

Other contemporaries also recognised the music hall as a potent force. For H. M. Hyndman the music halls were the most likely milieu of 'rampart chauvinism',[2] while Rudyard Kipling considered them to offer 'the very stuff of social history'.[3] For Kipling music hall performances represented an authentic popular voice, whose rhythms and sentiments he tried to match in his ballads and poems.[4] Historians have been fascinated by the music hall for a number of reasons. Its phenomenal growth in the 1870s represented the first great entertainment boom. It seemed, moreover, to appeal to all social classes, offering the same performers, often working-class in origin, in a great range of theatres with a wide spectrum of ticket prices. Above all, it reflected the dominant imperial ethos of the day in topical and chauvinistic songs, royal fervour, and patriotic tableaux.

Middle and upper-class attachment to the music hall developed out of its success among the working class. But it is the working-class devotion to the halls which has excited most attention. Popular writers from Max Beerbohm[5] to John Betjeman,[6] Harold Scott[7] to G. J. Mellor[8] and Mander and Mitchenson[9], followed Hobson in suggesting that music hall genuinely represented working-class views, although for all of them working-class jingoism was no more than an eccentric, if not engaging, foible, an amusing expression of popular patriotism. For Hobson, of course, it represented something much more sinister, a mass emotionalism with violent and aggressive tendencies, through which the proponents of imperialism secured popular support. Even if the links were not direct, they seemed to be part of the Rand magnates' conspiracy, with their political, financial, and press agents in Britain itself. Others have attempted to fit the music hall into a conspiratorial framework of a different sort. For Lawrence Senelick 'the halls were so much out of tune with popular sympathies that they might be regarded as pernicious instruments of propaganda'.[10] Some of the songwriters and singers had connections with the Conservative Party, while the Tory drink trade and Tory proprietors ensured that the music hall conformed to Establishment ideas. Music hall was a 'distorting mirror', which in no way provided an accurate reflection of the political opinions of the audience.[11] In the music hall, Senelick concludes, the working class heard sentiments that were contrary to their own class interests.

This is much too simple. No one made the working class attend the music hall, and its immense popularity cannot be explained solely as the successful duping of audiences by impresarios exploiting a mass craving for escapist entertainment encouraged by shorter working hours and the increase in disposable income. Penny Summerfield has argued more convincingly that there were official attempts to control the music hall, that fire and licensing regulations were used to mould it into a respectable pattern, that impresarios indulged in self-censorship in order to maintain respectability, and avoid the displeasure of the authorities.[12] Risqué and anti-Establishment songs were abandoned in favour of royalist, militarist, and nationalist outbursts. Music hall proprietors, eager to protect their licences, proclaimed themselves as being in the business of 'rational' entertainment, 'improving' their audiences with a nourishing diet of sentiment, patriotism, and encouragement to cross-class solidarity.

However, in order to explain fully the popularity of the music hall, it is necessary to place it in the much wider context of popular entertainment in the nineteenth century, as well as in the wider theatrical interests of the period. Some of its elements can be found in much older traditions, in the nineteenth-century taste for military and naval spectacle, as well as melodrama, which together developed into an extensive imperial stage by the end of the century, and culminated in the musical comedies in exotic settings of the late Victorian and Edwardian periods. None of these has ever been adequately analysed for imperial, military, and racial content. In this chapter, the music hall will be placed in that wider setting in an attempt to find a more convincing explanation for its popularity among the working, and indeed all other, classes.

Many writers have been concerned to contrast with the music hall a grittier tradition of popular culture in the early nineteenth century, embracing the radical politics of broadsheet ballads, and other evidences of class awareness and cultural class solidarity. But the ballad tradition was an ambivalent one. The ballad too was used in a propagandist manner, to disseminate moral tales, to propagate temperance ideas, and to convince the poor that conditions were not so bad. There was a 'culture of consolation', as one authority has described the music hall,[13] in this material too. Moreover, the national interest, and more particularly military events, were always a strong element in the ballads. The Napoleonic wars produced a 'ceaseless flow of poeticising upon international news and internal affairs'.[14] The theatre, like the ballad, also had a strongly topical content in the earlier nineteenth century, but its topicality was tempered and slanted by censorship. In the course of the century, censorship came to be accepted to the extent that few playwrights seem to have chafed under its restrictions or attempted to break out of it. In fact, censorship contributed to the general drive towards conformity which was a theatrical characteristic of the time. By the end of the century even the music hall, which was free of official restraint, was indulging in a form of self-censorship which extended, in effect, the Lord Chamberlain's conventions into areas where his writ did not run.

Censorship emerged from licensing legislation of the eighteenth century. When in 1843 the old patent theatre system was abolished, the *quid pro quo* was the extension of censorship through the increased authority of the Lord Chamberlain. By that time the social and political turbulence of the early nineteenth century had already ensured that there were a number of prohibited areas upon which the theatre could not trespass.[15] They included the Irish problem, reform legislation, Chartism, and the royal family. Historical plays which might contain veiled contemporary allusions were suspect, as were plays about the politics, particularly revolutionary politics, of other countries. No personalised political allusion and no impersonation of public figures, alive or recently dead (and sometimes not so recently), were allowed. The ban upon the portrayal of members of the royal family was the most vigorously imposed, perhaps not surprisingly, since the Lord Chamberlain was also the head of the royal household, and indeed survived to the 1950s if not the '60s. Bulwer-Lytton's *Oliver Cromwell* was banned because it contained slighting references to the court of Charles I. Such restrictions were intensified in the later Victorian and Edwardian periods and showed no signs of relaxation thereafter. In the 1920s a play about Queen Caroline, *Pains and Penalties*, was refused a licence, as was *The Queen's Minister*, which was about the relationship between Queen Victoria and Lord Melbourne. It was indeed difficult to portray Victoria at all until her last surviving son, the Duke of Connaught, died in 1942. It has been said that the portrayal of Queen Victoria in *The Glorious Days* in coronation year 1953 was permitted only because Anna Neagle *dreamed* in the play that she was Queen Victoria.[16] Yet Anna Neagle had of course played Victoria twice in 1930s screen epics. Royal bannings continued for two more decades.

The proscription of any work containing a dangerous social message or treating left-wing politics in a complimentary light was also standard practice. Indeed, between the 1870s and the First World War there were often strong suspicions that censorship acted essentially as a Tory instrument. W. S. Gilbert's *The Happy Land* (1873), which mercilessly satirised the Liberal government, was belatedly banned, but later permitted to run. In 1909 Shaw's *Press Cuttings*, which was deemed to contain references to Balfour, Asquith, Milner, and Kitchener, was refused a licence. 'Shaw himself was astonished,' writes Richard Findlater,[17] 'because the censor had accepted without demur his ridicule of Liberal politicians in *John Bull's other Island*, a play which by the Chamberlain's own standards was ultimately far more subversive than *Press Cuttings.*' In the 1920s a play which had depicted Gladstone in a less than favourable light, *Parnell and Gladstone*, was permitted (though only after intense lobbying), but another, specifically commissioned to portray Gladstone in a more sympathetic way, *Mr Gladstone*, stayed banned. *Versailles*, about the signing of the peace treaty, was forbidden in 1919, as were plays about the Russian revolution, *Red Sunday* and *Roar, China*. It was said that no play about Sir Roger Casement could ever have been licensed, while throughout the '30s no plays featuring Hitler, Mussolini, and fascism could be staged. Anti-war dramas, like Toller's *Hinkeman*, were also banned. In 1954 the Lord Chamberlain objected to a revue sketch featuring Eden and Churchill, while extensive cuts (including well authenticated events reflecting badly on the authorities) were required in *Guilty and Proud of it* (1953), a play which explored the resistance of Poplar Labour councillors in 1921 to rates regulations.

Censorship must of course be put into proper perspective. The Lord Chamberlain's jurisdiction did not run much beyond the West End (although his power had been increased by his right to license the theatres themselves), and unacceptable plays were put on at theatres outside his area. However, other licensing authorities were prepared to accept his lead, and plays which could not secure a West End run were unlikely to be financially viable. The music hall was free of official censorship, but by the time it had become a powerful entertainment medium it was, as we shall see, indulging in highly effective self-censorship. On the other hand, much of the most effective topical comment occurred in pantomimes (upon which the financial health of the Victorian theatre depended), and a good deal of such material escaped censorship. However, so far as one can judge, these topical allusions and the strong satirical vein of the period tended to be more affectionate than subversive, and indeed much of the satire merely reflected the familiarity of the audiences with the subjects mildly lampooned. If political censorship was, as J. R. Stephens maintains,[18] less obtrusive in the second half of the nineteenth century than in the first, the reason can only be that by then playwrights were clearer about what was likely to be permitted; in any case the powerful intellectual conformity of the period was such that few wished to challenge it. In 1912 the most notable Establishment actors, managers, and producers of the day petitioned the King in favour of the Lord Chamberlain (in response to an anti-censorship petition), and in the same year the British Board of Film Censors was established (see chapter 2). Moreover, many leading theatre critics were surprisingly passive towards censorship.

The thrust of the Victorian theatre can best be understood by examining its leading traditions and some of the 'uncontroversial' plays to which the censor raised no objection. The leading popular forms were melodrama and spectacle, which as the century progressed had a tendency to fuse. In both these traditions the military element was always strong, for the heroics and sentiment of warfare had long played an important part in all popular culture, stemming from the Napoleonic wars and receiving a significant new fillip during the Crimean War.[19]

Melodrama has been described as 'the most important theatrical form of the age'.[20] In melodrama it was possible to depict life as a titanic struggle between good and evil, a fantasy world in which the wildest dreams could be fufilled. Melodrama was a strongly non-intellectual tradition in which characterisation, subtle emotional nuance, or philosophic problems — as in the modern pulp romances — had no place. Plot, physical sensation, and stereotype were all. Melodrama neatly reflects the conservatism of the English theatre. The English tradition was based on French and German models, the former particularly potent in the Revolutionary period. But, as Booth puts it, English melodrama took from France and Germany the sensational elements and omitted the heartfelt radicalism.[21] The crude idealism and revolutionary ardour of French and German melodrama, the fervent libertarian spirit and stress on the rights of the individual, the genuine hatred of tyranny, became coarsened and vulgarised in the English version. Partly this was because the greatest English writers of the period did not write for the stage, partly it was because the British were engaged in a defensive struggle against the dangerous radicalism of the Continent.

Booth suggests that melodrama in Britain was very much a working-class taste, with melodrama theatres springing up in many working-class districts. It was also the stock-in-trade of the travelling troupes and 'penny gaffs', a genuinely popular theatre, and it was only later in the century that it came to have a middle and upper-class following. This has, however, been disputed. In Birmingham, at any rate, melodrama was the taste of all classes.[22] It certainly suited the dumb-show theatrical techniques necessary to evade the London patent system, but melodramas were also shown at the patent theatres, Covent Garden, Drury Lane, and the Theatre Royal Haymarket. Although the heyday of melodrama has been seen as the period 1800-1870, it survived until the 1920s, and must have filled many of the theatres of the theatre-building boom which developed from the 1860s. The Elephant and Castle Theatre specialised in the form for 140 years. It may well be that the audience for melodrama (the conventions of which were adopted by nineteenth-century opera) was extended as the opposition of the Churches to the theatre declined in the later nineteenth century, thereby encouraging more middle-class patronage.

If there was a shift in class patronage as the century progressed, it might be expected that this would be reflected in the subjects of melodrama. To a certain extent it was. Some plays from the early nineteenth century did display class tensions. By the end of the century such class antagonism had disappeared from melodrama. By then, imperial subjects offered a perfect opportunity to externalise the villain, who increasingly became the corrupt rajah, the ludicrous Chinese or Japanese nobleman, the barbarous 'fuzzy-wuzzy' or black, facing a cross-class brotherhood of heroism, British officer and ranker together. Thus imperialism was depicted as a great struggle with dark and evil forces, in which white heroes and heroines could triumph over black barbarism, and the moral stereotyping of melodrama was given a powerful racial twist.

If Victorian melodrama revealed a yearning for moral imperatives, spectacular theatre demonstrated the fascination with grandeur. The taste for spectacle emerges in almost all areas of Victorian culture — in public ceremonial, in the confident elaboration of urban architecture, in the vast canvases of some Victorian painters, in a general love of ostentation, reflected equally in the massive furniture and fussy detail of the middle-class interior, or in the treasured bric-a-brac of the working-class mantel, in the grand oratorios of Victorian composers, and in the exuberant use of cast iron and glass, extended from the Crystal Palace and Kew to markets, exhibition halls, and railway stations. In many respects, all these came together in the great imperial exhibitions (chapter 4) or in the planning, building, and pageantry associated with the Imperial Institute (chapter 5). Such spectacle was closely linked with pride in technological achievement, in engineering, lighting, and mechanical contrivance generally. The almost fanatical search for realism in Victorian spectacle arose precisely from the need to show off mechanical inventions, striking effects of shifting scenery and dramatic lighting. The theatre took up the spectacular effects achieved by panoramas, dioramas, and cosmoramas. Panoramas, long strips of unrolling picture, were displayed in public buildings from the 1790s; the diorama was invented by Daguerre in 1822; a cosmorama was opened in Regent Street in 1823.[23] Travel news, military events, and public catastrophes were the favourite subjects. There were, for example, monster panoramas of the Mississippi, the Nile, the overland route to India and others, some of them over 3,000 ft long, taking some two hours to unroll. Panoramas were also used to popularise emigration, for example to Australia and New Zealand, in the late 1840s and 1850s. In the theatre large armies of painters were employed to create vast effects, realistic backgrounds of Egyptian temples and the like.[24]

But it was the rapid translation of military and naval news to the stage which became the principal excitement of nineteenth-century theatre and one of its most enduring characteristics. Some theatres specialised in nautical and military spectacles, particularly the Surrey, south of the Thames, which was heavily patronised by sailors, the famous Astley's, and Sadler's Wells. As the century progressed the deeds of imperial expansion were found to fit perfectly the tradition of translating topical events into spectacular display, combining the Victorians' search for realism with an admiring self-regard in their own exploits.

There was a long pre-Victorian tradition of aquatic display in the theatre. Dryden's *The Indian Emperor* of 1665 may well have been produced with fountains and water effects. Sheridan's *Glorious First of June* opened only five weeks after the event, but with purely dry effects. In 1804 Sadler's Wells unveiled their magnificent new tank, 90 ft long and over 20 ft wide, and immediately presented *The Siege of Gibraltar* with working models of vessels built by Woolwich dockyard shipwrights.[25] Other nautical displays included *England's Glory, or British Tars at Spithead* and *The Defeat of the Dutch Fleet* at

Covent Garden in the 1790s, and *The Battle of Trafalgar* and *The Battle of the Nile* at Sadler's Wells. This naval tradition was continued in the decades after the Napoleonic wars with nautical plays by specialists like Cooke, Fitzball, and Campbell. Nelson was idolised, and the myth of the archetypal simple and heroic British tar developed. In all these there was repeated praise for the native land; ordinary people were portrayed in individual moral triumph through physical heroism against big historical backdrops. This identification of individuals with grand nationalist themes was heightened by repeated use of patriotic songs like *Rule, Britannia*, and by a constant evocation of the symbolism of the flag. In such plays the navy perpetually upheld freedom against oppression, whether personified by noble officers or heroic common sailors like Tom Topreef. There were literally dozens of them, with the Empire making an early appearance in *El Hyder* of 1818, set in India. The tradition remained virtually unchanged throughout the century, neatly combining patriotism and social deference, as in Tom Topreef's line 'Next to my captain's life, my country's liberty shall be my trust.'

The nautical tradition was continued with presentations of *The Armada* at Drury Lane in 1888, complete with fireships, while a late example of aquatic spectacle occurred in Blackpool during the Second World War when the *Graf Spee* incident was re-enacted in a flooded circus ring.[26] These two examples neatly embrace an imperial period which spent much energy seeking the nautical roots of world greatness. This maritime tradition was matched by extraordinary military and equestrian spectacle, which had its origins in the eighteenth century, particularly at Astley's circus ring, which carried on an unbroken tradition until burnt down in 1895.[27] Both the Surrey and Astley's had combined stages and circus rings in time for the Napoleonic wars, and trained troupes of horses came to be one of the theatrical marvels of the age. *Harlequin Mameluke, or, The British in Egypt* appeared in 1800 and was followed by many other Napoleonic events, like Waterloo, Badajoz, Vittoria, Salamanca, etc., all put on at Astley's many times. Wellington was idolised in the military tradition just as Nelson was in the naval. As the century progressed, imperial milieux began to predominate, becoming the essential backdrops to the national myth of success. The Burmese War was on the stage in 1826, as were two portrayals of South African frontier warfare (*Amakosa, or, Scenes of Kaffir Warfare* and *The Kaffir War*) in 1853.

The Crimean War produced the most popular military presentations, when theatre managers vied with each other to present thrillingly patriotic displays. *The Battle of Alma* ran at Astley's for four months, and as Bratton puts it, the image of the event became the reality for the audience.[28] Soon, however, the military stage reverted to the Empire with the staging of *The Indian Mutiny, The Storming of Delhi, The War in Abyssinia* (1868), *The Conquest of Magdala, The War in Zululand* and *The Kaffir War* (both at Astley's in 1879), the Khyber Pass in *Youth* (1881) and many others. For *Youth* the spectacle included the embarkation of troops at Portsmouth and fierce engagements near the Khyber Pass for which real Gatling guns were supplied by the Birmingham Small Arms Company.

Bratton has suggested that, by the Boer War, the taste for military spectacle of the type shown at Astley's had declined.[29] Astley's (latterly called Sanger's) had been burnt down, and in any case the inadequacy of the marriage of stage and circus ring had come to be apparent. However, Astley's function had been taken over by displays at Olympia, Earl's Court, the Crystal Palace, and in the great exhibitions reviewed in chapter 4. People turned out in large numbers to see the Volunteer Force drilling, as they did later to Aldershot tattoos and royal tournaments.[30] The appetite for military spectacle was now being satisfied by the real thing, particularly with the advent of newsreel film. Moreover, uniforms, weaponry, battle scenes, officer personalities, and medal-winning heroes had come to be the stock-in-trade of ephemera. Alternative visual representations were now available to satisfy a taste which was, if anything, growing rather than declining.

The Indian Empire appeared in both melodrama and spectacle from an early date. Eastern themes were developed in Restoration plays like Dryden's *Aurangzeb* (1676), and became common in melodrama from 1798. In Barrymore's *El Hyder* of 1818 British sailors uphold the cause of freedom against oppression in India. A 'noble chief' is helped against a 'usurping tyrant'; there is a desperate battle for Delhi, and the British flag is waved upon the ramparts. Good Indians are helped to overwhelm evil Indians in one of the most famous and spectacular of Eastern melodramas, Moncrieff's *The Cataract of the Ganges* (1823). There is much oriental spectacle — the rajah's palace, processions of the army and of priests, a temple, and so on — and after a battle scene in which good Hindus defeat evil Muslims, the victorious rajah thanks the British, whose 'battle is ever on virtue's side – your aim is charity — your victory peace; you ... carry the Christian spirit of your race through every clime to civilise and bless'.[31] Both these works beautifully convey propaganda about Britain's alleged mission in India at this period: acting as supporters of good rulers against bad, releasing Hindus from the Muslim oppression of the Mughal empire.

From at least the time of the Mutiny, plays and musical comedies set in India adopt a rather different tone. British rule is now an accepted fact, and there is less concern to contrast 'good' and 'bad' Indians. All are now evil, misguided, or figures of fun. Still, India offered tremendous scope for oriental display, and for that reason it continued to form a popular backdrop both to plays and, increasingly from the end of the century, to musical comedy. (It has continued to perform a similar function in modern romantic fiction.) Throughout the '80s and '90s titles like *The Great Mogul*, *The Nabob's Fortune*, *The Nabob*, *The Nabob's Pickle*, *Lalla Rookh*, *The Saucy Nabob*, *The Begum's Diamonds*, *The Stars of India*, and *The Mahatma* recur.[32] Now and again there were revivals from the past, reminders of military difficulty, such as *The Indian Mutiny* of 1892.

We can also identify a genre of generalised imperial sensation drama, like *The Defence of the Consulate* of 1883, which had scenes of British lads firing on 'fuzzy-wuzzies' against a vaguely oriental background.[33] By now empire had become its own melodrama, and had become inseparably mixed up with the late nineteenth-century craze for orientalism, which so perfectly fitted the taste for spectacle. As we have seen, African wars gave rise to military melodramas, and from the middle of the century the growth of African subjects inevitably came to reflect increased imperial activity in Africa. An analysis of the play titles in the Lord Chamberlain's collection for the late nineteenth century reveals a striking topicality. Several Zulu titles appear after 1879, and the visit of Cetewayo, king of the Zulu, to Britain was immediately celebrated in two plays (*The Zulu Chief* and *Cetewayo at Last*) in 1882. Britain's involvement in Egypt from 1882 and, above all, the fall of Khartoum, were swiftly represented on stage. There were various plays on emigration themes, and the Dominions featured from time to time, as in *Australia* (1881), *The Duchess of Coolgardie*, and *The Cousin from Australia*. South African subjects began to feature strongly, first from the Zulu War/Majuba Hill period, then again at the time of the Jameson Raid, and above all during the Boer War. Titles included *The Cape Mail*, *The Kimberley Mail*, *The Diamond Rush*, *The Raid on the Transvaal*, *Briton and Boer*, and as many as a dozen Boer War plays. The Sudan returned to theatrical consciousnesses in the 1890s with the new Sudan campaign, heralded in 1894 with *The Dancing Dervish* and *The Mahdi*. A number of plays on generalised imperial topics, with titles like *The Price of Empire*, *For the Crown*, *Under the British Flag*, *Our British Empire*, *H.E. the Governor General* and *The Viceroy* all appeared in the 1890s and the early years of the new century. China had made at least two appearances around the time of the second Anglo-Chinese war of 1859-61 with *The Chinese Insurrection* and *The Chinese Invasion*. At the end of the century Chinese, and above all Japanese, subjects became increasingly common, reminding the public of missionary heroism during the Boxer Rising, and of the stirrings of Japanese military and naval capacity in conflicts with China and Russia.

In the years before the First World War the stage perfectly reflected the military anxieties and crazes of the period. In 1909 the propaganda of the National Service League and of the Navy League was represented by plays called *Wake up England*, *Nation in Arms*, and *A Plea for the Navy*. Such military and naval exhortations, together with the contemporary invasion scares and plays on the new juvenile passion for Scouting, are featured until a veritable avalanche of war plays descends upon the London and provincial stages in 1914. No fewer than twenty four war plays and shows were licenced by the Lord Chamberlain in the brief period September–October 1914.[34]

The stage, then, reflected all the climacterics of imperial history in the nineteenth century. There were of course many more plays on domestic and romantic themes, but even some of them were placed in colonial settings or against a backdrop of imperial events. Titles are sometimes a poor guide to content: thus *A Life of Pleasure* (1893) included material on the most recent Burmese campaign, and *The Derby Winner* (1894) made reference to the Indian Empire. All in all, plays on colonial subjects, or including references to imperial events and territories, constitute a striking proportion of all those performed during this period. Many of them involved the rapid transfer of the most dramatic contemporary news to the stage. Imperial subjects were clearly convenient in offering the opportunity for spectacle, the chance to externalise the villains of melodrama and to concentrate on 'safe' military and naval topics, unlikely to draw down the wrath of the censor. In addition to these plays of topical interest, there were many more with a generalised oriental and colonial interest, which created opportunities to depict exotic peoples and a variety of colonial types — administrators, settlers and planters, missionaries, soldiers, and sailors — in a satirical or heroic vein.

An analysis of these plays from the imperial and racial standpoint would require a separate book. But an examination of just a few of them reveals some of the main obsessions of the popular playwrights of the period. *The Zulu Chief* and *Cetewayo at Last*, both of 1882, satirised the contemporary fascination with African rulers and offered stereotypes of their characteristics.[35] They are depicted as lightfingered, prone to irrational violence and rampant sexual desire. This racial satire is combined with domestic class comment. In both plays working-class figures are cured of social climbing ambitions through encounters with the supposed King, a blacked-up neighbour in each case.

The martyrdom of General Gordon, on the other hand, produced a spate of theatrical encomia on this classic hero. *Khartoum* was a spectacular drama in four acts performed at Astley's Theatre in 1885, with Gordon thinly disguised as General Morton.[36] Spectacular scenes included the departure of troops from Portsmouth, a street bazaar in Cairo, a bivouac in the desert, a battle scene, even cataracts, rocks, and boats on the Nile. The final scene took place in Khartoum itself. Characters include a British officer, wrongly accused of forgery at home; his wife eager to reach him in Egypt and clear his name; a disgraced, but fortunately rich, officer who has been removed from the regiment, but has a private yacht in which to reach Egypt and retrieve his honour; a villain called Mavrofordate who, in spite of being the Mahdi's agent, is in fact a Greek; a native reconciler figure, a chieftainess called Ayesha; and some working-class rankers who, as always, largely supply the comic relief. Again, all the classic ingredients of imperial fiction are present: good and bad natives, officers seeking to retrieve honour, good, simple, amusing troopers, a shifty southern European villain, and a great hero offering moral enlightenment.

In *The Fall of Khartoum*, a sensational military drama in five acts, contrasting working- and middle-class characters join General Wolseley to save Gordon.[37] The villain is a Frenchman, Le Vendre, who has abjured Christianity for Islam in order to secure position and wealth with the Mahdi. An Indian ayah called Zayda has arrived in the Sudan to avenge herself on Le Vendre, whose attempted violation of her in India had been thwarted by a British Officer, Richard Daring, also inevitably now in the Sudan. General Gordon actually appears in the play, offers his own biscuits to a starving woman, frees a slave, and refuses to believe that England has deserted him. The British army arrives too late, but nonetheless defeats the Mahdi and recaptures Khartoum in a piece of wishful thinking which anticipated the event by thirteen years. The dastardly Le Vendre is unmasked and confounded, and Lieutenant Daring gets the V.C. The play makes frequent use of what are described in the text as 'splendid pictures', tableaux of Gordon, marching troops, and the like.

There is no doubt that a strong vein of satire runs through imperial plays of the 1890s and the Edwardian period. Yet respect for flag, royalty, and authority emerge strongly, and of course the real moments of crisis, like Khartoum or the Boer War, are treated with high seriousness. In *Morocco Bound*,[38] a farce with musical numbers of 1893, there is a great deal of satire not only upon Moroccan rulers (including their names, Spoofah Bey and Sid Fakali), but also on capitalist exploits in Africa. The Grand Vizier of Morocco arouses excitement among London financiers by offering a concession for the erection of music halls in Morocco in the hope of recouping the fortunes of his treasury. If Moroccans could but be provided with music halls they would flock in their thousands and make fortunes for the English investors.

> This method will be speedier than anything the clergy says
> In turning rapacious Moors to peaceful Moors and burgesses,
> For quite a host of virtues and of unexampled pieties
> Are sure to flourish underneath a Palace of Varieties,
> With kangaroos in boxing shoes, a Palace of Varieties.

Smoking, drinking, promenading, and dancing will all be allowed (a satire on efforts to clean up the London variety). There is much dealing in shares, and Spoofah Bey dupes an English squire to part with £20,000 in the hope of finding 'fame, Praise, by civilising a barbarous country with music halls'. Scenes in Morocco offer opportunities for the usual oriental spectacle, and a wide range of targets are mocked, from Gladstone to Ibsen, the Salvation Army to the Eight Hours agitation. Thus a satire of home politics, theatrical developments, and capitalist investments is combined with spectacle, cultural conflicts over social customs, and ludicrous exotic rulers.

In *Cheer, Boys, Cheer* of 1895 satire on capitalism is developed in its most eminently satirisable milieu, southern Africa. The play puts together the topical military elements of the Matabele War of 1893 with the contemporary obsession with concessions, 'kaffir booms' and the bulling of dubious shares.[39] There is much in the play that the historian of southern Africa recognises: the ensnaring of aristocrats by City spivs to lend their names and their money for a gambling adventure in paper deals and remote concessions, the depredations of the Matebele (or Ndebele) on their allegedly subject Shona people in Rhodesia/Zimbabwe, the swashbuckling antics of Dr Jameson, administrator of Rhodesia, the so-called Victoria incident, and the ultimatum which precipitated the Matabele War and the extension of the British South Africa Company's territory by military conquest.

Perhaps the most interesting aspect of the play, however, is its racial content. It is suffused with anti-semitic, anti-Boer, and anti-black sentiment. The concession is owned by an 'Africander Jew' called Meckstein, a snivelling Jewish stereotype, who reveals his cowardice in declining to fight in the Matabele War, and is dispossessed by the B.S.A. Co. When a party of aristocratic Englishwomen arrives in

Matabeleland, accompanied by an escort of Boers, they are attacked by 'natives', and the Boers ('cowardly hounds') ride off. The climax comes with a final stand by some of the male aristocratic characters of the play, reminiscent of Major Wilson's last stand, one of the icons of late nineteenth-century imperialism. But in the last act all comes right. The nasty Jew is done down; the naughty but engaging City fiddler is arrested; aristocratic heroism is displayed in the face of the attacking blacks, who are finally defeated; and, for the principal characters who survive, Africa turns out to be a good thing. By the end, the satire on capitalism has been transformed into a patriotic reassertion of aristocratic values and the optimistic assumption that, despite Jews, Boers, and blacks, British involvement in Africa will be beneficial after all.[40]

In the following year the play *An Artist's Model* was principally notable for references to the Jameson Raid (illustrating again the manner in which titles are little guide to content).[41] A jingoistic song, 'Hands off', was prohibited by the Lord Chamberlain because it contained slighting references to the Kaiser (Victoria's grandson), and a number of other changes were also demanded. But the play remained a source of patriotic audience participation. References to the Queen, Dr Jameson, the B.S.A. Co., and Joseph Chamberlain were cheered to the echo, while any mention of the Kaiser was loudly booed. The gallery spontaneously gave cheers for Jameson and 'groans' for the German emperor.

By the late Victorian and Edwardian periods the spectacular tradition had come to be combined with a rather farcical musical comedy style. These have been described as a 'Plethora of escapist musicals, using exotic locales'.[42] but theatrical historians have always concentrated on story line and production mechanics, never on political and racial content. Most of the comedies do seem to have appeared at theatres in the West End, in Coventry Street, and in Shaftsbury Avenue, but hits from them secured a very much wider circulation. Many of them had strikingly long runs, among the longest of the period. *The Geisha* (1896) ran for 760 performances, *San Toy* (1899) for 768, *Chinese Honeymoon* for 1,075 from 1901 (the record run of the time), *The Cingalee* (1904) for 365, a naval comedy called *The Flag Lieutenant* for 381, *Mr Wu*, an Anglo-Chinese play for 403.[43]

In plays and musical comedies the Orient provided an unrivalled opportunity to portray not only spectacle in setting and costumes, but also peculiar people with funny names, odd laws and customs, and characters who were slippery, grasping, and, even more interestingly, lascivious. The Orient, after all, had become a source of anxiety and strain, a place of complex trading relations and periodic warfare. It should not be forgotten that, geographically, it was ill-defined. To the French it included North Africa, on which much of French orientalism earlier in the century was based. Gradually the Orient expanded. The British in India and Ceylon became an increasingly common subject, and growing contacts with China and then Japan shifted the European stage Orient from North Africa to the Middle East to the Far East in the course of the century. The geography of many works was strikingly indeterminate. There seem to be a number of reasons for the fascination with orientalism which produced an almost annual crop of works, both highbrow and lowbrow, with comic burlesques a link between the two.

The plays and musical comedies sought to define the position of their British audiences in that ever-extending and infinitely complicated oriental relationship by portraying the foibles of Eastern peoples, their iniquities, their mindless autocracies, and their general inadequacy in the face of an easy Western superiority. It is true that these works could be made the thinly disguised vehicle of satire on conditions at home, as in *The Mikado*, but generally they did set out to portray the East with all its — as contemporaries might have put it — silken warts. Even better, the audience could be titillated with a heady atmosphere of perfumed lust, repulsive yet attractive.

In musical comedies like *The Grand Mogul*,[44] *The Nautch Girl*,[45] *The Geisha*, *The Chinese Honeymoon*,[46] *San Toy*, and *The Cingalee*,[47] geishas, nautch girls, and dancing girls of one sort or another abound, offering feminine stage spectacle and constant sexual innuendo, the very stuff of the Naughty Nineties. There are usually autocratic and rascally members of oriental elites like Marquis Imari in *The Geisha*, Spoofah Bey in *Morocco Bound*, Rajah Punka in *The Nautch Girl*, and Boobhamba in *The Cingalee*. There are often classic instances of Westernised oriental gentlemen, like Chamboodhy in *The Cingalee*, who talks in a succession of ludicrous malapropisms. Asians speak funny languages which are sent up repeatedly in nonsense songs. The oriental is caste-ridden — the entire plot of *The Nautch Girl* satirises caste; he is superstitious — astrologers abound; he is litigious; he is lustful; he is trapped by a succession of enervating institutions and social customs, including his legal system and the extended family; in business he is shifty, obsequious and treacherous by turns, particularly if he is Chinese. The Indian is sunk in tropical indolence and oriental fatalism, as depicted, typically, in the opening chorus of *The Nautch Girl*:

> Beneath the sky of blue
> The Indolent Hindu
> Reclines the whole day long.

He scorns ambitious schemes,
He weaves no lofty dreams:
His glance is on the ground.

In all this, popular culture was actively engaged in the creation of racial stereotypes.

The English characters in such performances spend their time desperately trying to cope with exotic oddities. Trade, tea planting, commercial capitalism, naval bombardments, are all portrayed as a great adventure, occasionally as a means by which Europeans can achieve ease, a multiplicity of servants, upward social mobility, and, if not a fortune, at least temporary sexual liaisons. Rival imperialists like the French come in for much satirical treatment, and, as we have seen, capitalist imperialism is itself sent up, although invariably in a patriotic manner, and in such a way as to make a racial point. None of this satire is subversive. It makes fun of incidents only within the context of accepted norms, and reinforces those norms in the process. If 'colonials' were satirised, it is also clear that the audience was expected to feel some envy for the international set portrayed therein.

Clearly it is important to establish the relative influence of these plays and musical comedies. Did the Empire empty theatres as effectively as it was always said to empty the Commons? The answer seems to be no. The plays had respectable runs, and often moved from theatre to theatre on provincial tours. The musical comedies were smash hits in several cases, and new productions appeared repeatedly. It is true that musical comedy was very much a middle-class taste, but such works illustrate the climate of theatrical conformity and set the tone for music hall sketches and reviews. The music hall, in effect, created a digest of other theatrical material: jingoistic and satirical songs and sketches, tableaux of battle scenes (particularly popular in the Manchester and Bolton music halls); miniature melodramas, spectacular acts, and wildly patriotic concluding extravaganzas. Moreover, songs from musical comedies and from music hall were disseminated much more widely through the sheet music boom which developed in this period.

The popular songs of the later Victorian and Edwardian periods inevitably reflected the same concerns as the plays and musical comedies. Ronald Pearsall has divided the songs into three categories: comments on contemporary life and events, love and domestic, uplift and patriotic.[48] There is of course a clear connection between the first and third, and it was these songs which came to enjoy such a tremendous popularity in the music hall. Within the first category there were many racial songs, which depicted Asians in particular as strange-looking people with silly languages. Others concentrated on the military and naval preoccupations of the day and had an enduring interest. Leslie Stuart's song 'Soldiers of the Queen' of 1881 achieved its greatest popularity at the time of the Boer War. Arthur Reece's 'Sons of the Sea' was written by Felix McGlennon for the 1897 Jubilee, and Kipling's 'Absent-minded Beggar' was set to music by Sir Arthur Sullivan during the Boer War. 'War Songs of the Day' was a common title for concerts from the 1870s. Romantic and domestic songs may have formed the largest single subject area, but it is noticeable that the songs of class solidarity — most of which tended to be of an optimistic rather than a revolutionary nature in any case — declined after the 1860s. Moreover, topical songs formed a larger proportion of the whole as the century wore on.

The popular song tradition, like the plays, reflected the climacterics of contemporary history. MacDermott's famous jingo song, Tom Costello's patriotic songs, and the outburst of military song-writing at the time of the Boer War are but a few examples. The successful numbers were repeated in clubs and social gatherings, in the streets and at home throughout the country. This remarkable penetration had been facilitated by the extraordinary growth in the possession of pianos. *Chambers's Journal* of 1881 described every house as having 'an altar to St. Cecilia', where all were taught to serve.[49] This was of course a considerable exaggeration, but pianos had certainly penetrated to the homes of the aristrocracy of labour, and no place of public recreation or instruction would have been without one. Developments in lithography and printing, described in the introduction, led to dramatically increased sales of sheet music in the 1880s and after. If prices were such as to put it beyond any but the middle-class pocket, nonetheless pirated editions greatly increased its circulation.

Lively patriotic songs were also a feature of pantomime. The Drury Lane pantomime in 1911, *Hop 'o my Thumb*, contained the following number:

> There are enemies around us who are jealous of our fame.
> We have made a mighty Empire and they'd like to do the same.
> And they think the way to do it is to catch us as we nap.
> While they push our friends and neighbours from their places
> on the map.

There were several verses in the same vein, each ending with the refrain:

> And we mean to be the top dog still.
> Bow-wow-
> Yes, we mean to be the top dog still.[50]

A very successful pantomime of the inter-war and post-Second World War years illustrates the enduring nature of such material. *Aladdin*, by V. C. Clinton-Baddeley, was presented by Sir Nigel Playfair at the Lyric Theatre, Hammersmith, was produced at the Festival Theatre, Cambridge, and by professional companies in Amersham, Southport, Oldham, Worthing, and Guildford.[51] The Old Vic staged it in Bristol in the Christmas season of 1947-48, and in 1949 it was played on tour by the West of England Theatre Company. It contained many topical allusions and much imperial matter, including the song 'Chips of the Grand old Block', which apostrophised the 'Mothers of the Empire':

> Methinks I see beside the camp fire sitting
> Many an Empire Mother at her knitting.
> Take heart! The bonds of friendship draw us close—
> Soon we shall be one family — who knows?
>
> The Mothers of the Empire are mothers of us all,
> From humble cot or palace they hear Britannia's call.
> On Baffin's icy margin or Africa's sultry shores,
> They hear the call to duty and answer it by scores.
>
> See them trooping to the Standard, hear them answer to the cry
> Across our far-flung frontiers (theirs not to reason why).
> The hand that rocks the cradle is the hand that rocks the world,
> And it waves above each infant head a Union Jack unfurled.

This was to be sung to dramatic music in the minor key, and was following by the chorus:

> They are the Mothers of the Empire,
> The Sisters of the Free —
> Hands across the Sea;
> Girls of the Bulldog breed!
> From New Zealand and Australia, Ceylon and Wai-hai-Wei,
> Bermuda, Malta, and Bangkok,
> Chips of the Grand Old Block.[52]

The need for a rhyme for Block led the writer to extend the Empire to Thailand, but apart from this geographical peccadillo the song perfectly expresses both the imperial preference ambitions of the '30s and memories of imperial solidarity in the Great War. Topical allusions, dramatised references to contemporary events, and patriotic sketches were incorporated into all the traditional pantomimes throughout the period.

Defying convention, music hall has been left to the end in this chapter. It has too often been examined by historians in isolation because it was such a striking phenomenon. However, its power and the tremendous popularity it secured among a wide spectrum of social classes can only be fully understood if it is placed in a wider context, which has so far remained the preserve of writers on the theatre and popular music. The enduring popular interest in melodrama and spectacular theatre led directly to the topical, militarist, and patriotic content of the music hall. The well established tradition of topical imperial plays, and the orientalist musical, with all their racial and political overtones, fed off the music hall, in turn forming a wider environment in which music hall could flourish. The choral and brass band movements brought a new form of musical participation to the masses and developed the popularity of an outdoor music which was predominantly military and patriotic. Many of these were middle-class interests, but even the majority of the working-class who were not swept up into choirs and bands could scarcely avoid hearing them proclaiming patriotic themes, encouraging military recruitment, and adding to royal and civic pageantry.

A number of entertainment streams ran together into the great roaring torrent which was the late nineteenth-century music hall. Its tributaries were the song saloons paid for by the breweries and attached to public houses, the 'free-and-easies' of the 1850s and their middle-class equivalents, the song and supper rooms, as well as the working-class melodrama theatres. When Charles Morton turned his Canterbury Theatre in Lambeth into the New Canterbury Music Hall in 1854 his prospectus proclaimed his intention 'to form and refine the public taste', to bring a mixture of social classes to a poor area, and to offer a varied diet of popular entertainments.[53] Morton made sure that all classes were catered for: he offered nautical spectacles like Trafalgar, operetta, and acrobatics, as well as the usual music hall entertainments. There was also a library, and other music halls had exhibitions and emigration displays.[54]

Morton's venture was a huge success, and literally hundreds of music halls opened in the 1860s and 1870s. Despite the closure of some 200 after new fire regulations in 1878, there were no fewer than 500 in London alone in the 1880s.[55] By 1913 £5 million had been invested in music halls and 80,000 people were employed by them.[56] In the 1890s it was estimated that thirty-five of the largest halls were catering for an average nightly audience of 45,000.[57] At one stage there were as many as 242 in the twelve parishes of Tower Hamlets alone.[58] At a later date it was said that the total annual audience was some 25 million.[59] This tremendous growth turned the music hall into a highly capitalist venture, with, by the 1890s, a strongly monopolist tinge. A significant change in its character came about as a result. The music hall's antecedents had been small, informal oper-ations, often chaired by the proprietor himself, with the performances enlivened by the exchanges and general *rapport* between audience and performers. By the 1880s the stage had come to predominate over the auditorium, a process heightened by the intrusion of the proscenium arch, the development of strong lighting, and the new star status of many of the artistes. The chairman had disappeared, and with stabil-ised seating and the ban on drinks the audiences became much better disciplined. Moreover, the maximisation of the talents and profit value of the most famous stars through the 'turns' system (whereby they appeared in several houses on the same evening) led to tight schedules and the disappearance of ad-libbed asides and backchat with the audience. Indeed, by the 1880s, according to Peter Bailey,

> some managements obliged artists to sign contracts forbidding the direct address of the audience. House rules proscribed not only vulgarity but also offensive allusions to a long list of official figures and institutions, while audiences were invited to inform the manager of any breach of cen-sorship that escaped his notice. The audience themselves were put under restraint by uniformed commissionaires who stood in the audience pit regulating the number of choruses and otherwise policed the auditorium.[60]

It is clear that the music hall was censoring itself as effectively as if it had its own Lord Chamberlain.

The social range of such a large industry was of course diverse. There were many 'low' halls, some like Morton's with a diverse client-ele, and some in the West End which set their seat prices to attract a mainly middle-class audience. In a remarkable undergraduate disserta-tion Penny Summerfield has analysed the different types of music hall in London, their 'social tone', and the nature of the programmes. She categorises the halls into A, B and C, A being the multi-class halls of the West End, B the local halls of mixed upper working-class and lower middle-class composition, and C the working-class halls of the East End.[61] She suggests that a distinction must be drawn between the pat-riotism, which could often be combined with class solidarity, of the C halls, and the jingoism which was perhaps most pronounced in the B halls, and was also of course much in evidence at the A halls. In the C halls the working-class identified themselves with their fellows in the army and the navy, enjoying songs which expressed a traditional xenophobia as well as a degree of working-class consciousness.

If it is possible to analyse music hall material in these horizontal social bands, it is also possible to analyse it in terms of chronological change. In the 1870s a defensive nationalism was all the rage, expressed in songs and spectacles which gave prominence to the Eastern Question, the route to India and villainy of the Russian Bear. By the end of the decade a much more aggressive nationalism was becoming evident, coinciding significantly with the development of the 'New Imperialism'. Songs were strung together into 'song scenes' which owed a great deal to both the spectacular and the melodramatic traditions. These patriotic spectacles contained songs contributed by the most notable writers of the day. Clement Scott, the drama critic of the *Daily Telegraph*, wrote such songs, and they were incorporated in events like the 'New Patriotic Entertainment entitled Albion's Nationality' presented at the Oxford Theatre in 1878. G. W. Hunt, the creator of MacDermott's 'By Jingo' song, wrote many other patriotic numbers. One of them, 'If England to Herself be True' was a central feature of the 'Indianationality' spectacular performed again at the Oxford in 1879. The same theatre produced the spectacle 'Britannia' in 1885, and these are merely a few examples of dozens of such productions. Press reports indicate wildly enthusiastic audiences, with repeated demands for encores. All of them were underpinned by an ideology of pride in race, the brotherhood of the white Dominions of settlement, the justice of British rule in India, and the need to defend the Empire against aggressive rivals. Colonies could also be celebrated as places of emigration, escape hatches from poverty, social utopias across the sea. Other theatres soon followed suit, some of them stressing military elements. The Alhambra offered a 'Grand Military Spectacle' in 1886 and 'Our Army and Navy' in 1889.

Figures emerged who were closely identified with imperial themes, and their influence was encapsulated in the sobriquet 'statesmen of the halls'. MacDermott sang his jingo songs at many music halls, often on the same night, eventually bought himself a chain of music halls in the East End, and (although he was bankrupted on the way) died a rich man. Charles Godfrey appeared as Nelson, Wellington, and Major Wilson (of the Last Stand) at various halls, and espoused imperial federation and the brotherhood of the dominant imperial race in his songs. Many of Hunt's imperial and patriotic songs were parodied, but not in such a way as to strike an ideological blow at the originals, more to send up the characters they described and the performers who sang them. The parodies simply involved squeezing further entertainment value out of the songs, and were themselves a tribute to the fame of their lines and their sentiments. Parodies, after all, only work when the original is well known.

Between 1880 and 1914 the category A halls seem to have been the ones concerned with more sophisticated political ideas like colonial unity. During that period the category B ones rapidly emerged as the halls of the new suburbs, prone to the most rabid jingoism, while those in category C continued to express an essentially defensive nationalism. Whether this sophisticated social and class analysis works for the rest of the country is a moot point. There can be no doubt that different theatres had a variety of social tones, but Douglas Reid has established that in Birmingham the same theatre could have a different social tone on various nights of the week.[62] Moreover, the vast popularity of the material acted as a social leveller. The most popular songs, often the most rousingly patriotic, were popular in all social settings. By the end of the century the syndicates of Moss and Stoll, originating in the north, were establishing great chains of halls, enlarging and standardising the entertainment for a multi-class appeal.

The best clue to the working-class popularity of the music hall is, however, provided by the history of the working men's clubs. The Club and Institute Union had been founded in 1862. By 1867 there were no fewer than 300 clubs, many of them founded by socially conscious members of the middle classes in an effort to provide rational recreation for the working class.[63] The intention was to create a rival attraction to the pub, where workers could seek self-improvement through reading, debating, lectures and the like. The clubs went through a series of battles, first to introduce beer to encourage membership, second to secure independence from middle-class patrons, and third to politicise themselves in terms of working-class solidarity. From 1890, however, a significant shift took place in the emphasis of the clubs, from the old political, educational, and recreational style to a tradition of professional entertainment provided on a business basis. Entertainment had come to dominate club life: first, home-grown entertainment provided by members or visitors from other clubs; later, acts by thoroughly professional entertainers. Theatricals and melodrama had always been popular, but towards the end of the century music hall-style entertainment took over. Clubs were equipped with elaborate stage fittings; membership rose dramatically, and there was a great growth in their size and magnificence. Richard Price has cited them in evidence for the absence of working-class jingoism at the time of the Boer War,[64] but Stedman Jones,[65], Taylor[66] and Ashplant[67] have all pointed to the depoliticising of the clubs during the 1890s. In effect they became music halls, offering exactly the same sort of entertainment.

Those which failed to make this shift imperilled their very existence.[68] The South Bermondsey club found its membership declining in 1890, opened new premises providing music hall entertainment, and quintupled it within a year. The United Radical Club, one of the largest in London, closed in 1901, apparently because it had clung too tenaciously to its original political and educational purpose. In 1900 the Borough of Hackney club, once prominently radical, voted unanimously to do away with its political council, a decision which was apparently met with great cheering. By 1905 the secretary of the Club and Institute Union agreed that the clubs had fallen into political decay and that politics, far from being their *raison d'être*, had become no more than one of many hobbies which could be pursued there.[69] It is interesting to note that among these hobbies — catered for by the interest groups or sub-clubs — were several that reflected the growing militarism of the period: bayonet and rifle practice, interest in the services, and so on.[70] The collapse of the radical clubs, the popularity of militarist hobbies, and the universal popularity of patriotic music hall entertainment, all seem to run counter to Price's vision of the clubs as arenas for the serious discussion of Boer War issues, where the working class maintained independent attitudes towards the war itself and imperialism generally.

The evidence provided by the clubs is perhaps the best indication of working-class enthusiasm for the military and patriotic sentiments expressed in the music hall entertainment of the day. This is the more readily understandable when the music hall is seen not as an isolated phenomenon, an aberration in working-class culture, but as arising naturally from the theatrical and musical traditions of the nineteenth century. Perhaps the prime characteristic of both melodramatic and spectacular theatre was its responsiveness to topical events, in the equestrian and aquatic displays, in panoramas and lantern slide shows, and in plays which set ordinary characters, with whom the audience could identify, against a background of stirring national events. In addition to this precise topical context, much other popular entertainment was set against a more general background which took account of the great international developments of the day. What was true of the theatre was also true of popular songs, of band music, and of musical comedy and its spin-offs. Military, naval, and patriotic elements are not new in the late nineteenth century; they are part of a larger tradition. Charles Dibdin, manager of Sadler's Wells in the Napoleonic period, pointed out that the theatre always did well in time of war.[71] For the British, the great changes of the nineteenth century were in the locale of warfare, its shift from a defensive to an offensive posture, and the transformation of the enemy from Frenchman or Russian to African and Asian. The intellectual climate of the late century — aggressively self-confident, militarist, and racial — served to heighten long-standing trends in popular culture. The backdrop of stirring events was for a period almost exclusively imperial. Royal pageantry, warfare, sport, and even architecture, had all become imperial. The fact was that imperial exploits made good theatre.[72] They not only fitted into, they heightened military, patriotic, spectacular and melodramatic traditions. What, after all, could be more spectacular than the spread — as contemporary propagandists put it — of a global just rule, the destruction of barbaric villainy on a world-wide scale, and the defence of legitimately won possessions against aggressive and less beneficent rivals?

It has been said of Sir Edward Grey that he was a Liberal imperialist because he could see no other logical position in the conditions of the late nineteenth century.[73] To deny empire for Britain was to risk being overwhelmed by the empires of others. It was this approach to imperialism that lay behind much of the imperialism of the left. Better a free-trade and benevolent imperialism than the protectionist and autocratic imperialism of European rivals. That position communicated itself to the working classes and was indeed recommended to them by some of the leaders of the left, as well as by popular entertainers. Henry Mayers Hyndman, founder of the Social Democratic Federation, himself for many years an imperialist,[74] noted the patriotic fervour of the working classes in his reminiscences. He also observed that during the Boer War the poorest districts were more elaborately hung with bunting and patriotic decorations than even the West End.[75] The attempt to pin the jingoist expressions of imperialism on specific social classes, in particular the lower middle class, will not do. Nor will it do to see imperialism as a temporary aberration reaching a climax with the Boer War and undergoing swift decline thereafter. It was an enduring phenomenon, which from time to time produced jingoistic outbursts particularly associated with warfare. The ambivalence many Establishment figures felt towards it is again well represented by Grey. Not even his lofty, dispassionate temperament was untouched by imperial enthusiasm. In 1898 the war in the Sudan aroused in him 'the throbbing of a pulse which is stirred'.[76] Yet, in an anti-jingo mood, he also wrote, 'I should like to break the heads of all the Music Halls.'[77] Perhaps nothing better reflects the problems of definition, the thin dividing lines between patriotism, imperialism, and jingoism, together with aristocratic and liberal intellectual distrust of mob enthusiasm.

NOTES

1 J. A. Hobson, *The Psychology of Jingoism*, London, 1901, 3.
2 H. M. Hyndman, *Further Reminiscences*, London, 1912, 168.

3 Quoted in D. H. Simpson, 'Variations on an imperial theme', R.C.S. Library Notes, April 1965.
4 Charles Carrington, *Rudyard Kipling*, London, 1970, 415-16.
5 Max Beerbohm, 'Music halls of my youth', quoted in Lawrence Senelick, 'Politics as entertainment: Victorian music hall songs', *Victorian Studies*, XIX (1975), 150.
6 John Betjeman, foreword to R. Mander and J. Mitchenson, *British Music Hall*, London, 1965.
7 Harold Scott, *The Early Doors: Origins of the Music Hall*, London, 1946.
8 G. J. Mellor, *The Northern Music Hall*, Newcastle-upon-Tyne, 1970.
9 Mander and Mitchenson, *British Music Hall*.
10 Senelick, 'Politics as entertainment', 150.
11 Senelick, 'Politics of entertainment', 180.
12 Penelope Summerfield, 'The Effingham Arms and the Empire: deliberate selection and the evolution of the music hall in London', in Eileen and Stephen Yeo (eds.), *Popular Culture and Class Conflict, 1590-1914*, Sussex, 1981.
13 Peter Bailey, 'Custom, capital, and culture in the Victorian music hall', in Robert D. Storch (ed.), *Popular Culture and Custom in Nineteenth Century England*, London, 1982, 201.
14 J. S. Bratton, *The Victorian Popular Ballad*, London, 1975, 144.
15 John Russell Stephens, *The Censorship of the English Drama, 1824-1901*, Cambridge, 1980. Richard Findlater, *Banned! A Review of Theatrical Censorship in Britain*, London, 1967.
16 Findlater, *Banned!*, 156.
17 Findlater, *Banned!*, 102.
18 Stephens, *Censorship*, 132.
19 J. S. Bratton, 'Theatre of war: the Crimea on the London stage, 1854-5, in David Bradby *et al.* (eds.), *Performance and Politics in Popular Drama*, Cambridge, 1980.
20 Michael Booth, *English Melodrama*, London, 1965, 13.
21 Booth, *English Melodrama*, 46.
22 Douglas A. Reid, 'Popular theatre in Victorian Birmingham', in Bradby *et al.*, *Performance and Politics*.
23 Michael Booth, *Victorian Spectacular Theatre, 1850-1910*, London, 1981, 5-7.
24 Booth, *Spectacular Theatre*, 12. Photography probably contributed to the Victorian theatrical fascination with realism. Alan Thomas, *The Expanding Eye*, London, 1978, 116.
25 Derek Forbes, 'Water drama', in Bradby *et al.*, *Performance and Politics*, 99. Booth, *English Melodrama*, 100.
26 Forbes, 'Water drama', 107.
27 Antony D. Hippisley Coxe, 'Equestrian drama and the circus', in Bradby *et al.*, *Performance and Politics*. See also Booth, *English Melodrama*, 100.
28 Bratton, 'Theatre of war', 122 and 130.
29 Bratton, 'Theatre of war', 135.
30 Hugh Cunningham, *The Volunteer Force*, London, 1975, 1 and 120.
31 Booth, *Spectacular Theatre*, 62-3.
32 This analysis of titles is based on the lists in the Lord Chamberlain's plays collection in the manuscript collection of the British Library (B.L. MSS, L.C.'s Plays).
33 Booth, *English Melodrama*, 176.
34 Titles included: *England Expects, Call to Arms, God Save the Empire, British Soldier, War Declared, Sons of the Sea, To Arms, German Spy, In Time of War, Berlin, Allies, Your Country Needs You, Siege of Berlin, Soldier's Honour, Nation's Hymn, By Jingo if we do*. At the same time Sir Herbert Beerbohm Tree hastily revived the patriotic spectacular play, *Drake*, with himself as Sir Francis. Thomas Hardy's treatment of the Napoleonic Wars in three parts and nineteen acts, *The Dynasts*, was also performed. J. C. Trewin, *The Edwardian Theatre*, Oxford, 1976, 182. The list of war plays comes from the Lord Chamberlain's list of licensings, and could be continued in similar numbers for the rest of the war.
35 *The Zulu Chief* by W. Lowe and *Cetewayo at Last* by Robert Coote, B.L. MSS, L.C.'s Plays, both licensed 1882.

36 *Khartoum*, a spectacular drama in four acts, Astley's Theatre. B.L. MSS, L.C.'s Plays, 1885.

37 *The Fall of Khartoum*, a sensational military drama in five acts by Herbert John Stanely, B.L. MSS, L.C.'s Plays, 1885.

38 *Morocco Bound*, a farcical comedy in two acts by Adrian Ross and Arthur Branscombe, music by F. Osmond Carr, B.L. MSS, L.C.'s Plays, 1893.

39 *Cheer, Boys, Cheer*, a new drama for Drury Lane by Sir Augustus Harris, Cecil Raleigh, and Henry Hamilton, B.L. MSS, L.C.'s Plays, 1895.

40 It is surprising that, in an age so often described as one of economic and intellectual pessimism, so many stage performances had a strongly optimistic content. This emerges again in Hall Caine's *The Mahdi* of 1894. Caine's Mahdi is not the violent obscurantist of Sudan lore, but an Islamic revolutionary who brings Christ-like qualities of mercy, compassion, and freedom to the liberation of Islam. Caine developed these ideas further in *The White Prophet*, a novel of 1909. Islam, which had caused so much trouble in European expansion, would fall, if not to European arms, or European concession-seekers, then at least to internal religious reform. Caine's Mahdi can no doubt be seen as a personification of beneficent Western influence.

41 Stephens, *Censorship*, 130.

42 Ronald Pearsall, *Edwardian Popular Music*, Newton Abbott, 1975, 11. 'It was a time of unrepentant make-believe.' J. C. Trewin, *Edwardian Theatre*, 3. None of the historians of theatre has chosen to notice the racial and political ideas carefully concealed within this 'make-believe'.

43 Trewin, *Edwardian Theatre*, 155-9.

44 *The Grand Mogul, or, The Snake Charmer*, in three acts, composed by Audran, B.L. MSS, L.C.'s Plays, 1884. The original version by Henri Chivot and Alfred Durn was produced in 1877 in Marseilles. Mark Lubbock, *The Complete Book of Light Opera*, London, 1962, uses the French version, which is quite different from the English one, in B.L. MSS, L.C.'s Plays.

45 *The Nautch Girl: An Original Indian Opera*, libretto and lyrics by George Dance, music by Edward Solomon, B.L. MSS, L.C.'s Plays, 1891.

46 *The Chinese Honeymoon* by George Dance, music by Howard Talbot, B.L. MSS, L.C.'s Plays, 1899.

47 *The Cingalee, or, In Sweet Ceylon*, a two-act musical play by James T. Turner, B.L. MSS, L.C.'s Plays, 1904.

48 Ronald Pearsall, *Victorian Popular Music*, Newton Abbot, 1973, 40.

49 Quoted in Pearsall, *Popular Music*, 74.

50 Gyles Brandreth, *I Scream for Ice Cream: Pearls from the Pantomime*, London, 1974, 49-50.

51 V. C. Clinton-Baddeley, *Alladin, or, Love Will Find out the Way*, London, 1949, 3.

52 Clinton-Baddeley, *Alladin*, 39-40. At the climax of the song Widow Twankey appeared in Girl Guide uniform.

53 Penny Summerfield, 'The Imperial Idea and the Music Hall', University of Sussex B.A. dissertation, 1973, 9. I am very grateful to Ms Summerfield for permitting me to see this thesis.

54 Bailey, 'Custom, capital, and culture', 183, 185.

55 G. Stedman Jones, 'Working-class culture and working-class politics in London, 1870–1900', *Journal of Social History*, 7 (1973), 477.

56 P. Summerfield, 'The Effingham Arms', 222.

57 Jones, 'Working-class culture', 477.

58 Summerfield, 'Imperial Idea', 4.

59 Summerfield, 'Imperial Idea', 10.

60 Bailey, 'Custom, capital, and culture', 196.

61 Summerfield, 'Imperial Idea', 13-16.

62 Reid, 'Popular theatre', 73.

63 John Taylor, 'From self-help to glamour: the working-men's club, 1860-1972', *History Workshop* Pamphlet No. 7, 1972, 10.

64 R. N. Price, *An Imperial War and the British Working Class*, London, 1972, chapter 2.

65 Jones, 'Working-class culture', 480.
66 Taylor, 'From self-help', 59-69.
67 T. G. Ashplant, 'London working-men's clubs, 1875-1914', in E. and S. Yeo, *Popular Culture*, 241-70.
68 Ashplant, 'London working-men's clubs', 251-61. New club buildings were built as music halls, and their advertisements stressed this part of their existence, 269.
69 Ashplant, 'London working-men's clubs', 270.
70 Taylor, 'From self-help', 31. Taylor also charts the rise of the Conservative working-men's clubs.
71 Forbes, 'Water drama', 92-3.
72 In the late nineteenth century the form, the characters, the music, and the message of music hall entertainment were strikingly congruent. When in the twentieth century an attempt is made to ally the forms of pantomime and music hall to a negative message, as in the Royal Shakespeare Company's *Poppy* (1982-83), the political bite of the anti-imperial propaganda is destroyed by an attractive form which makes the characters unintentionally sympathetic.
73 Keith Robbins, 'Sir Edward Grey and the British Empire', *Journal of Imperial and Commonwealth History*, 1 (1972-73), 213-21.
74 Hyndman believed in 'the beneficent influence of the British flag and the glories of British rule all over the world, considering indeed that our expansion was good alike for governors and governed'. He repented his imperialism later. Hyndman, *Further Reminiscences*, 151.
75 'And among those who were most eager for the war and most jubilant at the slightest success were the wage-earners themselves in the very poorest localities. The insanitary pauper-inhabited court, then still standing at the end of the street I lived in, was more decorated with flags at the news of some "victory" than were all the fashionable parts of Westminster put together.' Hyndman, *Further Reminiscences*, 165.
76 Robbins, 'Sir Edward Grey', 217.
77 Robbins, 'Sir Edward Grey', 218.

—3—
THE CINEMA, RADIO AND THE EMPIRE

Historians of popular culture have frequently linked the decline of militarist or imperialist genres with the demise of the particular theatrical form they have studied. Military spectacle, we are told, was dead by the end of the nineteenth century.[1] In fact, it was the combined ring and stage form at Astley's (Sanger's) and the Surrey which had died. Military spectacle survived in the great Volunteer field days, at exhibitions, tattoos, royal tournaments, and eventually in the cinema. Melodrama was gone by the early 1920s, surviving only in opera and burlesque.[2] In fact it had taken up residence elsewhere, on film. Above all, the old patriotic and imperialist music hall died with the First World War, and for many commentators its passing marks the end of popular cultural imperialism.[3] But again, popular imperialism can be found surviving in both new and old forms, in exhibitions, in popular literature, in ephemera, in a whole range of propagandist and educational texts, and above all in the cinema. In each case the death of the form has been mistakenly identified with the demise of the content, which merely transmigrated into new popular vehicles.

Although film represented a technological revolution, the striking thing about its early history is the manner in which it swiftly adopted the traditional dramatic forms of popular culture, and indeed carried them forward into a new era. In doing so it probably gave the old conventions a longer lease of life than they might otherwise have had, for the conservatism of the material was obscured by the technical fascination of the new medium. Moreover, in silent films the dumb-show conditions of the pre-1843 non-patent theatre were reproduced. Once again it was not only melodrama but also spectacle which flourished best under such conditions. The early film industry proceeded to put on the screen the subjects which had proved such popular staples of the nineteenth-century theatre — warfare, royal events, exotica, orientalism, the drama of transport. This chapter attempts to demonstrate how an imperial world view, complete with the familiar range of military, racial, and technological perceptions, continued to be peddled to the public through the new medium. The great technical advances of sound and, soon after, colour may have led to a rapid sophistication in the treatment of subjects, but the old traditions survived. The cinema continued to draw its prime inspiration from a melodramatic and adventure genre[4] — which best fitted the box-office appeal of spectacle

in exotic settings — until the 1950s and 1960s. This tradition necessarily involved a world view often explicitly and always implicitly
rooted in nineteenth-century imperial perceptions. The dominance
of Hollywood in no way dented the supremacy of this world view.
American film-makers recognised its persistent drawing power,
generally accepted the United States' own post-1898 imperial role, and
certainly set out to pander to the British market.

Film was nurtured by the old entertainment forms before emerging
to consume them. It began life as an added attraction at the music hall
and as a sideshow at fairgrounds and exhibitions, thereby neatly
reflecting the exhibitions' role in marrying entertainment to the
revelation of technical advance. As soon as it had achieved its own independent outlets, however, its capacity to overwhelm the theatrical
entertainments on which it had been a parasite was swiftly apparent.
In 1913 a play with a prophetic title — Cinemania — was presented on
the London stage. In advance of the First World War many suburban
lower middle-class music halls were already being killed by the
cinema, which by 1917 already enjoyed an audience of twenty million
a week in 4,000 to 4,500 cinemas.[5]

The technical problems associated with early film made it unsuit-
able as a vehicle for major dramatic presentations. The shortness of the
reels, inadequate studio facilities, the primitive cameras and projectors
led to a concentration on outdoor filming. Once film had graduated
from its initial fascination with the sheer exhilaration of dramatic
movement — as in the endless train-entering-station scenes — it settled down to present great topical events, public pageantry and display,
exotic travelogues, together with short vaudeville and comic acts. An
examination of the early activities of British companies, the subjects
they treated, and the circulation they secured, reveals a continuation
of all the main themes which were explored in the previous chapter.
Before large-scale specialisation, some of the early film companies
were involved in a number of different media. The Bamforth company
in Yorkshire, for example, important dealers in lantern slides and
above all in picture postcards, took up cinematography at the turn of
the century and distributed humorous films in the north of England.[6]

The armed forces and warfare were one of cinematography's earliest
obsessions, and were to continue so throughout the history of the
cinema. The army, which had quickly seized upon the propagandist
opportunities afforded by military music, open-air band performances,
public displays, and the postcard collecting craze, seems to have been
alive to the propaganda value of celluloid from an early date. The
Adjutant General, Sir Evelyn Wood, made facilities available to the

film-maker R. W. Paul to produce a series of twenty films on army life in 1900.[7] In the same year Cecil Hepworth produced films on the army and the navy. Nineteen-hundred was of course a year which represented the periodic military climacterics of warfare in popular culture, and the Boer War did in fact provide a great fillip for the nascent cinematograph industry. Charles Dibdin had remarked (in Napoleonic times) that war filled the theatres; television viewing figures and newspaper circulations shot up during the Falklands War of 1982. The Boer War gave film its first great opportunity to prove its value in presenting 'actuality' material. People could now see images of war which purported to be captured reflections of the real thing, on a lighted screen, all the more enthralling because they represented the wonders of a new medium. The burning down of Astley's in 1895 was perhaps timely. Within a very few years film was giving a more convincing illusion of reality than the hundreds of extras storming the Heights of Alma on the Astley's stage could ever have done.

Rachael Low provides a list of the newsreels and Boer War films produced by British companies, most notably the British Mutoscope and Biograph Company and Urban & Paul.[8] All these films seem to have presented positive images of the war, carefully avoiding British reverses or the more controversial aspects of the British prosecution of the campaigns. Three films portrayed a skirmish between a troop of cavalry scouts attached to General French on his march to relieve Kimberley, *The Scouts in Pursuit of the Boers*, *Bringing the Maxims into Action*, and *A Charge and General Fusilade*. Boer surrenders were inevitably popular subjects, and titles included *The Surrender of Kroonstad to Lord Roberts* and *Cronje's Surrender to Lord Roberts*. *The signing of the Peace of Vereeniging* in 1902, however, was, like many other Boer War films, faked. The departures of troops, with all the opportunities they afforded for sentiment, spectacle, and transport interest, survived directly from theatrical traditions into film. The embarkation films included one featuring the departure of Sir Redvers Buller, *The Braemar Castle leaving for South Africa* and *The City Imperial Volunteers Marching aboard the S.S. Garth Castle*. The short dramatic films of the period also played on sentiment and heroism. In both *The Call to Arms* and *The Soldier's Return* of 1902, returning volunteers receive just rewards.[9] The first secures the acclamation of friends and the second rescues his mother from the workhouse and creates a model environment for her.

War and alarms of war continued to be a cinematic obsession up to the First World War. The Boxer rising in China, the developing industrial and naval might of Japan, and the battles of the Russo-Japanese

War were all the subject of films. The latter conflict helped to spread the many false perceptions, both professional and popular, of the nature of twentieth-century warfare, and fuelled the naval race which was kept prominently in the public eye by repeated newsreels of the launchings of dreadnoughts. Moroccan crises, imperial skirmishes and the Balkan wars also featured in the newsreels and may well have contributed to the apparent yearning for military action which was a characteristic of the period. 'Army life' films, like Hepworth's *In the Service of the King* and the Gaumont-distributed *British Army Film* of 1913 received a wide circulation.[10] The latter was explicitly propagandist, made with full official co-operation; it took six months to produce, and was publicised as widely as the Scott of the Antarctic films. In 1913 British & Colonial produced the timely *Battle of Waterloo*, a vast spectacular which neatly illustrates the transfer of Astley's material to the medium of the cinema. Such films contributed to the powerful militarism of the period, and helped to prepare the way for the massive working-class recruitment to the army on the outbreak of the First World War.

Film not only continued the nineteenth-century traditions of military drama but provided fresh material for the long fascination with nautical drama. Whole series of films were produced continuing the Jack Tar and Tom Topreef traditions, although it is interesting that in the Edwardian period the heroes became officers. Naval heroes like Lieutenant Daring and Lieutenant Rose appeared in a succession of films, and the cinema contributed as much to the 'Trafalgar cult' as to the 'Waterloo cult'. Traditional ballads were used in *Napoleon and the English Sailor* (1908). As in the media examined in other chapters, a general world view involving the acquisition and defence of a just empire, a natural superiority threatened by aggressive rivals whose claims were less solidly based both historically and morally, runs through all such films. It is true that many of them were burlesqued (for example, *Lieutenant Pimple*), just as MacDermott's jingo song had been, but not in such a way as to undermine the dominant ethos of the material. There were also factual presentations of naval subjects, including *A Dreadnought in the Making* (1911), which featured as its climax the launching of the *Princess Alice*, a Lion class battlecruiser, at Barrow, and *The Birth of a Big Gun*, the manufacture of a 12 in. gun at Armstrong Whitworth's in Newcastle. No doubt such films were made with official encouragement, but generally they were commercially inspired, designed to satisfy an existing, long-nurtured public taste.

If the forces and warfare were dominant themes, two others are germane to the core ideology of the period. These were the presentation of monarchy, and, at the other end of the imperial social spectrum, the presentation of the imperial monarch's more 'primitive' subjects at the outer reaches of Empire. Royal occasions saw the first successful application of the newsreel technique. Even static cameras and short reels could capture the spectacle of troops, horses, and personalities in the great royal pageants of the age. The 1897 jubilee was of course the first event so covered, followed in fairly rapid succession by the funeral of Queen Victoria, the coronation of Edward VII, the Delhi durbar of 1903, the state visits of Edward to Europe, and the next trilogy of funeral, coronation, and durbar on George V's accession. Paul Rotha's earliest film memories included going to see the film of the Delhi durbar.[11] Robert Roberts has described the enduring and detailed fascination royalty exerted on the Edwardian working class of Salford.[12] In the past that fascination could be satisfied only by visits to London, by provincial appearances of members of the royal family and other figures of the imperial personality cult, by the local pageantry associated with national events, or by theatrical presentations with actors and actresses standing in for the leading figures. The catalogue entries for the films of pageantry stressed two things: the effectiveness of 'close-ups' of members of the royal family, and the 'colourfulness' (which had of course to be painted in the imagination) of the great range of uniforms, accoutrements, and mountings of the colonial troops. Of the dozen 40 ft films issued by R. W. Paul of the 1897 jubilee, nine featured the troops in the procession, five of those involving named colonial troops, including the Canadians, the Cape Mounted Rifles, and the Indian escort. It was a relatively short step from this 'actuality' material to the large-scale historical reconstructions like W. G. Barker's epic *Sixty Years a Queen* of 1913. In 1911 Barker had contributed to the music hall patriotic tableau tradition with his 'Pageant of Empire' for the coronation of George V, which featured the colonies paying allegiance to Britannia enthroned.

Other nineteenth-century traditions carried over into film included the 'panorama' and the travelogue, offshoots of the lantern-slide lecture. Cinematographers were soon out and about in Japan, China, India, the Middle East, North Africa, and North America. There were panoramas of the Paris Exhibition of 1900 and (an enduring interest) of Egypt. The later 'scenics' were devoted almost entirely to India, the South Seas, and Tropical Africa. Expeditions were popular, like those of Cherry Kearton in India, Africa, and Borneo after 1908, although it was of course the films of the expeditions of Shackleton and of Scott to the Antarctic that received the greatest publicity.[13] Just as the exhibiting of the transplanted primitive village had become such a feature of late nineteenth-century and Edwardian exhibitions, so the film became a servant to dominant racial and Social Darwinian ideas of the time. Some of the earliest anthropological films, like those of Fred J. Nottage in North Western Rhodesia in 1913 or Major Shomburghe in West Africa in 1914, carried a powerful message of primitiveness assailed by the beneficent civilising mission of imperial rule, an imperial rule only very recently formally established in those areas.

The great imperial companies were as alive to the propagandist value of film as they were to other forms of advertising. In 1903 H. M. Lomas and the Charles Urban Trading Company produced a series of films shot in Borneo on the Urban Bioscope Expedition into North Borneo, paid for by the British North Borneo Company, the first of the modern imperial chartered companies, which received its charter in 1882 and ruled North Borneo until the Second World War. The journal *Era* urged other exploring and mining companies in uncivilised parts of the world to use the same technique to propagandise their work.[14] Other 'travel industrials' included seal-hunting in Newfoundland, whaling off Natal, and the date-growing in Egypt. Cadbury's, so adept at the other forms of commercial advertising, made a film in 1913 to celebrate the Gold Coast cocoa bean (the British West African territory had become the world's largest producer by that year), its chocolate derivatives, and the enlightened industrial welfare of Bournville. It is interesting to note that throughout the period before the First World War there are few, if any, feet of celluloid on social and industrial conditions in Britain apart from the positive propaganda of the Cadbury film.

All the films mentioned so far were distributed in a variety of ways. In the earlier period travelling showmen displayed them at fairs. London theatres like the Alhambra, the Empire, Leicester Square, the Hippodrome, the Lyceum, the Polytechnic, and the Tivoli showed them interpolated with more traditional theatrical fare. Films were also distributed to some of the great department stores, to Church mission halls, the Salvation Army, and many other outlets. There can be no doubt that many early film-makers considered the cinema to have an 'improving' role, to offer a satisfactory continuation of the late nineteenth-century search for 'rational' recreation, or at least liked to argue as much to gain acceptance for the new medium. Many of the films could be slotted into the lantern-slide lecture pattern, particularly those which dealt with travel and natural history. Film did not, however, develop along these educational/entertainment lines. By the First World War its story-telling and comic potentiality was becoming more apparent. Factual subjects rapidly declined as a proportion of the whole, and the public saw film as a source of escapism rather than of

instruction. Escapism did not, however, preclude the continuing obsession with royal and military subjects, and the imperial world view remained the central ideology of many of the adventure dramas of the
time.

Just as the outbreak of the First World War led immediately to the
flooding of the stages with military plays, so the film industry rapidly
geared itself to producing a plethora of army films. Titles included
*Ready, Aye, Ready, With the British Forces, Lord Kitchener's New
Army, Backbone England*, and many more, often including footage of
troops training. The war enhanced the cinema's popularity, and the
public needed little encouragement to attend in their millions. Cate
Haste has gone as far as to say that 'the pictures' were transformed
from 'an instrument for the amusement of the masses into an instrument for the manipulation of the masses'[15] Wartime film production in
fact simply developed and extended trends that were already there, and
the power of the cinema was well recognised. Northcliffe observed that
people forgot what they read in the newspapers, 'but no one can forget
what he has seen on the screen', which is presumably why he took care
to become closely involved in the newsreel industry.[16] The war saw a
considerable increase in official control of the industry, a recognition
of its great propaganda power, and the laying down of censorship
regulations which would continue to be influential in the inter-war
years. Once the government had set up formal machinery for propaganda in 1917, film became directly connected with State controls over
public information and opinion-forming. As in the Boer War, there was
renewed expansion of the production and popularity of actuality film,
newsreels, biographies, interviews, documentaries of royal tours of
inspection, films on the navy, and of particular battles.

From the beginning of the war, film production was subject to the
operations of the Defence of the Realm Act, restrictions on imports
and exports, as well as the regulations on trading with the enemy. Film
producers had never shown any disposition to produce material of a
socially controversial nature, let alone indulge in the most minor sub-
version, and it was highly unlikely that they would do so in wartime.
There were film biographies of Roberts and Kitchener, stressing their
imperial exploits throughout the world, and their role as recruiters.
Lloyd George was celebrated in *The Man who Saved the British
Empire*, written by Sir Sidney Low, lecturer in imperial and colonial
history at the University of London. The cult of the war personality
was developed by thirty-six filmed interviews with leading war figures,
a technique formerly reserved for tariff reform propaganda.

Large-scale propaganda films were produced, designed to form public opinion on war objectives and the threat posed by Germany. Among them was the massive *The Building of the British Empire* of 1917, containing historical information on the acquisition of the territories of the Empire; *What we are Fighting for* (1918), which depicted the German plot for world domination as principally exemplified by the Baghdad railway; *The Empire's Shield*, about the navy and based on Admiralty material; *Our Empire's Fight for Freedom* and *Sons of the Empire*, two films which dealt with the events of the war in 1914-15 and 1916-17 respectively, making elaborate use of titles; and, after the Armistice, *The World's Greatest Story*, which stressed the significance of war in the rise of the Empire, and its role in 'contributing to progress'. Catalogue descriptions of these and other films perfectly illustrate the capacity to romanticise and sanitise war. There is of course no hint of its horrors, only descriptions of excitements and thrills.

A number of army and navy films had been officially inspired before the war and in its early years, but interest in the propagandist value of the medium was given institutional form in the War Office Cinematograph Committee of 1916 and the War Office Topical Committee, which began to issue official films from November 1917.[17] Inevitably, royal visits played an important part in this output, but one of the interesting things about official war film activity is the prominence it gave to the Middle East as an important cockpit of hostilities. This fitted the contemporary propaganda about Germany's search for world dominion through the Baghdad railway; it resurrected the old bogey of the Ottoman Empire, provided exotic locations, and offered opportunities to refer to colonial troops and to the importance of the Indian Empire. Unlike the stark horrors of the Flanders battlefields, the Middle Eastern war could be depicted as a romantic one, set in Holy Land and Crusader locations. Such films included *With the Australians in Palestine, The British Occupation of Gaza, With the Forces on the Palestine Front, The 44th Remount Squadron on the Egyptian Coast, the New Crusaders, the Occupation of Es Salt, With the Forces in Mesopotamia.*

Outside the immediate area of war film production, many other films were issued in 1914-18 which reflected current preoccupations in dramatic form. Two films were made (with the encouragement of Baden-Powell) about the Boy Scouts, extolling the role of youth in the war. Fictional output inevitably drew on the adventure and imperial tradition, with several films from Henry Rider Haggard's works, historical reconstructions in *Florence Nightingale*, A. E. W. Mason's *The Four Feathers* (filmed twice during the war, with its recent memories of Sudan campaigns), and a continued output of Lieutenant Rose and Lieutenant Daring films. As with melodrama, certain plot sequences turned up again and again, contrasting 'cads' and 'heroes', cowardice and courage, dissipation and moral regeneration, the latter of course through the medium of recruitment and war. Moreover, numerous films made conscious allusions to the works of imperial writers like Henty and Steevens: *With the Indian Troops at the Front, With the Kut Relief Force in Mesopotamia, With our Territorials at the Front,* and so on.

Wartime film output drew upon and extended well established conventions rooted in earlier forms, in melodrama, in military and naval spectacle, juvenile literature, and patriotic tableaux as well as national pageantry. The repeated climacteric of war, in fact, caught these conventions and helped to perpetuate them. The Boer War struck film at an impressionistic and tender age and helped to ensure that it would not slip out of established entertainment modes. The First World War resurrected yet again the attachment of popular culture to warfare and patriotism, at just the time when film seemed to be diverting itself – much to the distress of the improvers – into more escapist forms. It is difficult to distinguish between the commercial output of the war and the more official material which emerged towards its end. The public were urged to see these films by leading political figures and by the press, and indeed all the evidence suggests that they were highly receptive to the message.

The film industry was unsure of its own direction in the early 1920s. It had emerged from the First World War clearly recognised as a significant medium, and discussion continued on its educational role and its capacity to create a national ideology. Early studies of the educational uses of film proved inconclusive. Commissions were established by the National Council of Public Morals in 1917 and by the Imperial Education Conference of 1923.[18] The latter reported in 1924, the former not till 1925. Neither reached any firm conclusions, and both recognised the problems of educational film-making, the provision of projectors and the like. Educational film companies were established, but it was not until the 1930s, when a report, *The Film in National Life,* appeared, that efforts to provide educational film were put on a firmer basis. The patriotic use of the medium was also under discussion in the 1920s. In 1926 the British Empire Film Institute was established, its aim being 'to promote and develop public interest in British films throughout the world'. This ambition was not, however, merely a matter of trade – to develop the British industry and encourage its exports – but also had a significant ideological dimension.

Foreign films, it was thought, conveyed messages inimical to the British Empire. The Institute would attempt to counter them by giving awards of merit to films of imperial value. The industry apparently scorned this encouragement, and Rachael Low concludes that 'there was no real, widespread, and deeply felt national preoccupation or theme seeking expression, despite the lip service paid to the ideal of Empire, which so many had tried unsuccessfully to wish upon the film maker.'[19] The idea that 'wholesome imperial sentiments' could be disseminated by an imperial film industry using the Empire as a protected market was repeated at the Imperial Conference of 1926, when Mackenzie King of Canada, Stanley Bruce of Australia, and Peter Coates of New Zealand all took up the idea[20] Given the fact that the American home market was almost twice the size of the entire Empire market, the fears both of imperial personalities and of the trade are perhaps not surprising.

The official propaganda machine had been closed down at the end of the First World War. Now the search for the educational and ideological applications of film seemed unavailing. But it would be quite wrong to conclude that the 'message' of the 1920s cinema was unfocused, that the public enjoyed free access to films of whatever national origin, bearing a wide variety of social, political, and moral views. In fact, the film industry, whether in Britain or in the United States, remained locked into a range of perceptions which seem to have changed very little as a result of the war. Moreover, the industry's own form of negative self-censorship operated in such a way as to compress the spectrum of subjects into a very narrow band indeed. Some of the most successful films indicate that popular demands continued in their old channels. But before examining popular interests, the manner in which they were supplied, and the consistent world view which they continued to convey, it is essential to look at censorship, for it is practice in this sphere which gives the lie to Low's suggestion that film industry escaped national direction and controls.

The industry's own system of self-censorship had been set up in 1912 to avoid the proliferation of licensing practices among the hundreds of local authorities empowered under the 1909 Cinematograph Act. The first president of the British Board of Film Censors (B.B.F.C.) was George Redford, who had been the Examiner of Plays under the Lord Chamberlain.[21] He therefore brought the principles of official theatre censorship into the 'self-regulation' of the cinema. In his first year twenty-two films were banned and alterations were demanded in another 166. Important in his criteria were taboos on the portrayal of royalty, judges, Ministers or high officials in an unbecoming or undignified manner; no living individual was to be lampooned, or public characters and institutions disparaged. His other concerns were mainly moral and religious. The Board issued certificates to films, and by the 1920s its certification was coming to be accepted by local authorities and magistrates throughout the country. The second president of the B.B.F.C., T. P. O'Connor, laid down a set of censorship rules in 1917, and it might be expected that in wartime political considerations would have been uppermost. Rachael Low has argued that censorship in Britain was primarily moral, but that view has recently been convincingly exploded.[22] Although the majority of the rules appear to be moral, the main thrust of the regulations was political, and it was the latter which were elaborated in the inter-war years.

Moreover, censorship was not, as has sometimes been suggested, exercised by non-official amateurs appointed by the trade. In fact, it was applied by a succession of figures expert in counter-propaganda and censorship techniques, all of whom had received their training during the war. Brooke-Wilkinson (secretary of the Board, 1913-49) Edward Shortt (president, 1929-36, formerly Chief Secretary for Ireland and Home Secretary), and Lord Tyrrell (president from 1936, formerly head of the Political Intelligence Department and Permanent Under-secretary at the Foreign Office, and chairman of the British Council) were all, in effect, highly qualified censors, who were closely identified with Establishment positions. Brooke-Wilkinson had been concerned with British film propaganda in the war, and was a member of the C.I.D.'s secret sub-committee on censorship. All these men saw to it that the film industry depicted only a positive view of Britain for overseas consumption and an uncontroversial one for domestic audiences. Controversial politics, disparagement of public figures and institutions, particularly royalty, or anything likely to encourage disloyalty among native peoples in the Empire or otherwise bring British prestige into disrepute were all banned. Censorship of the cinema was to be, in fact, even more effective than that of the stage. Yet it had been given unofficial, apparently amateur status.

Many of the regulations which may seem at first sight to be based on grounds of morality are in fact on closer examination political in purpose. The close connection between morality, politics, and the racial dimension of the imperial world view are readily apparent in the Board's rules. Amid the numerous prohibitions was the depiction of 'white men in a state of degradation amidst native surroundings'. Late Victorian attitudes to the social and sexual protection of white women found strong expression in rules which forbade 'equivocal situations between white girls and men of other races' and the casting of aspersions on the social life of wives of 'responsible British officials stationed in the East'. There were of course many other restrictions, on the portrayal of civil disorder, conflicts between capital and labour, and the like. The censors, in fact, were extremely active in imposing an Establishment and State view of what constituted politically and socially acceptable comment. No government officials could have been more effective in circumscribing the material available to the public. The censors were empowered to demand cuts in scenes, subtitle text, or, later, dialogue. With the advent of 'talkies' the technical problems of sound ensured that ideas and scripts were often submitted before a project was begun, in order to avoid expensive cuts later. Many were rejected.

Such stringent censorship would seem to leave little scope for anything but the most domestic and trivial of subjects. In fact the displeasure of the censors was felt in a very lopsided way. Strikes, poverty, or social disorder were unacceptable, but a film about a strike being broken so that a new ship could be built on Clydeside (*Red Ensign*) was passed with the comment that it contained 'a strongly patriotic note'.[23] The Conservative and Unionist Party was able to finance *The Soul of a Nation* (1934) without appearing in the credits.[24] The assassination of a pacifist M.P. was allowed to be seen as a laudable act (*The Four Just Men*), while white emigration to Rhodesia could be urged in *Rhodes of Africa*. In these ways censorship acted to produce a powerful negative propaganda.

Foreign films were of course subject to censorship too. The great Russian revolutionary classics could be shown only to intellectuals under club conditions. D. W. Griffiths's *America* (1924) was banned because its main theme was the War of American Independence, which was considered offensive to Britain. *Storm over Asia*, featuring an Asiatic revolt against British authority, of course incurred displeasure, and no doubt there were fears that imperial parallels might be drawn if *Battleship Potemkin* or *Mother* were shown. A projected British film entitled *The Relief of Lucknow* was proscribed in 1938 on the grounds that it might adversely affect the delicate relations between Britons and Indians, although, as we shall see, the depiction of African revolts was still acceptable at a time when African nationalist movements seemed to be at a much earlier stage of development. Until the death of George V it was difficult to get any film about Queen Victoria past the censors. Non-Establishment themes, such as pacifism were regarded as too controversial. Nothing that could conceivably give offence to a foreign country was permitted, and that included Nazi Germany in the late 1930s. All this sifting led one critic to describe the cinema as a political and social narcotic, superseding the Church in providing the masses with an escapist dream.

Yet the effect was not soporific at all. It only seemed so to those contemporaries who were inured to the dominant perceptions of the age. The conformity of one era is, however, the controversy of the next. In fact, much of the output of the '20s and '30s was highly contentious, constantly reframing a dominant world view derived from the previous century. In such areas as racial ideas, censorship had a positive effect. No film was banned for showing black people in an unpleasant or derogatory light. Intellectuals might have moved on, but the cinema, under the eagle eye of the censor, provided the masses with an anachronistic framework of political, social, and racial ideas which were to linger into the 1950s. It was the cinema which continued to rework the adventure, militarist, and imperial traditions of an earlier popular culture.

One of the great mysteries of the period is how far there was a genuine revulsion against militarism in the 1920s. The Great War is often said to have produced such a reaction, and given the fact that scarcely a household was without a casualty of some sort it would scarcely have been surprising. Nevertheless, warfare appears to have continued to be a popular subject for entertainment, particularly the aspects which could be romanticised in the true conventions of the adventure tradition. Censorship may again have played a part in presenting the armed forces and warfare in a favourable light. Among the B.B.F.C.'s many strictures were the prohibitions upon 'holding up the King's uniform to contempt or ridicule', 'bringing discredit on British uniforms' or 'scenes in which British officers and officials in India and elsewhere' were 'shown in ridiculous circumstances'. The censors expressed anxiety about any scene in which young officers became 'unpleasantly or discreditably drunk' or the ridiculing of colonial forces and governors. Forster, Maugham, Coward, and Orwell, in their very different ways, may have been unveiling some of the more ludicrous posturings of British military and civilian establishments overseas, but none of them could hope to reach a truly mass audience through the cinema. On the other hand, the portrayal of military or colonial officials in a sympathetic light was positively encouraged.

As we have seen, Lowell Thomas's exploitation of the Lawrence of Arabia myth was received with popular acclaim, and his lectures and publications were supported by film material. Indeed, there seems to have been no diminution in the popularity of the military film. From 1919 the war was the subject of a series of semi-documentary films which appeared for a decade. They combined actuality footage with 'boys' adventure stories' approach to war.[25] *Women who Win* and *Victory Leaders* appeared in 1919, the massive *World's Greatest Story* in 1920. Bruce Wolfe produced a whole series of films, including *The Battle of Jutland* (1921), *Armageddon*, about Allenby's campaign in Palestine (1923), *Zeebrugge* (1924), *Ypres* (1925), *Mons* (1926), and the *Battles of the Coronel and Falkland Islands* (1927). The latter, according to Low, was particularly popular, although it may be that the principal effect of these films was to bring the middle class, who had formerly regarded it as beneath them, into the cinema. All of them were made by British Instructional Films. New Era made the similar *The Somme* (1927), and *Q Ships* (1928). It is often asserted that documentaries had very little popular currency compared with feature films, but these war films seem to have been very successful, and they grossed large sums. Moreover, documentaries could influence feature film production. There seems to have been something of a vogue for war films in the later 1920s. Although King Vidor's *The Big Parade* of 1925 and the British *Tell England* and *Journey's End* (both 1930) could be construed as anti-war, others like *Mademoiselle from Armentières* (1926) and *Blighty* (1927) were nostalgic and sentimental. War was certainly good box office, although its popularity in the '20s makes its absence from the output of the next decade the more striking.

Expedition films and ethnographic films may not have had a mass following, but their treatment of the role of the explorer, and of the relationship between white observers and primitive peoples, certainly influenced the approaches of many feature films. There seems indeed to have been a plethora of expedition films in the 1920s[26] Some of them were spiced by the added excitements of the aerial exploits of the day. Titles included, in chronological order, *Nionga* (1925) made in East and Central Africa, which, although it purported to be an ethnographic film, contained curiously misplaced references to wife-burning on the death of husbands and used the word 'savages' (as did several others) in the subtitles; *Wildest Africa* (1923), *Wonderland of Big Game* (1923), *Senegal to Timbuktu* (1924), *Toto's Wife* (1924), *Pearls to Savages* (1924), *The Vast Sudan* (1924), *Kilimanjaro* (1924), *To Lhasa in Disguise* (1924), *Crossing the Great Sahara* (1924), *From Red Sea to Blue Nile* (1925), *With Cobham to the Cape* (1926), *Cape to Cairo* (1926), *Round Africa with Cobham* (1928), and *Stampede* (1930). In addition there were a number of stories in colonial settings, like *The Romance of Hine Moa*, a Maori story (1928), *Jungle Woman* (1926), *Pearl of the South Seas* (1927), *Samba*, set in South Africa (1928), and *Palaver* (1926). The latter was shot in Nigeria, which had been brought to the film-maker's attention by a royal tour. It set out to show the 'life of a

British district officer in a remote part of the Empire, administering justice, building roads and bridges, teaching the natives to develop the country and live peaceably together'. None of these offerings drew much attention from the critics, and few secured a wide showing, but they appear to have paid for themselves, and more of the same continued to be made.

Royal visits to the Empire, as well as playing an important part in the newsreels, continued to be turned into larger features. *50,000 Miles with the Prince of Wales* appeared in late 1920, the first of many such. The Prince of Wales may have been the Empire's most indefatigable royal traveller, but others were deemed worthy of cinematic treatment too. *Across India with the Duke of Connaught* appeared in 1921, and the silent imperial travelogue was capped with a *Tour of the Dominions by the Rt. Hon. L. S. Amery*. In 1923 the Imperial Conference decided that a tour by a Royal Naval squadron would give tangible evidence of imperial unity, and it was duly recorded in *Britain's Birthright* (1925), arranged by A. P. Newton, Professor of Imperial History at King's College, London, and a leading figure in the Imperial Studies movement. The Wembley exhibition of 1924-25 occasioned a number of films. 'Staid', 'excruciatingly dull', burdened by 'long indigestible factual titles'[27] many of these ventures may indeed have been, but they must be seen in the context of all the other media which kept an imperial world view constantly before the public.

Imperial achievements were celebrated in extensive footage. It is difficult to imagine *The Benguela Railway* or *The Opening of Takoradi Harbour* (both 1928) setting any cinemagoers alight, but aviation undoubtedly gripped the popular imagination. As we have seen, Cobham's flights were fitted into the expedition genre. Others placed aviation in an imperial context, like *Blazing the Airway to India* (1923) and various productions for Imperial Airways and Vickers Aviation. Rather more popular were films in the historical, adventure, naval and orientalist tradition. Some heroes never failed. *Livingstone* (1925) was sufficiently popular to be reissued in 1927 and 1928. Nelson was the subject of cinematic efforts in both 1919 and 1926. *Robinson Crusoe* was issued in 1927. Among popular writers, Rider Haggard, 'Sapper', and Sax Rohmer continued to provide the repertoire of possible subjects. Yet another *She* appeared in 1925. There were several Bulldog Drummond films, and a number of treatments of Rohmer's oriental villain Dr Fu-Manchu. The censors do not appear to have worried about the violently anti-oriental nature of the Fu-Manchu stories, though they did express anxiety about the Eastern setting of one of the 'Flag Lieutenant' films. The appearance of at least two of these, together with several about naval warfare (one examining the period 1789-1905, issued in 1926), revealed the continuing popularity of naval themes. Spectacle and orientalism survived too. The stage musical success *Chu Chin Chow* was turned into a cinema spectacular by Herbert Wilcox in 1923, and there were many other oriental subjects, including *A Chinese Puzzle* (1919), *The Chinese Bungalow* (1926), *The Romance of old Baghdad* (1922), *Shiraz* (1928), and *The Emerald of the East* (1929), many reminiscent of stage titles before the war.

By the late 1920s the idea was firmly implanted in many Establishment minds that here was a powerful medium of propaganda, particularly for the masses. As the Moyne Committee of 1936 put it, 'The propaganda value of the film cannot be over-emphasised'[28] The First World War propaganda establishment had drawn a distinction between influencing elite opinion, both in other countries and at home, and the influencing of the masses. Newspapers, pamphlets, books were appropriate to the former, the cinema to the latter. Lord Burnham reiterated the distinction in 1919, but by then of course the official propaganda machinery had been dismantled. Nevertheless, the use of film for propaganda purposes was a topic of discussion for the entire inter-war period. It has been suggested that propaganda had a somewhat more innocent meaning before its perversion by totalitarian regimes in the 1930s, that its proponents in the 1920s were thinking more in educational terms. Contemporaries were perhaps not so squeamish. They used the word freely and they understood it to mean a selection and slanting of the truth to a specific national end.

Its ablest proponent of the day was Sir Stephen Tallents, the first secretary of the Empire Marketing Board, who later moved on to direct public relations at the G.P.O. and the B.B.C. For him, education and propaganda were inseparably bound up with imperialism. Indeed, the question was so basic as to involve the country's very survival. He formulated these thoughts in a pamphlet, *The Projection of England*, in 1932. But it is clear that he had been thinking along the same lines from his E.M.B. appointment in 1926. The slump merely highlighted Britain's great dependence on the rest of the world. Four-fifths of her food came from overseas; a fifth of her population were maintained by exports. But her share of world trade was decreasing. Her well-being was at the mercy of events in distant countries, and action had to be taken to arrest decline, to capitalise upon the advantages of Empire, and compete in a hostile world. To these ends, Tallents extolled the work of the scientific research stations, describing it as 'a brilliant page in the history of Empire development'.[29] But this research had to be applied and disseminated around the Empire. He drew an analogy with the Elizabethan period. Hakluyt's *Voyages* had been propaganda for English participation in the exploratory work of Spain and Portugal, a participation necessary for survival in the seventeenth century. Two things were necessary for survival in the twentieth century. One was the exploitation of Empire resources and the other was to combat the idea that Britain was 'down and out'. Survival was now a matter of morale and international image. It was essential 'to throw a fitting presentation of England upon the world's screen'.[30]

Tallents was using no metaphor. He regarded the cinema as the most vital tool in this operation. It was 'the greatest agent of international communication', reaching an audience of 15,000 million a year throughout the world in cinemas alone, to which could be added an immense non-theatrical circulation. Both America and Russia had already discovered that 'the moral and emotional influence of the cinema is incalculable'. Every picture palace was in effect an American consulate, and among the great Russian films that were admired was *Storm over Asia*, which depicted an anti-British Asiatic rising. When he came to list the subjects appropriate to this projection of a new Britain, however, Tallents revealed the very conservatism which infused the film industry and other educational and propagandist bodies. Britain should project her monarchy, parliament, navy, literature, the distinctively English sports, ceremonies like Trooping the Colour, the media, and the Boy Scouts.[31]

When Tallents wrote *The Projection of England* he had already spent several years encouraging British documentary film makers to project the imperial economic nexus as the source of Britain's greatness and the prime means of her survival. In the dangerous world of the 1880s and 1890s that had been the argument of the chambers of commerce and trades councils alike of all the main cities, anxious about an increasingly hostile future.[32] Here it was being peddled yet again in a slightly more sophisticated form. This time, however, the medium lay ready to hand, and a band of British film makers, strongly influenced by Russian post-revolutionary film technques, were eager to exploit film to propagandist ends. That they should have been funded by an imperial body, the E.M.B., where Tallents established a film unit, and should have dedicated themselves to a form of imperial propaganda seems at first sight ironic, for in their own time they had the reputation of radicals, a reputation which most of them cultivated assiduously in memoirs and autobiographies. They made high claims for themselves, and have been described by one historian of the British cinema as Britain's most notable contribution to world cinema.[33] Inevitably such an inflated reputation has come under attack. More recently it has been suggested that they were neither radical nor influential, that they were always firmly under the control of Establishment figures, and that their output was little seen and even less understood.[34] As usual, reaction has gone too far. Certainly they were not radical, or at least such radicalism as they possessed was stifled by the form and content of their films. But their work was widely seen, if not always in the commercial cinema.

The leader of the movement was of course John Grierson, who, like that other great propagandist by stealth, John Reith, was of Scottish and Presbyterian origins. Both were possessed with the didactic yearning for improvement of middle-class Scots. To this Grierson added a background in the merchant navy and, while a student at Glasgow University, in Labour politics. As a postgraduate in the U.S.A. he had developed interests in mass communications and in cultural diffusion through emigration. He directed only one film, *Drifters*, but swiftly established such a reputation that he made important American contacts, won Tallents over to his film-making objectives, and gathered a significant school around him.

He had no doubts about his propagandist objectives or about his use of film as a pulpit.[35] He wished to dignify the labour and lives of common people while educating them for democracy, as he rather patronisingly put it. He was an indefatigable writer and lecturer, swiftly establishing an international reputation. His writings preached the same message over and over again: the State was inevitably going to play a more important role in education in the conditions of the modern world. That being the case, education should adopt a dramatic and entertaining rather than intellectual approach. There was, it is true, a strong strain of internationalism in him, but the message was confused. On the one hand he seemed to attack the adventure tradition which still suffused feature films, but nowhere in his writing does he attack the imperialism from which that tradition had partly sprung. On the contrary, Empire was part of the improving and purposive cosmology of his documentary movement. Empire was a fact of life in Grierson's world, a source of economic and moral improvement for both home and colonial populations. Far from being inimical to internationalism, it was in fact a sort of test-bed for the internationalism of the future, a view which was shared by the leaders of youth organisations and other opinion-formers. Hence he extolled the educational value of films in colonial dependent territories; he did a great deal of work for the Imperial Relations Trust; and he established the Canadian Film Board. As with so many Labour intellectuals of the day, he and his followers did nothing to question the fundamental tenets of the imperial connection. On the contrary, much of their work was devoted to the classic economic nexus of imperialism, which was precisely what the E.M.B., and their outside sponsors and subsequent employers, demanded. If they believed in a liberal, ethical imperialism, it was precisely through contemporary developmental, paternalistic, and educational ideas that such an Empire could be achieved.

The second contradiction of Grierson's position was his approach to commercialism. He deprecated Hollywood and the commercial cinema:

> The dogs of the commercial world are harried and driven to quick box office results. The dogs of the propaganda world are more wisely driven to good results, for half the virtue of propaganda is in the prestige it commands.[36]

Yet the documentary school he founded worked to commissions not only from the E.M.B., the G.P.O. and other government organisations (including colonial governments), but also from Gas, Shell, Anglo-Iranian, Imperial Airways, I.C.I. Not one of these would have been likely to commission work that assaulted the conventional imperial world view. The 'thousand Blimps' who accused the E.M.B. of going bolshevik, and the infiltration of a Special Branch man into the film unit, seem to have been entirely mistaken reactions, symptomatic of the paranoia of the right rather than the revolutionary intent of the film makers.[37]

Such radical content as there was in the films was so muted as to be almost unrecognisable. Both *Cargo from Jamaica* and *Song of Ceylon* (two of the 'imperial six' produced in 1933) are alleged to contain left-wing comment, but Raymond Durgnat sees *Song of Ceylon* as 'pure imperialist pastorale'.[38] In fact the films reflected the traditional approach to Empire, as did all the products of the documentary school in its varied guises from right to left. The pioneering, exploring spirit of Empire was promoted in such films as *Conquest* (1930), about the western exploration of Canada. The Empire as supplier of raw materials was depicted in *Cargo from Jamaica*, *Song of Ceylon*, *Gold Coast Cocoa* (1930, a poster film, one of several shown continuously at railway stations for the E.M.B.), *Windmill in Barbados* (1934), *Lumber* (1931), and *King Log* (1933). Even a film for the Southern Railway, *Rising Tide* (1934), was designed to illustrate the interdependence of Britain and the Empire. *Five Faces* (1938) was made for the Malayan colonial authorities. *One Family* (1930), *England, Awake* (1932), and *Contact* (1933) were all patriotic ventures made by the right-wing documentarists at British Instructional Films, a company which was overtly nationalist and imperial. Modern technology was celebrated in a series of films on flying, several of them made for Shell and Imperial Airways — *Airport* (1934), *African Skyways* (1939), *Air Outpost* (1937), *Air Post* (1934), and *The Future's in the Air* (1937), all of which dealt with imperial air routes, the air representing a new means of contact, and therefore of consolidation, among the peoples of the Empire. One of the most overtly propagandist films was *Men of Africa*, made for the Colonial Office in 1939 to demonstrate the work of imperial officials in spreading civilisation in Africa. Indeed, it was only a comparatively small step from the work of the documentary movement to the use of propagandist film in the Empire during and after the Second World War.

In retrospect, it is clear that the fervent Empire loyalism of Bruce Wolfe at British Instructional Films (of which one of the directors was John Buchan) is as characteristic of the British documentary movement of the 1920s and 1930s as the carefully masked 'radicalism' of Basil Wright or Paul Rotha. For all these reasons, the documentary movement found no difficulty in transferring itself into the propagandist film-making of the Second World War, seeking once more to present a consensual, traditionalist Britain fighting to preserve its way of life and protect its imperial possessions for tutoring in democracy. Several became members of the Crown Film Unit, and others (including the radical Paul Rotha) made propaganda films for other bodies.

Few of the productions of the British documentary movement were shown commercially. Grierson tried at first to break into theatrical exhibition with the 'imperial six' in 1933 and 1934. But none was given the registration to qualify for quota showing (that is, as part of the required British footage) under the Cinematograph Act of 1929, so he concentrated on non-theatrical distribution. He claimed that this audience was as large as that of the cinemas, and the scope and number of loans made by the Imperial Institute lend some credence to this view. Grierson argued in 1935 that the G.P.O. films reached an audience of four million, but a scholar has recently cast doubt on such a figure.[39] The documentaries were probably watched largely by involuntary audiences — schools, youth organisations, and the like. In 1935, 54% of film loans were to schools, 13% to youth organisations, and only 33% to adult bodies. Films were taken around the country in travelling roadshow vans. Historians have, however, largely ignored the Imperial Institute outlet. In 1937 the Institute's director, Sir Harry Lindsay, claimed that imperial films reached five million people through a wide range of organisations.[40] Even so, the importance of the documentaries lies principally in the insights they provide into the pseudo-radical approach of intellectuals to imperialism and popular culture at the time.

There can be little doubt that the mass audience of the 1930s was influenced principally by feature films and the newsreels that went with them. The newsreel companies were strongly conservative.[41] British Movietone News (in which Lord Rothermere had an interest) and Gaumont-British had close unofficial connections with Conservative Central Office. Together with British Talking News (which had a special Empire News Bulletin), British Paramount News, and Pathe News, they all presented a conformist approach to the issues of the day. They avoided controversy, promoted respect for established authority and ideas, as well as presenting a national self-assurance and confidence. These characteristics were well conveyed by famous commentators like E. V. H. Emmett for Gaumont-British and Leslie Mitchell for Movietone. It is true that the dominance of United States parent companies meant that American subjects were often given more prominence than imperial ones, but safe events like patriotic ceremonial and national ritual, transport technology (ships being launched, maiden voyages, developments in air travel), imperial events (often with jocular references to native peoples), and above all sport predominated. A survey in 1936 indicated that, after sport, royal, military, and imperial items together formed the next most important group (although the imperial did not figure strongly). Royal events were the greatest crowd-pullers. Queues formed outside cinemas everywhere at George V's jubilee in 1935, his funeral in 1936, and for the spate of coronation films which followed in 1937. It was at such times that the imperial monarchy was highlighted with large numbers of colonial troops in the processions.

Audiences grew steadily through the 1930s. In 1926 there were 3,000 cinemas in Britain.[42] By 1938 there were 4,967. In 1934 903 million tickets were sold; in 1940 the figure was 1,027. Although audiences contained a high proportion of women and young people, and although escapist romantic fiction remained the most popular genre, the continuing success of the imperial adventure tradition is striking. With the coming of talkies, all the favourite themes returned in new form. If there was any shift at all it was from the portrayal of exciting, violent, expansionist imperialism to an Empire of peace, democracy, and order. One of the most striking aspects of the long survival of imperial themes is their apparently powerful attraction to the movie moguls of Hollywood. Imperial epics flowed from the Hollywood studios, keeping a colony of English actors like Clive Brook and C. Aubrey Smith in work.[43] The screen tycoons seemed to recognise in Britain one of their most important markets. At the same time there was a valuable diplomatic effect, while American audiences had become sufficiently used to their own imperial role to be enthralled by the British experience.

In Britain the one serious attempt to match the scale and magnificence of the Hollywood studios, London Films, at Denham, also turned to imperial themes, and found them to be money-spinners, the ideal combination of 'Patriotism and Profit'.[44] From there the Hungarians-turned-British patriots Zoltan and Alexander Korda regaled their Anglo-Saxon audiences with films like *Sanders of the River* (1935), *The Drum* (1938), and *The Four Feathers* (1939). Meanwhile, at Gaumont-British, Michael Balcon produced *Rhodes of Africa* (1936), *The Great Barrier* (1936), and *King Solomon's Mines*. Noel Coward had long since shifted to the more patriotic mood of the '30s in *Cavalcade* (1933), made in Hollywood but described in *The Observer* as 'the best British film ever made'. Also from the U.S.A. came *The Four Feathers* (1929), *Clive of India* (1935), *King of the Khyber Rifles* (1929), *The Lost Patrol* (1934), *Under Two Flags* (1936), *Lives of a Bengal Lancer* (1935), and *Stanley and Livingstone* (1939). All transferred to celluloid the public school, militarist and racial stereotypes of late nineteenth and twentieth-century boys' fiction, and gave the adventure tradition a new lease of life long after it had lost respectability among serious writers. Moreover, Queen Victoria emerged from cinematic embargo to be celebrated on the hundredth anniversary of her accession in *Victoria the Great* and *Sixty Glorious Years*, representing her reign in heroic and expansionist vein.

The British films of the genre were not without official inspiration. Both Korda and Balcon had links with the Conservative Party Film Association and advised on the making of propagandist films.[45] Gaumont-British had close contacts with government, and its chairman had offered in 1935 to make, in effect, official films. Korda employed Winston Churchill as a script writer (although nothing seems to have come of it), while Sir Robert Vansittart, formerly Permanent Under-secretary at the Foreign Office, who had already scripted Herbert Wilcox's *Sixty Glorious Years*, worked on the later Korda imperial epics after he had failed to persuade the government to create its own propaganda film unit. Just as there was close, if veiled, official contact with censorship and its negative propaganda, so were significant public figures involved in the positive propaganda of imperial film-making. The imperial films hearkened back to late nineteenth-century events or were concerned with the allaying of native disaffection. The first type was devoted to the glorification of military courage and concepts of public school 'honour', the second with the portrayal of firm imperial government, symbolised by the Sanders figure putting down native revolt and establishing the order necessary for economic development.

The Second World War gave the imperial adventure tradition a further boost. *Our Fighting Navy* had appeared in 1937, and the war inevitably saw a wave of official films on the armed forces and their campaigns. The imperial productions of the '30s were repeatedly reissued during (and after) hostilities. The cinema readily placed itself at the service of State propaganda, which again set about promoting a consensual, class-free Britain coalescing around the monarchy, the armed forces, and a set of mythic imperial ideas enshrining concepts of freedom and development. No questioning of or controversy about British institutions, or Britain's imperial role, in its administrative, legal, or economic guise, was permitted in any popular cultural form. Hollywood produced *The Sun never Sets* and *Sundown* in 1940, but they were the last of their kind, for the American Office of War Information declined to allow further films to be made about the British Empire. Only the 'British spirit' could be celebrated, and as a result a version of *Kim* was held up until peace returned.[46]

In the post-war world the imperial epic continued to draw the crowds.[47] Kipling stories, for example, held their own, the cinema world apparently uninfluenced by the intellectual re-evaluation his reputation was already undergoing soon after his death. An adaptation of *Elephant Boy* appeared before the war, *Gunga Din* in 1939, *The Jungle Book* in 1942, and *Soldiers Three* and *Kim* in 1951. It may be that the true imperial apologia disappeared with the war, but the imperial world view continued in films like *King Solomon's Mines* (1950), *Storm over Africa* and *Storm over the Nile* (1953 and 1955), *Khyber Patrol* and *King of the Khyber Rifles* (both 1954), *West of Zanzibar* (also 1954), and *Yangtze Incident* (1957). The era of decolonisation produced a fresh wave of films of imperial nostalgia, in which, if the racial comment was somewhat more muted, nonetheless the moral force of imperialism, the justice of its wars, and the glorious exploits of its heroes remained unabashed — *North West Frontier* (1959), *Fifty-five Days at Peking* (1962), *Zulu* (1963), and *Khartoum* (1966) to mention but a few.

This survey of films with a military, royal, or imperial flavour admittedly covers only a fraction (perhaps no more than a quarter) of the total output of the period. But it does reveal a striking continuity from some of the obsessions of the years before and during the First World War. Far from seeing any diminution in the output of films of warfare, the 1920s witnessed a progression of successful military and naval films, semi-documentary and fictional, which revealed the durability of warfare in popular culture, even after the searing experience of the Great War. It was still possible to present romanticised images of war, and in feature films the censors saw to it that neither uniform nor flag was ever treated with disrespect. The existence of the censors ensured that an Establishment world view of the monarchy, industrial and transport achievements, imperial 'development' and race hierarchies continued to be peddled to the masses through the cinema. It may be that efforts to disseminate an explicitly imperial ideology, as proposed by the 1926 Imperial Conference or the British Empire Film Institute, failed, but the political, racial, military, and technological assumptions about the survival of Empire continued to be the implicit message of films. However unsophisticated the audience, however complex the problems of communications theory, one conclusion is unavoidable. Most of the plots of the adventure films, most of the newsreel, documentary, and actuality material remained incomprehensible except within the matrix of perceptions about the world shared by makers and audience alike. Censorship ensured that no efforts to break that mould were allowed, and indeed there is little indication that they would have been forthcoming in any case. Not even the 'radical' documentarists could escape the power of the core ideology. The public remained set in a late nineteenth-century view of the world, and popular preoccupations — military and naval adventure, oriental fascinations, racial condescension, deference to royal and patriotic symbols — survived from decade to decade, stimulated rather than stifled by warfare. The 1930s represented an extraordinary renaissance of the imperial adventure tradition, made all the more potent by Hollywood's eager participation.[48] The cinematic dramatisation of so many of the imperial classics created a popular cultural momentum — matched in children's literature and comics — which was to continue through the Second World War, and even into the 1950s and 1960s.

One other great technical innovation in popular culture, the wireless, made an equally effective and ubiquitous impact. Few developments contributed more to the conversion of pride in Empire into a domestic emollient than the royal broadcasts. Significantly, the first broadcast speech of George V was his opening address at the Empire Exhibition of 1924. In the ensuing years a dozen of the King's public speeches were transmitted, but it was not until 1932 that he was persuaded to make a set-piece Christmas broadcast to the Empire. The B.B.C. staff, still enthralled by the idealism of the new medium, by the image of the broadcaster as the honest, just, and pure sower of the seed, consciously sought to use the King's voice as a great advertisement for radio, a dramatic connecter of peoples all over the world. As Tom Fleming has put it, 'the B.B.C. believed that the British Empire, dominions, colonies and protectorates, that multiracial and multilingual community of nations, ought to become, with the harnessing of the international air waves, the worldwide exemplar and envy of all'.[49]

Indeed, the King's first Christmas message seemed to lend credence to such an idea. It was allegedly heard by 20 million people, and produced, it is estimated, 2,000 leading articles and 25,000 columns of newsprint throughout the world press. It was dubbed the greatest broadcast ever, preceded as it was by an hour-long programme on the Empire, including material from Canada, New Zealand, Australia, South Africa, ships on the Atlantic, and a cruise liner at Port Said. Each year more territories were added to the list, culminating in a massive extravaganza for the 1935 jubilee entitled 'This Great Family'. The tradition was of course maintained by George VI and Elizabeth II, although Neville Chamberlain refused to allow George VI to make annual broadcasts before the war on the grounds that over-exposure would destroy the mystique of the monarchy.

The talks were of course designed for the Empire, and to a certain extent as propaganda for the allies. The 1932 broadcast was received ecstatically in New York and Paris. During the war the Queen (now the Queen Mother) spoke to the women of the Empire, of France, and of the U.S.A. But in fulfilling that role the monarch inevitably presented an emollient and self-satisfied view of Britain's position in the world to the British public. By avoiding controversy his message could coalesce around the seemingly uncontroversial subject of Empire and later Commonwealth. Inevitably, the stress was upon history, on discovery, exploration, heroes, standing together in wartime, defending freedoms and the like; never on present discontents or future anxieties. In 1947 George VI made no mention of Indian independence. Instead, he asserted that the Commonwealth and Empire had 'not been disrupted by the stress and peril of war'.[50] In 1948 the war was invoked again: the Empire had 'stood alone in the defence of freedom'. In victory 'the unity and steadfastness of the British Commonwealth and Empire saved the liberties of the world'.

Given the necessity of avoiding anything with a party political content, it was inevitable that the speech writers should concentrate on such themes. But George V's first two broadcasts were almost certainly written by Rudyard Kipling,[51] and it could be argued that the repeated invocation of tradition, the avoidance of controversy, and the recurrent references to the armed forces and victory in war, by contributing to the conceit of superiority and success, did have a political import. Royal broadcasts aside, however, the accompanying Christmas Empire programmes certainly contributed to the same effect. Linking up white Dominions, India, Palestine, colonies, and protectorates in mutually congratulatory greetings masked the development of both Dominion and colonial nationalism. Broadcasts from aboard ship (a common feature) and from imperial garrisons gave an impression of world-wide commercial and military control. As with so many instruments of imperial propaganda, the royal broadcasts did not really change their tone until the late 1950s and early 1960s. Analysis of the texts reveals that the Queen was still referring to Empire, exploration and discovery, to heroes and deeds of the past, all linked by her own extensive tours, until that date.

Radio conveyed a sense of the unity of Empire, at least in the public mind, such as the Edwardian imperial societies had found unattainable. Leaders and newspaper articles rhapsodised to this effect, and it was given economic expression in the Ottawa agreements on imperial preference in 1932. Schools broadcasting (see chapter 7) contributed by concentrating on conventional approaches to history and geography. After the Second World War the B.B.C. continued to present a vision of a beneficent and regenerative Empire. At Christmas 1947 and again in 1948 the Empire broadcasts highlighted the groundnut scheme in Tanganyika.[52] The script in 1947 was read by Lawrence Olivier to a background of music by Benjamin Britten, and spoke of a project which would bring food to Britain and hope to Africa. In 1948 Robert Donat was to be heard describing the scheme in dramatic terms — 'In East Africa, the ground is being zipped open'. A great deal more work remains to be done on the content of the various imperial broadcasts, at Christmas time, on Empire Day, etc., but there can be little doubt that they proclaimed a confident, optimistic, self-congratulatory view of Empire to the public, rendered all the more potent by the intimacy and universality of the new medium.[53] By 1938-39 no fewer than 8·95 million wireless sets were licensed, one to every five members of the population.

NOTES

1 Bratton, 'Theatre of war'.
2 Booth, *English Melodrama*.
3 Senelick, 'Politics as entertainment'.
4 For a full examination of this tradition, see Martin Green, *Dreams of Adventure, Deeds of Empire*, London, 1980.

5 Rachael Low, *The History of the British Film, 1918-1929*, London, 1971, 47.
6 Rachael Low and Roger Manvell, *The History of the British Film, 1896-1906*, London, 1948, 15-16.
7 Low and Manvell, *British Film*, 55-6.
8 Low and Manvell, *British Film*, 66-8.
9 Low and Manvell, *British Film*, 94-5.
10 Rachael Low, *The History of the British Film, 1906-1914*, London, 1948, 164.
11 Paul Rotha, *Documentary Diary*, London, 1973, 3.
12 Roberts, *Classic Slum*, 182.
13 Low, *British Film, 1906-1914*, 153-5.
14 Low and Manvell, *British Film*, 60-1.
15 Haste, *Home Fires*, 45.
16 See note 41 below.
17 Haste, *Home Fires*, 46. Rachael Low, *The History of the British Film, 1914-1918*, London, 1950, 36-7 and 152-5.
18 Rachael Low, *British Film, 1918-1929*, 53-4.
19 Low, *British Film, 1918-1929*, 310.
20 Low, *British Film, 1918-1929*, 95-7.
21 Findlater, *Banned!*, 122-3.
22 Nicholas Pronay, 'The political censorship of films in Britain between the wars', in Nicholas Pronay and D. W. Spring (eds.), *Propaganda, Politics, and Film, 1918-1945*, London, 1982, 98-125. For censorship practice, see Jeffrey Richards, 'The British Board of Film Censors and content control in the 1930s: images of Britain', *Historical Journal of Film, Radio and Television*, 1 (1981), 95-116, and 'Foreign affairs', *Historical Journal of Film, Radio, and Television*, 2 (1982), 39-48.
23 Richards, 'Images of Britain', 113.
24 Pronay, 'Political censorship', 110.
25 Low, *British Film, 1918-1929*, 292-3.
26 Low, *British Film, 1918-1929*, 287-90. Karl G. Heider, *Ethnographic Film*, Texas, 1976.
27 Low, *British Film, 1918-1929*, 286.
28 Jeffrey Richards, 'Patriotism with profit: British imperial cinema in the 1930s', in James Curran and Vincent Porter (eds.), *British Cinema History*, London, 1983, 245-56.
29 S. G. Tallents, *The Projection of England*, London, 1932, 23.
30 Tallents, *Projection*, 39.
31 Tallents, *Projection*, 14-5.
32 William G. Hynes, *The Economics of Empire: Britain, Africa and the New Imperialism*, London, 1979.
33 Rachael Low, *Documentary and Educational Films of the 1930s*, London, 1979, 1.
34 Raymond Durgnat, *A Mirror for England*, London 1970, 106-23. Paul Swann, 'John Grierson and the G.P.O. Film Unit, 1933-39', *Historical Journal of Film, Radio and Television*, 3 (1983), 17-34. Stuart Hood, 'John Grierson and the documentary film movement', in Curran and Porter, *British Cinema History*, 99-112. For sympathetic material on the documentary movement, see, among many others, Rotha, *Documentary Diary*. Paul Rotha, *Documentary Film*, London, 1936. Elizabeth Sussex, *The Rise and Fall of British Documentary*, California, 1975. Forsyth Hardy, *John Grierson*, London, 1979.
35 Forsyth Hardy, *Grierson on Documentary*, London, 1979, a collection of Grierson's writings and speeches.
36 Hardy, *Grierson on Documentary*, 48.
37 Hood, 'John Grierson', 104. Hardy, *Grierson on Documentary*, 77.
38 Durgnat, *Mirror*, 119.
39 Swann, 'G.P.O. Film Unit', 27.
40 Sir Harry Lindsay, 'Romance and adventure in real things: the Imperial Institute and its film library', *World Film News*, July 1937.
41 Rachael Low, *Films of Comment and Persuasion in the 1930s: the History of the British Film, 1929-39*, London, 1979, 10-13. Nicholas Pronay 'The newsreels: the

illusion of actuality', in Paul Smith (ed.), *The Historian and Film*, Cambridge, 1976, 95-119. See also Anthony Aldgate, *Cinema and History*, London, 1979, 54-90.

42 I am grateful to Jeffrey Richards for permitting me to read in typescript his forthcoming *The Age of the Dream Palace: Cinema and Society in Britain, 1930-39*.

43 Jeffrey Richards, 'The Smith of Smiths', *Lancaster Comment*, 118, 1982, 14-15.

44 Richards, 'Patriotism with profit'. Richards has described the imperial films as being 'as successful as any of their period'. 'British feature films and the Empire in the 1930s', in J. M. MacKenzie and Patrick Dunae (eds.), *Imperialism and Popular Culture*, forthcoming. See also Jeffrey Richards, 'Korda's empire', *Australian Journal of Screen Theory*, 5-6, 1979, 122-37. For blacks in imperial films, see Peter Noble, *The Negro in Films*, New York, 1970, 109-36.

45 Richards, 'Patriotism with profit', 250-1.

46 Jeffrey Richards, *Visions of Yesterday*, London, 1973, 4.

47 Richards provides in *Visions* a full survey of all the imperial films, particularly those of Hollywood. 'The cinema of Empire', 2-220.

48 *The Times* remarked in 1937 that 'The Union Jack has in the last few years been vigorously and with no little effect waved by Hollywood'. Richards, 'Smith of Smiths', 14.

49 Tom Fleming, *Voices out of the Air: the Royal Christmas Broadcasts, 1932-81*, London, 1981, 2.

50 Fleming, *Out of the Air*, 47-50.

51 I am indebted to Mr D. H. Simpson for this point. Sir Henry Newbolt may also be a contender.

52 These quotations come from a Radio 4 programme on 'The ground nut scandal', broadcast on 28 July 1982.

53 Imperial broadcasting will be explored further in MacKenzie and Dunae (eds.), *Imperialism and Popular Culture*, forthcoming.

–4–
THE IMPERIAL EXHIBITIONS

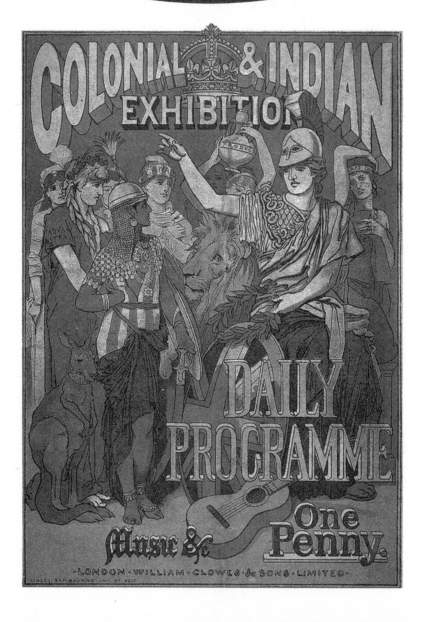

The great exhibitions which from the 1880s came to be dominated by the imperial theme offer the most striking examples of both conscious and unconscious approaches to imperial propaganda. The secret of their success was that they combined entertainment, education, and trade fair on a spectacular scale. By the end of the century they were enormous funfairs, coupled with, in effect, museums of science, industry, and natural history, anthropological and folk displays, emigration bureaux, musical festivals, and art galleries, together with examples of transport and media innovations, all on one large site. They were a wonder of their age, highlighted in the press and other contemporary literature. They seemed perfect exemplars of 'rational recreation', combining pleasure and instruction, and millions attended them. Even if most went for the fun, some at least of the imperial propaganda cannot have failed to rub off.

The exhibitions were, however, marvels that were ephemeral, constructed for a season, invariably dismantled and scattered at the end. That very transience heightened the sense of urgency to attend, and the need to capture them in leaflets, programmes, and photographs. They provided the greatest opportunity to disseminate printed and visual ephemera of all kinds, for the high point of these exhibitions, the almost continuous sequence from late Victorian times to the First World War, together with the great imperial and colonial examples between the wars, coincided with the peak of production of pamphlets, booklets, postcards, and advertising matter.

Much has been written about the manner in which the Great Exhibition of 1851 marked the apex of Britain's industrial and commercial supremacy, and conveyed an impression of overweening pride and self-confidence. It is perhaps the later exhibitions, however, that provide the best insights into national obsessions, character, and morale. Their theme was gradually transformed from the international industrial exposition, as in 1851 and 1862, to imperial and colonial display. They came to have a predominantly imperial flavour from the 1880s, precisely the decade of the new aggressive imperialism. During the Edwardian era there were almost annual exhibitions, run by commercial interests, and securing large attendances. By then the imperial ethos suffused even the exhibitions that marked diplomatic developments, like the Franco-British of 1908 and the Japan-British of 1910.

These were both celebrations of joint membership of the imperial club.

The great Empire Exhibition at Wembley in 1924-25 and its Scottish counterpart at Glasgow in 1938 signified the high points of an Empire gorged at Versailles on the mandate system. Even after the Second World War there were attempts to create colonial exhibitions in the Colonial Weeks of 1949. However, the 1951 exhibition on the South Bank was designed principally to propagate the ideas of the post-war Labour government on social and economic change. There was little direct imperial content, imperial exhibits being concentrated at another site, the Imperial Institute. To a certain extent it seemed to prepare the British for withdrawal into themselves in the period of abandonment of Empire after the loss of India, Ceylon, and Burma. The very title, Festival of Britain, reflected that. Thus all the exhibitions from 1851 to 1951 effectively chart the rise and fall of imperial sentiment.

The exhibitions of the mid-nineteenth century largely followed the classification originated by Prince Albert and Lyon Playfair for the Crystal Palace in 1851, in which exhibits were divided into raw materials, the manufactures created from them, and the arts that decorated the manufactures.[1] Geographical origins were at first almost incidental. In 1851 only 520 out of 14,000 exhibitors were colonial. The eastern wing of the Crystal Palace housed foreign and colonial goods, a mixture that would have been avoided later, with those from nearest the equator situated nearest the transept. There were two imperial representatives on the Royal Commission, Dr Royle for India and W. E. Logan for Canada. There were exhibits on India, Canada (according to Queen Victoria, 'Canada made an admirable show'), Australia, New Zealand, the South African colonies, Ceylon, the West Indies, and Malta.[2]

At the London Exhibition of 1862 this imperial content had already grown considerably.[3] There were 7,000 Indian exhibits which consumed 277 pages of the catalogue. Thirty other colonies as diverse as Bermuda, Borneo, and St Helena took part. Larger displays included Victoria, with 500 items, New South Wales with 400, and Canada. But the relative importance of the imperial possessions was beautifully symbolised in the fact that all the colonies took up only a quarter the space devoted to India. The event also showed how quick the exhibitions were to respond to the main economic news of the day. It featured an obelisk of gold to symbolise over 800 tons exported to Britain from Australia between 1851 and 1862.[4] In addition there was a Japanese display, only a few years after Commodore Perry had opened that country to the West. Eighteen sixty-two marked the beginning of regional categorisations that were to develop from the 1860s onwards. From 1886 the exhibition became almost entirely concerned with Empire, and as the Empire grew the balance with India was correspondingly redressed. In this the exhibitions were charting the growth of, and contributing to the development of national perceptions about, the Empire.

These exhibitions marked an imperial world-wide control, as expressed through the many displays on exploration, a new agricultural and geological understanding, and naval and military might; a capacity for global exploitation of resources, as exemplified by the plantation system (there was much emphasis on tea, sugar, tobacco, and later cocoa and rubber), and mining of all sorts; and the penetration everywhere of manufactured exports, particularly textiles, machinery, furniture, musical instruments, and all the other hallmarks of the civilised world. The companies that exhibited most frequently, and made themselves most visible by means of separate kiosks, often orientalist in architecture, were tea, tobacco, soap, and cocoa firms. Beef production and the canning and extractive industries associated with it were represented by Liebig's and Bovril, ever eager to be associated with topical imperial events. At Glasgow in 1938 there was a separate rubber pavilion, the only tropical product to be so honoured. Control over the natural world was exemplified in other ways. Stuffed animals first made their appearance in 1851 and aroused Queen Victoria's interest. Later, live animals representative of their region were to wander among the exhibits, as at the Greater Britain Exhibition of 1899 and the Coronation Exhibition of 1911. But it was living anthropological exhibits, villages of colonial peoples only recently 'pacified', that most reflected European man's control of his contemporary natural history. These will be examined in greater detail later.

Exhibitions were of course a world-wide phenomenon in the late nineteenth and twentieth centuries. In Europe they marked national self-confidence, and were occasionally a consolation for failure. Belgium in particular seemed to struggle to find a national identity through its many exhibitions.[5] Elsewhere they marked the coming of age of new States. American exhibitions from 1876 were both a commemoration and a signal of new economic and political power. In the Dominions exhibitions seemed to be a necessary rite of passage for pubescent responsible government, and were invariably held in the wake of notable economic advance. They were mounted in New Zealand (1865, 1906-07, 1924-26), Cape Town (1877), Sydney (1879-80), Melbourne (1888), Kimberley (1893), Brisbane (1897), and Johannesburg (1936-37).[6] British India produced exhibitions at Calcutta

(1883-84) and Bombay (1910); even smaller territories like Sierra Leone (1865), Jamaica (1891), Zanzibar (1905),[7] and Tasmania (1891-92 and 1894-95) got in on the act.

These colonial exhibitions were a celebration of the white man's successful transplantation to the farthest reaches of the globe, and his creation there of societies modelled on European lines. They were the peripheral expression of the larger-scale celebrations of the mother country, epitomising local control of the environment and its resources, and the capacity of responsible government colonial territories to attract exhibits from other colonies and neighbouring States. It is significant, perhaps, that imperial sentiment was powerful enough for more British companies to have exhibited at Sydney in 1879 than at Philadelphia in 1876.[8] The Dominion exhibitions also brought colonial settlers together in a sense of national unity, through the triumphs of travel that made such unity possible. The exhibitions in dependent territories like India or Jamaica presumably attempted to do the same for an indigenous middle class. The Calcutta exhibition was attended by more than a million people, presumably a combination of the British community and the educated and commercial middle class of Bengal that the British had largely brought into being. The French attempted the same thing at Tonkin (Hanoi) in 1902-03.

The move out of huge single buildings into a multiplicity of pavilions representing varied architectural styles began at Paris in 1867. It was this idea that led the Dominions and colonies to become the prime exhibitors at each of the British exhibitions from the Colonial and Indian of 1886 onwards. Just as the Dominions were to build in London the most impressive High Commissions on the choicest sites in Trafalgar Square and the Strand, so were the Dominion pavilions to dominate all exhibitions, both those nationally inspired and those commercially developed. Canada was particularly active, even building impressive pavilions at Wolverhampton (1902), Cork (1902), and many regional exhibitions where other Dominions were not represented.[9] The reason is clear: Canada was particularly active in encouraging migration, having to counteract the powerful pull of its neighbour, the United States. Canada was also impressively represented at most Continental, American, and colonial exhibitions. The Dominions presence was to reach its peak at the 1911 Sydenham Crystal Palace Coronation Festival of Empire, when three-quarter-scale models of all the Dominion parliaments were built to house the various exhibits, and at Wembley in 1924-25 and Glasgow in 1938.

It might be thought that the influences exerted by the exhibitions would be restricted mainly to the capital, but there were many provincial ones, and in any case individual exhibits often 'did the rounds'. Moreover, starting with Thomas Cook's famous activities in 1851, the exhibitions became a prime draw of cheap day trips to London, admission included, which at one and the same time boosted attendance, developed the travel companies, and encouraged the railways to promote cheap excursions for the masses. The exhibition technique was taken up by missionary societies, the army, and the navy on a local scale to raise funds or recruitment. All carried essentially the same message, and all were assiduous too in distributing leaflets, postcards, and magazines.

Some indication of the popular impact can be secured from the figures of attendance.[10] In 1851 and again in 1862 the exhibitions topped 6 million visitors. The Colonial and Indian of 1886 failed to match this figure, at 5½ million, but it was a smaller affair covering only half the area of 1851 and 1862. The Glasgow exhibition of 1888 actually surpassed it, with 5·7 million visitors. Later ones in that city in 1901 and 1911 were equally successful, the former drawing no fewer than 11½ million people and the latter 9·4 million. It is of course true that these figures would include some multiple attendance by locals, a habit which must have become more pronounced as the funfair aspect developed. The peak was reached at Wembley, with more than 27 millions, while the Glasgow Empire Exhibition of 1938 had 12 million visitors, although 15-20 million were expected. This may represent a decline of public interest in Empire and exhibitions, or it may be indicative of the anxieties of the period, both financial and international. None of the British exhibitions matched the great successes of Paris – with the whole Continent to draw on – in 1889 (32 million), 1900 (48 million), 1931 (Exposition Coloniale Internationale, 33·5 million), 1937 (34 million), or Chicago, 1893 (27·5 million) and 1933-34 (48·7 million). Figures for the great series of commercial exhibitions at the Crystal Palace, White City, and Olympia between the 1890s and the First World War are more difficult to come by, but as virtually annual events, open for months each year, they must have had a considerable impact on the population of London.

The propagandist intentions of the various exhibitions from the 1880s reflect a remarkable consistency. The Colonial and Indian Exhibition was planned by a Royal Commissioin in 1884, and its objectives were declared as 'to give to the inhabitants of the British Isles, to foreigners and to one another, practical demonstration of the wealth and industrial development of the outlying portions of the British Empire'.[11] When the exhibition opened on 4 May 1886 the second verse of the national anthem was sung in Sanskrit, and an ode by Tennyson, set by Sir Arthur Sullivan, was sung by Madame Albani from Canada. Both the Queen's address and the Tennyson ode highlighted the economic connection of Empire with a hint of imperial federation in a heady mixture.[12] There were no fewer than twenty catalogues for the Colonial and Indian Exhibition, together with reports on the individual colonies. A large number of booklets on the 'History, Products, and Natural Resources' of almost all the Dominions and colonies were produced, usually at 6d each.[13] The Colonial and Indian marks the beginnings of the popular exhibitions at which vast quantities of ephemera were produced at low cost for wide circulation. The educative and propagandist message could now be taken home.

The Colonial and Indian was the first of the imperial 'official' exhibitions, developed and funded with government support, that culminated in Wembley and Glasgow, but the striking thing about the period from the 1890s to 1914 is the role of popular commercialism in the management of the exhibitions. The tradition had already been established in the permanent displays at the Crystal Palace on its Sydenham site. In 1890 there was a Chinese Court, in which were displayed 'specimens collected by the Venerable Archdeacon Gray during a residence of 20 years in Canton'.[14] There was a 'Grand Panorama of the Battle of Tel-el-Kebir'; there was a permanent Dominon of Canada exhibit, and new displays were added in keeping with the latest developments of the day. In 1905, for example, there was an exhibit featuring the naval actions of the Russo-Japanese War, one of the many models of naval actions which appeared at exhibitions (there were also specialist naval exhibitions, like one at Chelsea in 1891).[15]

In 1895 the exhibition entrepreneur Imre Kiralfy and others founded a company, London Exhibitions Ltd. Despite his dominance of the movement over the succeeding two decades, Kiralfy is a somewhat shadowy figure. Neither his *Who's Who* entry nor the *Times* obituary mentions his origins or his age, but he seems to have been involved in exhibitions from the 1880s. In 1889 he was associated with P.T. Barnum in a spectacle, *Nero, or, The Destruction of Rome*. In 1891 he created an 'aquatic pageant' *Venice, the Bride of the Sea*, while in 1893 he produced the 'Grand Historical Spectacle' *America*, and in 1898 celebrated the United States' imperial status with *Our Naval Victories, an American Naval Spectacle*. Such activities neatly reflect the connections between the spectacular theatre tradition and the exhibitions.

The London company's first exploit was the Empire of India Exhibition at Earl's Court in 1895. Thereafter there were almost annual ventures on imperial themes, featuring India, Ceylon, Borneo, and Burma in 1896, the Jubilee in 1897, the Greater Britain Exhibition of 1899, with various regular spectacles like 'Savage South Africa' in 1899 (an unfortunate year to choose) and the Boxer rebellion in 1901. These were held at Olympia and Earl's Court, but by 1907 Kiralfy's ideas had outgrown their halls, and he began to erect his own great pleasure ground at Shepherd's Bush. He converted 140 acres into the Great White City and Stadium, and as *The Times* put it, 'the dazzling buildings and the colossal scale on which everything was carried out drew hundreds of thousands of people there'.[16] The First World War brought Kiralfy's operations to an end, and his Great White City became a drilling ground for recruits, a medical inspection centre, and an aeroplane factory. But by that time he was the acknowledged exhibitions expert. He became closely associated with Lord Strathcona and a number of other peers interested in exhibitions, and was honoured by them at banquets on several occasions.[17] When he died in April 1919 he left £136,680, so he seems to have secured better returns on his commercial ventures than the national ones, which invariably made a loss.[18]

His Greater Britain Exhibition of 1899 was a remarkable affair. It was perhaps Kiralfy's most ambitious effort, as is well demonstrated by the *Official Guide and Libretto*, 150 pages with maps, priced at 6d (2½p).[19] As though to demonstrate that showmanship had not entirely destroyed the educative aspects, the guide kicked off with a comprehensive list of all the colonies of the United Kingdom, complete with their surface areas and populations. The main buildings at the exhibition included the Imperial Court, the Queen's Court ('truly a regal spot'), with oriental facades, the Queen's Palace (which at one stage exhibited relics of the East India Company), the Central Hall, and the Empress Theatre, described as the largest in the world. There were also a 'Street of Nations', a Cairo Street (a common exhibition feature), a Grand Panorama, and a Royal Bioscope (presumably an early cinema). There was an International Mining Section, and exhibits of the natural resources of many colonies. That of Victoria, for example, included a large fruit exhibit together with displays on grain, butter, leather, education, wine, art, mining, wool, timber, refrigeration, and other aspects of agriculture. Victoria merited no fewer than five pages of statistical facts in the official catalogue. There was a special refrigeration exhibit on Australia and New Zealand, celebrating a technical advance that more than any other had served to tie those two economies to Britain. Recent additions to the Empire had their resources displayed to demonstrate their value to the imperial economy. There was a West African products section, and a Rhodesian Court, which contained everything from a 'stamp battery' for crushing ore from a Rhodesian gold mine to a display of postage stamps. The Rhodesian special commissioner, R. N. Hall — an amateur archaeologist who did untold damage to the Zimbabwe ruins — represented Rhodesian mining and farming interests, touted for migrants, and oversaw exhibits from as many as eleven Rhodesian gold belt regions, each listed in detail in the catalogue, together with displays on other mineral and agricultural prospects, all of it filling eleven pages of the catalogue.

Even more extraordinary was the 'Kaffir Kraal' and the 'Savage South Africa' display, 'A Vivid Representation of Life in the Wilds of the Dark Continent'. At the Kaffir Kraal there were 174 Africans, Zulus, Basuto, Matabele, and Swazi in four villages, infested apparently with strutting cranes and giant tortoises. A wide variety of activities could be seen here, for

> Unlike the Indian, the South African native is a restless active savage, and he will be seen to be very busy grinding corn, making the native drink, working beads, and most attractive of all, particularly to the fairer sex, the manufacture of kaffir bangles, which are said to be lucky amulets.[20]

There were five interpreters and headmen, and the public were reassured that the spiritual welfare of these exhibits was catered for by divine service each Sunday. Frank Fillis, a South African showman, contributed to this human natural history by a display in which 'baboons and bushmen take part', together with the Zulus, Basutos on ponies, ten picked Swazis 'magnificent of physique', some Transvaal Boers, two Malay families, some 'pretty little wildebeests', a 'battle of the elephants', and Miss Lillian Reiner, the champion lady shot of South Africa.

As if that were not enough, there were re-enactments of the Matabele War of 1893, complete with a long programme 'libretto' describing 'Lobengula's Indaba', the 'Grand War Dance', 'Throwing the Assegai', 'Lobengula's Army on the March', 'the Matopos Hills', 'the Plunge over the Cliffs', 'British Troopers', and 'Major Wilson's Last Stand'. Breathlessly the show rushed on to the Rhodesian revolt of 1896-97, featuring in particular 'Gwelo Stage Coach' in scenes entitled 'Infested with hostile Matabeles', 'The Last Cartridge', 'The Campbell Family', and 'Howling Matabeles'.

It may well be thought that such reminders of the dangers of white pioneer life might have counteracted the emigration propaganda elsewhere, but the impresarios seem to have assumed that any such fears would be allayed by the transformation of war, revolt, death, into sentimental spectacle and entertainment. The displays in fact reflect a striking topicality, a powerful application of Social Darwinism to entertainment, and an extraordinary illustration of the imperial exhibition's capacity to chain and tame people who a mere three years earlier had been enemies, now sadly acting out their former resistance. Representations like these contributed to the late Victorian taste for theatrical spectacle which, in the exhibitions, as in the theatres, set out to create living imperial icons. To Gordon's Death at Khartoum could now be added Major Wilson's Last Stand and The Gwelo Stage Coach. What has been described as a 'visual living taxonomy' was to be a feature of many exhibitions, as we shall see.

From 1908 Kiralfy moved his interests to the White City, and again mounted annual exhibitions, all with imperial connotations: the Franco-British of 1908, the Imperial International of 1909, the Japan-British of 1910, the Coronation of 1911, the Latin-British of 1912, and the Anglo-American of 1914. In 1911 there were no fewer than two imperial coronation exhibitions in London, the one at the White City and a rather more official affair at the Crystal Palace, as well as a Glasgow exhibition the same year. Kiralfy's style was strongly orientalist. The late nineteenth-century orientalist craze arrived in exhibition architecture from the 1860s and came to predominate by the '90s.[21] Many exhibitions had 'sets' that rendered them forerunners of Cecil B. de Mille epics. The epic of the exhibition was the contemporary world and all its wonders brought on to a single site, and expressed invariably in temporary wood-and-plaster architecture. It was at the White City that the Hollywood film-set characteristic was taken to its highest point, with white stuccoed oriental-style buildings which were used, like many of the amusement park features, over and over again. As with orientalism generally, the exhibitions created a vision of what the East ought to look like rather than the actuality. 'Moorish' kiosks and exhibits were to appear repeatedly, the Americans and British probably deriving the style from the French. The pronounced orientalism of Edwardian musical comedy must have conjured up in the popular mind the architecture of many of Kiralfy's exhibitions. These enormous sets contributed to the Victorian and Edwardian taste for spectacle, which reached a climax in the theatre at the time, and is also apparent in civic architecture, developments in transport, and public pageantry.

The Japan-British exhibition of 1910 was an interesting case of Anglo-oriental spectacle. It set out to produce a cultural and racial justification for the alliance of 1902 and to demonstrate the appropriateness of Japan's appearance as a commercial, naval, and imperial power. The official guide described 'tableaux giving a historic record of the

Japanese Empire'. It went on to demonstrate the racial acceptability of the Japanese.

> One curious similarity runs through the whole, that is, the striking simi-
> litude between the Japs and our own people. This resemblance manifests
> itself in manner, physical stamp, and shape of the head. To anyone ac-
> quainted with the principles of phrenology the resemblance is very mar-
> ked. This last point is indicated by the large proportion of the brain in
> front and above the ear. These structural conditions are distinctive in-
> dications of considerable mental power, and are emphasised by the por-
> traits of some of the most highly placed representatives. Taken as a
> whole, they constitute a good augury for the growth of sympathy be-
> tween the East and the West.[22]

There were huge exhibitions of Japanese art — probably the most considerable before the Royal Academy Great Japan exhibition of 1981 —
which were described as reflecting the Japanese people's 'natural in-
stinct for art'. The writer's only reservation was that Japanese painting
was judged inadequate because of its lack of realism. Perhaps more significantly, there were exhibits on the Japanese colonies of Korea, Man-
churia, and Formosa, and the exhibition attributed to Japan the same
self-congratulatory imperial ambitions as had been arrogated to themselves by Britain and France in the Franco-British Exhibition of 1908.
In these ways the exhibition was the means of Japan's admission to respectability in the imperial club.[23]

The Crystal Palace Exhibition of 1911 was intended 'to demonstrate
to the somewhat casual, often times unobservant British public the
real significance of our great self-governing Dominions, to make us
familiar with their products, their ever-increasing resources, their illi-
mitable possibilities'.[24] The exhibits were displayed in three-quarter-
size scale models of all the Dominions parliament buildings, and they
were connected by a train journey through the Empire in a series of extraordinary geographical juxtapositions. This trip was called, inevitably, 'The All-red Tour' and started in Newfoundland, passed a paper-
making plant and Newfoundland scenery before reaching Canada,
where wheat-growing and lumbering were featured. From Canada the
travellers passed through a Jamaican sugar plantation, a Malay village,
Indian jungle ('with a variety of animals running wild'), an Indian
palace with 'wonderful inlaid gold and jewel work', a 'typical Indian
bazaar', and, *mirabile dictu,* the Himalayas. The train continued past
Sydney harbour and the Blue Mountains, a sheep farm, orchards,
vineyards, and so on, to New Zealand, with its hot water geysers, a
'quaint Maori village', and much wool and mutton. The journey ended
in South Africa, with gold and diamond mines and the traditional

'native kraal' featured. The idea was that passengers would alight at each parliament building to see the exhibits within. As though that spectacle were not enough, 15,000 volunteers took part in an imperial pageant which featured landmarks in the history of the mother country together with, among others, the landing of Sir Humphrey Gilbert in Newfoundland, the 1820 settlers in South Africa, the rejoicings at Canadian confederation in 1867, and the 'Imperial Assemblage at Delhi and the Proclamation of Queen Victoria as Empress of India, 1877'. The pageant of Empire idea was repeated at Wembley in 1924-25, where it took place in the new stadium, and was so successful that it was decided to make seats free so that as many as possible could see it.

The official programme for the 1911 exhibition was filled with advertisements for emigration. The Tasmanian one described the colony as 'the most English of the Australian states', with 'quite a boom as regards the fruit-growing industry'. All this no doubt contributed to the last burst of emigration before the war, and demonstrated the continuing efforts, unavailing, at least in relative terms, to divert migrants from the United States. Many aspects of the exhibitions, including the pageants, were designed to reinforce the emigration appeal, and this was the reason the Dominions were prepared to put so much money and effort into them, including the purely commercial ones.

All the exhibitions emphasised the notion of Empire as an interlocking economic unit. Propaganda to this end was to reach a peak after the First World War with the creation of the Imperial Economic Committee and the Empire Marketing Board, which survived from 1926 to 1933. Imperial preference at last gained limited acceptability with the Ottawa agreements of 1932 under the influence of world depression, but efforts to achieve imperial self-sufficiency were an enduring theme of propaganda and of the various imperial institutions. The Empire Marketing Board took an active interest in exhibitions. It had a pavilion at Newcastle in 1929,[25] where the Dominions took it in turns to show off their products, and similar ideas were conveyed at Glasgow in 1938. But it was the Great Empire Exhibition at Wembley in 1924-25 which perhaps did most to further this imperial economic vision.

The idea of an Empire Exhibition had first been mooted by the British Empire League in 1902. The Liberal Party victory in 1906 killed the idea, but it was revived in 1913 by Lord Strathcona. He consulted Imre Kiralfy, thereby bringing the commercial and official streams of exhibition organisation together. The Metropolitan Railway had reached Wembley in the 1880s, and Sir Edward Watkin planned a great pleasure park and tower there. These ideas were taken over by the Metro Tower Construction Company in 1894, but the base of a tower which they constructed was dismantled in 1907-08. It was the Empire Exhibition which was to put Wembley on the map and lead to its rapid growth.[26] The exhibition idea was revived in 1919 at a luncheon at the British Empire Club attended by Premiers and High Commissioners from around the Empire. In 1920 an Act of Parliament empowered the government to become joint guarantor, and of the £2·2 million subscribed the government contributed half.

Wembley was the greatest of all the imperial exhibitons — in area, cost, extent of participation, and, probably, popular impact. The official guide described its primary purpose as:

> To find, in the development and utilisation of the raw materials of the Empire, new sources of Imperial wealth. To foster inter-Imperial trade and open fresh world markets for Dominion and home products. To make the different races of the British Empire better known to each other, and to demonstrate to the people of Britain the almost illimitable possibilities of the Dominions, Colonies, and Dependencies overseas.[27]

And the attractions of the single site were described much as in previous exhibitions:

> The grounds at Wembley will reproduce in miniature the entire resources of the British Empire. There the visitor will be able to inspect the Empire from end to end. From Canada it is but a stone's throw to Australia, from Australia a short step to India and the Far East, from Hong Kong a few minutes' walk to New Zealand or Malaya. In a single day he will be able to learn more geography than a year of hard study would teach him. And he will be able to see in each case the conditions of life in the country he is visiting. That is the importance of the British Empire Exhibition. It is a stock-taking of the whole resources of Empire.[28]

The buildings, which cost £12 million to erect and covered 220 acres, were rather more solid than those Kiralfy had erected at the Great White City. They were constructed largely of concrete, and they abandoned Kiralfy's orientalism for a stolid classicism. There were, however, attempts at more regional, indigenous styles. The Burmese pavilion was decorated with wood-carving executed in Burma. The Ceylon pavilion was described as being of 'Kandian' architecture, and the Malay site ('Moorist-Arabesque' style) included a replica of the residence of the Rajah of Sarawak (who was of course British, a member of the Brooke family). The West African building was designed as a mud-baked walled town, more appropriate to northern Nigeria than the Gold Coast and Sierra Leone, which shared it. In East Africa the exhibition again turned to a supposedly dominant Muslim culture, that of the Arab-Swahili people of the coast, by housing the exhibit in an 'Arab' building complete with a replica of a carved door from Zanzibar.

There were 175 Chinese active in the Hong Kong exhibit, and the West African section featured 'seventy representatives of the Yoruba, Fanti, Hausa, and Mendi tribes of West Africa, craftsmen — weavers, leatherworkers, brass-workers and others — who will carry on in the Exhibition the chief industries of the West African colonies'. Even in 1924 West Africa could be made to sound dangerous and unexplored, depicted in a new medium: 'A special camera party sent recently to the wilds of West Africa procured some 40,000 feet of film, which will be on view daily, showing the natural beauties of Nigeria and the Gold Coast'. The funfair at Wembley was thoroughly traditional, with its scenic railways, 'switchbacks', and water rides.

It is a striking illustration of the nature of Empire of the period that all the Commissioners for the 'dependent' colonies were British, including Lady Guggisberg, the wife of the Governor, for the Gold Coast.[29] Rudyard Kipling chose the name of the streets — Dominion Way, Union Approach, Atlantic Slope, Craftsman's Way, and so on — which cannot have taxed his imagination. The production of ephemera of all sorts was staggering in its scope, and the G.P.O. was very active in circulating these materials yet further afield. There were no fewer than fourteen official series of postcards, comprising more than 150 cards, together with dozens of series by commercial companies, individual colonies and exhibitors, running to many hundreds in all.[30] To these can be added large quantities of leaflets, programmes, maps, posters, and handbills. A special issue of postage stamps, a rare phenomenon at that time, together with a variety of cancellations and slogans — always a useful Post Office contribution to propaganda — were used. So extensive was the use of the site's post office that items franked there are still so common as to have little value to collectors.

Newspapers like the *Daily Telegraph* produced miniature editions, and *The Times* issued a series of special supplements which not only acted as souvenirs but carried articles by special correspondents from every part of the Empire, all stressing economic self-sufficiency.[31] The exhibition was featured in all the children's annuals for 1924 and 1925. A large imperial Scout jamboree was held there. Hugh Gunn, a member of the Imperial Studies Committee, issued a twelve-volume history and survey, *The British Empire*, in 1924, while the Royal Colonial Institute and the Imperial Studies Committee jointly sponsored an education conference at Wembley at the end of May 1924 to consider 'the Place of Imperial Studies in Education'.[32] The papers, edited by E. C. Martin under that title, were published; they considered in detail imperial studies in schools, colleges, adult education, libraries, and so on. In all these ways Wembley was not so much the grand climax of the imperial exhibitions movement as a consolidator of all the ideas prevalent before the war. Children's annuals, school textbooks, and films, taking their cue directly or indirectly from Wembley, were to keep them going to the 1950s.

Military events at the Exhibition included a 'Stirring Torchlight and Searchlight Spectacle' entitled *London Defended*, which featured aircraft and anti-aircraft guns.[33] There was also a Wembley Torchlight Tattoo, accompanied by 'the largest band ever seen in the British Empire', consisting of 1,000 military bandsmen. The Scout and Guide jamboree involved hundreds of thousands of Boy Scouts and Girl Guides, and its programme inevitably stressed the role of the Scouts in empire-building and in war. Mass concerts were held in which 10,000 voices and 500 instruments took part. The Empire Pageant involved no fewer than 12,000 performers, and included sections entitled 'The Pioneers', 'The Pageant of Newfoundland', 'Of Canada', 'Of South Africa', 'Of Australia and New Zealand', 'The English Fleet in the Mediterranean', and 'The Early Days of India'. The programme proudly announced that only the music of British composers was featured. Among the works performed were Elgar's Empire March ('1924'), Edward German's 'Long Live Elizabeth', Elgar's 'Crown of India', Alexander Mackenzie's 'Britannia Overture', Hamish McCunn's 'Livingstone Episode', and 'Camp and Kaffir Melodies'. A large number of popular songs were also written for Wembley with titles like 'Let's go to Wembley', 'Wembling at Wembley with you', 'You've got to come along to Wembley'. The Lyric Music Publishing Company issued Henry Pruden's 'The Wembley March' and 'The Australia Quick March'. Billy Merson sang 'In my Little Wigwam, Wembley Way', which included the lines:

> There you will find me in a costume gay
> In charge of the girls from Africa.
> All they wear is beads and a grin;
> That is where the exhibition comes in.

There were verses on 'Our ninepenny native meal' and 'Our Hoo-loo Cabaret', where 'dusky Eves' could be seen 'dressed in nothing but leaves'.

There were in fact a number of complaints about the representation of Africans at Wembley. The Union of Students of Black Descent (a mainly West African London student group) complained to the Colonial Office about the manner in which Africans were held up 'to public ridicule'.[34] Whatever the treatment of the entertainment aspects of the 'Races in Residence' (as the official guide called them), it is certainly the case that some of the publications of the exhibition took an essentially nineteenth-century line. The three-page leaflet distributed at the Anthropological Section referred to 'native customs' like human sacrifice and cannibalism, and to the '"town boys" of Africa who provide material for every political agitator in that Continent'. The fact that 'in the tropics there are large tracts of land imperfectly cultivated by natives or not cultivated at all' meant that European-led development was essential. The Oversea Settlement Gallery had a short guide designed to illustrate the importance of colonial produce and the necessity of British emigration within the Empire. Clear tables purported to demonstrate that while, between 1884 and 1893, 421,149 people emigrated from Britain to the Empire and 980,337 to the U.S.A., between 1904 and 1913 the position was dramatically reversed when 1,291,406 went to the Empire and only 622,773 to the United States. Trade with the Empire constituted more than a third of Britain's total trade, and the proportion was growing. In addition to items of propaganda like these, individual Dominions and colonies put out emigration pamphlets as well as information and samples illustrating the significance of their trade with Britain.

The publicity leaflet announcing the reopening of the exhibition in 1925 described it as 'the greatest Exhibition the world has ever seen', 'the greatest example of co-operative effort in history'. The new exhibition was described as 'brighter and better', to illustrate again 'the manifold products and resources of the British Empire', its 'unlimited but not yet developed resources and to encourage overseas settlement within the frontiers of the Empire'. Nevertheless, the attendance of 17½ million in 1924 dropped to 9¾ million in 1925. The loss on the first season amounted to £600,000, and the second was partly an attempt to recoup it. In fact it increased, but Dominions and colonies were convinced that the exhibition had had a dramatic effect upon their trade. The Australian pavilion almost covered its costs from the sale of samples of produce, and the Gold Coast cocoa campaign led to increased sales.[35] It is true that imperial trade rose as a proportion of British trade in the succeeding years, but this was a symptom both of depression and of continuing industrial decline.

Much contemporary fun was poked at the exhibition by *Punch*, the WGTW (Won't Go To Wembley) Society, by P. G. Wodehouse and Noel Coward, but these represented largely intellectual views, which are a poor guide to popular imperialism in the inter-war period.[36] Like royal ceremonials, the exhibition was a major commercial event. Huge quantities of bric-a-brac were produced and found their way into people's homes. There were plates, jewellery boxes, vases, spoons, medals, coins, all bearing the imprint of the exhibition's symbols or a variety of exhibits. There were even models of the pavilions themselves. Samples of colonial produce of all sorts were dispersed in appropriate tins or packaging. A large West African apparently distributed medallions bearing the legend 'Drink More Cocoa'. Certainly the reaction of one East European immigrant was different from that of the intellectuals of Hampstead.[37]

> The exhibition overwhelmed me. I remember it vividly, and will try to describe the colourful, bustling spectacle I saw, but the lasting impact it had on me cannot be conveyed in words. The nostalgic picture of this mightiest of all empires as displayed at Wembley is so deeply engraved on my subconscious that its influence still lingers after all the years that have passed.
>
> The more exotic the pavilions the more they thrilled me.... India held an irresistible fascination.... Nigerians in their colourful robes, cowboys from Calgary, dusky East African beauties, Indians, Malays, Chinamen, Australians, New Zealanders and Fiji islanders in an endless variety of human types, colour of skin and national costume, and in a profusion of tongues with which the Tower of Babel itself could not have competed — yet all were members of one great empire, united under one king and flag, linked by the English language, financed by sterling, ruled by British justice and protected by the Royal Navy. How proud they must feel, I thought, and how I envied them.[37]

Herbert Wilcox had suggested that Wembley should become the British Hollywood. Imre Kiralfy had created a 'dream palace' fantasy at the Great White City, and those other East European immigrants, Alexander and Zoltan Korda, were to be influential in disseminating popular imperialism through their films in the 1930s.

The Glasgow exhibition of 1938 was conceived in 1931 at the depth of the Slump as a conscious effort to provide employment and to advertise home-based depressed industries. Yet the exhibition remained imperial in appearance, in tone, and in name. By the time the scheme reached fruition, at a cost of £10 million, a new world crisis was about to break. Classical architecture was abandoned for a much more contemporary '30s style, although some pavilions, as in 1924-25, attempted to illustrate local styles, like the Dutch gables of the South African house or the carved teak of the Burma pavilion. Colonial products were again featured, the climax of two decades of intensive propaganda from the Imperial Economic Committee, the Empire Marketing Board, and the imperial preference movement, but there was also considerable emphasis on engineering and the staple industries of western Scotland. Shipbuilders and their shipping company customers seem to have been particularly active in producing booklets, advertising, and ephemera, although transport, with its obvious imperial connotations, was always a theme of all the exhibitions.[38]

The official guide book of the exhibition stressed that it was 'the greatest held anywhere in the world since Wembley 1924-25' (which was something of an exaggeration, given the size and massive success of the Continental and American exhibitions) and emphasised its accessibility to the public:

> It has been built by Great Britain, the Dominions, and close on forty of the colonies. Within 175 acres of parkland and a huge stadium, the Empire is presenting itself to the World. Although the exhibition contains over 100 palaces and pavilions, the admission charge to the Park – 1/- for adults and 6d for children under 14 — admits visitors to all but a few of the buildings.[39]

A map and descriptive guide was free on admission and it contained many of the now familiar references to imperial products and the nature of the imperial economic connection. In the case of Burma, for example, the significance of the oil industry was emphasised — 'the biggest oil-field in the Empire' — as well as the rice and teak exports. In one hall ordinary household articles were analysed and their components traced back to the colonies which produced them. 'An ordinary piece of blind-cord is traced to Tanganyika sisal, a hairbrush to Falkland Islands whalebone'. This was in the classic tradition of the Empire Marketing Board and the Imperial Institute (see chapter 5). So was the fact that 'another pavilion on Colonial Avenue has been built by the Empire Tea Market Expansion Bureau, and represents all the great tea-producing regions of the Empire'.

As always, the glories of the funfairs came in for particular treatment, including 'the latest and greatest devices that human ingenuity can devise', the Rocket Ride, the 'biggest dodg'em track in the world', the Brooklands Racer, and the Stratosphere Plane, the Trip to the Moon, the New Ride to Heaven, and the Flying Fleas, among many others. The Zulu Village and the Indian Temple were mentioned in the same breath, although the main village feature was the clachan or highland village. Nineteen thirty-eight can, then, be placed in the classic exhibition tradition, combining fun with information, economic propaganda with ethnic display.

The 'native villages' were in fact among the most enduring features of all the exhibitions from the 1870s. They repay closer attention because here was the prime way in which people in the metropolis were brought into contact with the conquered peoples of Empire. Here were racial stereotypes illustrated, Social Darwinism established in the popular mind, and control of the world expressed in its most obvious human form. Moreover, the numbers of programmes and postcards of these exhibits that can still be found seem to indicate that they caught the public imagination. Yesterday's enemies, the perpetrators of yesterday's 'barbarism', became today's exhibits, showing off quaint music, dancing, sports, living crafts, and food, but now set on the path to civilisation. In the exhibitions representatives of African and oriental peoples were brought cheek-by-jowl with all the trappings of the world-wide economy. It was a concentrated and speeded up version of what was happening in their own countries.

Usually these living exhibits were set against the backdrop of the 'primitive' village, but grander pieces of architecture, generally divorced from present-day inhabitants, were introduced in replica. One of the most popular French exhibits, which made its first appearance at Paris in 1889, and reappeared at Marseilles 1922 and Vincennes 1931, was a full-size model of the temple of Angkor Vat. The king of Annam made his first visit to France in connection with the exhibit in 1922. A replica of the Taj Mahal, rather surprisingly, was constructed in Philadelphia in 1926, but generally the message was primitiveness rather than splendour.

The practice of bringing peoples from overseas seems to have begun in 1867, when Parisians were served exotic products by those who allegedly produced them. Thus 'a Mulatto offered cocoa and guava' and there were 'even Chinese women with their little tea shop.'[40] The French fascination with North Africa was reflected in Tunisian and Egyptian architecture. In Paris in 1889 there was a large colonial section with several native villages and a Cairo Street, complete with belly-dancers and camel rides. The Cairo street was to reappear at Chicago in 1893, Antwerp in 1894, and St Louis in 1904, indicating the new accessibility of Egypt after the opening of the Suez Canal. Imre Kiralfy seems to have caught it between Belgium and the United States for his 1899 exhibition, but that extraordinary impresario may well have had his own.

In the British exhibitions the native villages always performed one function, to show off the quaint, the savage, the exotic, to offer living proof of the onward march of imperial civilisation. As we have seen, the 1899 Greater Britain exhibition had its astonishing southern African displays, but they did not reappear. No doubt a fresh outbreak of Zulu resistance in 1906 made them a rather less attractive proposition. Imre Kiralfy went on to create a Pageant of Women, complete with an Amazon Village, which must have helped satisfy an enduring fascination. (There were several plays and comedies about Amazons on the

[114]

London stage at various times.) The Bradford exhibition of 1904 attempted to book a group of Ashantis, overwhelmed even more recently than the Zulus and the Matabele, but the arrangements fell through and a Somali village appeared instead. The Somalis reappear in Dublin in 1907 and seem to have done the rounds of the resorts, for they were an attraction in Douglas, Isle of Man, in 1912. Kiralfy's White City Coronation Exhibitions of 1911 had an Iroquois village of Canadian Indians working at various trades and producing items for sale. There was also a Somali village under the command of Mohammed Hamid, who had been an interpreter for the British during the campaign against the so-called 'Mad Mullah' (whose revolt was to break out again after the First World War). These Somalis gave exhibitions of their war dances and their fighting methods, a neat example, as in 1899, of the search for military topicality.

The two most common villages, however, were from the French empire. These were the Senegalese and the Dahomeyan villages, which made frequent reappearances. The French had apparently perfected the organisation of travelling troupes of 'native' entertainers, who entertained by being themselves and pursuing supposedly normal activities. The Senegalese were at the Scottish National Exhibition in Edinburgh in 1908, exhibiting music, crafts, and wrestling; they (or presumably another team) were at the Franco-British in the same year, and they made a surprising come-back in Newcastle in 1929, together with 'members of the Fullah tribe'. The Senegalese also appeared as a attraction at seaside resorts in the years when they were not at exhibitions. The Dahomeyan village was a feature of the Imperial International Exhibition at the White City in 1909. It was joined there, most surprisingly of all, by a nomad Kalmuck camp from Central Asia, only recently incorporated in the Russian empire. At Glasgow in 1911 there was an 'equatorial colony' with 'West African natives' whose precise origins were not identified.

Booklets and dozens of postcards were published to commemorate these displays. The guide to the Senegalese Village at the Franco-British in 1908 was written by Aimé Bouvier and Fleury Tournìer, who described themselves as 'explorers' who had brought out 150 people from Senegal by permission of the Governor, after what seems to have been a sort of human 'Zoo Quest'. The booklet described the buildings and activities of the village, including the shop 'where goods of European merchants have penetrated to the remotest villages of Western Africa... tempting the native... by their brightness and cheapness' of the merchandise. This theme was pressed further:

Now take a hasty glace at the interior of this hut on your right, and make a rapid inventory of the contents. That will not be difficult. Inside you will see a bed of straw, nothing more. These primitive people have not yet adopted all the fashions and utensils of the luxurious life.[41]

So far as African eating habits were concerned, 'though you may be amused you will not be shocked'. The strength of the wrestlers ('two colossal negroes, who look like statues of ebony as they prepare to grip') is contrasted with the weakness of African education. A hierarchy of peoples, even within West Africa, is established, the Wolofs being described as superior to the Mandingoes. All this was presented with the help of Mr Victor Bamberger, 'who presents pictures of the life of India and its natives in the British Colonial section'.

The Dahomey Village at the 1909 exhibition had a guide book which stressed the recency of the conquest of the Dahomeyans, their 'bloodthirsty potentates', 'women warriors' (the Amazon interest again), and praised France in much purple prose:

Order and decency, trade and civilisation, have taken the place of rule by fear of the sword. France has placed its hand on the blackest spot in West Africa, and wiped out some of the red stain that made Dahomey a byword in the world.

Today Dahomey is a self-governing colony of France, with a revenue which exceeds its expenditure, a line of railway, rubber and cotton plantations, exporting palm oil and copra, maise, nuts, dried fish, cattle, sheep, pigs, and fowls. The days of savagery are passing away.... one day the European tourist will go to far Dahomey as he now does to Egypt in search of sunshine and merriment in the winter months. Until that time comes he must seek to find his amusement, instruction, and entertainment in this Dahomey village.[42]

It is a fascinating statement. Dahomey had been used in the late nineteenth century as a classic instance of a savage African polity that needed to be tamed by European rule, a principal apologia for the Scramble for West Africa. Now the Dahomeyans are turned into peaceful entertainers; the meaning of 'self-governing' is neatly stretched; and the ultimate virtue, the Gladstonian balanced budget, is attributed to their colony. A fresh stage in the penetration of civilisation will be achieved with the arrival of tourists.

The Kalmuck camp at the same exhibition illustrated the civilising activity of Russia, so recently the most feared of all imperial bogeys to the British. The Kalmucks afforded 'a page from the history of our own remote past', and to reach them one would normally have to cross Europe and Russia to the 'arid steppes and mountain ranges' on the 'borders of unknown Tibet'.[43]

For this summer, at least, the traveller and scientist are spared this long journey. Here, within the borders of civilisation, you may find a tribe of Kalmuck Tartars, actually encamped, with their tents and their camels, their women and children, their priests, and their praying wheels.

The peoples of the French and Russian empires were being used to sanctify and consolidate the Triple Entente in the popular mind. The message, however, was the same, whatever the empire: barbarism overwhelmed and beneficial commerce intruding to the remotest village. There is a sense in which that was what all the exhibitions of the period were about, and the native villages were but the most startling exemplification.

The villages are present in strength at Wembley, and, on a somewhat lesser scale, at Glasgow in 1938. But by the Second World War a new tradition was beginning to emerge. The last colonial exhibitions were to be small, mobile, and devoted to particular problems. Some of them were sent all over the country. They were, however, no less propagandist in tone. Indeed, during and after the Second World War, propagandist techniques had been developed much more thoroughly by the Ministry of Information and its successor the Central Office of Information. The exhibitions therefore accurately reflected the concerns of the time: the restoration of imperial trade, the overcoming of social and economic problems, and the development of constitutional advance.

In 1936 an exhibition called 'Peeps at the Colonial Empire' was held in Charing Cross Underground station.[44] In 1944 the Colonial Office and the Ministry of Information sent a touring Colonies Exhibition around the country. Several sections were devoted to the social and economic problems of colonial peoples and were no doubt designed to prepare the public for colonial development and welfare policies after the war. It became a semi-permanent exhibit at the Imperial Institute and was not dismantled until 1946.[45] In 1949 the Central Office of Information sent travelling exhibitions round the country in conjunction with the Colonial Month of that year.[46] Like the work of the Empire Marketing Board, this was principally designed to encourage the public to buy colonial produce.

The Imperial Institute mounted an exhibition entitled 'Focus on Colonial Progress' as part of the Festival of Britain in 1951.[47] A similar exhibition appeared in 1953 as a section of the 'Queen and Commonwealth Exhibitions' held in association with the coronation.[48] Others included an exhibition on the Colombo Plan and one on Christian missions. Several small travelling exhibitions were sent round the country in 1954 and 1955. They included displays on the Federation of

Rhodesia and Nyasaland, 'Progress in the Colonies', the British Caribbean, and Uganda.[49] With them the colonial exhibition movement seemed to peter out.[50]

The exhibitions, then, provide valuable insights into imperial propaganda. The early great exhibitions had very little imperial content, but as the nineteenth century progressed the Empire began to take over. As it did so the notion of a great interlocking economic unit, whose comprehensiveness and complementarity were heightened with the addition of each new colony, came to predominate. Exhibitions brought together both official and commercial efforts to propagandise the benefits of Empire. Several of them were officially inspired, but many were arranged by purely commercial interests, and it is this that explains the manner in which they came to combine funfair with trade fair.

They provide a valuable study because with them we have the rare opportunity to gauge public reaction, through press reports, and through the figures of attendance. They left behind large numbers of cheap publications of all sorts, which seem to have had a wide distribution, and these publications illustrate the predominant imperial ideas and racial attitudes that were disseminated for public consumption. None of these ideas show any sign of dilution in the years between the wars. The exhibitions of the period emphasised the economic justification of Empire all the more strongly, and continued to convey Social Darwinian views on race. Only after the Second World War did the tone of propaganda change, although by then it was in a sense even more overtly and officially propagandist, government agencies consciously preparing the public for colonial developments. By then, however, many of the popular attitudes towards Empire were deeply embedded and were to remain so into the era of decolonisation itself.

NOTES

1 C. H. Gibbs-Smith, *The Great Exhibition of 1851*, London, 1950.
2 D. H. Simpson, 'This insubstantial pageant faded', R.C.S. Library Notes, May 1974.
3 International Exhibition of 1862, London, Official Catalogue.
4 John Allwood, *The Great Exhibitions*, London, 1977, 40.
5 All the international exhibitions are covered in Allwood, *Great Exhibitions*.
6 The Official Catalogue, Empire Exhibition, Johannesburg, September 1936 – January 1937, indicates that the U.K., Canada, New Zealand, Australia, Northern and Southern Rhodesia, East Africa, the Bechuanaland Protectorate, Ceylon, and Nyasaland all had substantial exhibits there. The Dominions exhibitions were almost all 'imperial' rather than international. There seems to have been virtually no international representation at Johannesburg at all.
7 This was an exhibition of products from British East Africa, German East Africa, Portuguese East Africa, British Central Africa, Uganda, the Comoro Islands, Madagascar, Reunion, Mauritius, Italian Benadir (i.e. Somaliland), the Seychelles, and Zanzibar. See official catalogue.

8 Allwood, *Great Exhibitions*, 68.
9 F. A. Fletcher and A. D. Brooks, *British Exhibitions and their Postcards*, Part I, *1900-1914*, and Part II, *1915-79* (privately published, 1978 and 1979), provide useful plans and summaries of each exhibition.
10 Lists of attendance figures are supplied by Allwood. See also R.C.S. Library Notes, May 1974. Allwood's figures are sometimes at variance with those given in contemporary literature.
11 Reminiscences of the Colonial and Indian Exhibition, 1886, 1-2. See also the Official Catalogue.
12 The ode referred to 'Produce of your field and flood, Mount and mine and primal wood'. On imperial federation, Tennyson asked, 'Brothers, must we part at last?' and answered that the Dominions would 'cleave to one another still', making 'one Imperial whole'. The last line, 'One life, one flag, one fleet, one throne', was to be used as a slogan many times in the future, not least in the First World War. See also the Report of the Royal Commission on the Colonial and Indian Exhibition, 1886, C. 5083, 1887. Every Viceroy of India and all the Secretaries of State for India and the Colonies then alive served on the Commission under the chairmanship of the Prince of Wales. The membership is virtually a complete roll-call of late nineteenth-century imperial figures.
13 India had four such booklets, Canada three, Victoria, South Australia, the Cape of Good Hope, Natal, the Straits Settlements, and the West Indies two, and so on.
14 See the official guides to the Crystal Palace exhibits for the various years.
15 Official Programme, Royal Naval Exhibition, Royal Hospital Chelsea, 1891.
16 *The Times*, 29 April 1919. I am grateful to the British Architectural Library for additional information on Kiralfy.
17 *The Times*, 24, 26, 29 October 1908.
18 The will was published in *The Times*, 24 June 1919.
19 Greater Britain Exhibition, Official Guide and Libretto.
20 Official Guide and Libretto, 20.
21 When the American architect Louis Sullivan castigated the 1893 Chicago exhibition for its architectural conservatism he himself contributed a building of distinctly oriental flavour. Allwood, *Great Exhibitions*, 84, 89, 92.
22 Penny Guide to the Japan-British Exhibition, Shepherd's Bush, 1910, 10.
23 Fletcher and Brooks, *British Exhibitions*, Part I, 38-9. In contemporary exhibition literature Japan was described as having lifted her colonies out of 'their long sleep' and 'wiped out most of their corrupt courts'.
24 Festival of Empire, Imperial Exhibition, Pageant of London, Under the Patronage of His Majesty's Government, Crystal Palace, 1911, 7.
25 Fletcher and Brooks, *British Exhibitions*, Part II, 17.
26 Geoffrey Hewlett, *A History of Wembley*, Brent, 1979. Wembley History Society, *The British Empire Exhibition*, Wembley, 1974. Fletcher and Brooks, *British Exhibitions*, Part II, 9-10. Kenneth Walthew, 'The British Empire Exhibition', *History Today*, 31 (August 1981), 34-9.
27 In addition to the official programme, a free map and guide (from which these quotations are taken) was issued with the admission price of 1s 6d, children half-price. *The Times*, 30 September 1924, reported that no fewer than 5½ million copies of this map and guide had been issued. *The Times* extolled the role of the exhibition in issuing vast quantities of useful ephemera, including posters, handbills, leaflets, and postcards. By that date 10 million exhibition postage stamps had been sold.
28 Official Guide, Fleetway Press, 1s, and the Official Catalogue, Fleetway Press, 1s. There were also two souvenir picture albums, one at 1s and the other at 2s 6d.
29 Simpson, 'Insubstantial pageant'.
30 Fletcher and Brooks, *British Exhibitions*, Part II, 51-5. Huge numbers were issued for Glasgow 1938 also.
31 *The Times*, special supplements for the British Empire Exhibition, 23 April, 24 May, 29 July, 30 September 1924. These carried a full account of the pageant in the stadium, as well as numerous articles and advertisements that convey the atmosphere and intentions of the exhibition. The first supplement emphasised the economic

tone and range of products featured in the exhibition: 'Entering the Exhibition at Wembley, millions of British subjects will ascend the Heights of Empire. Spread before them is the wondrous reality of Britain's might and magnitude — her grandeur and her glory. Riches and romance, ancient civilisation flowering in modern enterprise, the limitless range of activity and achievement — the scene is without parallel in the history of mankind. Within the master-gateway of Wembley are a hundred inner gates of Empire. They give access to the five continents and all the seas: to the mystic East, the stirring West, the sterner North, the romantic South. They lead to tropical gardens, to groves of palm, banana and orange; to plantations of coffee, tea, sugar, rubber, and cotton; to goldfields and diamond mines, to ostrich farms and sheep stations; to busy Oriental bazaars and the lonely haunts of the trapper.'

32 Hugh Gunn, *The British Empire*, 12 vols., London, 1924. E. C. Martin (ed.), *The Place of Imperial Studies in Education*, London, 1924.

33 Collections of programmes, sheet music, photographs, and many other items relating to Wembley can be seen at the Grange Museum of Local History, Neasden.

34 P.R.O., C.O. 555/7, 1924.

35 Hewlett, *History of Wembley*, 188. An illustration of the Gold Coast medallion can be seen at the Grange Museum. There are also some oral recollections of Wembley deposited there.

36 James Morris, *Farewell the Trumpets*, London, 1979, 302.

37 Eric Pasold, *Ladybird, Ladybird*, Manchester, 1977, 77-9.

38 Transport was a constant theme at exhibitions because it incorporated engineering, machinery, and design, together with trade, emigration, and travel. Complete railway engines and coaches, ship models, turbines, even cross-sections through Atlantic liners, all appeared. Canadian Pacific and the Grand Trunk Railway of Canada, P. & O. and other shipping companies advertised themselves for travel and emigration purposes. Scale models of the Suez Canal, complete with model ships passing through, and later the Panama Canal made frequent reappearances. Handsome company brochures were issued like that of the Clan Line to advertise their exhibit at Glasgow in 1938.

39 'With the Empire in Scotland', free map and guide issued with admission. Note that the price of admission actually dropped by one-third from Wembley.

40 Allwood, *Great Exhibitions*, 45.

41 Franco-British Exhibition, The Senegal Village, Official Guide (price 2d), 2.

42 Imperial International Exhibition, White City, The Dahomey Village (price 2d), 2 and 16.

43 Imperial International Exhibition, White City, The Kalmuck Camp, official guide (price 2d), 2.

44 Imperial Institute, Annual Report, 1936.

45 Imperial Institute, Annual Reports, 1945 and 1946.

46 *Corona, the Journal of Her Majesty's Colonial Service*, Vol. 1, No. 7 (August 1949), 4-11. 100,000 people visited the exhibition organised by the Central Office of Information in Oxford Street. The writer in *Corona* criticised the model of the Masai warrior at this exhibition: 'There is, perhaps, still too great a tendency to over-emphasise the crude and the barbaric.' He went on to make the same criticism of a B.B.C. programme, 'Colonial Round-up'. There were nineteen special exhibitions in all, and *Corona* claimed they had reached millions. Shops throughout the country were encouraged to feature colonial products.

47 Imperial Institute, Annual Report, 1951.

48 Imperial Institute, Annual Report, 1953.

49 Imperial Institute, Annual Reports, 1955, 1956, and 1957.

50 There was a travelling colonial exhibition in 1950, a Commonwealth touring exhibition in 1959-60, and a City of London Commonwealth Exhibition in 1960.

–5–
THE IMPERIAL INSTITUTE[1]

The rise and fall of the Imperial Institute in South Kensington perfectly encompassed the last phase of Britain's direct imperial commitment between the 1880s and the 1960s. And its history provides a number of insights into 'formal' imperial propaganda. It was intended as a propagandist institution, but for the first forty years its record was one of almost complete failure. Not until it adopted the full range of modern propaganda techniques in the late 1920s did it begin to achieve some public influence. Its propagandist role was greatly enhanced by the Second World War, and by the time it was wound up in the late 1950s it was recognised as a successful 'educational' body. Its activities intersected with the creation of the later imperial exhibitions, with the rise of the documentary film movement, and with the provision of an extensive range of ephemera and visual aids. It was never, however, a popular institution. It largely abandoned its efforts to reach a 'voluntary' adult audience and concentrated instead on schoolchildren and, during the war, troops. The element of coercion no doubt limited its propagandist efficacy.

The Institute emerged from ideas mooted for a Colonial Museum in the 1870s and from the Colonial and Indian Exhibition of 1886. The ambition behind its foundation was to create a permanent exhibition, 'The Empire under one Roof', to which the populace could flock to wonder at the benefits colonial rule afforded them. It was planned and funded in a flush of high imperial sentiment, and opened in one of the most spectacular pageants of the age. Its florid architecture was intended to represent imperial economic, technical, and scientific achievement in physical form, a surrogate for the many imperial palace projects got up in the nineteenth century. But it rapidly became a mausoleum of imperial hopes, an expensive liability which caused some embarrassment as responsibility for its upkeep was shuffled from department to department. Instead of carrying a chorus of imperial harmony, its echoing halls became an arena for discordant British and colonial interests, a setting for Dominion jealousies and nationalist ambitions.

The Institute was fated because it began as a memorial, a memorial to the jubilee of 1887, a memorial to the Colonial and Indian Exhibition of the previous year, and in a very real sense yet another memorial to Prince Albert. Victoria actually brought herself to mention this

explicitly at the laying of the foundation stone in July 1887 when, referring to Albert and the Great Exhibition of 1851, she said, 'Even if we
refer to a never-forgotten sorrow,' the Imperial Institute would act as a
'fitting development and completion of the work thus wisely and usefully instituted'.[2] That Victoria — and the foundation stone — were
there at all was due to the vigorous importuning of the Prince of Wales
and his friends, the 'South Kensington gang' who together had been involved in the Colonial and Indian Exhibition (the Prince of Wales had
chaired its Royal Commission). They had seen to it that the Imperial
Institute became one of the principal fund-raising objects associated
with the Queen's golden jubilee. The organising committee suggested
that the Institute would exhibit 'the vast area, the varied resources,
and the marvellous growth during Her Majesty's reign, of the British
Empire'.[3] A memorial it began and in many ways a memorial it remained, concerned, like the Queen's opening speech, more with retrospect than prospect.

The ambitions of its founders were remarkably wide-ranging. The
organising committee described its purpose as being to illustrate the
great commercial and industrial resources of the colonies and India,
and to spread knowledge of their progress and social condition. It
would display the best natural and manufactured products, and circu-
late collections throughout the United Kingdom. There would be a hall
for the discussion of colonial and Indian subjects, and for holding re-
ceptions. There would be a library, and it was hoped that the Institute
would itself indulge in some successful imperialism by taking over the
Royal Colonial Institute, the Royal Asiatic Society, and the Emigration
Department. It would be charged with the collection and diffusion of
the fullest information about emigration, together with the industrial
and material progress of the colonies. Out of the latter emerged the
commercial and industrial intelligence department, designed to provide information on investment, labour, commercial and transport
arrangements for imperial economic projects and trade. The Institute's
laboratories and technical services would examine potential colonial
products, and the applications of those whose ecological suitability
was known. Moreover, the Institute would have a social purpose: there
would be rooms for fellows, including a bar, restaurant, billiard room,
and reading rooms. These could be used by 'colonials' visiting London
and by those concerned with imperial administration and commerce.

All this was to be achieved, it was hoped, by public subscription, by
a dramatic financial expression of the imperial sentiment of the late
1880s. The organising committee comprised many of the great imperial luminaries who had been involved in the Royal Commission for

the 1886 exhibition, together with Lord Rothschild, the Governor of the Bank of England, the Lord Mayor of London, the Lord Provost of Glasgow, the Archbishop of York, the President of the Royal Society, and — another link with 1851 — Sir Lyon Playfair. This breadth of representation was clearly designed to stimulate the flow of funds. As well as creating sub-committees to handle finance, building, organisation and liaison with the outside bodies which the Institute hoped to incorporate, the committee issued a prospectus and subscription form to be circulated throughout the Empire and the United Kingdom. By April newspapers were publishing long lists of subscribers, affording them an opportunity for a public affirmation of loyalty and generosity. The various companies of the Corporation of London produced £5,000; Coutts & Co., Rothschild's, Baring Brothers, and the Queen herself each provided £1,000. Sir Edward Guinness gave £2,500, the Marquess of Ripon and Sir Henry Holland £100 each, Lyon Playfair £50, Professor Dewar and Lord Crewe £10, among many others. A mere half-guinea subscription gave the right to be listed with the famous who were rich and the great who were, apparently, impecunious. Many a social and financial reputation must have been bruised in the process. The Incorporated Law Society of England and Wales made an arrangement by which its members could maintain ranks and preserve their reputations by subscribing two guineas each. Collections were made in regiments and on Royal Navy ships, ranging from H.M.S. *Duke of Wellington*, which raised £31 17s 3d, to H.M.S. *Iris* at £1 7s 6d. More than half the final subscription of £440,000 came from the United Kingdom, over £100,000 from that great milch cow, the Indian Empire, and rather less than that from all the other colonies. The public subscription in New Zealand raised £2,853 14s 4d, while the Maharajah of Mysore alone contributed 50,000 rupees (over £6,000), and the Bombay Parsi magnate Sir Cowasjee Jehangir gave two lakhs of rupees (about £27,000) to build the central meeting and reception hall, which was of course named after him.[4]

The organising committee investigated the purchase of various sites in central London, only to find that the price of just two or three acres would eat up almost the entire sum raised by the subscription. They turned, therefore, to the block of land in South Kensington which had been purchased from the profits of the Great Exhibition of 1851 and laid aside for the construction of buildings to glorify science and art. A site was acquired which had been used as the garden of the Royal Horticultural Society, lying between the Natural History Museum and the Royal Albert Hall. No fewer than sixty-six architects entered the competition for the design of a building required to incorporate the disparate elements of a large reception hall, a sizeable library, reading rooms, conference quarters, offices and laboratories, social accommodation, as well as the vast galleries which were to display both United Kingdom and colonial products — all for £250,000. Imperial and colonial woods and stones were to be used throughout.[5] The winner was T. E. Colcutt, whose entry, euphemistically described as 'a free rendering of Renaissance style', won a prize at an architectural exhibition in Paris. The final cost of his wildly extravagant building, £355,000, was to prove a burden from which the Institute never fully recovered. Of the £440,000 subscribed, £140,000 was placed in an endowment, earning a mere £4,000 per annum. The excess £55,000 had to be raised by mortgage. The ambitions of the organising committee, reflected in an over-elaborate building, had in fact outrun imperial financial sentiment.

Presumably few foresaw these problems at the brilliant foundation stone-laying ceremony, which took place on a curiously ironic date, 4 July 1887. An assembly of 10,000 people, which included a dozen of the most senior Indian princes, two European kings, two crown princes, and a host of other princes and princesses, together with all the leading political, imperial, and colonial figures available, heard Sir Arthur Sullivan conduct a grand processional march, together with an ode by Lewis Morris sung by the Royal Albert Hall Choral Society and the pupils of the Royal College of Music, composed, like the march, by Sullivan himself. The ode contained all the usual incantations, an 'Empire of a Thousand Years', spread not 'by war's red rapine, but by white-winged peace', trade and commerce, and emigration from Britain, where 'Labour crowds in hopeless misery' to 'a Happier Britain' "neath an ampler air'.[6] The charter of incorporation, like so many of the documents relating to the Institute's foundation, had strong overtones of imperial federation: the Institute's purpose would be to 'strengthen the bonds of union between all classes and races in Our Dominions and to promote a feeling of mutual goodwill, of a common citizenship...' of Empire.[7]

The opening ceremony, on 10 May 1893 (the building had already been informally opened in June the previous year) was even more brilliant.[8] Twenty-five thousand people were present; Morris contributed yet another ode and Sullivan conducted his specially composed Imperial March. The ode, like Tennyson's for the 1886 exhibition, concentrated on the economic benefits of Empire, 'the treasures of the wood, the sea, the mine, All kindly fruits over wide dominions bear, And corn, and oil, and wine', products of territories where 'commerce, smiling, calls'. Just as in 1887 he had written of a thousand-year empire, now he wrote of world dominion. Bonds would bind not only those of British blood, but also the peoples of subject realms, 'out great alien kinsmen', and 'Then, if heaven will, mankind!' The reaction of the European guests to these proto-fascist sentiments is not recorded, though they may have noticed that the music played was almost all German — selections from Mendelssohn, Wagner, Waldteufel, as well as the *Märchen aus dem Orient* by Johann Strauss and the coronation march from *Le Prophète* by Meyerbeer (born a German, Jacob Beer). After the usual address, the Prince of Wales completed an electrical circuit to the Queen's Tower bell chamber, and fifty changes were rung on an enormous peal of bells, known as the Alexandra peal, which had been contributed by an elderly Australian lady, who succeeded in giving her imperial sentiment aural form. The ten bells were among the largest then cast, and their position in the Queen's Tower made them second only to St Paul's as the highest peal in the Empire. They still survive in the Queen's Tower, now a free-standing campanile in the quadrangle of Imperial College, with the foundation stone of colonial granite at its base.[9]

In the succeeding months the rooms for fellows opened. For a subscription of £2 per annum they had access to the collections when not open to the public, as well as to an opulent suite of social rooms. They received all the reports and publications of the Institute and were entitled to the letters F.I.Inst. after their names. There were house dinners for fellows, meetings at which papers were read, and musical events of a distinctly non-colonial nature. The government used the Institute as a source of propaganda for royal and political visitors from overseas, many of whom were shown around in the 1890s.[10] The Department of Commercial and Industrial Intelligence was established in 1888, and corresponding agents were appointed in all the colonies.[11] Those in the Straits Settlements, the Australian colonies, and Canada were sought out by Sir Somers Vine, one of the organising secretaries, on a tour he made in 1889.[12] The Scientific and Technical Department followed in 1894, its laboratories funded by the Goldsmiths' Company and the Royal Commissioners of the 1851 exhibition. It built up large stores of colonial samples and made them available to commercial and industrial firms. A monthly journal was issued, together with trade circulars in eleven languages, and a branch was opened in the City.[13] Efforts to reach a wider public included courses of free lectures and the despatch of small travelling sample collections to schools and colleges.

Alongside this technical and intelligence work, the Institute was to become involved in language teaching.[14] A sub-committee of twelve was set up by the organising committee to manage the School for

Modern Oriental Studies, to be established at the Imperial Institute in association with University and King's Colleges of the University of London. This committee pointed out that there had been a School of Living Oriental Languages in France for 100 years, and that there were facilities in Germany and Austria-Hungary through the Imperial German School of Living Oriental Languages and the Imperial Oriental Academy in Vienna respectively. They were of great importance to the commerce of those States. The intention of the Imperial Institute was to co-ordinate and concentrate the Indian School of University College and the Oriental section of King's College to offer courses in oriental languages for candidates for the Indian Civil Service, existing members of that body, and people engaged in commerce. The languages were in fact offered from autumn 1889 in two divisions: an Indian section, comprising Sanskrit, Bengali, Pali, Marathi, Hindi, Hindustani, Tamil, Telugu, Punjabi, Gujerati, Arabic, and Persian, while the second section afforded study in colloquial Arabic, modern Greek, colloquial Persian, Russian, Turkish, Chinese, Burmese, Japanese, Malay, and Swahili. Three scholarships of £50 each were offered by the daughters of Colonel Ouseley, who had taught Arabic and Persian at Haileybury.

It was soon apparent, however, that the Institute was failing in all departments. As a club it was too far removed from central London. Companies largely failed to use its intelligence service or its laboratory facilities. The original conception had been that the entire north wing would be devoted to the manufactures of the United Kingdom, as an impressive showcase of exports set off against colonial products. Manufacturers declined to avail themselves of this opportunity, and for a long time the gallery remained empty.[15] The colonial exhibits were dreary and failed to stimulate the interest of the public. Both the Royal Colonial Institute and the Royal Asiatic Society wisely declined to amalgamate with the Institute. The Emigration Department was never transferred to it, as originally intended, and only a small emigration office was opened there. As with the original subscription, the most notable financial support came from the Asiatic territories of the Empire. The Indian government gave funds for research, and later the Ceylon administration and its Planters' Association provided a large sum for the building of a Ceylon Tea Garden and Rest House with the object of rehabilitating Ceylon teas with the 'well-to-do' classes of the capital.[16]

By the turn of the century the Institute was in a state of financial collapse. Its endowment of £4,000 per annum was hopelessly inadequate, and largely eaten up by parochial rates and government taxes. The small income from the fellows scarcely covered the cost of the publications and the social facilities available to them. In 1899 the government had no alternative but to take it over.[17] The social activities were immediately abolished, and the space allocated to them was handed over to the University of London to provide some rental income. By this arrangement the Institute lost its front entrance. For two more years the government considered what was to be done. As Kenneth Bradley, the last director in the 1950s, put it, the government had inherited an enormous baby, which it proceeded to starve of sustenance for the rest of its life.[18] He could have added that the government had no idea which nursery to send it to. In 1902 it was handed over to the Board of Trade; in 1907 it went to the Colonial Office; in 1925 it passed to the Department of Overseas Trade; in 1949 it was divided between the Colonial Office and the Ministry of Education.

In 1902 one writer considered the exhibits to be of little use either to the emigrant or to the practical man. They were merely 'emblems of an extinct greatness',[19] which failed to reflect economic and industrial change and could do real harm to a colony. The Dominions were reluctant to fund an institution of such dubious value. It was in fact this problem of funding which was to beggar the Institute for much of its life. India (at least until the 1920s) and a few better-off colonies could be milked of funds at will. The dependent territories which most required its technical services were the least capable of funding projects, since most of them operated on an administrative shoestring. The Dominions, on the other hand, having control of their own resources, saw little reason to put money into a London institution providing employment, conducting research, and making available information and exhibits which could perfectly well be supplied at home.

The Imperial Institute Act of 1902 listed its purposes as being to display the resources of the Empire together with the 'comparative advance made in other countries', to establish a commercial museum and sample rooms in London and throughout the Empire, to collect and disseminate information, to advance trades and handicrafts, promote technical and commercial education, further systematic colonisation, and promote conferences and lectures.[20] There was thus no attempt to focus the Institute's role, and it was to continue with its multifarious, ill-matched activities. The first director, Sir Frederick Abel, a military chemist who had been particularly identified with the ceremonial and social aspects of its work, died in 1903.[21] His successor, Professor Wyndham Dunstan, also a chemist, set about emphasising the scientific and educational functions.[22] The publications provide evidence of the quickening of scientific activities, but little seems to have been done to brighten the public displays, which were no more attractive as a source of popular recreation than they had been before. The confusion about the true role of the Institute was illustrated in its transfer to the Colonial Office in 1907, on the grounds that the colonies were contributing considerably to its upkeep. But the Colonial Office proved no more capable of resolving whether its value lay in scientific work, commercial intelligence, the promotion of raw materials for industrial use, or propaganda for colonial produce and emigration.

The First World War, which set in motion the powerfully conflicting pressures of imperial sentiment and Dominion nationalism, presented the Institute with both great opportunities and even greater dangers. In 1915 it tried to regain the rooms occupied by the University of London to extend its laboratories for the study of rubbers, resins, gums, oils and oilseeds, fibres, feeding stuffs, tobacco, cotton, drugs, and essential oils, together with facilities for assay, cement testing, and the examination of ores and minerals, all connected with the war effort.[23] On the outbreak of war a Technical Information Bureau had been set up. Experimental work was undertaken on dyes for khaki cloth, which had formerly been supplied entirely by Germany, and through the Institute's efforts coal had been discovered in West Africa. In 1916 Lord Sudeley pressed the government in the House of Lords to provide more funds.[24] The Institute's total income was £17,000, and to prosecute its work properly an additional £40,000 was required.

Neither the extra accommodation nor the increased funding was forthcoming. Instead, the Institute was under threat. It had been brought into a closer relationship with the Colonial Office through the Imperial Institute (Management) Act of 1916, and the Dominions Royal Commission of the period now proceeded to consider its contraction or closure.[25] In early 1917 the views of the Royal Commission were leaked. Its report would reveal the Institute's shortcomings and propose that responsibility for colonial displays should be handed over to the Royal Colonial Institute, that Dominions research should be conducted at home, and that the Institute should be restricted to a rump of scientific work on India, the Crown colonies, and protectorates. The commission was attempting, in fact, to resolve the conflict between democratic and autocratic funding. These recommendations had the effect of rallying support for the Institute. Its executive council launched a vigorous defence and aroused much press support. Both *The Times* and *The Telegraph* were delighted to attack Haldane, the chairman of the commission, and accused him of misunderstanding the purposes and value of the Institute.[26] The English sector of the Indian press was even more vociferous in its support. A series of articles in *The Pioneer of India*, *The Times of India*, *The Madras Weekly Mail*, and

Indian Engineering listed its achievements and urged its continued funding on the Indian government.[22]

Nevertheless, the years between 1917 and 1923 the Institute was under real threat of closure. When post-war boom turned to slump in 1921, many Dominions and colonies cancelled their already small contributions. Milner and Churchill, succeeding Secretaries of State for the Colonies, made appeals for funds, Milner threatening that the Institute would be closed if his appeal were not met. The Ormsby-Gore Committee, which reported on the Institute in 1923, was specifically charged with considering closure.[28] Yet not only did it survive, it succeeded in finding a new role in the 1920s and 1930s, when its commercial, scientific, and technical work came to be subordinate to its role as a source of public propaganda on the Empire. It was this 'educational' function which was to prove more attractive, to the Dominion governments at least. The Institute now became caught up in various propagandist efforts, the Empire Marketing Board, the Colonial Empire Marketing Board, the great exhibitions, including those on the Continent, and the use of the full range of propaganda techniques, the cinema, ephemera, lectures, slides, film strips, and special exhibits.

Before the Institute could find this new purpose, however, it had to weather a succession of storms. Following the Dominions Royal Commission of 1917, a report was prepared by a committee under the chairmanship of W. A. S. Hewins, M.P. It recommended the closure of the technical laboratories in favour of the Institute's educational role. Although Hewins was eventually proved right, the council of the Institute refused to carry out the recommendations and asked the Secretary of State for an increased grant. Nothing was done until Milner became Secretary of State in 1919. He persuaded the Treasury to increase the parliamentary grant from £2,500 to £10,000, provided the £10,000 were matched in donations from overseas governments, and he issued an appeal to the colonies.[29] In 1918-19 the income of the Institute had come from a variety of sources in the following percentages:

Endowments	19·9
Dominions	9·7
Colonies and protectorates	32·1
India	8·1
Parliamentary grant	14·5
Other (fees for technical work, etc.)	15·7

So far as the Dominions were concerned, Milner's appeal fell on deaf ears. Only Canada complied, and shortly afterwards India, now enjoying greater financial autonomy, withdrew, 'dissatisfied with the amount of assistance received in the past'. The Ormsby-Gore Committee's report recommended that the Institute should take a direction diametrically opposite to that which in fact proved its salvation. They wanted it to become a purely technical establishment; the galleries should be closed, the South Kensington building sold, and the laboratories move to new premises. The High Commissioners for both South Africa and Australia recommended winding-up, and four members issued a minority report on the preservation of the galleries. The mixed voices of the Ormsby-Gore Committee were somehow incorporated into a new Imperial Institute Act of 1925, which handed the Institute over to the Department of Overseas Trade.[30] Although the main emphasis of the new legislation was on scientific and technical work, the galleries were to survive and indeed be broadened in scope. Curiously, the Institute was now on the verge of its most successful period.

The Ormsby-Gore Committee's recommendations were frustrated by private donors and by the development of propagandist institutes and techniques. The galleries survived only because Viscount Cowdray, a civil engineering contractor who had made a fortune from Mexican oil, donated £25,000 in 1924 (the critical year between the report and the new Act) to the display and educational side of the Institute's work.[31] In 1926 the newly created Empire Marketing Board provided funds (£6,000 capital cost and £1,000 per annum) for a cinema at the Institute which opened in 1927.[32] Sir Robert Hadfield, metallurgist and steel-maker, provided money for metallurgical investigations.[33] In 1932 Viscount Wakefield, another oil millionaire, gave £25,000.[34] Wakefield was actively concerned with imperial solidarity and propaganda, particularly among the young. He supported the imperial cadet movement, and was honorary colonel of the imperial cadet yeomanry. Potentially the largest gift was from Benjamin Drage of the Oxford Street firm of house furnishers.[35] In 1931 he offered £36,000 over six years to the Empire Marketing Board for its film work at the Imperial Institute. He made two payments, secured his knighthood in 1932, and from 1933 defaulted when he transferred the bulk of his estate to his wife. He made token payments thereafter, but steadfastly declined to fulfil his pledge despite voluminous annual correspondence. The Institute failed to take legal action, and discovered on his death in 1952 that under the statute of limitations it had lost its recourse to law. Nevertheless, Drage gave, in all, £16,000. Moreover, after 1933 the film work continued to be supported by an unnamed Scottish donor. Besides all these private donations, a number of commercial companies associated with the Empire contributed to exhibits. They included Lever

Brothers, the Elder Dempster shipping line, Canadian National Railways, Turner & Newall, Courtauld's, the rubber growers' and tea associations, and many others. Not for nothing did the retiring director of the Institute lament in his 1933 report that it had survived only through private gifts.

Funding from the Dominions and colonies was drummed up by invoking imperial sentiment at imperial conferences and the conferences of colonial governors. In 1921 Churchill, then Secretary of State, browbeat the members of the imperial conference on the question of contributions.[36] At the 1923 Imperial Economic Conference a new scale of contributions from the Dominions was organised.[37] In 1927 the entire Colonial Governors' Conference, held under the auspices of Leopold Amery — like Milner, an enthusiast for the Institute — visited the exhibitions, and colonial contributions improved thereafter.[38] Renewed financial crisis in 1930-31, when almost all the Dominion and colonial subventions were stopped during the depression, was weathered, and, after badgering from Colonial Office circulars in 1933, contributions resumed again in the middle '30s only to decline once more as war loomed.[39] It was, however, no thanks to the Empire that the Institute survived. The crises of the '20s and '30s were overcome by the large private donations already mentioned and by ever-increasing Treasury grants. In 1919 the grant of H.M. government had amounted only to 14·5% of total income; by 1930-31 it constituted 29·1%. After the Second World War the British contribution reached 45·6%. Throughout the period the Dominions' contribution, compared with those of the Crown colonies and protectorates, was out of all proportion either to their wealth or the amount of space their exhibits took up in the galleries. By the late '30s the Dominions' grant had almost faded away while the colonial contributions had increased steadily.

It is ironic, therefore, that the scientific and technical work, which could benefit the colonies and protectorates, steadily became less prominent in the Institute's work compared with the propagandist and educational objectives. The shift was apparent from the appointment of Sir William Furse as director in 1926. In his first report he wrote, 'My hope and belief is that these galleries, if made sufficiently attractive, will be of immense value to the public, especially to the younger generation, as a permanent "Wembley" from the educational point of view.'[40] He regretted that more of the exhibits from Wembley had been dispersed before he was appointed, so that he had been unable to secure as many for the Institute as he would have liked. Once again, the Institute was seen as a permanent imperial exhibition.

The new policy was heralded in a number of ways. In September

1925 a meeting of 1,200 headmasters and headmistresses at the Institute was addressed by Ormsby-Gore and the Duchess of Atholl. The King and Queen visited the galleries in December in an attempt to bring them to public notice, an event which marked the beginning of a series of annual royal visits, particularly by Queen Mary, who took an interest in the Institute until her death. The Premier of New Zealand and the Maharajah of Burdwan made visits from the Imperial Conference of 1926, though none of the other colonial Prime Ministers could find the time.

Immediate steps were taken to brighten the galleries, to provide livelier exhibits, in particular dioramas of imperial economic activity. The emphasis was to be on the utilisation of raw materials, the transformation of imperial products into finished articles, demonstrating the importance of Empire to British industry and the manner in which everyday articles were dependent on tropical raw materials. The message would be driven home through sets of postcards, leaflets on Empire products, specimens for school use in teaching 'Empire development and economic geography', and exhibits which would be made available to museums.[41]

The Institute embarked on a publicity campaign in the belief that it was the 'least known of the museums'.[42] Part of the problem was that the main entrance had been taken over for the accommodation rented by the University of London, and public access was by a side door. London Transport's celebrated publicist, Frank Pick, commissioned Imperial Institute posters to be displayed at Underground stations. There was a press campaign, and leaflets were distributed in selected London areas (noticeably middle-class ones, in fact).

In the following years new displays in new courts were gradually completed, the South African court being opened in 1927 despite the fact that South Africa made no contribution to its cost.[43] New dioramas were added featuring, for example, the clove industry of Zanzibar, tin mining in Malaya, cotton in the Sudan, cocoa and manganese in the Gold Coast, tobacco in Southern Rhodesia. Funds for an improved exhibit on Nigeria were swiftly found after the visit of the Governor. Exhibits were sent out to many outside exhibitions, the British Industries fairs, Ideal Homes exhibitions, building trade exhibitions, schoolboys' exhibitions, Empire Shopping Weeks and the like. Marshal Lyautey paid a visit in 1930 in connection with the Colonial Exhibition in Paris. Moreover, by the 1930s the Institute had embarked upon a policy of taking itself out into the country. Lectures were organised for schools, both by recognised imperial lecturers in Britain and by colonial officials home on leave. Travelling displays for use in schools were arranged, and some portable ones were sold. In the galleries themselves there were travelogue displays like 'A trip down the Irrawaddy', 'Round Barbados', 'Up Like Nyasa', and so on. Inevitably, there was a new emphasis on aerial transport. The 'new story method of display' was adopted, describing the manner in which raw materials were transformed into manufactured items, for example, jute into linoleum. More traditional methods of displaying imperial history were also used. The galleries were festooned with silk banners of the arms of the colonies and Dominions, and statuettes of Empire builders appeared with all the relevant displays.

But by far the more important element in the Institute's new devotion to imperial propaganda was the cinema. The economic approach the Institute adopted, which arose naturally from its original concern with the technical problems of imperial production and its displays of Empire products, fitted perfectly with the objectives of the Empire Marketing Board, founded at the Imperial Conference of 1926.[44] However, the link with the E.M.B. came in an unexpected form. The Secretary of the E.M.B., Stephen Tallents, one of the foremost exponents of propaganda techniques recognised the great power of the cinema in reaching the public. He was responsible for establishing the E.M.B. film unit, and offered the Institute funds to establish a cinema which could show, among others, E.M.B. films. The cinema opened its doors on 1 July 1927, and immediately became the setting used by the head of the E.M.B. film unit to lecture on film as propaganda, and to show the Russian propagandist films which had such a significant effect on the work of the British documentary film movement.[45] In its rather more humble guise, showing imperial films four times a day, the cinema rapidly became the most important attraction the Institute could offer.

Indeed, the cinema proved so popular that it threatened to overwhelm the Institute's other features. A pamphlet advertising the Institute's educational facilities — 'The Empire under one Roof' — plaintively admonished visitors that 'the cinema should not be used as the sole object for visiting the Institute. The cinema is intended to be used as a supplement to visits to the galleries.'[46] In addition to the E.M.B.'s films (some of which, it must be said, had a rather dubious, or non-existent, imperial content), the Institute was supplied with films from the Dominion High Commissions, and various commercial sources. Titles included *Peoples and Products of India, Romantic India, Monsoon Island – Ceylon, British West Africa, Airport*, etc.

In 1933 the E.M.B. was wound up, but by then its film unit had in effect transferred to the G.P.O. The Institute continued to be the repository of Empire and G.P.O. films, and this was regularised in the creation of the Empire Film Library in 1935.[47] The Institute received subsidies in turn from the E.M.B., the Post Office, and the Treasury, as well as from private donors, to carry on the work. Its central place in propaganda was assured when the Empire Film Library became the Central Film Library in 1940. By 1937 it was claimed that the library had 1,300 films, made 24,600 loans, and reached a total audience of five million, in addition to those who saw the programme of films entitled 'An Empire Storyland' in the Institute's cinema.[48] Even if the figures are somewhat inflated by a director anxious to demonstrate the propagandist value of his organisation, nonetheless its activities all showed remarkable growth during these years, as Tables 1 and 2 indicate.[49]

Table 1
Attendance at the Institute

1927	326,435
1928	345,967
1929	397,598
1930	608,900
1931	732,455
1932	1,121,199
1933	738,718
1934	775,314
1937	600,000 *

*No figures are available for 1935 or 1936. During the last three years staff shortages made adequate counting difficult, perhaps conveniently, since the trend seems to have been downwards.

Table 2
Imperial Institute Film Library

Year	No. of films	No. of loans	Estimated audience
1931	189	–	–
1932	550	–	–
1933	696	9,560	2,005,600
1934	800	14,550	2,900,000
1935	1,000	17,001	3,675,000
1936	1,000	22,785	n.a.
1937	1,300	24,600	5,000,000

By the late 1930s propaganda had come to dominate the activities of the Imperial Institute, and took up a large amount of space in the annual reports. It had come to be the best argument for survival and funds. The Dominion governments were now prepared to donate films, even if no more inclined to increase their subventions. The Secretary to the Canadian High Commission, Vanier, told the director,

Sir Harry Lindsay, in 1935 that he believed 'very strongly in a development of Empire propaganda by films.'[50] In 1933 the sources of films included Canada (fifty-nine films), Australia (twenty-nine), New Zealand (twelve), South Africa (fifteen), India (seventeen), Canadian National Railways (twenty-three), Southern Rhodesia (one), East Africa (eight), Malaya (four), the West Indies (six), Cyprus (one), and the Crown Agents (two).[51] Borrowers that year make a fascinating list. In addition to more than 500 schools, there were religious bodies, Scouts, Boys' Brigades, Girl Guides, film societies, army schools, Workers' Education Association, Toc H, hospitals and unemployment centres.

During the same period thousands of postcards and picture sets of Empire products were sold and many more thousands of leaflets on imperial raw materials were issued. Moreover, from 1929 the Imperial Institute embarked on a programme of lectures. These were to build up to extraordinary numbers during and after the Second World War, and used both film strips and slides, which were sent around the country for the use of lecturers. Just as the Institute was building up its library of the new medium, films, particularly sound films, in the 1930s, it was also building up vast collections in the apparently obsolete medium of slides. Dominion and colonial governments, the Victoria League, commercial organisations and private individuals donated slides at this time. Large collections of slides and photographs of the Empire were also deposited during the war by the Ministry of Information, but in 1941 the Ministry, perhaps not surprisingly, informed the Institute that it was rather sceptical about the effectiveness of lantern slides as propaganda and was unwilling to spend money on them.[52] This was perhaps just as well, for the Institute's collection had by then reached 20,000.

Although the Institute seemed to have achieved some real propagandist successes in the 1930s, it must be remembered that a high proportion of visitors were in fact involuntary ones, members of school parties. There can be little doubt that film had the greatest impact, although the photographs of the displays do reveal them to have been remarkably modern and well designed. The message of the films was by no means clear. Few carried the economic emphasis on changing colonial raw materials into metropolitan manufactured goods that was the Institute's prime concern. Judging by the titles, a large number were on economic subjects, but there were many travelogues, often simply in the 'pretty picture' category. Some of the E.M.B. and G.P.O. films had only a tenuous imperial connection. Nonetheless, the Institute cannot have failed to convey to visitors, school parties, borrowers of exhibits and films that the Empire was large, diverse, and useful.

This developing propagandist activity was in no way checked by the war.[53] The cinema and galleries were closed from August 1939 to 1943 except for organised parties. The Institute soon found a new source of 'involuntary' visitors at a time when most schoolchildren had been evacuated from London. For British as well as colonial troops the Institute was a recognised part of the educational programme. Well over 100 organised parties of troops were shown round each year, reaching a peak of 192 in 1945. Despite shortages of manpower, the Institute continued to improve its displays, adding new techniques like Stillograph and Informograph machines (press the button for lighted information) in 1941. As in the First World War, the Institute's scientific departments became closely concerned with investigating alternative sources of raw materials to those which had formerly come from enemy or occupied territories.

Early in the war, however, the Institute decided to take itself out to the country even more effectively than it had done in the 1930s. Its work was now recognised as an important element in wartime propaganda. Dioramas and 'stories' of products were turned into posters. New sets of stories, picture cards, story posters, travelogues and transparencies were produced each year. Many more slides were acquired from a variety of governments and commercial companies, and sets were sent out to schools, Women's Institutes, literary societies, and village halls. The Institute also became involved in overseas propaganda. Material was sent to the New York World's Fair in 1940. It established a link with the National Council for British Commonwealth Propaganda Overseas. Sets of slides were prepared for the use of the British Council, and picture talks were produced in collaboration with the Colonial Empire Marketing Board.

Many more new films were added to the Central Film Library, including films of India contributed by G. D. Birla, together with others from Cadbury Brothers, the Empire Tea Bureau, Canadian Pacific Railways, British Columbia Salmon Packers, the Irrawaddy Flotilla Company, B.O.A.C., I.C.I., and Cable & Wireless. A grant for new prints of films was given by the Imperial Relations Trust. Borrowings continued to grow, and the film librarian discovered that there were two types of new borrowers, air raid shelter marshals, and army officers lecturing to troops. In 1944 the film library consisted of 15,000 prints of 900 films, 237 of them specifically Empire films, the rest being United Kingdom, G.P.O. and Ministry of Information footage, some of which also had imperial content. The Institute's annual report described the library as the largest collection of documentary and educational films in the Empire and probably in the world. In 1942 4,500 organisations borrowed films, and loans during the war reached a peak in 1943.[54] (Table 3).

Table 3
Empire films loaned

1941	29,000
1942	34,048
1943	35,909
1944	33,242
1945	29,881
1946	28,012

But perhaps the greatest effort went into the lecture scheme. At the outbreak of the war, 100 Empire lecturers were recruited, and the figure increased greatly as the war wore on. They were gathered together in an annual lecturers' conference, and received material for lectures with titles such as 'Trade with our Colonial Empire'. Freelance lecturers were also employed. One of these was Harold Heap, a professional lecturer and ex-schoolmaster who was adept at self-publicity and operated between 1940 and 1948.[55] He produced his own posters and ran a lecture agency, frequently giving more than seventy talks a year on the Empire. The Institute prepared a pamphlet entitled 'The Imperial Institute Scheme for Empire Lectures to Schools', recommended A. P. Newton's *History of the British Empire* for historical background, and a series of Oxford pamphlets on the British Empire published at 3*d* each. It succeeded in securing grants for the lectures from the Leverhulme Foundation (which gave £1,000 each year for several years), the Rhodes trustees (also £1,000 per annum), the committee of the Empire Day Movement (£500 per annum), and the Imperial Relations Trust (£500 per annum) as well as the Royal Society of St George. The lectures were given to schoolchildren, troops, and a variety of organisations, but by now the Institute was convinced that its main propaganda role was among schoolchildren. The annual report for 1944 reiterated the commitment to 'the educational needs of the rising generation', 'on the principle that the youth of today is the Empire-builder of tomorrow'. If that seems like a curiously antiquated objective, at least the lecture scheme was alive to contemporary developments. The lecturers' conference the same year was devoted to the 'new concept of Empire', 'its development as a free association of peoples and its potentialities for good in a post-war world'.

The geographical spread of the lecturers' activities is difficult to ascertain, but such evidence as there is seems to indicate a concentration on the south, west, and Midlands of England. Nonetheless, the figures are impressive (Table 4).[56]

Table 4
Imperial Institute lecture schemes

	1941-42	1942-43	1943-44	1944-45	1945-46
No. of lectures delivered	768	1,476	2,177	3,044	3,553
No. illustrated with slides or films	557	1,201	1,565	2,099	2,544
Total audience	126,098	241,648	329,349	436,832	511,529

The Institute emerged from the war a recognised propagandist body. It had really only developed its propagandist activities to the full in the late 1920s and 1930s with its ephemera, its greatly improved displays, its films, film strips and slides, its specimens, and travelling exhibitions, its role in all imperial and colonial exhibitions, and finally its lecture schemes. In 1949 this achievement was recognised when all its educational functions were transferred to the Ministry of Education, the surviving technical laboratories passing to the Colonial Office.[57] The Institute's techniques were now well established, and in the post-war world it continued to operate, with some new developments, on the educational pattern of the past two decades.

At the end of the war conferences of head teachers were held, and contacts were made with all local education authorities and teacher training colleges. The general secretary of the Institute visited seventy-five of the 140 L.E.A.s in England and Wales. Conferences of British Empire lecturers were held in January and July 1947, and a British Empire panel of H.M. school inspectorate was established. A co-ordinating committee was set up, with representatives of the Colonial Office, the Commonwealth Relations Office, the Central Office of Information, the London representatives of colonial governments, the Empire Societies and the Institute to produce a catalogue of information services available on the colonies.[58] This appeared in 1948.

The Institute's role in the establishment of colonial exhibitions was now widely acknowledged. Its change of direction had really emerged from Wembley. In the 1930s the director had been chairman of the Standing Committee for Colonial Trade Agencies, concerned with advertising the colonies through international exhibitions.[59] It had played a significant role in the establishment of the British Empire Exhibition in Glasgow in 1938, and had been the setting for colonial exhibitions at the end of the war.[60] Now it was closely involved with the Colonial Months and the British Industries fairs.[61] The director, Sir Harry Lindsay, was on the council for the Festival of Britain, and all the colonial aspects of that festival were in fact held at the Institute.

Nonetheless, financial problems remained. The private donations of the '20s and '30s had come to an end, as had the grants from the various trusts during the war. Colonial contributions continued to decline as a proportion of the whole, and the Institute survived on its Treasury grant (more than 50% of the total in the early 1950s) and funding from the Central Office of Information for the Film Library. Nevertheless, colonial territories continued to use the Institute for their own purposes. Increases in grants from various Indian states are most marked at the end of the war. In some cases, new displays were actually created for Indian princely states on the eve of their demise, such as Udaipur, Hyderabad, Mysore, Travancore, Jaipur and Baroda.[62] It is clear that they were trying to assert their individual identity before the lapse of British paramountcy. Surprisingly, Indian donations actually increased after independence, to improve the quality of the Indian exhibit.[63] In 1953, the newly created Federation of Rhodesia and Nyasaland supplied no less than £5,000 for a new display.[64]

Almost all the courts at the Institute were reconstructed in an impressively modern manner, as the photographs in the annual reports show. Visiting children were presented with Empire quizzes to complete on their tour of the building. Colonial stamps were given as prizes. Folding dioramas were produced for schools. Colonial officials on leave were asked to tour schools giving lectures, though the schools proved unresponsive. No fewer than twenty-four 'Stories of Empire Products' were produced in leaflet form, as well as a series of pamphlets entitled 'The Colonies Today'. Conferences of grammar school sixth-form pupils and students in teacher training colleges were held from 1952. There were five in 1953, fifteen in 1954, and twenty-four in 1955. In 1952 a Saturday morning boys' club was founded to promote the study of Empire geography, and it soon had several hundred members (even in 1952 girls were not expected to be interested). In December 1955 a Scottish branch was established and was provided with a grant-in-aid of more than £3,000 by the Scottish Education Office. At the Institute itself a schools' reception centre was established. By 1954 the Institute was claiming that it had reached 1¼ million people, a million of them schoolchildren.[65]

The cinema continued much as before, films being donated from the usual sources. At the end of the war films were made in African colonies by the Ministry of Information for the Colonial Office. Several were set in Tanganyika. A dozen films made in East Africa by Kingston Davies were added to the collection. The Institute became the repository for the films of the Colonial Film Unit of Northern Rhodesia, and commercial companies like Cadbury's and the Aluminium Union continued to supply their own propaganda. Under the directorship of

Lindsay the Institute had also begun to make full use of the B.B.C. In 1933 and 1934 the latter had produced a series of programmes for schools entitled 'The Life and Work of the British Empire', divided into a series on Science and Agriculture and another on the Peoples of the Empire. The director had broadcast frequently in connection with the various exhibitions with which the Institute had been associated, including the fresh burst of colonial exhibition activity at the time of the coronation in 1953. In the 1950s the B.B.C. Children's Hour produced a 'Children of the Commonwealth' series in collaboration with the Institute.[66]

On the eve of its closure and demolition, the Institute seemed to have reached a new statistical peak in its propagandist activities (Table 5), although not matching the success of the 1930s.[67]

Table 5
Imperial Institute activities

Year	Attendance	Cinema	Sale of leaflets	Postcards
1947	138,964	–	–	–
1948	162,404	–	–	–
1949	155,577	76,150	18,033	13,874
1950	215,745	93,325	12,456	9,606
1951	274,949	147,885	13,017	6,653
1952	388,000	229,423	10,921	6,271
1953	407,000	292,901	13,242	2,132 *

*The imposition of 100% purchase tax on postcards in 1952 destroyed sales.

In 1950 a new committee was established to investigate its work under the chairmanship of Lord Tweedsmuir.[68] In 1945, in a House of Lords debate, Tweedsmuir had spoken of the need to avoid duplication with the work of the Royal Empire Society and the Royal Institute of International Affairs.[69] The committee, which included the historian Gerald Graham among its members, while commending its successful educational work with schools nonetheless considered that the Institute was little known to the public. It found the concentration on the economic connections of Empire no longer appropriate and suggested that there should be a shift of emphasis from products to peoples, that the Institute should become a cultural centre where there should be displays of the art and cultures of Commonwealth peoples, a centre for artistic events, painting, sculpture, crafts, dance, theatre, even Commonwealth cuisine. The Institute should be a centre not for imperial economic geography but for Commonwealth arts. In 1955 Lord Home announced in the Lords that the country's need for scientists necessitated the considerable extension of Imperial College.[70] The Imperial

Institute would be demolished and resurrected as the Commonwealth Institute at a new site.

As though to soften the loss of one of South Kensington's more florid museum buildings, the chairman of the council, Lord Hudson, described its architecture in 1955 as 'perfectly abominable'.[71] At the same time he lamented that the Institute had been 'disgracefully neglected' throughout its life. For twenty-odd years the Treasury had given only £16,000 per annum to educate the British people on the meaning of the Commonwealth. 'It is fantastic to think of it.' Now the government was giving £24,000, and 'to run the show properly we want to add a naught to the end of it'.

Hudson's breast-beating at its demise epitomised the government's failure throughout the Institute's existence to put any real effort into imperial propaganda. Yet the Institute had survived. Propaganda had come to be its main activity from the late '20s, just when the 'Projection of Britain' was coming to be important overseas. Some large private donations and a few energetic individuals had kept it alive in order to promote the imperial economic propaganda of the inter-war years. That it won through was no thanks to the Dominions, whose exhibits took by far the most space, and which could have hoped to benefit most from emigration and trade. Dominion nationalism thwarted repeated appeals. Instead, the captive governments of the colonies and protectorates provided the bulk of the income. It is difficult to judge what return they received in the scientific work of the Institute, but so far as propaganda was concerned there can be no doubt that they subsidised the infinitely wealthier Dominions. Indeed, at just the time when the latter were reducing their commitment the Institute turned from scientific investigation to propaganda, which was more likely to benefit them.

The Institute's scientific vicissitudes neatly reflected the position of science in British society. The research laboratories were set up out of a conscious desire to ape Germany's systematic approach to science and colonial production. But the scientific objectives were lost in the dissipation of effort into exhibition and display so that neither worked. Even in time of war the Institute received no extra encouragement or funding, but instead came under threat. The social and scholarly side of its work was finally doomed by the continuing refusal of the Royal Colonial Institute to contemplate amalgamation in 1900 and 1912. The members of the R.C.I., proud of their central site in Northumberland Avenue, declined to transfer to 'the dreary wastes of South Kensington'.[72] In the late nineteenth century the Institute became in fact a source of fun. In Arthur Wing Pinero's play *The Gay Lord Quex*

(1898), one of the characters describes the Egyptian handmaidens in the painting 'Moses in the Bullrushes' as being 'rather like the girls in the ballet at the Empire'.

> *Lady Owbridge.* The Empire?
> *Lord Quex.* A place of popular entertainment.
> *Lady Owbridge.* The only place I have been to of that kind is the Imperial Institute.

The British public remained more disposed to visit Moss Stoll's Empires than the Imperial Institute, but nonetheless it enjoyed greater success after the First World War. Yet its influence on the public remains difficult to assess. In the 1930s, during the Second World War, and up to the mid-1950s, its statistics of attendance, sales, and above all loans of films and provision of lectures were impressive. But the assimilation of its message must have been inhibited by the involuntary nature of the visits by schoolchildren and troops. The films no doubt reached the largest and most eager audience, and in this respect the Institute did much to make the work of the E.M.B., G.P.O., and colonial film units more widely known. Commercial companies, Dominion governments, and private film makers used the Institute as a vehicle for their own particular propaganda. Although the message was a highly complex and often divided one, the ideas that the Empire was extensive, was peopled by curious and strange peoples, provided valuable raw materials and foodstuffs, and above all was 'ours', must at least have sunk home.

In the wider context of British imperial history, the phases of the Institute's life reflect contemporary colonial concerns. In the first, before the First World War, it was set up in a mood of self-congratulation; it was an elitist body, and its prime concerns in commercial and technical developments were often ignored by those whom they were designed to benefit. In the inter-war years, almost by accident, and on the basis of private rather than public financial support, it propagated the economic vision of the time, the Empire as a self-sufficient unit capable of withstanding the economic storms of the age. It was a short step to propaganda for war aims during the next conflict, and in the post-war world it was diverted to a new vision of Empire as an association of free peoples, among whom mutual understanding could best be fostered by an appreciation of their distinctive arts and customs.

NOTES

1 The records of the Imperial Institute are deposited in the Public Record Office at Kew, and are contained in the files P.R.O. 30/76/1-309. I am grateful to the Director of the Commonwealth Institute, James F. Porter, for arranging the waiving of the

thirty-year rule, so that I could follow the story to the Institute's demise.

2 Programme and speeches of the ceremony of laying the foundation stone, P.R.O. 30/76/13. For the Prince of Wales's involvement, see Lant, *Insubstantial Pageant*, 124-43.

3 Reports of the Organising Committee to the Prince of Wales, P.R.O. 30/76/13.

4 Details of the appeal for funds are contained in P.R.O. 30/76/13. See also Kenneth Bradley, 'The Imperial Institute', *Journal of the Royal Society of Arts*, 105 (1956-57), 871/87. Imperial resistance was encountered too. One report complained that 'the result of the organising appeals in Ireland is not so favourable as could be desired'.

5 These and subsequent details of funding and building come from the Reports of the Organising Committee, P.R.O. 30/76/13.

6 Programme of the Ceremony of Laying the Foundation Stone, P.R.O. 30/76/308.

7 Charter of Incorporation of the Imperial Institute, 1888, P.R.O. 30/76/308.

8 Programme of the State Inauguration of the Imperial Institute, 10th May, 1893, P.R.O. 30/76/308.

9 I am grateful to Mrs J. Pingree, College Archivist, Imperial College of Science and Technology, for details about the bells. They are rung by the Ancient Society of College Youths to commemorate the birth of an heir to the throne.

10 In 1892, for example, the Institute was visited by the Prince of Wales, the King of Roumania, the Prince of Hohenzollern, and the Duke and Duchess of Edinburgh.

11 Memorandum by Sir Frederick Abel on the Nature and Progress of the Work of the Imperial Institute, December, 1897, P.R.O. 30/76/308.

12 Correspondence on Vine's mission is to be found in P.R.O. 30/76/13.

13 The Imperial Institute *Yearbook* was published from 1892 to 1894, the Imperial Institute *Journal* from 1895 to 1902; the *Bulletin of the Imperial Institute* from 1903 to 1948. The changing concerns of the Institute are well reflected in the pages of these journals. The *Yearbook*, for example, reflected a concern primarily with commercial and financial matters; technical and scientific work became more important later, but the frequency of the publications declined. The half-hearted British approach to science was well illustrated in the history of the Institute. Selected technical reports and scientific papers were also published between 1903 and 1914. A series of Imperial Institute handbooks on commercial products were published in the 1890s. The annual reports of the Institute were published as Command papers between 1906 and 1914.

14 A special sub-committee of twelve for the management of the School of Modern Oriental Studies was established with a view to opening the school of Oriental Languages in the autumn of 1889 for officers of the Indian civil service. See also the Syllabus of Lectures of the School for Modern Oriental Studies, 1890, P.R.O. 30/76/13.

15 Memorandum by Sir F. Abel, December 1897.

16 P.R.O. 30/76/108.

17 Correspondence on the transfer of the Institute to the government and its partial use by the University of London can be found in the records of the Ministry of Education (Ed. 26) and of the Office of Works (Works 17) in the Public Records Office.

18 Bradley, 'Imperial Institute'. See also K. Bradley, 'The Commonwealth Institute', *Corona*, X, 6 (1958), 222-4.

19 A Norman, 'The Imperial Institute, its genesis, history, and possibilities, *Imperial Argus*, 1, 8 (January 1902), 393-407.

20 A copy of the Imperial Institute Act (1902) can be found in P.R.O. 30/76/308.

21 It is perhaps indicative of the Cinderella status of the Imperial Institute that the *Dictionary of National Biography* entry on Sir Frederick Abel does not mention his association with the Institute, which extended from 1887 to 1902.

22 Sir Wyndham Rowland Dunstan (1861-1949), Director of the Scientific and Technical Departments of the Imperial Institute; Director, 1903-24; chairman of Committee for National Memorial to the Earl of Meath.

23 Memorandum by the Chairman of the Advisory Committee, November 1915, P.R.O. 30/76/308.

24 Parliamentary Debates, House of Lords, XXIII, 20 December 1916, 991-7.

25 Dominions Royal Commission (Cd 8462), 1917, X, 1.

26 *The Times*, 27 March 1917; *Daily Telegraph*, 26 February 1917.

27 *Pioneer of India*, October 1918; *Madras Weekly Mail*, April 1918. *Indian Engineering*, November 1917 and February 1918.

28 Imperial Institute, Report of the Committee of Enquiry (Cd 1997), 1923, XII, 197.

29 Documents on the financing of the Institute are to be found in P.R.O. 30/76/79-97.

30 Imperial Institute Act, 1925.

31 Lord Cowdray's gift, P.R.O. 30/76/149. Cowdray (1856-1927) is described in *D.N.B.* as 'little known in public life', but he was a munificent donor to the R.A.F. Club, the R.A.F. Memorial Fund, the Imperial Institute, and to Aberdeenshire, where he had estates. He also supplied substantial funds over a five-year period from 1909 to the Round Table. He was Liberal M.P. for Colchester 1895-1910, and President of the Air Board in 1917.

32 Relations with the Empire Marketing Board can be found in P.R.O. 30/76/152, 206, 212, 292, 294.

33 Sir Robert Hadfield, bart. (1858-1940) was interested in the history of metallurgy and also in experimental work. He was himself a Fellow of the Royal Society as well as a Sheffield steel magnate.

34 Viscount Wakefield (1859-1941) was, according to *D.N.B.*, interested in fostering imperial strength and friendship. He was also interested in aviation and financed Cobham, Amy Johnson, as well as R.A.F. projects and attempts on the land speed record. He endowed the Raleigh lectures at the British Academy. He was contemptuous of covenanting arrangements for the remission of income tax on charitable donations. Irked by negotiations on such an arrangement with the Imperial Institute, he sent a cheque overnight for the full sum of £25,000.

35 P.R.O. 30/76/150. Mr Benjamin Drage: deed of gift, correspondence 1931-1952.

36 Proceedings of the Imperial Conference of 1921, P.R.O. 30/76/201. Churchill announced, 'the £250 that comes from South Africa, although very welcome so far as it goes, is, I think, a little below the dignity of that El Dorado of gold, diamonds, and all the luxuries most desired by men'. It was proposed at this conference that the Institute building should be turned into an Imperial War Museum.

37 The Ormsby-Gore Committee report contains a useful history of the financing of the Institute.

38 Imperial Institute Annual Report, 1927.

39 Correspondence on the crisis in colonial contributions associated with the depression can be found in P.R.O. 30/76/189 and 191. A great deal of haggling went on among the Dominions on the scale of contributions related to the number of square feet allocated at the Institute. See, for example, P.R.O. 30/76/190, 192, and 193.

40 Imperial Institute Annual Report, 1926. A new handbook was designed and issued in 1926, with academic help. See P.R.O. 30/76/222.

41 It is an interesting reflection on official attitudes to 'ephemera' that the Institute did not keep a collection of its own postcards. They were, however, carefully collected by a member of the Victoria League, who subsequently donated her albums to the Institute, P.R.O. 30/76/14.

42 Annual Report, 1926, 40. The Institute subsequently became closely involved with the E.M.B. poster competitions, P.R.O. 30/76/206.

43 Annual Report, 1927, 22.

44 I am indebted to Dr Stephen Constantine for information on the E.M.B. and the opportunity to read an unpublished paper based on his research on that body.

45 Forsyth Hardy, *John Grierson: a Documentary Biography*, London, 1979, 46. Hardy, *Grierson on Documentary*, 22-8.

46 Pamphlet to indicate the Educational Facilities offered by the Imperial Institute Galleries, 'The Empire under one Roof', P.R.O. 30/76/223, 1928-34. These pamphlets also listed the postcards, leaflets, and samples of empire produce available.

47 P.R.O. 30/76/152. Annual Report, 1935.

48 Annual Report, 1937. See also Lindsay, 'Romance and adventure'. Here Lindsay extolled the virtue of real romance and adventure in inspiring the young, but spoilt the effect by suggesting that romance lay in raw materials and finished articles, the commercial geography of Empire. The same issue of *World Film News* carried a large

advertisement for the Empire Film Library, describing its collection and hiring services. The catalogue of the collection was issued at 3*d*.

49 These tables are compiled from the annual reports, contained in P.R.O. 30/76/72-6. The reports were also issued as Command papers. There was no report in 1931 because of financial difficulties.

50 Sir Stephen Tallents to Sir Harry Lindsay, 22 February 1935, P.R.O. 30/76/152.

51 P.R.O. 30/76/152.

52 P.R.O. 30/76/234.

53 The annual reports, 1940-46, reflect a quickening of propaganda activity to transmit war aims to the population.

54 Figures compiled from annual reports.

55 At times the Institute found it difficult to control Harold Heap. See correspondence in P.R.O. 30/76/254.

56 Figures compiled from annual reports.

57 Details of post-war reorganisation and finances are in P.R.O. 30/76/306. The disappearance of the Institute's scientific work had been predicted by the Imperial Committee on Economic Consultation and Co-operation, 1933 (the Skelton Committee), paragraphs 274-84, which had indicated that the Dominions would be unlikely to support scientific research at the Institute in future.

58 P.R.O. 30/76/239.

59 P.R.O. 30/76/160 and 204. The Institute had also been involved in the compilation of the Economic Survey of the Colonial Empire between 1933 and 1939, P.R.O. 30/76/228.

60 For the Institute and imperial exhibitions, see P.R.O. 30/76/161-70.

61 Annual Report, 1949.

62 See the annual reports for the war years.

63 P.R.O. 30/76/192. *The Madras Mail*, 23 May 1948, carried an encomium on the Institute's work for India.

64 Annual Report, 1954.

65 All the developments mentioned in this paragraph can be found in the annual reports, 1947-57.

66 The Institute's relations with the B.B.C. and the texts of talks given by the director can be found in the annual reports, the files dealing with the various Empire exhibitions and in P.R.O. 30/76/224, 229, 237, 249.

67 Figures compiled from annual reports, 1947-53, and from the articles by Sir Kenneth Bradley.

68 Ministry of Education, Report of the Committee of Enquiry into the Imperial Institute (the Tweedsmuir Report), 1952.

69 House of Lords, 31 January 1945, debate on 'Knowledge of the Empire'.

70 Annual Report, 1955, 10.

71 Rt. Hon. Viscount Hudson, 'The future of the Imperial Institute', *United Empire*, XLVI (1955), 8-10.

72 Reese, *Royal Commonwealth Society*, 81-4.

God prosper your affairs
Shakespeare

Raphael Tuck & Sons, Empire Postcard Nº 250

H.M.S. CAMPERDOWN.   10,600 TONS.

GOD GIVE US VICTORY!

We've shut the gates by Dover Straits,
And North, where the tides run free,
Cheek by jowl, our watchdogs prowl,
Grey hulks in a greyer sea.
And the prayer that England prays to-night—
O Lord of our destiny!—
As the foam of our plunging prows, is white
We have stood for peace, and we war for right.
God give us victory!

JAMES BERNARD FAGAN.

BY PERMISSION OF "THE DAILY TELEGRAPH."

The foundation of the Royal Colonial Institute in 1868 has often been seen as a significant event in the rise of late nineteenth-century imperial sentiment. In 1886 the planners of the Imperial Institute hoped to engross the Royal Colonial Institute, together with other bodies like the Royal Asiatic Society, under its aegis, to create a great central institution for Empire study and propaganda. They failed, and instead colonial (in both metropolitan and peripheral senses) activists and propagandists created a surprising range of imperial organisations between the 1880s and the First World War. In doing so, they prevented imperial propaganda from becoming institutionally ossified, as it might well have done had it been entirely centralised under the Imperial Institute. Each new society represented not so much a dissipation of effort as a fresh infusion of energy at critical moments. In this, as in Christian missionary endeavour, strength does seem to have come from diversity.

All these organisations were middle-class and elitist; only one or two enjoyed a wider, more popular membership. But all addressed themselves to the task of influencing public opinion, particularly through the medium of education. Most of them used propagandist techniques — leaflets, pamphlets, and posters — and several sought to produce and distribute textbooks to schools. An examination of their activities, therefore, constitutes a necessary prelude to the study of school textbooks. They were active also in the creation of exhibitions with imperial themes, and in influencing areas of popular culture like film-making. Moreover, these various societies were the means by which the committed elite could establish contact among themselves, influence politicians and academics, journalists and other opinion-formers, as well as act as conduits for the flow of funds from commercial companies and private subscriptions to propagandist activity. Some had highly specific aims, others a more general desire to spread imperial propaganda. But all, in some sense or another, were concerned with imperial unity — constitutional, defensive, or cultural. Such unity was to prove elusive, and in that sense most of them can be said to have failed. Yet their activities undoubtedly contributed to the imperial world view which was propagated through the popular cultural media and education.

The activities of all these societies overlapped with official imperial propaganda and with the imperial studies movements. Historians have generally concentrated on the latter in attempting to establish the relationship between imperialism and education.[1] These pressure groups were concerned to develop imperial studies at all levels of education, but they directed their main efforts towards the tertiary sector, desiring to establish Chairs and create courses of studies in the universities and the teacher training colleges in order to secure 'downward filtration' to the public at large. They flourished in Edwardian times, appeared to receive a tremendous stimulus from the First World War, secured a limited success, but withered away in the new climate of the inter-war years. The history of these movements has contributed powerfully to the idea that imperial propaganda secured, at best, only very limited success in Britain, and was destroyed by the intellectual holocaust of the post-First World War re-evaluation of nineteenth-century ideologies. But their activities can be understood only in the wider context of imperial propagandist organisations of all sorts.

There has, moreover, been no study of the extent to which imperial ideas were diffused to the schools independently of imperial societies or imperial studies organisations. Such bodies have in fact left something of a false trail. They envisaged the dissemination of a sophisticated concept of Empire, notions of imperial unity, constitutional and defensive, developed out of the Imperial Federation League, the Round Table, and other bodies. But if we take our wider definition of imperialism, as an imperial world view, replete with racial, cultural, and economic values, imperial ideas do indeed seem to have been widely distributed through formal education. In this chapter a survey of the imperial societies will be followed by an examination of the imperial studies movements, and in the next an effort will be made to assess their influence on school textbooks from the late nineteenth century to the 1950s. These texts seem to indicate that imperial notions, if not necessarily the sophisticated ideas of the imperial pressure groups, were a prime staple of school studies. The Empire was used as a focus for inter-disciplinary approaches, as a means of integrating the moral and informational aspects of education, by concentrating children's minds on the world in which their society survived through contemporary patriotic and military excitements. Looked at from the perspective of the schools, the imperial studies movements do not seem to have been such a failure. Moreover, among the educational establishment, the First World War did not herald the intellectual revolution so often attributed to it.

The Primrose League did more perhaps than any other society to generate an emotional and uncritical enthusiasm for Empire. The

League has seldom received the attention it deserves, partly because the standard work on its early history was published in New York in 1942.[2] The League had none of the precisely focused constitutional or economic ambitions of the other imperial societies and may indeed have derived strength from its generalised approach. But it set out quite consciously to apply imperialism to the domestic political situation, in the promotion of Tory democracy and the creation of class conciliation. It was founded by Lord Randolph Churchill, Sir John Gorst, and Sir Henry Drummond Wolff in late 1883 and sought to capitalise on the Disraeli cult which had begun soon after the imperialist statesman's death in 1881. It was alleged that the primrose was Disraeli's favourite flower, and on the anniversary of his death, 19th April, primroses were worn or carried by those who revered his memory. Hotels and shops were decorated with the flower, and London cabbies, no doubt mindful of their clientele, wrapped them round their whips. There were annual celebrations at Disraeli's statues, and the Primrose League converted these into mass political demonstrations, culminating in pageantry with banners, floral symbols, music, and speechifying at the Royal Albert Hall. The leaders of the party were reluctantly swept up into this mass emotionalism.

The Primrose League was organised on medieval lines to capture the interest of its membership. Its local branches were 'habitations', its subscriptions were 'tribute', and its full members were Knights and Dames. For an additional 'tribute' it was possible to become an Imperial Knight, and orders, badges, and certificates were issued by the movement. The working class were enrolled as 'associate members'. The membership mushroomed in the 1880s and by 1891 it was claiming one million members. By 1901, the figure had reached 1·5 million, of which 1·4 million were said to be working-class.

Like so many of the imperial societies, the League claimed to be non-party, although its foundations were firmly Tory (originally 'Tory' appeared in its title) and it re-embraced the party in 1913. It professed itself as admitting 'all classes and all creeds except atheists and enemies of the British Empire', and its declaration of faith, to which all members subscribed, enshrined 'the maintenance of the Imperial Ascendancy of the British Empire' at its core. Its greatest significance lay, perhaps, in its perfecting of propaganda techniques. It exploited each of the imperial climacterics of the 1880s and 1890s, notably the death of Gordon at Khartoum, the Home Rule agitation, the Sudan campaign of 1896-98, and the Boer War. Large numbers of leaflets, with direct and simple messages, were issued on imperial, as well as domestic, questions. It dressed up its propaganda in the garb of popular entertainment through *tableaux vivants*, magic lantern displays, lectures, and exhibitions. Children's fiction was issued for the 'buds' of the movement, and images like the death of Gordon were reinvoked annually at its 'Grand Habitation' (or national meetings) and in village and church halls throughout the land. Lantern-slide lectures on 'Our Glorious Empire', the problem of the Sudan, and the navy were much in demand. Both middle-class and working-class speakers set out to convince the populace of the benefits of Empire, and from 1894 the League became closely connected with the Navy League.

The Imperial Federation League had the most precisely specialised, and the grandest, objective of all the imperial organisations.[3] It had powerful proponents, including leading members of the Primrose League, but it was short-lived, surviving only nine years, from its foundation in 1884 to its winding up in 1893. It issued a journal for eight years, and in the late 1880s the reviews, such as *Fortnightly, Nineteenth Century, Westminster, Macmillan's Magazine*, were full of articles on the prospects of some form of imperial unity.[4] Rosebery described imperial federation as 'the dominant passion of my political life', but the League expired shortly before his arrival at the premiership.[5] Its propaganda was directed mainly to the political elite and to the Dominions, but its constitutional proposals were too precise to gain wide acceptance and its political purpose was confused by its premature espousal of imperial preference. Its significance for domestic imperial propaganda lies in the fact that it gave birth to other organisations which were to attempt to influence the British public more directly. Among them was the British Empire League (B.E.L.) started by a group which had opposed the dissolution of the Imperial Federation League.[6] The founders included Sir John Lubbock (Lord Avebury), Lord Roberts, Lord Strathcona, and the Canadians Tupper, Brassey and Denison. It took upon itself the 'duty of informing and educating the public mind' on the Empire.

The League's objects were sufficiently vague to secure a wide spectrum of support. Balfour, Sir Edward Grey, and Bonar Law were all vice-presidents, its presidents included the Duke of Devonshire and the Earl of Derby, and it secured extensive support from the City of London. Among its treasurers was Lord Rothschild. It was active in establishing branches of the Royal Naval Reserve around the Empire; it played a social role in the imperial conferences of 1897, 1902, 1907, and 1911, and it campaigned for an imperial penny post (introduced in 1898, with further reductions in 1907). The League was also interested in exhibitions. In 1902 it pressed for the creation of a great imperial exhibition to celebrate the coronation of Edward VII. The idea was not in fact brought to fruition until Wembley in 1924, but the League co-operated instead with Kiralfy's series of exhibitions. Lord Derby, as president of the League, became president of the Franco-British Exhibition of 1908, and it was asserted in 1916 that without the active encouragement of the B.E.L. establishment 'in all probability the White City would not have been built'.[7] In 1905 the League created the British Empire Club, and opened premises in St James's Square in 1910. It paid for imperial statues to be erected in London, and raised troops for the Boer War and the First World War. Like all such organisations it received a tremendous infusion of membership during these wars.

The Victoria League (V.L.) was founded in 1901 during the Boer War.[8] It prided itself (as all such bodies claimed) on being non-party, and numbered Balfour and Asquith among its vice-presidents. Its original committee (set up at a meeting in 10 Downing Street) was entirely female, although it later accepted men. It remained, however, predominantly a women's organisation. The wives of successive Colonial Secretaries, such as Lyttelton and Harcourt, were closely involved, as were some of the great ladies of both parties (Jersey, Crewe, Selborne, and Emmott). It employed ten paid workers, and soon opened its own rooms. Its organising secretary toured the Empire setting up branches, and links were formed with the Imperial Order of the Daughters of the Empire in Canada and the Guild of Loyal Women in South Africa, both founded the same year. The League dedicated itself to spreading accurate information about the history and general conditions of the Dominions 'to all parts of the kingdom and all classes of society'. Before the First World War it had held more than a thousand meetings throughout the country, and had carried its message in lectures to (among others) the Boy Scouts, girls' clubs, the W.E.A., the Co-op Union, the Working Men's Club and Institute Union, teachers' conferences, shop assistants' groups, and army camps. It amassed a collection of thousands of lantern slides for use in lectures, and persuaded 500 schools to become affiliated. Correspondence schemes were arranged between children in Britain and the Dominions. It established a Ladies' Empire Club in Grosvenor Street, and became involved in settler schemes, as well as artistic, industrial, and town planning projects.

The Victoria League received annual grants from the Rhodes trustees, and found little trouble in raising money for specific projects. During the First World War, it threw itself into the propaganda effort. A Special Publications Committee was established, and a million pamphlets were sold for $\frac{1}{2}d$ to $2d$ or distributed free. Sir Edward Cook's pamphlet 'Why Britain is at War' was translated into nine languages and sent around the Empire, to the United States, and to neutral countries. A Club for Overseas Forces was opened in London, and membership (including junior associates and affiliated schools) greatly expanded during the war. The League survives to the present day.

The most overtly propagandist of the Boer War societies was the Imperial South Africa Association (I.S.A.A.).[9] It was founded 'to uphold British supremacy and to promote the interests of British subjects in South Africa, with full recognition of colonial self-government', and pursued these objectives 'by the publication and distribution of pamphlets and leaflets, and by organising public meetings'. It numbered among its general committee Rider Haggard, Edward Carson, Lord Charles Beresford, and the future Colonial Secretary, Alfred Lyttelton, as well as dukes and peers, several of whom were shared with other imperial associations. The Association issued over a hundred broadsheets and pamphlets during the war, including handbills on the Outlander grievances, speeches by Chamberlain, Milner and others, attacks on Germany as well as the economic policies of Kruger, and 'Handy Notes on South Africa for the Use of Speakers and Others'.[10] There was also advice for settlers in South Africa, material on land settlement, a defence of concentration camps, exposés of pro-Boers, and lists of missionaries (and their writings) who supported the war. 'Vigilance Papers' No. 1 contained declarations by the governing bodies of the Congregationalist, Presbyterian, Wesleyan Methodist, Baptist, Lutheran, and Anglican Churches in South Africa, unanimously supporting imperial policy. The Rev. J. S. Moffat, who had himself held an official British position in Bechuanaland, argued in one pamphlet that the Boer War was akin to the American Civil War, that the British were fighting for the rights of blacks against the illiberalities of the Boers, and listed Boer persecutions of missionaries. After the war the Association illustrated its commitment to black rights by issuing pamphlets devoted mainly to the question of black labour in the post-war reconstruction, including a vigorous defence of the Chinese labour policy. It wound itself up in 1907 with a dinner in honour of Louis Botha and an encomium on the policy of 'reconciliation and appeasement' in South Africa.

Other societies which devoted themselves to encouraging popular support for the armed forces and to recruitment had close links of ideology and personnel with the imperial organisations. The Imperial Federation Defence Committee (I.F.D.C.) was active between 1894 and the First World War, and was yet another successor body to the I.F.L.[11] Some members of the latter founded the I.F.D.C. to promote a common interest in the maritime defence of the Empire and encourage the

Dominions to share its cost and administration. It acted as a pressure group at the colonial conferences of 1897, 1902 and 1907. It printed and circulated pamphlets, and proposed, during the Boer War, an Imperial Council and an Imperial Fund for Defence, as well as the establishment of colonial territorial forces and a general service army. From 1908 it changed its name to the Imperial Co-operation League. The Navy League, founded in 1895, was much more active in the field of public propaganda.[12] It also issued pamphlets, encouraged the issue of postcards and cigarette cards about the navy, held displays and exhibitions, organised public meetings and lectures, and issued a textbook which was circulated to schools. It published the *Navy League Journal*, which included a women's page. By 1914 it had no fewer than 100,000 members.

But it was the National Service League (N.S.L.) that was to be the most notable of these imperial defence organisations.[13] It was founded in 1902, shortly after the publication of George Shee's book *The Briton's First Duty*. Shee proposed not only compulsory military service, but also the creation of a pan-Britannic militia, with a peacetime strength of 450,000, and a wartime reserve of 2½ million. Thus imperial manhood was to be marshalled for service throughout the Empire, divided into four age groups: eighteen to twenty-three, the first (active) class; eighteen to twenty-five, first reserve; twenty-five to thirty, the second reserve; and thirty to forty, the third reserve. Lord Newton arranged for the book to be republished by the Army League; Shee gave lectures to the Royal United Services Institute, and such was the interest in the book and the lecture that the N.S.L. was founded with Shee as its secretary. From 1903 the League issued the *Journal of the National Service League*, which adopted in 1905 the more vivid title *The Nation in Arms*. It sold 47,000 copies a month, while the N.S.L. *Notes* sold 40,000.

The League brought together a wide variety of contemporary concerns, the quest for national efficiency, the health of the race, drill associations, rifle clubs and the like. It incorporated Lord Meath's Lads' Drill Association of 1899, school cadet corps and more than 1,000 rifle clubs. In 1906 it found its ideal leader in Lord Roberts, who resigned from the army to become its president. He epitomised the Christian soldiering traditions which had developed from the 1860s and had been active in the Army Temperance Association. Roberts transformed the N.S.L. into a mass movement which utilised every propaganda technique available at the time. There were lantern slide shows and lectures, national campaigns, public meetings, displays featuring the Volunteers and from 1908 the Territorials, Church Lads'

Brigade bands, performances of melodramas of invasion, as well as pamphlets, broadsheets, and other forms of ephemera. Between 1910 and 1913 there was a drive to increase working-class membership, and by the outbreak of the war the League claimed 220,000 members and adherents. It held an average of 240 meetings a month in 1911-12, and organised 2,500 up and down the country in the months leading to the war.

The connections between the N.S.L. and a disciplined labour force as well as discipline in the classroom were explicit. The League wished to see compulsory military training and military drill in all schools, as well as two months' training under canvas or in the navy for all eighteen-to-twenty-two-year-olds. This programme was designed to improve national physique and instil a sense of citizenship among the young, as well as to inculcate cleanliness, punctuality, order and discipline, in order to improve the industrial and commercial efficiency of nation and Empire. The League sought to enlist the Church too, through the participation of churchmen in its observances, through the Anglican Church Lads' Brigade (which moved into khaki uniforms in this period) and through the publication of a pamphlet entitled 'Religious Thoughts and National Service'. Associated organisations like the Naval and Military Bible Society provided New Testaments to all troops, each containing a Message from Lord Roberts. Proposals for the amalgamation of the N.S.L. with the R.C.I. were discussed in 1916 and, according to Reese, 'nearly succeeded'.[14] However, the draft agreement was unacceptable to the Institute's council and the League was in fact disbanded in 1921. The move does, however, reflect the close association between military and imperial propaganda, particularly in time of war.

The League of the Empire (L.E.), yet another Boer War foundation, directed its efforts principally towards education.[15] From 1903 it sought the affiliation of schools throughout Britain and the Empire, and began to work with education departments to establish imperial co-operation in education. In 1907 it organised a conference in London of colonial education departments and administrators, including colonial officials as well as delegates from universities, learned societies, and educational institutes, at which it called for a quadrennial imperial educational conference. The first was instituted by the government in 1911, and set about the interchange of teachers, the establishment of uniformity in curricula, mutual recognition of teachers' certificates, and the like. In 1912 the League held the first Imperial Conference of Teachers' Associations throughout the Empire, attended by over 600 representatives, which led to the setting up of the Imperial Union of Teachers in 1913. The League also embarked on a series of textbooks, prepared under the direction of a historical committee chaired by J. B. Bury, Regius Professor at Cambridge, and including in its membership H. E. Egerton and H. A. L. Fisher, the cost of publication borne by a fund set up by Louis Spitzel. The first volume was A. F. Pollard's *The British Empire: its Past, its Present, and its Future*, compiled with the help of contributors from all over the Empire, and published in 1909. Two other volumes, for secondary and elementary schools, were published, as were series of lectures (with lantern slides) on 'British Colonies and Empire' and 'Empire Builders'. The League collaborated with George Philip & Son in the issue of a 1s *Philip's Primary Atlas of the British Empire*. It ran essay and art competitions, educational exhibitions, school exchanges, an Agency for the Migration of Teachers, as well as a Bureau of Educational Information. The Correspondence Comrades branch, which had 30,000 members by the First World War, established links with young people around the Empire. Booklets were published on imperial territories and their economic products and potential, and the League attempted to establish schemes for new projects in the smaller territories.

The L.E. published articles, bibliographies, and syllabuses on the various countries of the Empire in its journal *Federal Magazine*, and established schemes for the study of imperial history in training colleges, secondary and elementary schools, evening classes, and among private students. Its Imperial History Scheme was launched during the First World War and received an encouraging response from headmasters and headmistresses throughout the country. From 1909 the League was closely associated with the organisation of the Empire Day parades in London. Lord Meath was one of its vice-presidents (as was the former Viceroy, Lord Curzon, Lord Selborne, and the High Commissioners of the Dominions). Each year up to the war, the Empire Day celebration took the form of parades of youth organisations in Hyde Park, at which Lord Roberts took the salute. In order to maximise its membership the League kept its subscription low. Five shillings secured full rights, including receipt of the magazine, and children could be associate members for a shilling or sixpence. The League claimed branches throughout Britain and the Empire, many of them numbering their membership in thousands.

Just as the Boer War had spawned the Victoria League and the League of Empire, the patriotic fervour of the Great War gave rise to yet another association, the British Empire Union (B.E.U.).[16] It was founded in 1915:

> to inculcate a greater interest in and knowledge of the Empire; to

strengthen Empire Unity of Purpose and to make our people increasingly Empire-minded; and to create a fuller realisation of what the Monarchy – the unifying influence of the Crown – means to the British peoples, to the Empire and Commonwealth of Nations, and to our British Way of Life.

The Union devoted itself to spreading imperial propaganda by the 'spoken and written word', increasing knowledge of the Empire's 'vast undeveloped resources', and promoting the teaching of Empire history in schools. It sought to secure a wider acceptance of Empire Day, organised Empire Day gatherings, and distributed thousands of medals and flags to schools. From the late 1930s it also adopted Empire Youth Sunday as a means of emphasising the role of religion in the Empire. Panels of speakers were enrolled to address open-air, group, and other meetings on the economic significance of the Empire to the welfare of British workers, to encourage migration, and to instil in the young a realisation of the achievements of the Empire in maintaining peace and bringing 'order, health, knowledge, improved conditions of life to formerly ignorant and primitive peoples'[17] The language used by the B.E.U. indicates that it was less squeamish than its rivals in linking Empire to capitalism and conservatism. Like all the others it proclaimed itself to be non-party, but it devoted pages of its annual reports to attacks upon socialism and communism. Later it took up the cudgels against nationalisation and argued for the restitution of corporal punishment. In 1959, still surviving, it attacked the nationalist movement in colonial territories, argued against further decolonisation, and sent speakers to support Conservative candidates in the general election of that year.[18] It cannot have liked the results of the Conservative victory. Yet it was no fringe group. In the 1920s and 1930s it shared presidents and vice-presidents with other Empire societies, Establishment figures like the Duke of Grafton, Lord Carson, the Earl of Mansfield, the Earl of Derby, Admiral Earl Beatty (who was for a time president), and Lord Lloyd. Although the R.C.I. was wary of contacts with it, nonetheless it shared the concerns of all the imperial societies in spreading knowledge of Empire history, and in promoting Empire preference in the inter-war years. As late as 1959 it continued to argue that Commonwealth trade was central to British prosperity and should constitute 50% of Britain's total trade. Throughout its existence the Union was supported by a large number of commercial firms. Early annual reports listed at least fifty, including Castrol, Firestone, Hoover, Houlder Bros., J. Lyons, Morris Motors, Plessey, Tate & Lyle, Ty-Phoo Tea, and several brewers.

This examination of the imperial societies has been by no means exhaustive. There were a number — like the United Empire Trade League, the Empire Parliamentary Association, and the Society of Comparative Legislation — devoted to highly specialised activities, which played little or no part in public propaganda. A number of these emerged in the new protectionist atmosphere after the First World War. The Britannic Industrial Alliance was founded to devote itself to the development of the Empire's resources and the promotion of imperial unity, and the Empire Resources Development Committee and the Empire Industries Association of the same period had similar economic aims. Others were less precisely directed in their imperial work, or were more concerned with membership in the Dominions. In 1910, Evelyn Wrench founded the Overseas Club, which pledged itself to a belief in the 'justice, freedom, order, and good government of the British Empire', and to the maintenance of the 'heritage handed down to us by our fathers.[19] It added an Empire verse to the national anthem and soon had 100,000 adherents, mainly in the Dominions. In 1914 Lord Selborne, prominent in several other imperial societies, founded the Patriotic League of Britons Overseas, which amalgamated with the Overseas Club in 1922.[20] Although these last two bodies were primarily concerned with membership in the white Dominions, they devoted themselves also to the support of the various imperial societies in Britain. The First World War also produced the British Empire Land Settlement League, and in the 1930s the Kipling Society devoted itself to sustaining its master's ideals.

Imperial propaganda can, moreover, be discovered in the work of societies which were not explicitly imperial in their objectives. Brian Harrison has demonstrated the centrality of imperialism in such bodies as the Girls' Friendly Society and the Mothers' Union during this period.[21] They pursued an ideal of motherhood which would reconcile town with country, and class with class, and which saw imperialism as 'a means of eradicating the selfishness of the individual'.[22] Empire, says Harrison, was the Girls' Friendly Society's first love: its colonial (from 1911 imperial) committee was founded in 1896, and co-operated extensively with the Mothers' Union and with Anglican missionary and emigration societies. These societies formed close connections with leading imperialists of the day, such as Milner, issued propaganda on the righteousness of the First World War, as well as furthering the nineteenth-century ideal of the Christian soldier.

Imperialism also suffused the eugenics and motherhood movements of the Edwardian era.[23] All imperialists were disturbed by the falling birth rate of the late nineteenth century and the revelation in the Boer

War of the physical inadequacy of a third of all recruits. Notions of national efficiency linked to the eugenics of Karl Pearson and others were influential across the political spectrum. The majority of Fabians, together with the leading Liberal imperialists, supported a programme to keep mothers at home, educate them in motherhood, encourage 'eugenic' marriage, and provide State inducements to procreation, nutrition and health. In 1907 Sidney Webb published a pamphlet advocating such State involvement. The British Medical Association petitioned the Board of Education in 1904 for elementary instruction on health in primary schools, and educational authorities and theorists proceeded to emphasise schooling for motherhood in girls' schools, stressing needlework, cooking, laundry, housewifery, and so on. One of the dedicatees of this book, educated in that period, remembers that a building in the playground of her school was converted into a 'house' in which girls were instructed in the domestic virtues, spending, indeed, most of their time there. In 1908 the president of the B.M.A. wrote that mothers should teach children the 'importance of self-control, of obedience, and of patriotism'.[24] Prominent churchmen were swept up into eugenics arguments, and a whole range of societies came into being whose propagandists travelled and lectured on motherhood, couched in terms of rearing healthy sons to protect and expand the imperial race.

The dominant ideology had become the central justification of social engineering and renewed emphasis on woman's role as child-rearer, home-maker, and imperial propagandist. If the 'science' of eugenics was ultimately discredited through its use by the Nazis, arguments about the maintenance of the imperial race, both in numbers and in quality, were to continue between the wars. Leopold Amery was prominent in such work, and echoes continued to sound in the Beveridge Report of 1942. Other women's societies promoted the role of women in class conciliation through an emphasis on patriotic and imperial concerns. A society called the Women's Imperial League has eluded all efforts to crack its history, but the Women's Guild of Empire is rather better known.[25] It was founded about the time of the First World War, and aimed to 'uphold King and country', to spread knowledge of imperial questions in order to create an atmosphere of tolerance and mutual understanding in politics and industry', and thus 'overcome class and party prejudice and unite the British people'. It pledged itself to work for economic unity within the Empire and restore industrial prosperity. Its founder and controller-in-chief was Mrs Flora Drummond and its national organising secretary Lady Muriel Gore-Browne. It appointed organisers for all the main regions of

Britain as well as for Australia, New Zealand, and Canada, but its activities remain shadowy. Its objects were, however, symptomatic of a general belief in the role of Empire in British domestic affairs which was promoted by all the imperial societies, the press, by medical and educational authorities as well as by a wide range of travelling propagandists satisfying a contemporary craving for entertainment through meetings and lectures.

No study of imperial propaganda would be complete without some consideration of emigration. This is an area which has been blessed with some excellent scholarship, which has demonstrated just how pervasive and long-lasting emigration schemes were between the 1870s and 1950s.[26] Such schemes, for children, women, and other groups considered to be disadvantaged in Victorian Britain, began with a philanthropic and Christian revivalist tone. By the 1870s they had become much more overtly imperial. Emigration rhetoric adopted a strongly racial and patriotic ring; the emigration societies became willing instruments of imperial policy; and emigration was promoted in terms of its role in creating imperial unity, fostering imperial defence, and providing labour and servants for the colonies. Whereas Lord Shaftesbury's child emigration plans of the late 1840s and 1850s had used the language of saving individuals, both spiritually and economically, by the end of the century emigration schemes were depicted as saving the Empire, combining philanthropy with imperialism, love of children with love of empire. Child emigrants were 'bricks of empire building' assuming 'the natural heritage of the British race.'[27] Female emigration was seen as a feminine civilising mission, a means of keeping the British Empire for the British race, while 'gentlemen' emigration not only helped to solve the 'younger son' problem at a time of declining agricultural and land revenues, but also raised the social tone of the colonies and increased the size of the 'officer class' within them.[28] Emigration had become an imperial duty: to maintain the loyalty of the colonies, provide labour and human material for enlistment, transfer late Victorian and Edwardian concepts of motherhood and eugenics to the Dominions, together with the gentlemanly, public-school, adventurer ethos. Emigration, which Cecil Rhodes had seen as the only alternative to revolution, was transformed by Edwardian times into the essential bridge between the cult of National Efficiency and Social Imperialism.

Organised children's emigration began, according to Wagner, in 1869-70, and between that date and 1930, 100,000 children were the victims of involuntary emigration ('philanthropic abduction', as one authority has put it)[29] to Canada. A large number of societies, including

Dr Barnardo's and the Salvation Army, became involved in this movement, which received the support of all the leading imperial figures of the day. From 1896 Australia, and from 1902 South Africa, became important destinations for the emigrant children. In the South African case, both children's and women's emigration were seen as a crucial part of Milner's anglicisation policy, and John Buchan acted as his emigration secretary. A whole range of women's societies were involved in female emigration, including the Women's Emigration Society (1880), its offshoot, the Colonial Emigration Society (1884), the South African Colonisation Society (1902), the British Women's Emigration Association (originally 1884), and the Colonial Intelligence League. All this activity engendered much propaganda, in parish magazines, in girls' schools and clubs, through the Mother's Union and the Girls' Friendly Society, as well as in the juvenile literature and comics of the period. Gentlemanly emigration became something of a craze among the middle and upper classes, complete with books, handbooks, journals, agencies, extolling its virtues as a means of recreating social status in a colonial class hierarchy, and offering advice and often exploitative services. Some journals, like the *Imperial Colonist*, were specifically devoted to emigration.

Reginald Brabazon, the Earl of Meath, had repeatedly advocated State colonisation schemes in the 1880s.[30] Although emigration remained in private hands it received considerable official support, both moral and financial. It was encouraged by the Imperial Conferences of 1907 and 1911 and by the Dominions Royal Commission of 1912. The colonial enlistment of the First World War seemed to offer ample justification for all this support, and the war was followed by a variety of emigration schemes.[31] Indeed, emigration activity tended to mirror the rise and fall of imperial sentiment. If some of the momentum left the emigration schemes during the late 1920s, there was a resurgence during the '30s. After the Second World War a fresh burst of migration, including more schemes for child emigration, was to continue into the 1950s. It is true that emigration from Britain reached a peak in the 1880s,[32] and that the intensity of emigration propaganda thereafter tended to be a symptom of decline. Nevertheless, in the context of this book, imperial emigration propaganda should be seen as much for its effect on domestic attitudes towards imperialism as for the process of emigration itself. As is so often the case, the Labour Party provides a vital clue. When doubts about childhood emigration were raised in 1924 Margaret Bondfield, parliamentary secretary to the Ministry of Labour, was sent to Canada to investigate the situation. Her report was couched in conventional imperial rhetoric and recommended that the emigration of children, particularly girls, over school-leaving age should be positively encouraged.[33] In the late 1940s a Labour government could become entrammelled in the preparations for the creation of a Central African Federation because Attlee and his Cabinet imagined that the post-war emigration boom could lead to a massive increase in the white population there. All this had echoes in school teaching methods and in textbooks, as we shall see in the next chapter, as well as in other areas of popular culture like the cinema.

This survey of the imperial societies has demonstrated that several of them devoted considerable attention to education and the teaching of Empire history and geography. We now turn to the imperial studies projects of this period, which were specifically designed towards educational ends. The promotion of imperial studies had been started by the R.C.I. in the 1880s and 1890s, when that body tried to encourage schools to incorporate Empire material into the curriculum (see below).[34] It became a constant lament of the imperial elite that the message of Empire was not reaching the population of Britain. Imperial sentiment, it was frequently asserted, was stronger in the Dominions.[35] This elite was of course thinking in terms of a sophisticated imperialism, linked to concepts of national efficiency, imperial federation, and the permanent survival of empire. The protagonists of imperial studies repeatedly identified turning points, great national events from which imperial ideas could be expected to take a hold. The accession and coronation of Edward VII were one; the coronation of his son a second; the outbreak of the First World War a third.

It was on the first occasion that the Colonial Office embarked on the one instance of formal, official imperial propaganda. This was the Colonial Office Visual Instruction Committee, (COVIC), which was set up in 1902, partly at the suggestion of Professor M. E. Sadler, the Director of Special Enquiries at the Board of Education.[36] The idea was to provide for the people of the United Kingdom, the Dominions, and colonies 'a more vivid and accurate knowledge than they possess of the geography, social life, and the economic possibilities of the different parts of the empire'. This was to be achieved through the provision of lectures and accompanying lantern slides for use in schools, an idea Sadler had derived from the extensive use of lectures and slides in New York State. Sadler and a Colonial Office official later to be prominent in non-official imperial studies, Sir Charles Lucas, laid the idea before Joseph Chamberlain, who received it enthusiastically and was prepared to support it if the scheme were genuinely reciprocal. Lectures should be prepared on Britain as well as on the imperial possessions, and the lectures on the mother country should be paid for by the colonies and vice versa. Chamberlain set up a committee to oversee the project, consisting of representatives of the various imperial societies, including the Royal Colonial Institute, the Imperial Institute, the Victoria League, the League of the Empire (the two latter only recently founded), the India Office, the Colonial Office, the Crown Agents, the Board of Education, and the Scottish Education Department, as well as the ubiquitous Earl of Meath and the director of the National Gallery. The latter's presence indicated that the project was to be an artistic as well as educational one.

As was usual with formal imperial propaganda (cf. the Imperial Institute), the first move was to raise money from the colonies, particularly those in reasonable financial condition whose governors could be expected to be sympathetic. In 1903 the colonial administrations of Ceylon, the Straits Settlements, and Hong Kong agreed to fund (offering £300 each) a course of seven lectures, illustrated by lantern slides, on a journey from the East to England 'descriptive of the United Kingdom and the defences of the Empire'. In 1904 the geographer Halford Mackinder provided a specimen lecture at a fee of £200, and by the following year fifty copies of seven lectures, two complete sets of lantern slides and two lanterns and apparatus had been supplied to the three contributing colonies. The next stage was to adapt the lectures for use in other colonies, an arrangement under which India, the West Indies, West Africa, Mauritius, and later Canada and South Africa entered the scheme. Chamberlain's successor as Colonial Secretary, Lyttelton, sent out a circular despatch urging colonies to participate in April 1905, and as a result no fewer than 26,000 slides of Britain and of the armed forces of Empire were sent out. Australia and New Zealand, belying their reputation for imperial loyalty, declined to be involved.

The scheme had been launched without any expenditure of British money, except in providing the secretary to the committee, who was funded by the Treasury until 1908. In that year the Treasury refused further assistance, and the secretary's salary had to come from the colonies. By then, however, the permanent under-secretary of the Colonial Office, Sir Francis Hopwood, had interested the Princess of Wales (later Queen Mary) in imperial visual instruction, and a fundraising committee under her patronage and chaired by Lady Dudley was established. In 1907 the project to unveil the colonies to Britain was inaugurated, and to this end Lady Dudley's committee raised £3,715 18s, which was augmented in 1910 by a £500 grant from the Rhodes trustees and £205 from City companies. The scheme had found its feet with captive colonial finance, and was now to be continued by the power of royal patronage to tap private sources.

The visual and artistic part of the project was developed during the succeeding few years. An artist, A. Hugh Fisher of the *Illustrated London News*, was appointed to work with Mackinder and travel the Empire for three years taking photographs (he had to be given a crash course in photography), as well as painting and sketching. Sir Owen Phillips of the Royal Mail Line offered free travel on the company's ships, an arrangement which took Fisher on three journeys embracing (October 1907 to June 1908) Ceylon, India, Burma, Aden, Somaliland and Cyprus; (July 1908 to May 1909) Canada, Newfoundland, Wei-Hei-Wei, Hong Kong, Borneo, and Singapore; (October 1909 to August 1910) Gibraltar, Malta, Australia, New Zealand, and Fiji. West, east, and southern Africa were missed because the Royal Mail Line did not operate there. While Fisher travelled the Empire, Mackinder was preparing the Indian lectures, slowly and, despite handsome fees, with much complaint. Chivvied by members of the committee, he complained of the great labour of preparing eight lectures on India, and the repeated need for 'much revision, both official and unofficial'. In 1909 he gave a specimen lecture with slides before the Princess of Wales, but it did not prevent the Earl of Meath, later the same month, from chiding him on the slow progress of the textbooks. The same summer Fisher was given several weeks at home to travel the United Kingdom, taking photographs. Mackinder regarded this as vital to provide Canada with an idea of the magnitude and power of industry in the Old Country, so that the Canadian of the far west 'should not think that we have been completely outdistanced by his neighbour the United States'.

The Indian lectures were published by Waterlow in 1910, with a popular school edition brought out by the educational publisher Philip & Son.[37] Mackinder pleaded illness and forsook the project. The preparation of the lectures on the Mediterranean colonies, the Far East, British North America, and Australasia were taken over by A J. Sargent, the Professor of Commerce in the University of London. By now the COVIC was assessing its achievement after eight years' work, and found the results disappointing. Slides had been distributed around the Empire in large numbers (though how often they were used will never be known), but interest in Britain was slight. Only 124 copies of the India lectures were sold, and a mere ten sets of slides were distributed, of which one went to the War Office and one to the *Daily Mail*. These figures were to improve only during the First World War. The identification of the COVIC with the Colonial Office was held to have seriously inhibited the whole scheme. Since the project appeared to be under government aegis, the lectures had to be minutely revised to avoid any controversial matter. The COVIC was merely a backwater of the Colonial Office, entirely dependent on the personal interest of one or two officials. Since imperial studies had been vigorously taken over by other bodies, it seemed appropriate to hive off the visual project to one of them. The Imperial Institute, the Royal Colonial Institute (now actively in the lecturing field), the Victoria League, the League of the Empire (which had set up the Imperial Educational Trust and began publishing textbooks in 1909) were all considered. But if the committee ceased to be official, it was thought that the patronage of the Queen (as the Princess of Wales had now become) and the support of the imperial Establishment would no longer be forthcoming. The rival claims of the various imperial organisations and the fear of losing official and royal support ensured that the project stayed with the Colonial Office, with Lucas as a private member (having resigned from the Colonial Office), and its driving force. Harcourt sent out yet another circular despatch to encourage colonial support, and Sargent continued with the preparation of the lectures. In 1912 he was also asked to prepare a South African set, for which illustrations were to be procured by correspondence. Sir Algernon Aspinall, who had published a very successful guide to the West Indies in 1907, was asked to prepare lectures on the West Indies, and he prepared lists of subjects for which he required photographs. In 1914 A. Wyatt Tilby agreed to write the COVIC's seventh volume of lectures, on tropical Africa, but it was never published because the whole scheme was overwhelmed by the war.

The COVIC was now privatised. It was transferred to the Royal Colonial Institute, whose membership grew dramatically during the war, and which had become the leading organisation in co-ordinating the publishing and lecturing activities of the various imperial studies groups. The R.C.I. in effect became the visual and documentary archive of the COVIC, but no further productions were undertaken, and the commercial side of the scheme fizzled out. The COVIC was an extraordinary attempt to provide, on a semi-official basis, visual aids for the education of an imperial people. It was the only peacetime exercise in official imperial propaganda, but no government finance was forthcoming. Money had to be extracted from the colonies, or secured by private donations encouraged by royal and aristocratic patronage. The visual techniques adopted were doomed to rapid obsolescence (a definite decision was taken in 1908 not to use a cine camera or 'bioscope') and the content of the lectures was thoroughly anodine. Mackinder's lectures on India stressed the religious and the picturesque, while the 480 slides which accompanied them were a 'tourist's eye view' of India — temples, scenery, caves, bazaars, stations and railway trains, with a few imperial icons like the Black Hole of Calcutta and scenes of the Mutiny. The slides were costly, and schools and local authorities everywhere pleaded poverty. The COVIC represented a mixing of governmental and commercial elements ill suited to the original propagandist objectives.

In the years just before the First World War a number of other organisations joined the COVIC in the development of imperial studies. These, however, were bodies which sought to propagate a highly sophisticated concept of Empire and therefore concentrated on the elite and on the tertiary sector of education. Nevertheless, there were some attempts to translate ideas into textbooks, and efforts were made to reach the working class through the Workers' Education Association, the Working Men's College, and the university settlements. Moreover, the leaders of these movements were sufficiently influential for their ideas to be found filtered down, as we shall see, into many of the textbooks of the inter-war period.

A number of strands of elite activity originating at the beginning of the century came together in the formation of the Round Table in 1909.[38] In 1902 the Coefficients Club had attempted to bring together members of different parties (including the Fabians) in the pursuit of imperial objectives. Joseph Chamberlain's tariff reform arguments had broken them asunder, and there emerged from the fragments the Tariff Reform Compatriots' Club. In the early years of the century F. S. Oliver, later associated with many of the leading lights of the Round Table, was one of the ablest imperial pamphleteers and publicists. His work on Alexander Hamilton and the creation of the United States was in fact a 500 page paean of praise to imperial federation and has been described as influencing a whole generation of imperial publicists. When Alfred Milner returned from South Africa in 1905 he used his powerful position among the Rhodes trustees to direct finance in the direction of schemes for the study of the Empire. Milner's autocratic, anti-democratic temperament was, however, averse to the creation of mass movements, and his weight and Rhodes's money were therefore placed behind elite bodies and advanced research. Leopold Amery's *History of the Boer War* was financed from this source, as were the literary activities and travels of members of Milner's kindergarten. In 1908 there was a scheme to raise a fund for Halford Mackinder (as we have seen, already active in the COVIC) to study the problems of the Empire. Later the Rhodes trustees contributed to the expenses of the Round Table organisation (together with many private donors) and the publication of its journal. Influential political coteries like those of the Astors at Cliveden and the Salisburys at Hatfield were drawn in, the latter reflecting the move of the Cecil family from the great marquess's high-minded reluctant imperialism of the late nineteenth century to a more strenuous imperial commitment in the twentieth. *The Times* underwent a similar progression. At this period, under the influence of Leo Amery, Edward Grigg, and Geoffrey Robinson (later Dawson), it fell into the idealistic imperialist camp.

The Round Table was an elite body of influential writers, administrators and politicians, all of whom had had considerable colonial experience. Its driving force was Lionel Curtis, who, particularly when he became Beit Lecturer in Colonial History at Oxford for a year in 1912, was able to influence a generation of students and co-opt a range of scholars to the movement. The members, some of them drawing on their experience of constitution-making in South Africa, were concerned to approach the question of imperial unity from the standpoint of the Dominions. An organic union, they believed, would emerge from Dominion independence, and the sense of equality so formed between Britain and the Dominions. With a common defence and foreign policy, the Empire, internationally speaking, would be one State. The Round Table was in consequence little concerned with commerce, and avoided taking sides on tariff reform, although many members were individually committed to it. They developed some of the constitutional preoccupations of the Imperial Federation League, but their prime vision was essentially a mystical one, a vision of imperial States acting as 'trustees of civilisation in its highest form'. Theirs was, like that of their imperial federationist predecessors, essentially a racially bound concept, the brotherhood of Anglo-Saxons around the world. Later, however, Curtis's ideas extended to embrace the 'dependent' empire. He became convinced during the First World War that India should become a full self-governing Dominion, and that ultimately Malaya, East Africa, and West Africa could also achieve Dominion status.[39] The members of the Round Table divided on the multi-racial question, but those who adhered to Curtis developed close links with the ethical imperialists in Exeter Hall and the Labour movement.

Curtis, like Seeley, believed in the severely practical approach to history, and in the historian as prophet. In the preparation of a succession of studies on imperial questions he enlisted many of the most distinguished historians of the day. Arnold Toynbee, Seton-Watson, H.A.L. Fisher, Reginald Coupland, and Lewis Namier were all in one way or another induced to help, together with overseas scholars like

Samuel Beer in New York. Namier and several other Balliol scholars organised a W.E.A. summer school on imperial topics in 1914. The First World War brought many of the most influential members of the Round Table to positions of power — Alfred Milner, Philip Kerr, Leo Amery, Edward Grigg — and they hoped that the imperial sentiment engendered by the war could enable the Round Table to achieve its objectives, at least in so far as they related to the white Dominions. They failed to recognise the manner in which the war would develop a very different, and separatist, Dominion nationalism from that which they envisaged.

Some of the ideas of the Round Table do turn up in textbooks of the inter-war period, and there can be no doubt that several of the most influential of rising historians were influenced in such a way that an essentially Seeleyan view of history, closely connected with imperialism, was transmitted to the 1920s and 1930s. Many of the scholars associated, directly or indirectly, with the Round Table were also active in the imperial studies movement, which emerged from the collapse of the Imperial Federation League, and from a desire to ginger up and extend the membership of existing imperial bodies like the Royal Colonial Institute.[40] In 1909 the Institute extended its publishing activities by amalgamating its periodic journal and its annual proceedings into the monthly *United Empire* (which from 1910 faced competition from the Round Table's own eponymous journal). This was followed in 1912 by the *Royal Colonial Institute Yearbook*. In 1910 the R.C.I. instituted an appeal to establish a fund for Empire lectures to be given mainly in centres outside London. It was from this new concern with lectures that the R.C.I. decided to adopt professional techniques in which the form, in effect, would become more influential than the actual message. It employed W. Herbert Garrison, an evangelical orator, to provide talks for young people, talks which would express, as J. G. Greenlee put it, the Kiplingesque notions of the grandeur, romance, moral benefits, duty, and self-sacrifice of Empire.[41] Imperial heroes were identified and held up as models, sometimes living ones like Lord Strathcona. Garrison became a popular figure at music halls and public meetings, and he was also capable of filling the Albert Hall, particularly if his lectures were accompanied by lantern slides, musical fanfares, and patriotic songs. His activities were ideal for wartime conditions, and probably helped to develop the wartime membership campaign of the Royal Colonial Institute.

Presumably somewhat less histrionic techniques were envisaged by those who argued for an extension of imperial studies in the tertiary sector. In November 1912, in a paper to the British Academy, Sidney

Low advocated the creation of an imperial seminary, if not as a separate institution, at least as the co-ordinator of courses in the various colleges of the University of London.[42] In 1914 the Imperial Studies Committee of the university was established under the chairmanship of Milner and with A. P. Newton as secretary. This body was closely associated with the R.C.I. — which gave it a continuing existence after the war — the Victoria League and the League of Empire. A pamphlet on imperial courses in the University of London was produced within a few months, and was followed by the publication of the King's College imperial lectures. Sir Charles Lucas published his lectures on the British Empire in 1915, dedicating them to the members of the Working Men's College.[43] The university also set about supplying speakers to give academic lectures at provincial universities and other educational institutions, work in which they were closely allied with the R.C.I.

In 1916 Sir Charles Lucas published an article in *United Empire* in which he laid out the objectives of imperial studies, and appended an impressive list of lecturers involved in the scheme.[44] It included many of the writers of imperial texts and activists in Edwardian imperial associations — H. E. Egerton, A. B. Keith, Sidney Low, Charles Lucas, Halford Mackinder, Ramsay Muir, A. F. Pollard, A. J. Sargent, Alfred Zimmern — several young historians yet to make their names — R. Coupland, Basil Williams, Basil Worsfold — together with scholars noted in other fields — H. A. L. Fisher, Richard Lodge, R. S. Rait, Sir Walter Raleigh, H. W. V. Temperley, Sir Herbert Warren and W. Pember Reeves (Mackinder's successor at L.S.E. and an adherent of national efficiency).

The work of the Imperial Studies Committee was greatly extended during the war. Three sub-committees were formed covering the three sectors of education, and these set about influencing the Board of Education to establish Empire studies at every level in schools, training colleges, universities, and other educational establishments. In 1918 a deputation was received by the President of the Board of Education, and letters were sent to education authorities, public schools, libraries, and other institutions suggesting that English history should be taught as imperial history. The Imperial Studies Committee was also charged with considering the use of visual aids, and the materials of the COVIC were handed over to it and deposited in the R. C. I. Library.

It has often been said that these activities represented no more than a temporary aberration induced by the patriotic fervour of the war. Lucas, for example, thought that the war had helped to convince the working class of the need for Empire.[45] Historians have enjoyed the paradox that the imperial studies activists, as well as the Round Tablers, saw the war as their great opportunity when in fact it was to bring Dominions nationalism of age and destroy·Edwardian idealistic imperialism. Nevertheless, even within its own terms, the movement achieved some results. The Rhodes Chair of Imperial History at the University of London was established in 1919 (the first incumbent was A. P. Newton). Halford Mackinder created a series of Empire lectures for teachers in the 1920s, and the R.C.I.'s own propagandist activities spread into the Empire Day movement and the creation of a cinema sub-committee. Moreover, if the evidence of school texts and teaching handbooks is to be believed, the Imperial Studies Committee succeeded in breaking out of its apparently elitist approach. The policy of 'downward filtration' worked. Basil Williams[46], A. P. Newton and others continued to publish popular imperial works, and their ideas were taken up, as we shall see in the next chapter, by the writers of school texts.

Between the wars the Imperial Studies Committee became primarily the responsibility of the R.C.I., although it included representatives of the Board of Education, the London County Council, and the Victoria League, and developed an association with the Universities Bureau of the British Empire.[47] A succession of Imperial Education Conferences in the 1920s and 1930s stimulated the development of new approaches to imperial education both in the colonies and at home. As Lord Eustace Percy, President of the Board of Education in the second Baldwin administration, put it, 'After the war a hardly noticed revolution took place in British policy. For the first time in her history Britain became obscurely conscious that she had created not only an Empire but a civilisation.' After the 1923 conference an agreed syllabus for the teaching of Empire history and geography was produced in association with the various historical and geographical societies, and was circulated throughout Britain and the Empire. After the 1927 conference Newton published his *British Empire since 1783* for use in history, geography, commerce, economics, and colonial history classes in secondary schools, universities, and the W.E.A.[48] It drew on the resources and facilities of the Imperial Studies Committee, the Federation of Chambers of Commerce of the British Empire, the Imperial Institute, the Empire Marketing Board, and the R.C.I., reflecting the highly co-operative nature of these ventures. The Imperial Studies Committee also prepared bibliographies for students and teachers, and instituted in 1926 the publication of scholarly monographs to be known as the Imperial Studies series. The Royal Empire Society (as the R.C.I. became in 1928) continued to be active throughout the '30s in publishing handbooks and pamphlets for those involved in imperial studies, in campaigning in the universities, in holding meetings, lectures, and summer schools. By that time, however, the Imperial Institute had perhaps become the main propagandist body in reaching the schools and youth adult organisations, and the late nineteenth-century imperial world view was firmly lodged in all history texts in use in the schools. Even if, as has so often been said, many of the societies reviewed in this chapter failed in the pursuit of their specific objectives, nonetheless they ensured the central and continuing role of an imperial world view in public propaganda, entertainment, and above all in education.

NOTES

1 See, for example, J. G. Greenlee, 'Imperial studies and the unity of the Empire', *Journal of Imperial and Commonwealth History,* VII (1979), 321-35.

2 Robb, J. H., *The Primrose League, 1883-1906,* New York, 1942.

3 W. Basil Worsfold, 'The Imperial Federation League, 1884-1893', *United Empire,* VI (1916), 263-73.

4 A list of such articles would take up almost an entire bibliography in themselves. See, for example, *Murray's Magazine,* January, 1887, 66-80; *Nineteenth Century,* March 1887, 351-61; *Nineteenth Century,* April 1887, 507-16; *Westminster Review,* July 1887, 484-94; *Edinburgh Review,* July 1887, 247-57; *National Review,* October 1889, 184-99 and 200-7; *United Services Magazine,* May 1890, 118-36.

5 Worsfold, 'Imperial Federation League', 263.

6 C. Freeman Murray, 'The British Empire League', *United Empire,* VI (1916), 431-9.

7 Murray, 'British Empire League', 437.

8 E. B. Sargent, 'The Victoria League', *United Empire,* VI (1916), 588-94.

9 Collections of the pamphlets of the Imperial South Africa Association can be found in the Royal Commonwealth Society Library.

10 R.C.S. Library, I.S.A.A. Pamphlets, Vol.1.

11 Arthur H. Loring, 'Imperial Federation (Defence) Committee, 1894-1906', *United Empire,* VI (1916), 341-6.

12 Anne Summers, 'Militarism in Britain before the Great War', *History Workshop,* 2 (1976), 106.

13 R. MacLeod, 'The National Service League', *United Empire,* VI (1916), 893-901. Summers, 'Militarism', 104-23.

14 Trevor R. Reese, *The History of the Royal Commonwealth Society, 1868-1968,* London, 1968, 147.

15 Sir Frederick Pollard, 'The League of the Empire', *United Empire,* VI (1916), 736-41.

16 *Annual Reports of the British Empire Union* (from 1960, the British Commonwealth Union).

17 This phraseology was still appearing in the forty-second Annual Report of the B.E.U. in the late 1950s.

18 *Annual Report,* B.E.U., 1959.

19 Reese, *Royal Commonwealth Society,* 148.

20 Reese, *Royal Commonwealth Society,* 144 and 148.

21 Brian Harrison, 'For Church, Queen, and family: the Girls' Friendly Society, 1874-1920,' *Past and Present,* 61 (1973), 107-38.

22 Harrison, 'Church, Queen, and family', 126.

23 Anna Davin, 'Imperialism and motherhood', *History Workshop,* 5 (1978), 9–65.

24 Davin, 'Imperialism and motherhood', 55.

25 A badge of the Women's Imperial League has come to light, but no other evidence of its existence can be found. For the Women's Guild of Empire, see Hutchinson's

Women's Who's Who, 1934, 591.

26 A. James Hammerton, *Emigrant Gentlewomen,* London, 1979. Joy Parr, *Labouring Children,* London, 1980. Gillian Wagner, *Children of the Empire,* London, 1982.

27 Parr, *Labouring Children,* 143.

28 Patrick A. Dunae, *Gentleman Emigrants,* Vancouver, 1981.

29 Parr, *Labouring Children,* chapter 4.

30 Brabazon, Earl of Meath, 'State-directed colonisation', *National Review,* 1887, 525-37.

31 There were ex-servicemen's schemes to Africa and the Dominions, together with schemes for children orphaned in the war. It was in this period that the Dominion governments were most active in issuing postcards and pamphlets on emigration. See, for example, 'Australia for the Farm Labourer', Government of the Commonwealth of Australia, 1926.

32 Charlotte Erickson, *Emigration from Europe, 1815-1914,* London, 1976, tables 27-9.

33 Wagner, *Children,* 225-8.

34 Reese, *Royal Commonwealth Society,* 84-7.

35 George T. Denison, *The Struggle for Imperial Unity,* London, 1909. Lord Meath also referred to this in his efforts to establish the E.D.M.

36 The account of the COVIC is based on the report of Sir Charles Lucas on the Visual Instruction Committee printed for the use of the Colonial Office, miscellaneous No. 265, September 1911, and on the summary of the COVIC reports held at the R.C.S. Library.

37 H. J. Mackinder, *Eight Lectures prepared for the VIC of the C.O., India,* London, 1910.

38 Walter Nimocks, *Milner's Young Men,* London, 1970, 123-216.

39 Deborah Lavin, 'History, morals, and the politics of the Empire: Lionel Curtis and the Round Table', in J. Bossy and P. Jupp (eds.), *Essays presented to Michael Roberts,* Belfast, 1976, 117-32.

40 Greenlee, 'Imperial studies', 321-35

41 Greenlee, 'Imperial studies', 324

42 C. P. Lucas, 'Imperial studies', *United Empire,* VI (1916), 665-9.

43 C. P. Lucas, *The British Empire: Six Lectures,* London, 1915.

44 Lucas, 'Imperial studies', 668-9.

45 Lucas, *British Empire,* 1-2.

46 Basil Williams, *Cecil Rhodes,* London, 1921, and *The British Empire* in the Home University Library series, London, 1928.

47 Reese, *Royal Commonwealth society,* 138-9 and 144.

48 A. P. Newton and J. Ewing, *The British Empire since 1783,* London, 1929.

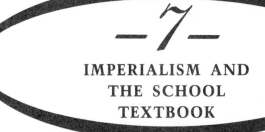

–7–
IMPERIALISM AND
THE SCHOOL
TEXTBOOK

There have, unfortunately, been few studies of school textbooks, and the textbooks themselves can be difficult to obtain, since librarians, even of the great national collections, have regarded them as eminently disposable. Until very recently neither booksellers nor collectors have regarded the frayed and ink-stained mementoes of classroom *ennui* as quite holding their own against competing interests like the attractively illustrated juvenile literature considered in chapter 8. Valerie Chancellor's work on nineteenth-century school history texts stands out as a notable landmark in this scene of neglect, but the single-discipline approach is inadequate for a full understanding of the manner in which a 'core ideology' came to dominate school texts in the late nineteenth century.[1] Moreover, the end of Chancellor's period of study, the Edwardian age, marks not so much the end of one tradition as the beginning of a new one. And while the school texts themselves are fascinating, the many manuals for teachers published from the turn of the century are perhaps even more illuminating.

If we are to discover the manner in which imperialism came to dominate school studies in the humanities, we need to look not only at history, but also at geography, English, and the teaching of religion. Every teaching manual from the 1890s pointed to the close affinities between history and geography. The geography taught in late nineteenth-century schools was primarily human and historical. It was a more popular school subject than history because it was regarded as more likely to stimulate children's interest, and was in any case an invaluable basis for historical understanding. One teaching manual suggested that the geography of the geographer was not the geography which should be taught in schools.[2] The latter should be about world problems, political, economic, and historical, and contemporary travel works and geographical fiction (Kipling, E. S. White, Jack London) constituted good sources. School geography texts, in fact, became in many ways virtually indistinguishable from history texts. Moreover, English 'readers' likewise came to depend upon a contemporary adventure, military, and travel literature which had proved itself through the successes of commercial publishing. Thus the great voyages, episodes of exploration, scenes of colonial military activity, and passages from the writings of missionary heroes, came to be a vital source of cross-disciplinary material, appropriate to history, geography, and English. In religious instruction the expansion of Christendom, with stories of missionary heroism, neatly dovetailed with the central themes of history, geography, and English readers.

Such pedagogic techniques did not, however, spring full-blown with the arrival of the 'new imperialism' in the 1870s and 1880s. It took at least two decades, and much intellectual propaganda, for teaching methods to concentrate on the late nineteenth-century world view. The experience of the Royal Colonial Institute in its efforts to promote imperial studies in the schools demonstrates this very well. In 1883 the R.C.I. offered money prizes for essays on imperial topics to be submitted by schoolchildren and university students.[3] The response was so disappointing that the idea was dropped in 1885. It was not revived until 1913, and thereafter it became a continuous feature of the Institute's work until modern times. The R.C.I. also exerted pressure on the education system to introduce imperial studies. In 1883 letters were sent to the headmasters of public schools and other secondary schools attempting to persuade them to place colonial history and geography on the school curriculum. In 1892 the same technique was used to encourage the development of studies of the Indian Empire. Although the schools at first reacted in a noncommittal way, such activities began to bear fruit in the 1890s. The Education Code of 1892 incorporated suggestions for instruction on British colonies, and school inspectors were urged to develop studies from the fourth to higher standards. Lectures on imperial topics began to appear on the curriculum of the Cambridge local lectures syndicate and in university extension summer schools. The Geographical Association recommended the study of Empire geography in secondary schools in 1896, and the Library Association introduced a section on colonial literature in the library assistants' examination from 1904. The R.C.I. was also active in promoting the writing of textbooks. A set of textbooks began to appear from 1889, covering in successive volumes the West Indies, Canada (one historical and one geographical), and southern Africa. These were all adopted by the management committee of the Schools Board of London, and the first at least ran to several editions.

Nevertheless, history took some time to become acceptable as a school subject, although, paradoxically, by the time it did the approach to other disciplines had also become historical. Arnold introduced history to Rugby, but the subject was little known in State schools before 1875. In that year it became one of the possible optional topics in primary schools, but for a long time it remained the least favoured of such subjects, unpopular among pupils and teachers alike. These attitudes were reinforced by working-class parents, who regarded history and geography as superfluous, and wished to have their children educated only in the basics of writing and arithmetic.[4] Only from 1895 was history commonly taught in standards IV to VI of elementary schools. By that time strenuous efforts were being made to brighten up the teaching of history and geography, and an Empire context was seen as the best way of doing it. J. R. Seeley had in effect argued for this in dilating at length on the excitements of history in *The Expansion of England* (see below).[5] However, as late as 1899 only 25% of elementary schools taught history, although 75% found geography more congenial.[6] In secondary schools, however, history had developed in popularity in the later years of the nineteenth century, and in 1900 it became compulsory. New texts were produced each time a new Educational Code was promulgated, and it was this need for repeated renewal in the 1890s which helped to produce a dramatic shift in the tone of the texts.

At the beginning of the century, history texts were written only for an elite. In them, the working-class were viewed with scorn, and depicted as largely responsible for their own problems.[7] By the end of the century the working-class had ceased to be an object of abuse (such attitudes had by then shifted to other races). By the last half of the century, the Whig interpretation reigned supreme in most texts: commerce and business were extolled, and the history of England was seen as the rise and triumph of a middle class securing freedom and reform. Moreover, significant shifts had taken place in attitudes to specific historical figures. Warlike characters moved from denigration to respect, and the reverse occurred for any politician who had failed to maintain the imperial momentum. Certain periods and incidents came to be glossed over — like the Civil War, the slave trade, and times of sexual licence — while patriotism, militarism, adulation of the monarchy, and of course imperial expansion came to be the central concerns. A significant shift took place, too, in the authorship of texts, from upper middle-class amateurs to schoolteachers, and finally to academics. Almost all the texts written to respond to the Education Codes at the end of the century were by academics.

School texts do in fact undergo a drastic shift in both method and tone in the 1890s. Before that decade, the main concern seems to have been with the organisation of knowledge, the production of large compendia of facts, often lacking any real interpretative thrust. It was against this approach that so many imperial propagandists and writers of textbooks of teaching method railed at the end of the century. It is at this time that a single ideological slant is introduced to all such texts. Older ones, like James Hewitt's *Geography of the British Colonies and*

Dependencies[8] (in print from the 1860s to the late '80s), William Francis Collier's senior class books *The History of the British Empire*,[9] and William C. Pearce's misnamed *Analysis of English History*,[10] proceeded year by year, fact by fact, reign by reign. The latter work, indeed, seems to be the prototype of Sellar and Yeatman's *1066 and all that*. Victoria's reign did indeed largely consist of 'a wave of justifiable wars'. The 1855 campaign against Persia was due to 'the intrigues of Russia', the Chinese war of 1859 broke out 'chiefly in consequence of the arrogance of the Chinese Commissioner Yeh'.[11] These texts certainly allowed imperial events to predominate in their accounts of the eighteenth and nineteenth centuries; they skated over awkward events in the long march to imperial dominance; they consistently shifted moral responsibility for conflict on to others; but they had not yet developed a concept of empire as the consummation of the development of the British state. The *Fourth Book of Lessons for the Use of Schools*,[12] published in 1870, carefully skirted round the loss of the American colonies, perhaps not suprisingly, since it was published by Collins in the 'Irish National School Books' series, 'printed by Authority'. 'The World at Home', 'a new series of geography readers adapted to the latest Code', published in 1885, shifted the blame for the opium wars on to the government of India, almost as though it were an independent power: 'The disgrace of having forced a market in China for the sale of opium lies with the Government of India.'[13]

The reaction to this blow-by-blow approach was to stress the utility of history. Joseph H. Cowham's *A New School Method* of 1900 contrasted the technique of commencing history teaching with the remote past and working down to modern times with the new method of starting from the present and working backwards.[14] It was only through the new technique that history could achieve its proper purpose, which was the inculcation of patriotism and good citizenship as well as the provision of moral training. These three objectives appear in all the works on teaching methods of the succeeding decades. James Welton's *Principles and Methods of Teaching* (1909, still in use in the 1920s after a new edition in 1924) quoted Stubbs on the necessity of history to the training of a new generation 'who will know how to vote' and 'bring judgement . . . to help in all the great affairs of life'.[15] For Welton progress, the process of reform, the constant need to develop and change institutions, could not be satisfactorily achieved without historical understanding. In *The Teaching of History in Elementary Schools* (1916) R. L. Archer pointed out that all citizens required such an understanding. Only small numbers of people need know about science, but everyone required some knowledge of history.

[177]

'Even the highest intellects are liable to grievous mistakes through not taking account of the warnings of history in human affairs.'[16] History was now enshrined as a central school discipline through this inflated vision of its utility. And that attitude was to survive through the 1920s and 1930s, as Board of Education publications and new series of textbooks repeatedly indicated.

If history was to be popular and useful, then it had to be simple. Teachers were repeatedly enjoined to select from the materials of history those facts, periods, and individuals important to an understanding of the present. In 1927 the H.M.S.O. *Handbook for Teachers* asserted that children should not be 'harassed' by complicated issues, thus carrying forward this idea to a new generation of teachers who would remain influential in the post-Second World War period.[17] In honing down the essentials of history and geography to a series of stark and simple statements about 'development', 'progress', and racial superiority, teaching methods ensured that those historical figures whose careers could best be portrayed as a consistent drive on the route towards the world of the late nineteenth century would be highlighted. Thus it was easier to teach Disraeli's romantic imperialism, his association of the monarchy with Empire, and flamboyant actions like the purchase of the Suez Canal shares, than it was to consider sympathetically the complex political thought and actions of Gladstone. It was perhaps inevitable that Disraeli should win the battle of the reputations which went on in school texts in the late nineteenth century. Thus in his teaching handbook of 1916 R. L. Archer described him ('a Semitic genius, brilliant, imaginative, self-conscious, a lover of the pomp of Empire and not without a medieval capacity for clever intrigue') as symbolising British imperialism ('the spirit that dictates honest spade-work on the borders of Empire, sane but unimaginative, scrupulously fair, disdainful of show, unconscious of merit'), while Gladstone represented 'English middle-class Philistinism — slow to recognise an evil till it lies straight before its eyes and then remedying it with an inevitable growl of dissatisfaction, over-cautious, suspicious of ideas, elevating consistency into a vice'.[18] Disraeli fitted better the list of heroes which stretched from the Elizabethan sea dogs through Cromwell, Clive, and Livingstone. It was this same congruence of simple thought (at least perceived as such) and direct action which suffused all the juvenile literature and stories of heroes of the period.

Events were also fitted into this pattern. R. L. Archer suggested that in approaching the seven great wars of naval and colonial supremacy after 1689 teachers should disregard the European continental aspects and concentrate on the rise of naval power and the 'utmost importance' of our colonial Empire. Catherine Firth, in a teaching manual first published in 1932, similarly advised that the complexities of eighteenth-century domestic history should be avoided in favour of the events vital to the development of the British Empire and Commonwealth.[19] In 1935 a set of three school texts perfectly conveyed these concepts of utility and simplicity through their title *Today through Yesterday*. These 'three books . . . have been written to help you to understand the present better by learning about the past, for it is out of the past that the present has grown.[20] The Tudor period, in volume 1, was described as 'the most important period in the story of the British nation' because it was the one which marked the beginning of the British Empire.[21] Throughout the three volumes, the drive towards the consummation of empire was the central theme and climax of national history. School texts developed a habit of quoting the classic nineteenth-century historians, probably because the teaching manuals urged teachers to use them for their own preparation. Froude, Lecky, Macaulay, the Seeley were perhaps the most frequently quoted, and maintained their grip upon school history teaching until after the Second World War.

Among this group there can be no doubt that Seeley was the most important. The great sea change which took place in the writing of popular and school history at the end of the nineteenth century owed most to him. Valerie Chancellor noted that the alleged gloom and pessimism of the late Victorian period is not borne out in school texts.[22] In this they followed Seeley's approach to the uses of history. For him it was to be deliberately employed as an uplifting moral force, to stimulate exertions, and raise the morale of the nation.[23] History should be treated as a rewarding interaction of past and present, in which imperial expansion should be seen as the moral of British history, ultimately acting as the key to the future. It was a means of uplift from the anxieties of the late nineteenth century, a route to a national class and party consensus, enabling the country to escape from the social conflict and political division which seemed to be developing in the 1880s.

Moreover, Seeley was the great simplifier *par excellence*, who insisted on a selection from the past which would chart the rise of the nation State, and in particular present the British Empire as achieving the apotheosis of the State through the first great world political order. He had a contemporary practical objective in the ill-starred imperial federation movement, but although that particular application of his ideas failed, his approach to history became standard in teacher training and in school texts. As a historian he did no original research, but set about creating syntheses with a message. As the German G. A. Rein put it in his work on Seeley, published just before the First World War, Seeley was interested in 'uniformities', in generalisation, large considerations, broad coherences, general principles, comprehensive ideas.[24] The writing of history was a matter of periodisation, classification, and short formulae, and in the onward march of the State war acted as a civilising agent and as a teacher of morals. Thus Seeley directed the Victorian intertwining of politics, history, and religion towards a vision of the patriotic and militarist expansion of the State. His most influential book, *The Expansion of England*, published in 1883, sold 80,000 copies in its first two years, and continued in print through many editions in the decades that followed. In 1915 an advertisement priced it at 4s, with an abbreviated version at 1s.[25] It was still in print in 1956.[26]

Robert Roberts recognised the extraordinarily successful downward filtration which Seeley's ideas achieved:

> Teachers, fed on Seeley's imperialistic work, *The Expansion of England*, and often great readers of Kipling, spelled out patriotism among us with a fervour that with some edged on the religious.[27]

We have seen the manner in which Seeley's moral and patriotic approach, and his criteria of a directed historical selection, can be found in the teaching manuals and the school texts of the succeeding decades. That his ideas were also given official sanction is apparent from the H.M.S.O. *Handbook* issued in 1927. History, the writer averred, was for children 'pre-eminently an instrument of moral training.' If the teacher made history live to the children through the lives of individuals.

> they will learn naturally in how many different ways the patriot has helped his country, and by what sort of actions nations and individuals have earned the gratitude of posterity. Without any laboured exhortations they will feel the splendour of heroism, the worth of unselfishness and loyalty, and the meanness of cruelty and cowardice.[28]

Here Seeley's morality and State patriotism are combined with the biographical approach of Thomas Carlyle. For Seeley, history was the biography of the State rather than of individuals, but teachers and the writers of textbooks tended to follow Carlyle's dictum that 'history is past biography'. All official and unofficial teaching handbooks stressed the importance of 'story-telling' to the teaching of history and geography, and that meant vivid personal life histories. Children's interest had to be stirred as they were prepared for the threefold patriotic obligations of the vote, work within the industrial system, and military duty. And that interest could best be stirred by stories of great men.

Here educational ideas overlapped with commercial publishing practices. Again, this nineteenth-century idea enjoyed a long currency in the twentieth. The Board of Education's *Handbook* asserted that 'children like to hear or read about the lives of great men and women'[29] (the list that followed consisted only of men). In 1949 an Oxford junior series comprised two texts, *Stories of Great People* and *Stories of Great Deeds*.[30] Moreover, both texts and teachers' manuals recommended the 'books of heroes' and the works of Henty and his imitators which contained the names of 'great men' in their titles. Archer recommended 'modern' works like G. W. Steevens's *With Kitchener to Khartoum* and Conan Doyle's *Boer War* in his lists of works of value in the teaching of imperial history.[31] Passages from Steevens appeared in Harrap's *Readers of Today*, advertised in successive H.M.S.O. handbooks, together with Jack's 'Children's Heroes' series on General Gordon, Livingstone, Lord Roberts, Bishop Patteson, and others. Kipling continued to be recommended until at least the 1940s.

The ideal hero combined piety, adventure, and military prowess, in the tradition of Christian militarism created in the 1860s and '70s, which reached its apotheosis in Gordon. Again there was a congruence between the imperial world view and the use of personalities in 'moral training'. Warfare came to be seen in a beneficent light at the end of the century, and war stories became a prime staple of English and history 'readers'. In the 1899 Revised Code, twelve out of thirty stories from 1688 to the present for standard V were devoted to war and war heroes.[32] The Cambridge University Press readers of 1911 contained twenty-four military figures out of forty historical personalities selected for study, including the by then inevitable litany of Drake, Grenville, Marlborough, Wolfe, Clive, Nelson, Wellington, Havelock, and Gordon. In the 1920s one of the most popular series of readers in general use were known as 'The Patriotic Readers'. British history became a sequence of commercial and territorial wars through which world-wide dominion was achieved, and those who waged them became the heroes of British expansion. The history of England was invariably taught, as one teacher's manual put it, as 'a series of unavoidable wars', from which pupils could learn patriotism, good citizenship, and moral training.[33]

The beneficent effects of these wars lay, of course, in their opening of the world to the civilising effects of trade, technology, and Christianity. The tremendous quickening of the process in the nineteenth century contributed to the textbook vision of the Victorian age as the great moral climax of human history, in which British imperial power constituted 'the end of history', a grand plateau to be defended against the new aggressors (rival European empires) toiling dangerously up the foothills. Both imperial federation and an adequate defensive provision were seen as vital to the maintenance of this Anglo-Saxon Olympus, and dire warnings about the dangers to the British Empire, and therefore to civilisation itself, appeared in manuals of instruction for the young. The idea that imperial federation represented salvation was developed by Edward Salmon, one of the most active propagandists for imperial studies, editor of *United Empire*, and a leading member of the R.C.I., in his *The Story of the Empire* (1902), specifically written for schools and young people.[34] For him the history of the Empire was like a three-volume novel, the first volume to the loss of the American colonies, the second to the achievement of imperial unity, and the third on the achievements of federal Britain. Similarly, Queen Victoria's reign was a trilogy of periods: it opened with a 'dark prospect'; the middle was characterised by revolts and wars; and the final represented 'Progress All Round'. Victoria's reign was a sort of Pilgrim's Progress from slough of despond to bright prospect. In 1911 *The Story of the Empire* was republished in a new edition, to which the only addition was Salmon's suggestion for an imperial peripatetic monarchy, an idea he developed in articles elsewhere.

The 'bright prospect' had to be defended. Teachers were urged to teach the significance of the army and navy in the patriotic duty of defence. These exhortations reached a peak in the textbook published by Fletcher and Kipling in 1911, a book which was in fact an extended paean of praise to the National Service League.[35] For Fletcher and Kipling, although Cromwell was a great hero (Protestant, anti-Dutch, uniter of the race, and extender of the Empire), the drawback of the Protectorate was the distrust of the army it engendered in British minds:

> Unfortunately, this reign of the Sword left on Men's minds an unreasonable hatred and fear, not only of this Puritan army, but of all armies; and that hatred and fear has [*sic*] too often paralysed the arm of England, and is not wholly dead today. It has prevented men from seeing that to serve King and country in the Army is the second best profession for Englishmen of all classes; to serve in the Navy, I suppose we all admit, is the best.[36]

Each Prime Minister from the younger Pitt, who 'neglected the army and the navy', was judged according to whether he increased or reduced spending on the armed forces. It was a yardstick from which, particularly in the period closest to Fletcher and Kipling's own times, Tories fared best. For them, as for Salmon, the Empire constituted a grand climactic final act to history, which they could celebrate in patriotic tableau illustrations to the text and the inevitable reddened world map on the endpapers. If the younger generation did not prepare itself for defence, the Empire would be lost.

In Bristol, and presumably elsewhere too, the Navy League distributed a textbook to schools indicating the importance of the navy in British history, and by implication to Britain's future.[37] The Navy League also instituted prize essay competitions 'to stimulate the scientific study of sea power', and encouraged the development of the Nelson cult. These activities were in no way inhibited by the First World War. In 1919 the League sent circulars and leaflets to all education authorities requesting that Nelson Day should again be celebrated on 21 October.[38] All schools should be asked to devote half an hour to a discourse on the sea services, and the debt of the Empire to the Royal Navy and the merchant marine. The naval essay competitions were resumed in the same year, and schools were officially urged to continue the savings schemes which had proved so successful during the war.[39] In 1916 12,500 schools had been in the War Savings Association, and those which passed the 1,000 mark in sales of war savings certificates were allowed a day's holiday. In 1919 the Board of Education considered that this fostering of thrift and patriotism should be continued in peacetime, and schools were instructed to substitute Post Office or Trustee Savings Bank savings arrangements.

Patriotism and militarism were also encouraged through the iconography on school walls.[40] The Nelson/Trafalgar and Wellington/Waterloo cults ensured that illustrations of these events received pride of place. There seems also to have been a cult of St George, and representations of the patron saint slaying his dragon were a common classroom adornment. Teachers used 'free gifts' offered with magazines and other products to brighten the dreary walls of Victorian and Edwardian classrooms. In one school, for example, 'Lord Roberts and the Innkeeper's Child', a supplement to the *Christian Globe* of January 1901, from the original painting by Cress Woollett, was framed and hung. At Abbeystead School in north Lancashire there were wall hangings of Portsmouth harbour, featuring Dreadnoughts, of 'A Naval Ship' by W. J. Wyllie, both published by Edward Arnold. Educational publishers also put out wall pictures of 'Famous Figures', 'Ships', 'Areas of the Empire', 'Empire Types', and many on 'Trade Routes'. The shift towards economic subjects was pronounced in the inter-war years when the Empire Marketing Board published and distributed a series of posters (150 in all) featuring products from around the Empire.

Fletcher and Kipling's book is notable for its strident racial tone, which, it must be said, was criticised in reviews at the time. This criticism sprang, perhaps, from their unpleasant strictures on the

Irish.[41] Judging by the prevalence of racial ideas in other texts of the time it may well be that their references to blacks and slaves were taken somewhat less amiss. Geography texts were the prime conveyers of racial ideas. One teacher's manual asserted that it was the role of the geography textbook to apply evolution to humans. Each text laid out the conventional progression from hunting to pastoral to agricultural and finally to industrial societies, larding this Social Darwinism with a strong dose of ecological determinism. Thus 'The inhabitants of the savannas are superior to the forest tribes, who have many degraded customs and superstitions'.[42] The nineteenth-century vision of Africans as children sunk in tropical abundance was perpetuated into the twentieth century. In Nelson's *The World and its Peoples* (c. 1907) the African was described as 'an overgrown child, vain, self-indulgent, and fond of idleness. Life is so easy to him in his native home that he has never developed the qualities of industry, self-denial, and forethought.'[43] Fletcher and Kipling considered that blacks had carried these characteristics across the Atlantic with them: in the West Indies they were 'lazy, vicious and incapable of any serious improvement, or of work except under compulsion'.[44]

> In such a climate a few bananas will sustain the life of a negro quite sufficiently; why should he work to get more than this? He is quite happy and quite useless, and spends any extra wages which he may earn upon finery.

In one text it was explained that the 'Dark Continent' was described as such because of the 'barbarous condition of its inhabitants'.[45] As if to prove the point, the *Chambers's Geographical Reader* repeated an old, and entirely inaccurate, *canard*: 'Many of the Central African tribes are so savage as still to be cannibals'.[46]

Contemporary texts prepared their young readers for the final acts of the partition of Africa. In one, published between 1905 and 1910 and still in school use in 1919, the impending collapse of Morocco, 'a monument of barbarism', was predicted, its ruler described as 'racked with anxiety', going 'in daily fear of assassination'.[47] In *Chambers's Geographical Reader* of 1904 Morocco was 'terribly misgoverned', ruled by a few who 'suck the life-blood of the nation and make enterprise impossible'.[48] But it was not just Africans who were denigrated. Asia was described as a continent of dying nations rapidly falling back in civilisation, while the Chinese were 'cruel and vengeful', a people of dubious and unpleasant appearance.[49] Of all the Afro-Asian peoples, only the desert Arabs of the Middle East occasionally got a good press, reflecting the rediscovery of Arabian Islam by the famous Arabists of the period.

Social Darwinian ideas always emerged most forcibly in the descriptions of hunter-gatherer peoples. A veil was usually drawn over the fate of the Tasmans, but geography texts invariably predicted a similar outcome of the contact between whites and aborigines in Australia or bushmen in southern Africa. 'The wretched bushmen, the lowest and most debased human beings on the face of the globe' were 'a rapidly disappearing race' in one text,[50] while in another the 'degraded' Hottentots and bushmen were diminishing in numbers and strength.[51] Even the Maoris were said to have been in danger of extinction at one stage, although by 1905 one text was acknowledging that this danger was now past.[52] Sometimes the moral dimension of this evolutionary process was made explicit. A. J. Herbertson, who prepared a number of school geographies in the Edwardian period (many of them remaining in print into the inter-war years) suggested a quasi-legal justification for the white settlement of Australia:

> ... the natives of Australia ... were among the most miserable of men. They roamed nearly naked, and were ignorant of everything except the chase. The explanation of their degraded condition lies in the arid climate of Australia... Their great poverty led them to practise vices like cannibalism and the murder of the sick and helpless.[53]

And he went on to describe 'the many shocking charges brought against them by the early colonists'. The aborigines were found guilty and consequently dispossessed.

This moral justification became inextricably bound up with economic exploitation (in its non-pejorative late-nineteenth-century sense). One text described the English as 'the only successful colonists of modern times'.[54] 'We have succeeded,' wrote Meiklejohn, 'by moral influence alone, in establishing the Pax Britannica in one of the most fertile regions on the surface of the earth, and have left man and nature free to do the rest'.[55] He was writing of the Straits Settlements, but it was the kind of sentiment expressed even where moral suasion had been backed up by considerable physical force. This entwining of economic and moral purpose appears in all the history and geography books. In creating world economic integration Europeans were 'spreading a hard-won civilisation', demonstrating Western man's 'dynamic power, possessing the forces of progress by which he can change his whole mode of life and mould his environment to his needs.'[56] Societies were to be judged by the extent of their commercial life. 'Trade led to the spread of more progressive economic, social, and political ideas and institutions'.[57] In such a value system, clearly, only industrial societies were distinguished by total command over the civilising effects of world commerce.

To highlight this global interaction, teachers were enjoined to stimulate children's interests in the value of the Empire by revealing the manner in which their diet and clothing relied on supplies of food-stuffs and raw materials from it. A common visual aid were the boxes of samples which were used in 'object lessons'.[58] One such box included raw cotton, gum arabic, raw coffee, loaf sugar, saffron, rice, and camphor, among many others. School log books in Lancashire indicate that these object lessons took up a significant proportion of school time, and may well have been partly designed with the knowledge that many of the pupils would go into the shop and distributive trades where a knowledge of such materials, their origins and uses, would be valuable.

In a number of school geography texts the economic role of each territory, down to the very smallest, was emphasised in order to demonstrate the variety of the interlocking parts of economic imperialism. The questions asked of pupils in such books were expected to elicit specific economic responses. If asked, for example, why Labuan was important to the Empire, the answer would be its large coal mine. The poets were marshalled to contribute to this vision of Empire. Tennyson's

> Sons and brothers that have sent from isle and Cape and continent,
> Produce of your field and flood, mount and mine, and primal wood

was quoted in one geography text, while even a German *Lebensraum* statement was considered appropriate, at least in 1891. Goethe's

> To give space for wandering was it
> That the world was made so wide

was quoted to preface a consideration of the two classes of colonies, the 'colonies of exploitation' and the 'colonies of settlement'.[59]

Such texts were eager to *organise* knowledge, and the varied resources of Empire were perfectly amenable to such treatment, made all the more attractive by the sense of patriotic self-satisfaction in possession. J. M. D. Meiklejohn's *The British Empire* was divided into material in bold type that was to be 'got up' by the pupil and material in small type which was supplementary. It contained a glossary largely of the more unusual products of the Empire, like coir and copra, both derived from coconuts and produced in the Laccadive Islands and the South Sea Possessions, or plumbago, mined in Ceylon, the value of which could be brought home to pupils by reminding them of its use in pencils and in black lead for the iron grates and fireplaces which were found in every home.[60]

In 1911 Kipling supplied a poem for the Fletcher textbook which perfectly represented the supreme expression of this economic imperial relationship, linked with maritime sentiment embracing both a great merchant marine and naval defence.[61]

Big Steamers
'Oh, where are you going to, all you Big Steamers,
    With England's own coal, up and down the salt seas?'
'We are going to fetch you your bread and your butter,
    Your beef, port, and mutton, eggs, apples, and cheese.'

'And where will you fetch it from, all you Big Steamers,
    And where shall I write you when you are away?
'We fetch it from Melbourne, Quebec, and Vancouver,
    Address us at Hobart, Hong-Kong, and Bombay.'
                    . . .

'Then what can I do for you, all you Big Steamers,
    Oh, what can I do for your comfort and good?'
'Send out your big warships to watch your big waters,
    That no one may stop us from bringing you food.

For the bread that you eat and the biscuits you nibble,
    The sweets that you suck and the joints that you carve,
They are brought to you daily by all us Big Steamers,
    And if anyone hinders our coming you'll starve!'[61]

The Empire means food; the steamers represent technical control (celebrated elsewhere in the same book by another Kipling poem, 'The Secret of the Machines'); and the Royal Navy is presented at the most basic level of survival, starvation.

Valerie Chancellor argued that school history texts stressed the moral duties of Empire rather than its economic benefits. This seems scarcely borne out by the evidence of a wide range of geography and history texts examined for this study. In convincing schoolchildren of the need to secure and to hold Empire, it was the economic value of all the component parts that was stressed. Robert Roberts noted this in his memories of his Salford school in the years before the First World War.

And how, indeed, did the nation's poor profit from the possession of empire? Compulsory State education had been introduced with overt propagation of the imperialistic idea . . . What the undermass got materially from empire, old or new, is hard to see, unless it was the banana . . .[62]

Moreover, late Victorian and Edwardian under-classes could be made to feel particularly fortunate when contrasted with the new colonial 'undermass'. As one East End autobiography put it:

The American War of Independence, indeed the existence of the United States of America, was hushed up ... Geography was confined to the British Empire and countries were assessed not by their peoples but by the magnitude and wealth of their products. The only reference to people that I remember was 'the Indian can live on a handful of rice a day', which made us feel a particularly opulent race when we were enjoying our Sunday dinners.[63]

This concentration on the economic benefits of Empire did not diminish after the First World War. On the contrary, the propaganda (including the Beaverbrook campaign) which led to the Ottawa agreements on imperial preference in 1932 had its expression in the school textbooks of the period. A Cambridge geographical reader, first published in 1920 and reprinted in 1924 after it had been recommended by circular No. 1320 of the Board of Education, was entirely historical in approach, and carried forward many of the dogmas of the nineteenth century.[64] Notions of tropical abundance and the resulting tropical indolence abound (Africans in South Africa 'lapse into idleness'; in East Africa they have 'no need for exertion'); while all young people in Britain are taught the virtues of patriotism, 'no such feeling inspires the natives of India'.[65] But the main thrust of the book is the attempt to depict the Empire as economically self-contained. In some cases, this self-sufficiency is potential: cotton for the Lancashire textile industry could be produced entirely 'in lands where the Union Jack flies'.[66] Other commodities reveal the immense value of Empire: late nineteenth-century imperialism ensured that all wheat imports were imperial; and the source of tea shifted from China to India.

Texts of the 1930s moved the emphasis from Empire to Commonwealth in the wake of the Statute of Westminster, and stressed the role of the Commonwealth as a precursor of the League of Nations, demonstrating the manner in which a multi-ethnic world-wide community could be made to work. In this element of idealism they were echoing a phrase of Smuts that the British Empire was the only truly successful League. But the economic message remained just as prominent at a time when imperial trade for the first time represented 50% of the British total, and imperial projects were being pursued as a means of alleviating unemployment at home.[67] The H.M.S.O. handbooks for teachers and a variety of texts continued to affirm the necessity of the imperial connection to the supply of foodstuffs and raw materials for industry. Teachers were advised to show children the value of raw materials, and make the point vivid to them by drawing attention to basic articles of clothing and of foodstuffs.[68] Geography pupils should also be taught the concepts of development and undevelopment in 'the regions inhabited by civilised and uncivilised peoples.'[69] The 1927 handbook expected that the British Empire was most likely to be the selected subject of geography courses, and no fewer than four of the six *Chambers's Regional Geographies* in use at the time concentrated on it.

A senior course history textbook of 1932 took as its starting point the vision of an economically interdependent Empire.

> We began by saying that once upon a time men in this country provided themselves with almost everything that they wanted. Nowadays we get much of what we want from overseas. A great many of the things come from different parts of the empire. There are, for instance, meat from New Zealand, wheat for flour from Canada, wool from Australia, tea from Ceylon, fruit from South Africa, and so on. We could easily make a long list of the things in our own homes which were sent to us by men living in the empire.[70]

This and other texts of the period echoed the message of the displays and films at the Imperial Institute in the years before and following the Second World War. The Institute's propaganda was reflected in another way. The school texts frequently referred to the opportunities for emigration and settlement provided by Empire. Children were reminded that new schemes had been instituted after the First World War, and that relatives and friends had already gone to many imperial territories.[71] They were urged to correspond with them so as to find out about the different ways of life and economic activity prevailing in the dominions.[72]

Nor did the emphasis on warfare seem to decline in the interwar years. The dilemma was faced squarely by Catherine Firth in a teachers' manual of 1932. 'The history teacher cannot possibly omit the story of wars. Whatever he thinks about them, they happened. Men got many things by fighting and wars had long results.'[73] 'Children,' she went on, 'care primarily about action . . . to shut out the great warriors is to go far towards emptying a child's Valhalla.' Further, 'No one can stand for a few minutes watching small boys at play without recognizing that to attempt to rob physical conflict of glory, is to ignore young human nature.' War was an essential part of the foundation and growth of the Empire, and was therefore the source of British greatness. Moreover, the Empire was vital to the defence of the mother country. In her school history text published in the same year (and edited by Firth), Nunn wrote of the peoples of Empire, 'Some of them are black, some are brown, some white . . . But all of them are subjects of the same king as we are, and if any danger threatened England, all of them would come to her help.'[74]

A new influence of the period was schools broadcasting. It too harped on old interests and approaches. The *B.B.C. Year-Book* of 1932 commented on the great success of a history series entitled 'Tracing History Backwards'.[75] So far as geography was concerned, the schools service asserted that to attempt to teach conventional geography over the air would be tedious and unnecessary. Radio could better bring famous travellers into the classroom, and provide children with excitements like Allan Sullivan on his visits to the Eskimos, Clifford Collinson and his Cannibal Island, and Ernest Haddon on the peculiarities of the pygmies.[76]

Not only did the new school history and geography created in the 1890s survive the First World War, its resistance to change was so great that, in all essentials, it survived the Second too. School texts had a remarkable shelf life, not only in schools, but in the offices of their publishers. The Nelson series *The House of History*, in four volumes, first appeared in 1931.[77] In reached its eighteenth impression in 1968, when it was still standard in the schools of many local authorities. The Macmillan junior histories, first published in 1939 were reprinted every third year or so, and were still in print and in use in the 1960s. [78] Joseph H. Stembridge's *The World: a General Regional Geography*, published in 1939, was still in print in the late 1950s.[79] The Collins series 'The Thrill of History', which came out just after the Second World War, reached its seventh impression in 1959.[80] G. W. Southgate's standard post-war texts *An Introduction to English History*, in three volumes, first published in 1947, were reprinting as late as 1969.[81]

The history contained within these texts represented merely a modified version of the late nineteenth-century 'new history'. The racial tone is, perhaps, rather less pronounced, but they were still nationalist and patriotic, devoted to stories of great men and of significant events (usually wars) in a national march to greatness. Muriel Masefield's 'House of History', used in schools for more than forty years, adopted the usual approach to the eighteenth century. The narrative was hung on the lives of figures like Pitt, Clive, Wolfe, and Cook, and England's 'progress' in inventions and colonial acquisition was contrasted with the backwardness and failures of France. Macaulay was quoted more frequently than any other authority. 'The ardour of [Pitt the Elder's] soul had set the whole kingdom on fire.' 'With Pitt at the head of affairs,' Masefield went on, 'it seemed as if a new spirit of hope and courage ran through the army, navy, country, and colonies.'[82] For Clive ('a hero and a rich man') she recommended Henty's *With Clive in India* for further reading. Similarly Steevens's *With Kitchener to Khartoum* and standard Gordon hagiographies appeared in her reading lists, together with Jack's 'Children's Heroes' series, Petrie's *Poems of South African history*, Rider Haggard, Buchan, Newbolt, and Mrs Lowndes's *Told in Gallant Deeds*. The great-man approach appears in all the other texts too. In I. Tenen's *This England* (in print from 1939 to the 1960s) there is a conventional approach to the Elizabethan and seventeenth-century periods as the crucial source of the British Empire.[83] As well as the usual heroes, Tenen attempted to take up the cause of some lesser known ones. For example, Sir James Lancaster, he contended, should be regarded as one of the founders of the British Empire, making up in his Eastern exploits for the South American 'disappointments' of Drake and Hawkins.

B. I. Magraw's *The Thrill of History* contained hero-worshipping chapters on Livingstone, Rhodes, Baden-Powell, and Lawrence of Arabia, although modern heroes like King Khama (perhaps the most effectively incorporated of all African chiefs), Lenin (an account clearly influenced by Russia's role as ally in the Second World War), and Gandhi do appear. Magraw offered short plays for performance in class. In one of these, Rhodes meets the Matabele, and an old Matabele woman counsels peace to her people. Rhodes, she says, is a great chief who will be father to the Matabele, and will bring them peace, justice, and plenty.[84] Children are thus presented not only with a highly favourable vision of empire, but with a dramatic expression of African acquiescence in imperial rule. There are similarly dramatised accounts of B.-P. at Mafeking, Lawrence, Prince of Mecca, in Arabia, and so on. Book 3 of the same series, Magraw writes in his introduction, might have been entitled 'From Great to Greater Britain, the "growing up" of the British Empire'. Exploration and acquisition are the prominent themes, and once again the tone of the book is best conveyed in its little plays. In one of these Cook meets the Maoris and tells them they have nothing to fear, 'We'll plant the British flag here . . . New Zealand shall be a Britain of the South Seas.'[85] Pitt was, as always, the greatest figure in the development of Empire, Clive the bad boy who made good. At a somewhat more senior level, Southgate also proceeded by the 'famous people' approach.

The best key to the general world view of these later texts can be found in their accounts of that central event of imperial history, the Indian 'Mutiny'. In Muriel Masefield's *The House of History*, the Indian atrocities like Cawnpore are described in detail, but British retribution is passed off in a phrase. 'After the Mutiny was quelled, the governor showed great mercy.'[86] But 'the heroism of the recapture of Delhi, the tragedy of Cawnpore, and the long defence of Lucknow will never be forgotten'. To ensure that they were not forgotten in the 1950s, Mase-field made a number of suggestions for questions and class activities. 'What has British rule in India done for its people?' is her recom-mended essay topic, and she proposes Fitchett's *Tales of the Great Mutiny*, Strang's *Stories of the Indian Mutiny*, Tennyson's 'The Relief of Lucknow' and Whittier's 'The Pipes of Lucknow' as further reading ('Learn some verses by heart'). The class should conclude its studies of the Mutiny with a rousing rendering of 'The Campbells are Coming'.[87]

Southgate's account is in some respects even more striking. The great benefits Bentinck and Dalhousie brought to the Indian people is contrasted with the obscurantism of the latter, who 'preferred to live ... without railways, post offices, schools'.[88] 'The Mutiny,' he goes on (inaccurately), 'was not a rising of the Indian people but only of the sepoys of the Bengal army ... this was probably because there were many races in India, some of which hated one another much more than they disliked the British.' Here half-truths are neatly dressed up to re-flect the progress and peace represented by British rule. The post-Mutiny history of India is dismissed in a few sentences (in a work first published in 1947):

> Since the Mutiny India has been ruled by a line of Viceroys who have done much for the good of the people. India has been peaceful, and Indian peasants have been left to cultivate their little plots of land without hav-ing to fear that they would be slain and their homes burned by invaders.[89]

In *History: Mankind and his Story* (1948) the British were described as introducing material improvements to early nineteenth-century India which were 'meteoric compared with the past'.[90] The Mutiny was due to 'suspicion, wounded pride, and religious bigotry'.

Independence had done little to change textbook views of India. In-deed, the achievements of British rule and the 1947 partition were fre-quently expressed in terms of India's great disunity of race, language, and religion.[91] In the early '50s, of course, a large dependent Empire continued to require justification. The Odhams textbook *Mankind and his Story*, which consisted of a series of regional contributions, two of them by advisers to the Foreign Office, was in fact almost en-tirely about European mankind and his effect on the rest of the world. The African section particularly emphasised the abolition of the slave trade, and the concepts of trusteeship and partnership, by which Empire could be seen to be devoted to the well-being of the subordinate peoples. The 1956 edition of Jasper Stembridge's *The World* empha-sised throughout the 'developmental' aspects of European rule. The be-neficent influence of imperialism on Africa was particularly stressed:

To-day, under the guidance of Europeans, Africa is being steadily opened up. Roads and railways are being built and air routes are being extended. Doctors and scientists are working to improve the health of the Africans, who, on their part, are increasing in numbers; missionaries and teachers are educating the people; and traders and trading companies are extending their operations. The rights and wrongs of 'the scramble for Africa' on the part of the European Powers lie outside the field of geography. But the significant fact remains that the Europeans have brought civilization to the peoples of tropical Africa, whose standard of living has, in most cases, been raised as a result of their contact with white peoples. Look at the picture from whatever angle you will, there is no escaping the interdependence of the various races of Africa, and especially that of the black and white peoples, for only by partnership between them will the economic and social development of the continent be assured.[92]

In a test question (p. 384), pupils were asked to discuss the importance to the homeland of the colonial territories in Africa.

Thus the imperial and patriotic mould, formed at the end of the nineteenth century, was not broken until at least the late 1960s and 1970s. Even then, financial constraints ensured that texts whose approach was formulated in the 1930s remained basic school material in an era when their message bore little relationship to the real world. A late nineteenth-century world view continued to be transmitted long after an elite literary culture had moved on. The formulation of history syllabuses and historical method, even more significantly of the geography equivalents, occurred just at the time when they were likely to be most susceptible to the imperial core ideology. A generation of imperial thinkers at the end of the century influenced the imperial idealists of the Edwardian period and set up ripples through manuals of teaching method, Board of Education handbooks for teachers, and school texts, which, periodically agitated by the two world wars, survived at least until the 1950s and 1960s. In these ways the ideas on the uses of history promulgated by Seeley, Stubbs, and others survived for decades until a revolution in the writing and teaching of history took place in the late 1960s. The result was a world view similar to that of classical China. As A. H. Halsey has put it, the village classroom he remembered from the 1920s

> was steeped in officially sanctioned nationalism. The world map was red for the Empire and dull brown for the rest, with Australia and Canada vastly exaggerated in size by Mercator's projection. The Greenwich meridian placed London at the centre of the world. Empire Day and 11 November ritualised an established national supremacy.[93]

It is, as always, difficult to assess the effect on pupils of all this patriotic history and imperial geography. However, there are some useful pieces of evidence. A few children's jotters have survived in Lancaster from the period before the First World War (c. 1909).[94] Most of the little essays in them are about military heroes. Stephen Humphries, in his oral history of working-class childhood and youth 1889-1939, found that while children saw Empire Day as an excuse for a holiday, imperialism itself was taken much more seriously:

> However, interviews reveal that working-class children were generally much more responsive to lessons and activities that were inspired by imperialism than they were to any religious influence in school. In part this success was due to the stimulation of children's interests and energies by the introduction of an element of variety into an extremely restricted curriculum based on the three Rs. Many children clearly welcomed games lessons, colourful stories of heroism and national glory and imperial celebrations as relief from the monotony of the school routine. Most important, however, the ideology of imperialism made a direct appeal to working-class youth because it reflected and reinforced a number of its cultural traditions, in particular the street gangs' concern with territorial rivalry, and the assertion of masculinity.[95]

Higher up the social scale, Clement Attlee remembered that at the time of the 1897 jubilee 'most of us boys were imperialists . . . with an immense pride in the achievements of our race'.[96] While his father, as a Gladstonian Liberal, was shocked by the Jameson Raid, 'to us Dr. Jim was a hero'. Empire appealed to 'adventurous and idealistic youth', who were convinced that 'other people were not so good at the game as we were'. Quite apart from this evidence of educational influences, the effects of the patriotic and imperial approach to the teaching of history and geography can be understood only in the context of the transmission of the dominant ideology through all the other media examined in this book. In every case the message was a highly simplified one, of racial and cultural superiority, breeding a sense of self-satisfaction only rudely shattered in the most recent decades.

NOTES

1 Valerie E. Chancellor, *History for their Masters*, London, 1970.
2 James Welton, *Principles and Methods of Teaching*, London, 1924, 283-4.
3 Trevor Reese, *Royal Commonwealth Society*, 84.
4 J. S. Hurt, *Elementary Schooling and the Working Classes, 1860-1918*, London, 1979, 31 and 180.
5 J. R. Seeley, *The Expansion of England*, London, 1883, 293-309.
6 Welton, *Principles*, 283-4.
7 Chancellor, *History*, 33-4.
8 James Hewitt, *Geography of the British Colonies and Dependencies*, London, n.d. The earliest edition appears to have been published before 1869; it was brought up to date by the Rev. Canon Daniel after 1887.
9 William Francis Collier, *History of the British Empire*, London, 1880 (first published

1869). This was described as 'suitable for preparation for papers for Military and Civil service examinations', so it was not a school text.

10 William C. Pearce and Samuel Hague, *Analysis of English History*, London, 1878, (19th edition).

11 Pearce, *Analysis*, 168.

12 Collins, *Fourth Book of Lessons for the Use of Schools*, Glasgow, 1870.

13 Nelson, *The World at Home*, London, 1885.

14 Joseph H. Cowham, *A New School Method* (Complete), London, 1900, 342.

15 Welton, *Principles*, 225.

16 R. L. Archer, *The Teaching of History in Elementary Schools*, London, 1916, 3.

17 *Handbook of Suggestions for the Consideration of Teachers and Others concerned with the Work of Public Elementary Schools*, Board of Education, H.M.S.O., 1927.

18 Archer, *Teaching of History*, 245.

19 Catherine B. Firth, *The Learning of History in Elementary Schools*, London, 1932, 208.

20 C. F. Strong, *Today through Yesterday*, London, 1935, v.

21 Strong, *Today*, 20, 170-7.

22 Chancellor, *History*, 46.

23 Peter Burroughs, 'John R. Seeley and British imperial history', *Journal of Imperial and Commonwealth History*, 1, (1972-73), 192.

24 G. A. Rein, *Sir John Robert Seeley: A Study of the Historian*, ed. and trans John L. Herkless, Dover, N.H., 1983.

25 This advert appeared at the back of C. P. Lucas, *The British Empire*, London, 1915.

26 H. John Field, *Toward a Programme of Imperial Life*, Oxford, 1982, 78.

27 Roberts, *Classic Slum*, 142.

28 H.M.S.O. Handbook, 1927, 139. Pupils should be taught to admire such personalities as the Lawrences, Nicholson, Havelock, and Outram (133).

29 H.M.S.O. Handbook, 121.

30 E. J. Boog-Watson and J. I. Carruthers, Oxford Junior Series, *Stories of Great People, Stories of Great Deeds*, Senior Series, *Building the Empire*, 1949. Boog-Watson and Carruthers published a *Teacher's Companion* to accompany these texts. It recommended a strongly late nineteenth-century approach to history teaching.

31 Archer, *Teaching of History*, 127. So popular was Steevens that a special school edition of *With Kitchener to Khartoum* was published in 1925.

32 Chancellor, *History*, 73-4.

33 Cowham, *School Method*, 340-8.

34 Edward Salmon, *The Story of the Empire*, London, 1902, new edition, 1911. See pp. 154, 164.

35 C. R. L. Fletcher and R. Kipling, *A School History of England*, Oxford, 1911. Kingsley Fairbridge used to read this book daily to his boy emigrant charges at his farm school at Pinjarra, Western Australia. Wagner, *Children*, 197.

36 Fletcher and Kipling, *History*, 162.

37 Humphries, 'Hurrah for England', 183.

38 Rear Admiral Ronald A. Hopwood, General Secretary, the Navy League, to Chairman of Education Committees, September 1919, and enclosed Navy League leaflets. Lancaster Judges' Lodging Collection.

39 Board of Education circular on the War Savings Movement, No. 1133, 10 October 1919.

40 All the following examples of school wall-hangings are taken from the collections of the Judges' Lodging, Lancaster.

41 Fletcher and Kipling, *History*, 21. The Irish problem, they went on, stemmed from the fact that the Irish had never been conquered by the Romans. As a result, they had 'never gone to school' and had remained like 'spoilt children' ever since.

42 A. J. Herbertson, *The Junior Geography*, the Oxford Geographies, VII, Oxford, 1905, 232.

43 Nelson, *The World and its People*, London, n.d.

44 Fletcher and Kipling, *History*, 240.

45 Nelson, *The World*, 237-8.

46 Chambers's Geographical Readers of the Continents, *Africa and Australasia*, 1904, 30.

47 Nelson, *The World*, 297.
48 Chambers's Geographical Readers, *Africa*, 55.
49 Nelson, *The World*, 135 and 206.
50 Nelson, *The World*, 240-1.
51 Chambers's Geographical Readers, *Africa*, 30.
52 Nelson, *The World*, 411. By 1924 the Maoris had achieved their position as one of the most favoured of the indigenous peoples of the Empire. C. F. Bosworth, Cambridge Geographical Readers, *The British Empire*, 1924, 121-2.
53 A. J. Herbertson, *Man and his Work*, London, 1902, 1-2. This text, 'an introduction to Human Geography', reached its fourth edition in 1920 and remained in use in schools for several decades.
54 Hewitt, *Geography*, 10.
55 J. M. D. Meiklejohn, *The British Empire*, London, 1891, 169. This reached its fifth edition in 1899, and was issued as a paperback in an abridged version in 1897 (price 6d). In 1907 it reappeared as *A New History of England and Greater Britain*. See also Longmans Geography Series, *The World for Senior Students*, London, 1907.
56 Welton, *Principles*, 306.
57 Welton, *Principles*, 303.
58 There is a good example in the Judges' Lodging collection. I am grateful to Rachel Hasted for information about this.
59 Meiklehohn, *British Empire*, 1891, introductory quotations.
60 Meiklejohn, *British Empire*, 331-6.
61 Fletcher and Kipling, *History*, 235-6. This poem was recommended for use in schools in the 1940s in Boog-Watson and Carruthers, *Teachers' Companion*, 147. It also appeared in *Princess Mary's Gift Book* in 1914.
62 Roberts, *Classic Slum*, 143.
63 Fred Willis, *101 Jubilee Road, London, S.E.*, London, 1948, 76-7.
64 Bosworth, *The British Empire*, 1924.
65 Bosworth, *British Empire*, 17.
66 Bosworth, *British Empire*, 3. Oceans do not separate, but unite, wrote Bosworth, and this notion that a seaborne empire could be stronger than a landward one like Russia continued to appear in texts until the 1940s.
67 Ian M. Drummond, *British Economic Policy and the Empire, 1919-1939*, London, 1972. Stephen Constantine, *The Making of British Colonial Development Policy, 1914-1940*, forthcoming.
68 Welton, *Principles*, 309, and several other textbooks.
69 H.M.S.O. Handbook, 153.
70 Catherine B. Firth, *History*, Senior Course, Book One, *The Growth of the British Empire*, by Elsa Nunn, 1932, 11.
71 Robert M. Rayner, *A History of England*, III, *1784-1930*, London, 1931, 401, and Firth, *The Learning of History*, 203-4. Geography texts continued to carry emigration propaganda after both both world wars. Bosworth, *British Empire*, 2.
72 A. J. Herbertson, *Preliminary Geography*, Oxford, 1901, 1.
73 Firth, *Learning History*, 171.
74 Nunn, *Growth*, 12.
75 *B.B.C. Year-Book*, 1932, 167.
76 *B.B.C. Year-Book*, 1931, 234.
77 Muriel Masefield, *The House of History*, London, 1931.
78 I. Tenen, *This England*, Macmillan Junior Histories, London, 1939.
79 Joseph H. Stembridge, *The World: a General Regional Geography*, London, 1939.
80 B. I. Magraw, *The Thrill of History*, 4 vols., 7th impression, 1959.
81 G. W. Southgate, *An Introduction to English History*, Books I-III, London, 1947.
82 Masefield, *House*, Third Storey, 58.
83 Tenen, *This England*, 132, 270-3.
84 Magraw, *Thrill*, Book 4, 97-102.
85 Magraw, *Thrill*, Book 3, 106.
86 Masefield, *House*, Third Storey, 262.
87 Masefield, *House*, Third Storey, 326.

88 Southgate, *Introduction*, Book III, 310.
89 Southgate, *Introduction*, Book III, 311.
90 Max Beloff (ed.), *History, Mankind and his Story*, London, 1948, 264.
91 Stembridge, *The World*, 278.
92 Stembridge, *The World*, 347-8.
93 *The Listener*, 6 January, 1983, 10.
94 Lancaster, Judges' Lodging collection.
95 Stephen Humphries, *Hooligans or Rebels?* Oxford, 1981, 41.
96 Earl Attlee, *Empire into Commonwealth*, London, 1961, 3, 5, 7.

The search for an improving juvenile literature demonstrates perhaps better than any other field the manner in which the core ideology of imperialism solved the many problems which had been identified during the nineteenth century. Anxieties about the extension of literacy and the provision of a distinctively juvenile literature, both in books and in periodicals, were resolved by the development of the adventure tradition, replete with militarism and patriotism, in which violence and high spirits became legitimated as part of the moral force of a superior race. The public school ethos, embracing athleticism and chauvinism, was disseminated through these works to classes who would never enjoy such an education. By the 1880s adult opinion, politicians and social reformers, clerics and missionaries, parents and schoolmasters, found this tradition entirely acceptable, and fostered its growth by plying the young with its by then manifold products.

The recognition that literacy might prove to be a two-edged sword came first in the late eighteenth century, and societies were founded to deliver improving material into the hands of the newly literate, particularly the young. During the first half of the nineteenth, however, the success of these activities was limited, partly because the publications were too heavy-handed in their didacticism, partly because rival publishing attractions continued to secure an avid readership. From the middle of the century the purveyors of an improving literature began to attempt a new approach, to convey their morality in more appealing secular forms. At the same time, the morality itself began to change. The emphasis moved away from faith to works, from submission to improvement, self-help, aggressive individualism. By the 1880s that new morality had come to be wedded to the late nineteenth-century world view and was suffused with the patriotic, racial, and militarist elements which together made up the new popular imperialism. This occurred just as the revolutionary expansion of publishing and popular readership began to take place. The result was the creation of a well tested mould of popular juvenile literature which continued to form the products of this very considerable market until the 1950s.

These developments can be fully understood only in the perspective of a century and a half. It is a perspective that has been missed because so many studies of juvenile literature have been limited to the hugely popular juvenile journals of the late nineteenth century and the few better-known adventure writers of that period, in other words to the so-called 'golden age' from the 1880s to 1914. In this chapter an attempt will be made to examine the tradition through to the mid-twentieth century, and the sources will be extended to embrace the popular biographies of military, imperial, and missionary figures, the ubiquitous 'books of heroes', and the 'annuals' put out by so many publishers eager to tap the rapidly expanding market for prizes and presents.

Anxieties about the dangers of a developing literacy emerged in the 1790s. Evangelical Christianity regarded literacy as a vital key to faith, but recognised that it could be a dangerous tool in the hands of the working class.[1] In consequence, the Sunday school movement, which had its origins in that period, embarked on the publication of reading matter which might direct and control the reading habits of the newly literate. These publishing activities demonstrated the self-confidence of a movement which grew with extraordinary speed and reached a remarkable proportion of the population. The 1851 census indicated that 50% of children in the five-to-fifteen age group had some contact with Sunday schools.[2] By 1901 the movement's activities had become important throughout the Empire. In that year there were two million Sunday scholars in Britain and 22 million in the Empire.[3] Evangelical publishing societies, the Society for the Propagation of Christian Knowledge (S.P.C.K.) and the Religious Tract Society (R.T.S.) were founded in the 1790s and set about publishing tracts, penny histories, little books of heroes, children's stories, and Sunday magazines in order to control the much-feared spread of insubordination, irreligion and revolutionary activity. By 1818 25 million tracts had been published.[4] In 1819 *Youth's Magazine* appeared, followed in 1824 by *Children's Friend*. These efforts tended to be heavy-handed improving tales, in which the somewhat macabre genre of pious children's deaths was prominent. It may well be, however, that the latter did more to contribute to the contemporary fascination with the ghoulish than to frighten children into Christian concepts of goodness or efforts to save their souls.

The evangelical societies used the normal outlets of the time to disseminate their wares — itinerant traders, street ballad sellers and the like — and, despite the great volume of tracts produced, it must be suspected that their output was swamped by the other temptations such traders had on offer. At any rate, the reading public was only too ready for the 'penny dreadful' craze when it came, and the provision of a proper improving literature for the young continued to be a much-discussed problem through the middle period of the century.

[200]

The 'penny dreadfuls', recounting tales of Gothic horror and criminal 'heroism', enjoyed their boom period between the 1830s and the 1880s.[5] They highlighted historical and contemporary criminals, smugglers, pirates, highwaymen, and murderers, as well as extolling the tradition of rough, rebellious-spirited youths resisting authority. The symbols of order, employers, teachers, the police, were held up to ridicule or depicted as oppressive tyrants. It is an interesting fact that the heyday of the penny dreadful coincides precisely with the period, from the 1850s, when public school headmasters attempted to control their unruly charges through organised sport.[6] Clearly there was much implicit class dissent in penny dreadful tales, and they could therefore be converted into an explicitly political instrument. G. W. M. Reynolds, the founder of *Reynolds' Weekly Newspaper*, wrote penny dreadfuls with a Chartist message.[7] The influence of the penny dreadful seems to have excited almost as much concern among the middle class as television today, and studies of their effects were instituted which have a familiar ring. Research was conducted in prisons into the influence of popular literature on the criminal mind. A variety of leading figures and institutions turned their attention to the problem of making more satisfactory provision for the young. Various societies were founded, like the Society for the Propagation of Useful Knowledge and the Pure Literature Society. Lord Shaftesbury was a patron of the latter, and on one occasion addressed the R.T.S. on the dangers of sensational literature.[8] A succession of articles on children's literature appeared in the great journals of the time, the *Contemporary Review*, the *Fortnightly Review*, and *Nineteenth Century*, including several by the young Edward Salmon, later to become such an influential imperial propagandist as editor of *United Empire* and author of imperial textbooks.[9] However, by the time Salmon was writing, in 1886, the problem was already close to solution. It was, in fact, the expansion of penny dreadfuls from the adult to the juvenile market, and the appearance of weekly 'dreadful' papers for boys, which had provided the clue. *The Bad Boys' Paper*, the *Boys' Standard*, the *Boys' World*, and *Our Boys' Paper*, together with the *Wild Boys of London* series (which was eventually suppressed by the police) were all in the 'dreadful' tradition. But by now a new tradition was growing in popularity, and was poised to take over fully in the 1880s.

J. S. Bratton has identified a shift in publishing styles in the evangelical houses in the 1850s. The R.T.S. published *The Leisure Hour* from 1852 and *Sunday at Home* from 1854. These were much more secular in tone than their predecessors, and announced themselves as desirous of inculcating 'watchwords of patriotism' in their readers. They exhibited a 'stirring, chatty, bustling air... a thrusting optimistic appeal to Smilesian self-confidence and healthy patriotism'.[10] At the same time, commercial publishing was also experimenting with new magazines. S. O. Beeton produced his *Boys' Own Magazine* in 1855, readily acknowledging that it might be considered 'too high, too solid, too good' compared with the dreadfuls. But, he claimed, the higher he pitched the magazine the more readers he secured. Even so, the circulation was no more than 40,000 (his own, probably inflated, claim) in 1862.[11] W. H. G. Kingston, a notable transition figure in the development of imperial children's literature, published his *Magazine for Boys* in 1859, but it swiftly proved a failure, and was absorbed by Beeton. The Rev. J. Erskine Clark published *Chatterbox* in 1866, and this was followed by a succession of publishing ventures which represented the conversion of penny dreadful publishers to this new type of 'improving' journal. E. J. Brett, a former radical, and W. L. Emmett vied with each other in producing new boys' titles over a number of years. They included Brett's *Boys of England* (1866), *Young Men of Great Britain* (1868), *Rovers of the Sea* (1872) and Emmett's *Young Gentleman's Journal* (1867) and *Rover's Log* (1872). These were followed by *Sons of Britannia*, *The Young Briton*, *The Young Englishman* (all Emmett), and *Boys of Empire* (Brett). Other penny dreadful publishers followed suit, with titles like *Boys' Standard* (1875), *Boys' Champion* and *Boys' Leisure Hour*. There was a considerable overlap between all of them and the penny dreadful tradition, but, as the titles imply, more patriotic and imperial, and therefore also historical and military, matter was creeping in. Most used the new marketing techniques of competitions, prizes, illustrations, as well as the usual serial methods of inducing addiction. Few of them, however, gained full parental acceptability, and none aspired to the staggering circulations of the 'new wave' of magazines at the end of the century. Figures like Sir James Barrie, H. G. Wells, and Havelock Ellis admitted to being influenced by them, but their readership probably remained largely middle-class. However, the new breed of fictional heroes and anti-heroes — such as Jack Harkaway and Ching Ching — emerged from them, and in many ways they set the tone for the truly popular journals of the '80s, '90s, and Edwardian era.

They set the tone in another important respect. As the titles indicate, publishers now chose to divide their wares not according to class background or educational attainment, but according to sex. The sharp division between boys' and girls' literature became the norm, providing the opportunity to relate the patriotic-imperial ideology to a sexual stereotype: aggressive, individualistic adventure for the boys, submissive domestic service and child-rearing for the girls. The problem of contact between the sexes, sexual or otherwise, was solved by the simple expedient of separating their worlds, and rendering relations between them a source of embarrassment and tension, or an inspiration to service and defence. The fact that so much of the new fiction was to be set in the separated worlds of the public schools or in military and imperial milieux greatly facilitated the process.

Although patriotic and imperial subjects were becoming more common between the 1850s and 1880s, the full-blown ideology of these journals had not fully emerged until the last two decades of the century. It has been suggested that, in the earlier tales of adventure and warfare, Empire constituted only a 'bizarre backdrop' rather than a fully developed ideological context.[12] That had to await the emergence of a new wave of high-circulation journals from 1879. *Boys of England* had pointed the way, claiming sales of 250,000 in the 1870s, but truly spectacular results were achieved only when the new imperial philosophy penetrated every organ of entertainment, literature, and education. The new wave of journals presented imperial ideas, in all their nationalist, racial, and militarist forms, in adventure stories and historical romances. These journals represented the distinctive late Victorian alliance of Church, State, and military, and succeeded in finding the ingredients which would at the same time turn them into vehicles of the dominant *Zeitgeist* and secure a truly mass, cross-class following through excitements acceptable to Establishment, parents, and children alike. The R.T.S. led the way with the *Boys' Own Paper* in 1879, a journal which had a life span which coincided precisely with the era of the 'new imperialism', expiring only in 1967. Within a few years it claimed a circulation exceeding one million, and had received the endorsement of *Punch*, the critics in the reviews, and, so it claimed, parental approval.[13] It enjoyed a unique editorial continuity, for its first editor, G. A. Hutchinson, continued in office until 1912.

It was swiftly followed by imitators. W. H. G. Kingston founded *Union Jack* in 1880, shortly before his death, and was succeeded as editor by G. A. Henty. It proceeded to marshal some of the best-known boys' and adventure writers of the period, including Jules Verne, Conan Doyle, and R. L. Stevenson, as well as Henty and Kingston themselves. *Union Jack* only survived until 1883, but by the end of the decade the apostles of a popular journalism were active in the juvenile market. Alfred Harmsworth, whose *Answers* (1888) was designed to compete with George Newnes's *Tit Bits* for adult readership, entered the boys' field with *Comic Cuts* (1890) and developed a crusade against the lingering penny dreadfuls with weapons like *Halfpenny Wonder* (1892),

Halfpenny Marvel (1893), *Union Jack* (which survived for forty years), *Pluck* (both 1894), and *The Boys' Friend* (1895, which survived thirty-two years). Newnes responded with *Captain* in 1899, at a time when the Boer War was generating further avid readership for boys' papers. *Boys' War News* appeared for a year, in 1899-1900; *Chums* (founded in 1892) became closely identified with events of the war; and Harmsworth's Amalgamated Press brought out *Boys' Realm* in 1902. (Unusually, the *Boys' Own Paper* was silent on the subject of the Boer War, because of the influence of the Baptists, who opposed it, on the R.T.S.; the magazine lost a great deal of circulation as a result.[14]) Still the market was not satisfied. The *Boys' Herald* appeared in 1903, *Gem* in 1907, *Magnet* in 1908, and (at the height of the naval race) the *Dreadnought* in 1912.

These journals' recipe, approved by parents and children alike, was to blend much of the violence, boisterousness, and cruelty which had poured from the penny dreadfuls with the late nineteenth-century world view. Whereas the dreadfuls had largely internalised crime and conflict in terms of domestic society, the new journals externalised them. The world became a vast adventure playground in which Anglo-Saxon superiority could be repeatedly demonstrated *vis-à-vis* all other races, most of whom were depicted as treacherous and evil. Many of the stories contained grisly description, not just in details of violence, but also in practical hints on the pursuit of blood sports, taxidermy, and the like, but it was acceptable because they could be depicted as necessary adjuncts to the spread of civilisation, Christianity, and Just Rule. Moreover, the journals became explicit disseminators of middle-class values. School stories were always set in public schools, and efforts to depict State schools were invariably judged a failure. Heroism was displayed in middle-class sports (cricket, rugby, hunting) and professions (army and naval officers, missionaries, colonial administrators, and the like). The stories developed cults of super-boys and super-men who succeeded against overwhelming odds. They acted as a barometer of international affairs, responding at once to the high pressure of war and invasion scares. Colonial wars, historical and contemporary, were fought and re-fought; great conflicts like the Boer War and the First World War inevitably came centre-stage; and fantasies of invasion by the French, Russians or Germans haunted their pages. No doubt some of these effusions were a comfort to their adult authors — French, German or Russian invaders turned back by real characters like Roberts and Buller offered a vision of future national heroism — or satisfied yearnings for revenge, as in 1905 when one journal carried a story of a punitive expedition to Russia to avenge the Dogger Bank incident (when the Russian Baltic fleet fired on Hull trawlers).[15] This strongly xenophobic strain infected the detective story craze which burgeoned in the same period. The villains thwarted by Sexton Blake, Nelson Lee, and others, were invariably foreign, their villainy underlined by evil-sounding names, strange accents, and implied racial disabilities.

Scarcely a story appeared which did not carry some form of patriotic message, reverence for royalty and all authority, particularly in its military form. Havelock Ellis wrote of the fever the earlier versions induced in their readers, while Robert Roberts commented upon the extraordinary attraction of middle-class stories and middle-class heroes for his working-class contemporaries in Salford.[16] The Amalgamated Press regarded the boys' journals as

> aimed from the first at the encouragement of physical strength, of patriotism, of interest in travel and exploration, and of pride in our empire. It has been said that the boys' papers of the Amalgamated Press have done more to provide recruits for our Navy and Army and to keep up the esteem of the sister services than anything else.[17]

The Boer War stimulated a direct connection between boys' literature and the patriotic association. Howard Spicer, who published *Boys of our Empire* between 1900 and 1903, founded the Boys' Empire League (Bs'.E.L.).[18] It was designed to be an imperialist boys' movement dedicated to ideals of patriotism and Christian manliness. Spicer intended it to be, like the *Daily Mail*, the 'embodiment and mouthpiece of the imperial idea', which would be supported by a series of British Empire League pamphlets. The Bs'.E.L. soon claimed 10,000 members, under the presidency of Conan Doyle, with Lord Strathcona, Hector Macdonald and other imperial figures as 'guardians'. The members were taken on patriotic visits, subjected to imperial lectures and sermons, and were expected to develop an interest in, and collect information about, one particular colony. No doubt this was intended to encourage emigration, and indeed there was much emigration propaganda in the juvenile journals.[19] Sometimes it took the form of stories about young emigrant heroes, sometimes factual (if often highly romanticised) accounts of emigration and western backwoodsmanship. In these ways the journal brought together colonial war and colonial settlement in a manner to be later characterised as 'war scouting' and 'peace scouting' in Baden-Powell's *Scouting for Boys* (see chapter 9).

The Boys' Empire League developed the well tried marketing technique of the competition to further its emigration propaganda. Soon after its foundation, it sponsored a contest in *Boys of our Empire*, entitled 'A Free Start out West'.[20] The competitors were expected to answer questions on the history, geography, resources and constitution of Canada. Sir George Parkin, principal of Upper Canada College and a patron of the League, judged the entries, and the most successful candidates followed Peacock's *Canada, a Descriptive Textbook* (which had been commissioned by the Canadian Department of the Interior in 1899) in stressing the egalitarian, utopian, and romantically western aspects of Canadian life. The idea was later followed by the Agent General for South Australia, who offered a similar prize for an Australian competition, also organised through the Bs'.E.L. in the pages of *Boys of our Empire*. Unfortunately Canadian propaganda had been so effective that the winner used his prize to emigrate to Canada instead.

Neither the Bs'.E.L. nor *Boys of our Empire* long survived the Boer War, but the former merged with the Boys' Life Brigade, and the latter was absorbed by *Young England*, published by the Sunday School Union. By this time the penny dreadful was effectively dead. The new journals had, in Patrick Dunae's words, acceptably reorientated youthful aggression: 'The themes expressed in the old dreadfuls had been tamed, politicised, and re-directed to serve the needs of empire'.[21] But of course the journals had not been alone in this. The decline in the unit costs of printing had facilitated the appearance of a vast range of books for the juvenile market. If some of the journals could claim a circulation in excess of a million a week (which always suggests a much wider *readership*), the books of the most popular boys' writers often sold more than 150,000 a year. It has been suggested that this juvenile market accounted for at least a quarter of the entire publishing industry.

Whereas the penny and halfpenny journals were bought and exchanged by the young people at whom they were directed, books were designed primarily to be given as prizes or as presents by adults anxious to form their reading habits. The prize system, which came to be such an important means of distributing books at the end of the century, had a long pedigree in the 'rewards' techniques of the Sunday schools and the National schools.[22] The evangelical publishing houses had of course been the main source of such rewards in the past, and purely religious works, Bibles, prayer books, tracts and the like were the staple fare in the first half of the century. From the middle of the century, juvenile fiction came to be acceptable, and by the 1870s it was virtually the norm. The National schools, the school boards set up under the 1870 Act, Sunday schools, and other agencies were all distributing prizes of this sort by the end of the century. A wider readership was reached through the lending libraries of Sunday schools, Board schools, and local authorities.

The works of W. H. G. Kingston, R. M. Ballantyne, R. L. Stevenson, G. A. Henty, Manville Fenn, F. S. Brereton, Gordon Stables, and the many lesser luminaries who imitated them all shared and developed certain common characteristics. The schoolboy hero was central to all their works, and they prompted their readers to identify with him. Many of them approached the ideology of the present through the medium of historical romance. All celebrated self-reliance and individualism, competing now not with other classes in their own society but with other races and nationalities in a world-wide context. Boy heroes were invariably placed in the setting of great contemporary or historical events, thereby personalising details of colonial wars and imperial expansion. Morality came to have both a class and racial dimension, for integrity, courage, loyalty (all subsumed under the concept of 'character') were generally identified with a particular type of public-school, middle-class, sporting, and of course Nordic, ideal. For such heroes war was, as Seeley had argued in *The Expansion of England*, a purifying experience, heightening contemporary moralities in making huge demands upon bravery, physical endurance, group loyalty, and ultimately patriotic self-sacrifice. There is even evidence that W. H. G. Kingston, who had written in a much more evangelical vein in the middle of the century, elaborated the military aspects of his stories in later editions in order to follow the new fashion.[23] And of course, since way lay at the centre of so much of this writing, it was inevitable that it should be a male-dominated world.

Such an approach to war was perhaps only possible in a century entirely free, after 1815, of any experience of 'total war'. Apart from the relatively remote Crimea, wars became generally brief colonial excursions, in which the horrors of killing and the unheroic aspects of death were masked by the relatively low level of white casualties and the fact that the enemy were of another, often despised, race. A fearless foe might be admired, like an animal which bravely resisted the hunt, but non-European deaths were considered lightly. By the last decade of the century Social Darwinian precepts ensured that the destruction and elimination of 'inferior peoples' could be predicted, described, and condoned. Hence the warfare that accelerated the process was not destructive, but an evolutionary imperative. With races and nationalities that could not be expected to disappear, such as the Bantu-speaking and most oriental peoples, warfare's constructive end was in spreading 'civilisation' and implanting through subordination and discipline faint traces of the character traits so admired in the dominant racial and class paradigm.

Most of the boys' writers had experience of colonial life or of warfare and war reporting. W. H. G. Kingston was editor of a journal called *The Colonist* and author of a manual entitled *How to Emigrate*. R. M. Ballantyne worked for the Hudson's Bay Company in northern Canada. R. L. Stevenson's personal myth was greatly enhanced by his later years and death in Samoa. G. A. Henty had been a war correspondent, covering campaigns from Russian central Asia to West Africa, and in 1885 he became editor of the *United Services Gazette*. G. W. Steevens, seeking to turn a brilliant academic record into a career where he could influence his contemporaries, also chose journalism and in particular war reporting. Many of the later school of adventure writers had been in South Africa and found the wars of 1879-81 and 1899-1902 a formative experience which they turned to propagandist account. Rider Haggard arrived in 1875 in time to be caught up in the 1877 annexation of the Transvaal. Edgar Wallace was the South African correspondent of Reuter's and of the *Daily Mail*. Conan Doyle went out in 1899 as senior physician. John Buchan was assistant private secretary to Milner. Several of them sought to combine a professional career, the writing of propagandist fiction, with political activities through which they could more directly apply their ideology to contemporary events. Several stood for Parliament, demonstrating the manner in which imperialist ideology transcended political affiliation, since there were both Conservatives and Liberals among them.

The names of all these writers, with rare exceptions, appeared in the many juvenile journals of the day as well as on the spines of books, and as participants in contemporary events. It was this range of activity, as both doers and reporters, exemplars and propagandists, that made them such fascinating figures, epitomising the ubiquitous energies of a master people. Like the journals of the Amalgamated Press, they acted as recruiters, not just to the army and the navy, but also to the nationalist and patriotic ideals, inseparably intertwined with imperialism, which the armed forces were dedicated to protect. They derived their common allegiance from related sets of dominant influences, the great public schools, a few influential academics at Oxford and Cambridge, powerful publishers, and the new enlightened despotism of the imperial proconsuls, and they clustered around influential and symbolic personalities like Oscar Browning, Alfred Harmsworth, W. T. Stead, Alfred Milner, and W. E. Henley, who dedicated his *National Observer* to the creation of democratic popular support for imperialism. Some, it is true, were 'outsiders', but they gained success by aping and propagating those same schools (both literally and figuratively) of thought and action.

A number of developments lay behind this emergence of a successful juvenile fiction at the end of the century. The nautical adventure tales of Captain Marryat, the location of heroism in the life of the average Englishman in Kingsley's *Westward Ho!* (1855), and the central position of the school in *Tom Brown's Schooldays* (1857), were the early models on which a simple, direct adventure fiction was based by the 1880s. Its appearance was facilitated by the rise of publishers like Blackie, Nelson, and Macmillan, specialising in this kind of literature, and by the convergence of interests which developed between these commercial houses and the evangelical publishing societies. W. H. G. Kingston stands in many ways as the pioneering figure, linking developments in serious fiction with the new juvenile tradition, as well as evangelical purpose to commercial enterprise. But it was his misfortune to be writing before the popularity of such material had fully developed, although his boys' books continued to be published after his death in 1880. His works (and he published over 100 books for boys between 1850 and 1880) were firmly rooted in his particular concern with emigration, in which he was active as a propagandist in the 1840s.[24] He took notions of 'improvement' into the colonies of settlement, and located the Englishman's opportunities there, in exploration, conquest, sport, missionary activity, and settlement. He set out to fuse Christian and imperial beliefs, attempting to create a single ideology of evangelical action and material success. But his message was too complex to be widely assimilated, and it pre-dated the imperial events of the last two decades of the century, which enabled boys' writers to exploit lurid and violent deeds to the full.

The process of simplifying Kingston's message was really begun by his somewhat younger contemporary, R. M. Ballantyne.[25] Ballantyne declared himself to have been called to write morally uplifting boys' books as a divine vocation, and a didactic tone persisted in them, but his stories were briefer and altogether faster-moving than those of his predecessors. He developed the tradition of gory description of the hunt, a characteristically central aspect of late nineteenth-century writing, and he created a fantasy world of 'daring action, triumph, and adventure'.[26] Like Kingston, he was involved in emigration movements, particularly children's emigration schemes. Like Kingston too, he wrote travel books, and blended fact and fiction in a manner which was to become standard by the end of the century.

No one achieved that blend more successfully than Henty. In his

[209]

writing the military tradition overwhelmed the evangelical purpose of predecessors like Kingston and Ballantyne. A great deal of attention has rightly been lavished on Henty, for no other writer matched his output, his sales, or his influence.[27] Son of the owner of a coal mine and ironworks in Wales, he devoted his life (rather like Cecil Rhodes) to compensating for a sickly childhood. He attended Westminster School, and developed his health and strength by boxing. Both school and sport were to figure strongly in the making of all his boy heroes. Before he began to write boys' stories, however, he had visited the Crimea, become a purveyor to the forces, and, as a war correspondent, witnessed most of the conflicts of the period, including the Austro-Italian war of 1861, the Abyssinian campaign of 1867, the Franco-Prussian War of 1871-72, the Siege of Khiva in the Russo-Turcoman war of 1873, the Ashanti War of 1873-74, the Carlist insurrection of 1874 in Spain, and the Turco-Serbian war of 1876. He was present at the opening of the Suez Canal in 1869, was a spectator of the Paris Commune, and accompanied the Prince of Wales to India in 1875. He knew Garibaldi and was a friend of Sir Garnet Wolseley. He had observed, in other words, many of the most important events of the age, and had come into contact with several of its leading personalities. He edited the *Union Jack* between 1880 and 1883, contributed to Beeton's *Boy's Own Magazine* 1888-1890 and the *Every Boy's Annual* of 1886, and founded another annual, *Camps and Quarters*, in 1889.

He was best known, however, for his full-length boys' stories. He published some eighty-two, of which more than a third can be regarded as being about the British Empire or loosely about imperial ideology. A similar proportion chart imperial events in British history, and demonstrate, as Seeley would have wished, the important elements that went into the rise of the imperial race. It is noticeable that imperial themes became more prominent towards the end of his career, not surprisingly perhaps, in view of the weight of events in the 1890s, culminating in the Sudan campaign, the Ashanti War, and the Boer War, which rounded off his life. Henty's Empire was the Empire of the soldier rather than the administrator or the missionary, and his racial and militarist views had hardened by the time of his last imperial works. His boy heroes, who participate in the great events of the age, are middle-class competitive stereotypes. They have been described as garrulous prigs, paragons of gentility, devoted to boxing, improvement, and money-making.[28] They invariably express upper middle-class disdain for the values of the lower middle class. Clerks are frequently objects of derision, yet his works were read by large numbers of clerks and other members of the lower middle class.

The snobbery and search for fame, money, and position of his leading characters clearly stimulated a desire to emulate them among Henty's readership.

Henty's racial ideas were merely an expression in heightened form of the principal, and oft-repeated, racial notions of the late nineteenth century. He was antisemitic. He condemned miscegenation. And he considered blacks unfit to govern themselves (a theme he explored in his examination of the Haiti revolt in *A Roving Commission*). References to the childlike nature of Africans abound, just as they do in a host of missionary works and school texts of the period.[29] Moreover, Henty propagated to a wider public the climatic determinism of the nineteenth century, concepts of tropical abundance and tropical indolence, which were, so the argument ran, the prime cause of the laziness of African and Asian peoples.[30] Many of his stories are concerned to contrast the vigour, energy, self-reliance, and ambition of Anglo-Saxon heroes with the lethargy, fatalism, and lack of competitive individualism of other peoples. (Such ideas were still being instilled into settler children in Africa in the 1950s.) Not all the butts of Henty's racial distaste were black or brown. He despised the easy racial tolerance, including sexual tolerance, of Latin peoples, but he reserved his greatest vituperation for the Boers. By the end of his life, imperial exploits constituted in his writings a sequence of acts of revenge by a righteous and wronged people. Thus Omdurman avenged Gordon's death; the Ashanti campaign assuaged past near-humiliations; and the Boer War expunged the follies that had succeeded the disgrace of Majuba Hill in 1881, an event which, it is said, caused Henty to cry.

If occasionally he portrayed African and Asian peoples in a favourable light, he was still giving popular currency to dominant contemporary ideas. He reserved an admiration for 'martial races' who had the guts and energy to resist imperial rule, and the even greater good sense to act as its auxiliaries after their defeat. The individuals who are admired are invariably chiefs, kings, or princes. Henty transferred his snobbism of rank, and his delineation of moral purpose and physical prowess as attributes of a particular social class, to non-European peoples. The faithful servant stereotype, so common in many works, represented the acceptable face of colonial races, since such figures sought to ape their masters, and were capable of remarkable displays of trust and loyalty. In every case, mental capacity was a devalued attribute. Like his contemporaries, Henty had little regard for intellectual abilities, which served only to inhibit purposeful action in sowing self-doubt and sapping moral and physical self-confidence.

In all these respects he was of course entirely unoriginal. He merely dressed up the attitudes of the age in tales of adventure-with-a-purpose, campaigns and deeds connected with State-building and empire-forming. The same ideas can be found in all the children's literature of the period. Dunae has identified a number of approaches to race in the juvenile journals.[31] All such material peddled the concept of a racial evolutionary hierarchy, with the aborigines at the bottom, and other peoples in an ascending scale to the Anglo-Saxons at the top. In the earlier period (1850s-1870s), African and Asian peoples principally constituted threatening or comic background (precisely the role that the working class had often filled earlier in plays and other works). By the end of the century the alleged failings of other races are much more sharply distinguished. They are gluttons, who look alike, and whose main, and risible, inclination is to imitate their betters. They are sunk in witchcraft, fetishism, and superstition, and were therefore ripe for missionary treatment. The missionary societies themselves promoted such views, and some of them, notably the R.T.S. and the S.P.C.K. were active in this kind of publishing for boys (the S.P.C.K. published some of Henty's short stories). It was this mix of racial attitudes which led both Henty and Stables to condone slavery, and express sympathy with the South in the American Civil War.

Juvenile literature reflected shifts in attitudes to specific races as much as it charted the progress of imperial events. The Chinese, for example, moved from a position of relative respect, still evident in the 1870s and 1880s, to one of abhorrence at the beginning of the twentieth century. Inevitably, the Boxer rising was the crucial turning-point. Violent resistance to civilisation was always the snake by which a people could slide down the racial scale. Even before the rising, the Chinese had been depicted as brutal and benighted, or as buffoons who perpetrated ludicrous social customs like feet-binding. The Boxers transformed the Chinese into a Yellow Peril, a source of evil genii against whom Anglo-Saxon supermen could pit their wits in the succeeding decades. With few peoples was it necessary to put racial images so swiftly into reverse. The noble Japanese, successful imitators of Western civilisation, a people whose samurai warrior caste and bushido law could be held up by Baden-Powell as worthy of emulation by his Scouts, turned the Chinese in the 1930s into hapless victims, led by a new order of civilised Christians, the Kuomintang elite.[32] Views of the Japanese, or course, underwent a corresponding somersault. If the 1857 'Mutiny' had been to Indians what the Boxer rising was to the Chinese, by the late nineteenth century its effects seem to have worn off. By that time British self-confidence in the sub-continent had turned the juvenile literary image of Indians into a loyal race, supplying great armies of domestic servants and splendidly attired regiments for the British military pantheon. Nevertheless, late Victorian and Edwardian children were still regaled with stories of sati and thuggee, and the 'Mutiny' incidents, as well as accounts of Afghan wars and North West Frontier exploits, remained staple fare of school texts as well as of fictional works.

Another layer of popular publishing lies beneath this much mined seam of popular children's fiction. Many of Henty's titles reflected contemporary hero-worship: in them the names of imperial and military heroes stood forth like totems identifying the milieu and the allegiances of the contents of the books. Such hero-worship was pursued in other ways too. As in so many other respects, the evangelical houses had shown the way. Penny histories of heroes had been part of the tractarian publishing activity of the early nineteenth century, and the S.P.C.K. had repeatedly issued lives of Nelson, Mungo Park, and other celebrated figures. By the end of the century such 'hero publishing' had become a considerable industry. There were several popular series of biographies of military, imperial, and missionary figures, highly condensed lives, some of them suitable for juvenile consumption. They often shared publishers' lists with imperial works, the popularity of which was illustrated by, or perhaps ensured by, cheap imprints. Churchill's *Malakand Field Force*, Durand's *Making of a Frontier*, Grogan's *Cape to Cairo*, G. W. Steevens's *With Kitchener to Khartoum* (no doubt a conscious copying of Henty's titles), and Edmund Candler's *The Unveiling of Lhasa* rubbed boards in the Dent Everyman's Library with lives of great imperial personalities like Sir John Nicholson. Nelson had their own cheap series of imperial lives; Clarendon issued (for a mainly adult audience) its Rulers of India series; and imperial figures predominated in Macmillan's English Men of Action. Some of these retailed remarkably cheaply. Collins's Wide World Library, for example, sold for 7*d* (just over 2½p) per volume. It included such titles as *With Stephenson in Samoa*, *The Life of Baden-Powell*, *Uganda to Khartoum*, *Life of Lord Kitchener*, and the *Life of Lord Beaconsfield* (but none of Gladstone), and the *Life of Lord Strathcona*. Central figures like Gordon and Livingstone were the subjects of multiple biographies, many of them anonymous, as a range of publishers attempted to secure part of the prime prize and present market.

In addition to single biographies, there were many books of heroes. One, published in 1884, opened with the obligatory Gordon, and left him gallantly holding on in Khartoum with the eyes of the world upon him.[33] Longman published *The Red Book of Heroes*; Frederick Warne had *The Pictorial Treasury of Famous Men and Famous Deeds*;

Heinemann offered *British Soldier Heroes* and *British Sailor Heroes*, each in two volumes at 1s 6d (7½p); T. C. and E. C. Jack produced The Children's Heroes' series of biographies at 1s each; while the R.T.S. published *Brave Sons of Empire*. With only slight variants, these lists of heroes invariably included Raleigh, Drake, Cromwell, Gordon, Cook, Livingstone, Chalmers of New Guinea, Speke, Stanley, Bishop Patteson, Anson, Burke and Wills, and heroes of the Indian Mutiny. The National Sunday School Union had its 'Splendid Lives', economically printed on cheap paper to secure maximum circulation. Rather larger ventures included Cassell's *Heroes of Britain in Peace and War* in two volumes;[34] Marcus Ward issued a series of 'Heroes of Discovery' in 1877; Blackie published Sir Harry Johnston's 'Pioneer Library' of pioneers in West Africa, India, South Africa, Canada, and Australia. T. Fisher Unwin's 'Stories of the Nations' published in the late 1890s, had a strongly imperial tone. Each highly publicised imperial campaign was followed by a wave of publications in much the same way as the Falklands War became a publishing event in 1982. The Boxer rising is a perfect instance, because, despite the fact that it coincided with the Ashanti War and the Boer War, it produced a number of children's stories, biographies of leading participants, and tales of missionary heroism. At least one of the latter went through nine editions, and was continually in print until the 1930s, reaching a print figure which would place it today in the category of best-sellers.[35] The death of a major figure produced a crop of popular biographies. Soon after the death of Lord Roberts at the outbreak of the First World War, A. J. Costain published *Lord Roberts: his Life-Story for Boys* (1915). It was, significantly, dedicated to 'the fourth form'.

The continuity of these publishing activities is well represented by Collins's 'Brief Lives'. Andre Maurois's *Cecil Rhodes* appeared in this series in 1953, and was indistinguishable from the many hagiographical biographies of the arch-imperialist published in the Edwardian period and the 1920s. Lionel Curtis's *With Milner in South Africa*, published as late as 1951, offered an intriguing echo of the titles of Henty, Steevens, and many others.

It may be that none of the biographies or books of heroes enjoyed the popularity of a Henty or a Ballantyne, but they often ran to several editions, and seem to have been distributed widely (if surviving bookplates and inscriptions are any guide) as Sunday school and day school prizes, or as presents from improving maiden aunts. It is a form of distribution which may well have diminished their attraction to their readership, but covers, pictures, and titles adequately conveyed their message. Moreover, children were encouraged to participate in hero-worship at school and through competitions. When the *Girls' Own Paper* (founded in 1880) asked for biographical notes on one hundred famous men in 1884 they received almost 5,000 entries.[36] In 1885, the *Boys' Own Paper* was active in raising money for the General Gordon fund.

Almost as common as the lives of heroes were series which included 'Romance' in their titles. The 'Romance of Empire' series of T. C. & E. C. Jack included works on Canada, Australia, New Zealand, India, South Africa, West Africa, and 'The Outposts of Empire'.[37] The same publisher brought out H. E. Marshall's 'Our Empire Story' series, histories of the various territories for boys and girls at 1s 6d each. George Newnes, a publisher very active in royal and patriotic subjects, brought out the lavishly illustrated *Outlines of the British Empire* by the indefatigable Sir Harry Johnston. Judging by publishers' advertisements, all these were extensively reviewed in the national press. Jack particularly highlighted their children's Empire series, together with their volumes of 'Children's Heroes', in their special catalogue, 'Books for Prizes'. Seeley Service had a complete Library of Romance, including *The Romance of Modern Pathfinders, The Romance of Savage Life*, of *Missionary Heroism*, of *Missionary Pioneers*, of *Modern Exploration*, of *War Inventions*, and of *Modern Mining*. Most of these works, no less than the popular biographies and the books of heroes, featured individual lives, many of which fitted perfectly into the Samuel Smiles tradition, for nothing better pleased their writers than the opportunity to recount stories of relatively simple origins transformed by self-reliance, courage, or piety, and the mystic ingredient 'character', into exemplary heroism, or great wealth and power. Livingstone perfectly fitted the first category, Donald Alexander Smith, Lord Strathcona, the second. Others, lacking humble birth, could be depicted as upholding family tradition and honour, or rescuing a family from social or financial ignominy.

Another striking characteristic of the late Victorian and Edwardian ages is the popularity of poetry, a poetry of romance, patriotism, and war. Tennyson turned his hand to imperial war ballads in the 1880s, as well as poeticising on the great imperial events of his time. His successors as poet laureate developed the imperial theme, although the imperial ideology became cruder as the quality of the poetry declined. Kipling demonstrated that poetry of high quality could sell in large quantities, and for a period his various collections of poems enjoyed a voguish, though perhaps largely adult, popularity throughout the world.[38] But it was perhaps Sir Henry Newbolt who gave the imperial idea its supreme poetic expression for the young. His first volume of poems appeared in 1897, and his career subsequently brought him into contact with many of the luminaries of the age. He was a friend of the mystic imperialist, Sir Francis Younghusband; he collaborated with John Buchan in wartime propaganda at the Ministry of Information in 1918; and he and Buchan planned the provision of imperial text-books to be published by Nelson after the war.[39] His naval history of the First World War appeared in 1920, and he worked with Cromer, Milner, and Haldane on a book about post-war reconstruction. He played an active part in broadcasting between the wars, as a consultant to the B.B.C. on lectures and talks, and as a contributor to the annual Empire Day and royal Christmas broadcasts.[40] He also suggested a wireless service of imperial news. But it was his naval verses which were to imprint themselves on a whole generation of children's minds. *Admirals All and other Verses*, including his most famous poem, 'Drake's Drum', was published in 1897, a time when, Newbolt later wrote, his generation felt like heroes and heroines in a great national saga, dreaming 'an impossible but not ignoble dream of world leadership'.[41] Throughout his career he was concerned to transfer that dream to the young, and was gratified that his poetry secured such an audience among them. In the 1890s he had worked for a boys' club in Notting Hill and proclaimed that the youngsters had 'enlarged ' his 'sense of patriotism'. He continued his role as the unofficial poet laure-ate of the Navy League with *Songs of the Sea* (1904) and *Songs of the Fleet* (1910). Many publishers responded with cheap editions of natio-nal and patriotic verse designed for school and juvenile use. An excel-lent example, published on the eve of the First World War, was Heinemann's *Our Glorious Heritage*, 'a Book of Patriotic Verse for Boys and Girls', which included sections entitled 'Songs and Ballads of the Sea' and (on the Dominions) 'The Mother and her Sons'. Such poe-tic compilations were continued with John and Jean Lang's *Poetry of Empire*, Arthur Mee's *The Book of the Flag*, and Stephen Leacock's *Our British Empire*. Imperial poetry contributed to imperial hero-wor-ship and to the invoking of central historical episodes like the relief of Lucknow.

The First World War, far from restraining this publishing activity, accelerated it. The excitements of the war led to what can only be de-scribed as a wave of patriotic marketing. The Amalgamated Press issued free 'cigarette' cards of regiments, British and colonial, war heroes, naval engagements, royal occasions and the like. Nor was this material directed solely at boys. Girls' papers like *Girls' Realm* and *Sunday Stories* gave away 'silks' of similar subjects with instructions for stitching them up into cushion covers. Thus girls were encouraged to scatter items of patriotic propaganda about the house, while accepting their domestic role in stitching and sewing. The *Daily Telegraph* issued a whole series of 'war books' priced at 1s. By the middle of 1915 there were already twenty-three titles, and many more followed. They included books on the fleet, various regiments and actions, and the role of Indian and colonial troops. Two in the author's possession were given as Band of Hope prizes in Preston in 1915 and 1916.[42]

Above all, the boys' papers, which for years had been featuring invasion stories of one sort or another, could now concentrate on the real thing. Not only did they consciously become recruiters, they also highlighted the activities that could give the members of the youth organisations a significant part in the war effort. Baden-Powell's ideas for the Scouts had of course emerged from the efforts of youths in Mafeking, as messengers, carriers of mail, and the like. One of the central sections of *Scouting for Boys* concentrated on observation, which could be turned into spy-hunting, deserter-spotting, and a variety of civil defence roles. Members of the youth organisations were indeed urged to hang around railway stations, making sure recruits joined their trains, and watching for deserters.[43]

Most studies of popular juvenile literature, like so many on imperialism generally, end with the First World War. A whole generation was wiped out; the naivetes of the Edwardian era were no longer possible; 'total war' had induced a recognition of its true horrors that was lacking in the period 1870-1914. The public became more inward-looking, caught up in the fierce fluctuations of the economic cycle in the inter-war years. A new generation of intellectuals and writers, Robert Graves, H. G. Wells, George Orwell and others, wrote in an anti-imperial spirit. War was treated in a new and very different light in works like R. C. Sheriff's *Journey's End*, Remarque's *All Quiet on the Western Front*, or Siegfried Sassoon's *Memoirs of an Infantry Officer*. The war, too, far from bringing about the imperial institutions so eagerly looked for by the imperial federationists and the Round Tablers, heightened the Dominions' nationalism, and led to their virtual independence in the Statute of Westminster of 1931. For all these reasons, patriotic imperialism as a popular concern has been discounted in the aftermath of the First World War.

Historians who have taken this view have been influenced primarily by such intellectual and historical developments. It may be true that sophisticated ideas about imperialism were now more difficult to sustain, that the elite societies of the late Victorian and Edwardian periods had lost momentum or died, but the levers of public influence were still controlled by those who maintained an essentially imperial world view. Much commercial advertising continued in its old forms; a patriotic, royalist, and consensual press continued to preach a doctrine firmly focused on imperial economic self-sufficiency; and school textbooks, teaching manuals, and official educational advice, as well as the new medium of broadcasting, perpetuated the imperial world view. Above all, juvenile literature continued in its old forms. The difference between the pre-war and post-war worlds is that in the former high and popular culture to some extent converged, while in the latter they diverged. In each case, 'the energising myths of imperialism' were forcibly carried through popular cultural forms. The intellectual critique which developed between the wars was not to gain a hold on the popular mind — and then probably only insubstantially so — until the 1960s, primarily through the medium of education and some, not always the most successful, elements of theatre, film, and television.

The stories in all the boys' papers continued largely in the established mould, highlighting the deeds of public-school sporting stars, reliving colonial wars, recreating super-boy heroes and supermen, and featuring detectives and Secret Service agents battling with sinister and dangerous foreigners. J. A. Mangan has described the long, lingering decline of the anti-intellectual ideology of athleticism in the public schools, still surviving in some places into the 1950s.[44] E. S. Turner has demonstrated the essential changelessness of boys' literature.[45] Several of the boys' writers survived into the inter-war period, purveying many of the attitudes so prevalent before 1914. Frank Richards, Edgar Wallace, Hugh Lofting, Percy F. Westerman, W. E. Johns, and 'Sapper' (Cyril McNeile) all continued to instil middle-class patriotic, militarist, and xenophobic, occasionally tinged with racist, ideas to the Second World War and beyond.[46] The late nineteenth-century classics remained in print, and some were given fresh currency in school readers and in geographical teaching, which highlighted an adventurous understanding of the world through works of exploration and 'geographical fiction'.

During the years immediately following the First World War, adult obsessions continued to find expression in boys' journals. In 1921 one carried a story about the suppression of a communist revolt in a school; in 1922 another launched a serial on Germany's future war of revenge.[47] Meanwhile, the Empire continued to play a central role in the world of Greyfriars in *Gem* and *Magnet*. More boys from the Dominions appeared as Greyfriars pupils. Each year Harry, Bob and Co. embarked on imperial adventures during the holidays. They encountered cannibals in Africa and wild Crees in western Canada.

At the same time it became apparent from the pen pal columns that they were tremendously popular throughout the Empire, and by no means solely among people of Anglo-Saxon descent. Not only had the working class been incorporated into middle-class culture at home: a colonial middle-class imitative elite (which we must presume constituted the *Gem* and *Magnet* readership in the 'dependent' Empire) had also come to ape its imperial masters.

Despite the massive popularity of *Gem* and *Magnet*, it may seem that the first generation of boys' journals suffered setbacks during these years. *Boys' Friend* died in 1927, *Union Jack* disappeared in 1933, and *Gem* followed in 1939. *Magnet*, like many others, vanished with the paper restrictions of the war in 1940. But a new breed of comic had come to replace the old. They were the products of D. C. Thomson & Co. of Dundee, who launched *Adventure* in 1921, *Rover* and *Wizard* in 1922, *Skipper* in 1930, and *Hotspur* in 1933. Amalgamated Press answered with *Champion* in 1922, and *Triumph* in 1924. The firm of D. C. Thomson has excited a good deal of interest precisely because it has always shrouded its activities in secrecy. It is, and has always been, a non-union firm, which has never allowed scholars access to its archives, and has declined to participate in exhibitions of juvenile literature. One employee, however, recollects no political directives being issued by D. C. Thomson or his successors.[48] The firm adopted and developed well tried and tested formulas to create large circulations for its papers. The writers of their children's adventure stories merely kept the old traditions of juvenile literature alive. Science fiction gradually became more prominent, but world wars and colonial campaigns continued to be fought in the pages of the Thomson boys' papers until the 1950s and 1960s. They continued, too, to carry recruitment advertising for the armed forces. Some have seen them as best exemplifying George Orwell's strictures on gutter patriotism[49] or Hobson's 'spectatorial passion'.[50] The company's publishing philosophy can perhaps best be defined today through its highly successful newspaper, *The Sunday Post*, which blends working-class conservatism with Presbyterianism, prudery, and sentimentality.

During the inter-war years the popularity of Henty remained legendary among schoolmasters and others connected with the young. In 1905 he had been described as 'the god of a lad's literary idolatry' in a book on Manchester boys.[51] In at least one public school his books were so popular that the boys had to be limited to borrowing only three a week. Henty's friend and biographer, Manville Fenn, claimed that the stories taught more history than all the schoolmasters of the period, a view recently reaffirmed by A. J. P. Taylor and by others of his generation.[52] It is difficult to put exact figures on this popularity. Sales ranging from 150,000 to 250,000 a year have been estimated for the late 1890s. Agnes Blackie reckoned in the 1950s that her family's publishing house had sold up to 25 million copies during the total period of their printing.[53] More precise figures are expected in the bibliography by Peter Newbolt. All the Henty titles were still in print in 1955, and some were reprinted in the 1960s. Certainly any number of public figures — writers, politicians, soldiers, businessmen, churchmen, even trade union leaders — all admitted to his influence on their way of thinking. C. S. Forester, Howard Spring, Harold Nicolson, Henry Miller, Field Marshal Lord Montgomery, Harold Macmillan, Lord Home, Maurice Bowra, Airey Neave, J. Paul Getty, A. J. P. Taylor, and Tom Jackson wrote or spoke of his influence on their lives and attitudes. The Bishop of London admitted in a speech to the House of Lords in 1963 to having Henty still in his system.[54]

If the boys' journals and the classic boys' authors continued as popular after the First World War as before, so too the publishers stuck to well tried formulas. The lists of prize-and-present works from all the leading patriotic and juvenile publishers retained much of the flavour they had had in late Victorian and Edwardian times. Seeley Service, for example, maintained long lists and series of missionary, exploration, and imperial titles suitable for children. Books stayed in print for many more years than would be normal today. Catalogues of the 1920s and '30s reveal the durability of series like the Library of Romance, the Missionary Library for Boys and Girls, the Library of Adventure, Remarkable Missionary Books, Heroines of Missionary Adventure, Heroes of the World Library, the Wonder Library, the Daring Deeds Library, and Adventures of Missionary Explorers, and so on. Each contained at least a dozen titles, all of them redolent of the message within. Titles like *Arnot, a Knight of Africa, Missionary Crusaders, Missionary Knights of the Cross, Modern Crusaders*, etc. linked their subjects to medieval historical romance, now gaining new currency in the cinema. The word 'hero' inevitably appeared more frequently than any other: *A Hero of the Afghan Frontier, Judson, the Hero of Burma, Missionary Heroes in Asia, Missionary Heroines in India, Heroes of the Indian Mutiny, Livingstone, the Hero of Africa*. Other titles contrived to encapsulate attitudes to other peoples: *Winning a Primitive People, Among Wild Tribes of the Afghan Frontier, Bishop Patteson of the Cannibal Islands*, and so on. Some of these series sold remarkably cheaply. Missionary Lives for Children sold at 1s each, Missionary Heroes for Boys and Girls at 2s 6d, and the Wonder Library for 3s. All the missionary societies continued to produce their cheap imprints, and works for children on the army, the merchant navy and Royal Navy abounded.

The new medium of broadcasting lent a hand in this perpetuation of pre-war attitudes. The radio gave a new fillip to royal popularity in bringing, from 1924, the voice of the monarch to every fireside (see chapter 3). During these years, publications on the royal family maintained or even increased their popularity. The tradition of photographic essays on royal lives developed from Queen Victoria's jubilees. G. A. Henty wrote a book about Queen Victoria for the 1897 jubilee. Each subsequent coronation, jubilee and death offered publishers, including the missionary houses, the opportunity to issue books on the new or late monarch, his consort and family. The accession of Edward VII brought a plethora. The Educational Supply Association issued *King Edward's Realm*, 'The Story of the Making of an Empire'. The account of the rise of the Empire culminated in chapters on 'The Progress of the Empire in the Nineteenth Century' and 'The Unity of the Empire' (which was symbolised by the monarch and likely to be solidified under his rule).

Although Edward VII had paid visits to India and Canada when Prince of Wales, it was really only from the journeys of George V that the direct imperial experience of the monarch was stressed in celebratory publications. George V had travelled extensively round the Empire, both as naval midshipman and as Prince of Wales. The climax of these imperial progressions came with the great oriental extravaganza associated with the Delhi durbar and imperial coronation of 1911.[55] The central role of the monarchy in the propaganda of the First World War was greatly helped by the fact that the king was relatively young, yet had sons just old enough to be independently effective. The 'exploits' of the Prince of Wales, the future Edward VIII, in France were duly featured in the press, boys' journals, war books, and in ephemera. In the post-war era, the Prince of Wales emerged as the main thrust of royal and imperial propaganda. In the space of a few years he travelled more widely than any other monarch, to Canada in 1919-20, Australia, New Zealand, the West Indies, and the Pacific islands in 1920, to India, South-east Asia and the Far East in 1921-22, and to West and southern Africa in 1925. Each of these journeys prompted the appearance of stories and accounts in the juvenile press, extensive publications of ephemera, and numerous descriptive and illustrated books. Hurst & Blackett, Methuen, Hodder & Stoughton, and Odhams were all closely connected with this royal publishing activity.[56] Each subsequent occasion, the jubilee of George V, his funeral, the accession of Edward VIII, and the coronation of George VI, produced a minor avalanche of material, designed for both the adult and juvenile market.

The publication of children's 'annuals' began in the late nineteenth century. As we have seen, Henty founded one or two of them. But it was in the inter-war period that they became a particularly characteristic aspect of juvenile publishing. Ward Lock had begun to publish 'Wonder Books' before the First World War, and they continued to appear throughout the years between the wars and after the Second World War. Titles included *The Wonder Book of Railways, of the Navy, of Ships*, and others which emphasised contemporary technical developments. Perhaps the most popular was *The Wonder Book of the Empire*. It started before the First World War. The fifth edition, issued just after it, contained a special supplement on the 'ex-German and Turkish colonies now occupied and administered by Great Britain and her dominions'. The annual contained mainly factual articles on the history and resources of Dominions and colonies, with particular stress on individuals like Rhodes, Livingstone, and Stanley. Some changes were made from year to year, mainly in the illustrations, but generally the contents were reprinted decade after decade. Generally, the illustrations were of a patriotic or military nature. In 1919 the frontispiece was a painting by S. Begg, 'Under one Flag', containing no fewer than seventy-eight figures representative of the peoples of the Empire, while that of the seventh edition a few years later consisted of 'Sons of Empire' by Frank Aveline, another montage of imperial stereotypes, with upstanding colonial frontiersmen prominent at the front. To back up these images of ethnic diversity, each issue was full of pictures of 'picturesque and primitive native life'.

The fourth edition of *The Wonder Book of Soldiers*, published in 1919, emphasised the romantic, adventurous, and glamorous side of combat. Trench warfare was described as a 'wonderful development', 'much fuller of interest and excitement than might seem possible', while the withdrawal from Gallipoli represented 'one of the most brilliantly successful operations recorded in military history'.[57]

The annuals were not restricted to boys. *Every Girls' Paper* issued *The Empire Annual for Girls*, containing 'Tales of Adventure, Sport, Holidays, School Life', in Edwardian times. It reached its twenty-second edition in 1930, and its subtitle seems to indicate a degree of convergence between boys' and girls' interests. The *Boys' Own Paper* launched a *New Empire Annual* in the 1930s, edited by M. Marshall, and offering 'Stories of Adventure and Informative Articles on Life within the Empire'. The editions of the 1930s contained an introduction by Percy F. Westerman, described as the author of popular books 'who needs no introduction to the new generation. He is a man who can tell a good yarn, a sportsman — and a friend of youth'.[58] For Wester-man, the *New Empire Annual* was a training ship of Empire to qualify the young for service in the much larger craft of the Empire itself. He urged his readers to become administrators, nurses, explorers, pioneers, civil engineers, and soldiers. 'It may be that you will have to defend your heritage against foreign aggression.' After Kipling's Empire toast ('not only a toast, but a prayer; not only a prayer but an ideal') the annual began with a descriptive survey of royal tours in the Empire. In another article, 'Mysterious Zimbabwe', the ruins in Southern Rhodesia were described as 3,000 years old. The writer linked them directly with Rider Haggard's *King Solomon's Mines* and *She*, still very much juvenile reading matter, after all, and asserted, 'There are no na-tives today living in South Africa who could have erected such monumental structures. The blacks possess nothing but little huts made of wood and boughs.' The medieval and African provenance of the ruins of Zimbabwe had been conclusively demonstrated by Randall McIver in 1906 and Gertrude Caton-Thompson in 1928.

The same blend of fact and fiction, with some of the fiction mas-querading as fact, continued to appear in the *Empire Youth Annuals* of the 1940s and 1950s, published by P. R. Gawthorn and edited by Raymond Fawcett. By that time the Second World War had stimulated a fresh wave of patriotic, naval, and imperial propaganda. Indeed, res-trictions on printing and the shortage of paper ensured that the pub-lishing industry was, in effect, directed principally towards the patrio-tic war effort. As always, large numbers of works appeared celebrating the navy and the merchant navy. Blackie published *The Navy of Today* at the outbreak of the war.[59] Sampson Low and Odhams produced lavishly illustrated volumes on the merchant navy and the Royal Navy during the war.[60] Sir Archibald Hurd, who had written several of the *Daily Telegraph* war books during the Great War, contributed articles. The Wonder Books continued to appear from Ward Lock, with a par-ticular wartime slant towards the forces and the Empire. Collins embarked on a new series entitled 'The British Commonwealth in Pictures' in 1943 and 1944. Short volumes were issued on Australia, Canada, India, South Africa, and New Zealand, and the colonial Empire, at 4s 6d each. The authorship was largely in the hands of impe-rial propagandists, Lady Tweedsmuir, Sarah Gertrude Millin, Elspeth Huxley. At the end of the war Collins issued George Blake's *British Ships and Shipbuilders* in their 'Britain in Pictures' series. All these concentrated on the traditional, and by now anachronistic, message of Empire and seapower, that the navy remained the only sure shield of Britain's security, while the merchant navy and the shipbuilding industry were crucial to economic survival. The children to whom the illustrated works were directed were urged to prepare themselves to man these vital services, crucial in the maintenance of 'empire life-lines' along which the mother country could be supplied with Dominion and imperial support in fighting men, foodstuffs, and raw materials.

A great deal of work remains to be done on the juvenile literature of the inter-war years, the period of the Second World War, and the years that followed, but it is at least possible to suspect strongly that there was a real continuity of fundamental ideas from the late nineteenth century to the 1950s. Clearly, listing titles is not enough. We need more information on sales, and as always it is difficult to gauge the real impact of these works. But the fact remains that publishers' lists looked much as they had done before the First World War; boys' and girls' journals continued on the traditional lines; and new media like the cinema and broadcasting conveyed essentially the same world view. As with the school texts, late nineteenth-century developments laid down powerful influences which survived for decades. A range of classics emerged which proved equally acceptable to both parents and children, classics which were firmly rooted in contemporary events and sought to disseminate the ideology through which those events could be understood and controlled. Long after contemporary realities and intellectual thought had moved on, the same complacent self-con-fidence, sense of national and racial superiority, and suspicious xenophobia continued to be the principal characteristics of children's literature. In *The Lion and the Unicorn* and his famous 1940 article in *Horizon*, George Orwell noted the influence such materials had on the working-class mind.[61] It was an attitude well expressed by one of the boys in William Golding's *Lord of the Flies:* 'After all, we're English, and the English are best at everything'.[62]

NOTES

1 J. S. Bratton, *The Impact of Victorian Children's Fiction*, London, 1981.
2 N. Abercrombie, S. Hill, and Bryan S. Turner, *The Dominant Ideology Thesis*, London, 1980, 125.
3 Bratton, *Victorian Children's Fiction*, 15.
4 Bratton, *Victorian Children's Fiction*, 34.
5 Patrick A. Dunae, 'Penny dreadfuls: late nineteenth century boys' literature and crime', *Victorian Studies*, 22, 2 (1979), 133-50. Patrick Howarth, *Play up and Play the Game*, London, 1973, 34.
6 J. A. Mangan, *Athleticism in the Victorian and Edwardian Public School*, Cambridge, 1981, 19-34.
7 E. S. Turner, *Boys will be Boys*, London, 1975 (first edition 1948), 25.
8 Dunae, 'Penny dreadfuls', 139.
9 Edward Salmon, *Juvenile Literature as it is*, London, 1888: 'What Boys Read', *Fortnightly Review*, 45 (February 1886); 'What the Working Class Read', *Nineteenth*

Century, 20 (July 1886), 108-17, and 'What Girls Read', Nineteenth Century, 20 (October 1886), 515-29.

10 Bratton, Victorian Children's Fiction, 45.

11 Turner, Boys. For a survey of the new journals, see also Louis James, 'Tom Brown's imperialist sons', Victorian Studies, 17 (1973), 89-99, and Patrick A. Dunae, 'Boys' literature and the idea of Empire', Victorian Studies, 24 (1980), 105-21.

12 Dunae, 'Boys' literature', 107.

13 Turner, Boys, 88. Bratton, Victorian Children's Fiction, 135. Dunae, 'Boys' literature', 108.

14 Dunae, 'Boys' literature', 115. The Boer War caused serious splits in evangelical approaches to militarist imperialism. The Methodist Times fiercely supported the war, while The Methodist Recorder maintained 'an embarrassed silence'. Stephen Koss, 'Wesleyanism and Empire', Historical Journal, XVIII, 1 (1975), 114.

15 Turner, Boys, 179.

16 Roberts, Classic Slum, 160-2.

17 Turner, Boys, 115.

18 Dunae, 'Boys' literature', 112-13.

19 Patrick A. Dunae, '"Making Good": the Canadian west in British boys' literature, 1890-1914', Prairie Forum, 4, 2 (1979), 165-81. See also Dunae, Gentlemen Emigrants.

20 Dunae, '"Making Good"', 175-7.

21 Dunae, 'Penny dreadfuls', 150.

22 Bratton, Victorian Children's Fiction, 17-18. Later in the century obscure publishers specialised in prize materials. For example, Robert Brown's The Story of Africa and its Explorers was originally published by Cassell. It was later reprinted by C. Combridge of Birmingham, 'Publisher of Prize Literature', and copies were issued as prizes by the Pleasant Sunday Afternoons Brotherhood.

23 Bratton, Victorian Children's Fiction, 123.

24 M. R. Kingsford, The Life, Work, and Influence of W. H. G. Kingston, Toronto, 1947. Bratton, Victorian Children's Fiction, 115-33. Kingston's books continued to be issued in prize editions after his death. A copy of My first Voyage to Southern Seas, published by Nelson in 'the Kingston Library for Boys' in 1887 was given as a present in 1900.

25 Eric Quayle, Ballantyne the Brave, London, 1967. Bratton Victorian Children's Fiction, 138-47. Howarth, Play up, 38-45.

26 Bratton, Victorian Children's Fiction, 138.

27 Guy Arnold, Held Fast for England: G. A. Henty, Imperialist Boys' Writer, London, 1980. Mark Naidis, 'G. A. Henty's idea of India', Victorian Studies, 8 (1964), 49-58. J. O. Springhall, 'The rise and fall of Henty's empire', Times Literary Supplement, 3 October 1968. Jeffrey Richards, 'Spreading the gospel of self-help: G. A. Henty and Samuel Smiles', Journal of Popular Culture, 16 (1982), 52-65.

28 Arnold, held Fast, 43-68.

29 See chapter 8 for school textbook discussions of the childlike character of Africans. Andrew C. Ross has examined the idea in a missionary context, 'The African — "A Child or a Man"', in E. Stokes and R. Brown, The Zambesian Past, Manchester, 1966.

30 For an extended discussion of the theories of tropical indolence, see P. D. Curtin, The Image of Africa, Madison, Wis., 1963, 60-2, J. M. MacKenzie, 'African Labour in South Central Africa', unpublished Ph.D. thesis, University of British Columbia; 1969, 452-6, and J. M. MacKenzie, 'Colonial labour policy and Rhodesia', Rhodesian Journal of Economics, VIII (1974), 1-15. School textbooks continued to emphasise notions of tropical abundance and tropical indolence between the two world wars. See Bosworth, Geographical Readers, Africa, 141 and 176.

31 Patrick A. Dunae, 'Boys' literature and the idea of race, 1870-1900', Wascana Review, spring 1977, 84-107.

32 It is intriguing to discover that The Mikado of Gilbert and Sullivan was banned from performance by the Lord Chamberlain in 1907-08 on the grounds that it might cause offence to Britain's Japanese allies. See p.32 above.

33 Mrs G. W. Tooley, *Lives Great and Simple*, London, 1884.

34 Cassell's were vigorous in patriotic publishing. In 1897 they produced a lavishly illustrated twenty-four-number part-book, *The Queen's Empire*, edited by H. O. Arnold-Foster. There is a set in the collections of the Judges' Lodging, Lancaster. Arnold-Foster, a Unionist M.P. and member of the Imperial Federation League, also 'prepared six educational handbooks designed to propagate a wise patriotism' for Cassell's, together with *The Citizen Reader*, which went through many editions between 1885 and 1904. Field, *Imperial Life*, 94.

35 A. E. Glover, *A Thousand Miles of Miracle in China*, London, 1900, remained continuously in print until at least 1948. It reached its seventeenth edition in 1931, and was translated into Swedish, German and Arabic.

36 Ford and Harrison, *Hundred Years*, 36-7.

37 The South African volume in this series was by Ian D. Colvin, the biographer of Dr Jameson. A similar series, 'The Story of the Empire', was published by Horace Marshall at 1s 6d (7½p) each around the turn of the century. *The Rise of the Empire* by Sir Walter Besant was followed by *The Story of India, Australia* (by Flora Shaw, Lugard's wife and a *Times* correspondent), *Canada, South Africa* (by Basil Worsfold), *New Zealand, The West Indies*, and *West Africa* (by Mary Kingsley).

38 Dunae, *Gentlemen Emigrants*, 115.

39 William Buchan, *John Buchan: a Memoir*, London, 1982, 182.

40 Empire Day Movement Annual Report, 1929, *B.B.C. Year-Book*, 1930, 229. Haworth, *Play up*, 10.

41 Haworth, *Play up*, 12.

42 Archibald Hurd, *The Fleets at War*, London, 1915. Charles W. Domville-Fyfe, *Submarines, Mines, and Torpedoes in the War*, London, 1915. The latter work passed through five editions in less than a year.

43 Springhall, *Youth*, 62.

44 Mangan, *Athleticism*, 217-8.

45 Turner, *Boys*, 223-34.

46 For examples dating from this period, see Bob Dixon *Catching Them Young*, London 1977, Vol. 2, Political Ideas in Children's Fiction, 99-109.

47 Turner, *Boys*, 185.

48 I am grateful to James Clark, an editor of *Adventure* in the 1930s for information about D. C. Thomson.

49 George Orwell, 'Boys' weeklies', Penguin *Collected Essays, Journalism and Letters of George Orwell*, vol. 1, London, 1970.

50 Hobson, *Psychology of Jingoism*, London, 1901, 12.

51 Springhall, 'Rise and fall of Henty's empire'.

52 B.B.C. Radio 4 programme on Henty, 'The world of Henty', 23 December 1982. See also Bratton, *Victorian Children's Fiction*, 200.

53 Agnes C. Blackie, *Blackie and Son : a Short History of the Firm, 1809-1959*, London and Glasgow, 1959.

54 Arnold, *Held Fast*, 1979, and B.B.C. Radio 4 programme.

55 Both the 1903 and 1911 durbars produced a flood of publications, ephemera, and other illustrated materials.

56 Charles Turley, *With the Prince round the Empire*, London, 1926. *The Prince of Wales African Book*, 1926. *The Prince of Wales Eastern Book*, 1922. Odhams published lavishly illustrated volumes for each royal occasion between the wars.

57 Harry Golding (ed.), *Wonder Book of Soldiers*, 83, 142-3.

58 M. Marshall (ed.), *The New Empire Annual*, Stories of Adventure, and Informative Articles of Out-of-the-way Interest in Life within the Empire, Boys' Own Paper Office, 1934, 7-8.

59 Lt.-Com. K. Edwards, *The Navy of Today*, London and Glasgow, 1939.

60 Sir Archibald Hurd (ed.), *Britain's Merchant Navy*, n.d., but clearly published during the war. Francis E. McMurtrie, *Ships of the Royal Navy*, London, 1942.

61 Orwell, 'Boys' weeklies', 505-31.

62 William Golding, *Lord of the Flies*, Penguin, 1960, 42. The remark is made by Jack Merridew, who proceeds to lead his 'hunters' back into savagery.

Notions of imperial patriotism and military preparedness were not, however, the sole preserve of formal classroom disciplines or popular juvenile literature. Deliberate efforts were made to suck working-class children into a consciousness of imperial and military destiny, both through the curriculum and through drill and exercise. In the public schools the same effects were achieved by relating sport to the imperial obligation, and by ensuring that the message was potently carried through the paraphernalia of school magazines, memorial tablets, speech days, and chapel services. Outside school, efforts were made from the 1880s to seize children with the same world view through youth organisations, often associated with the Churches. In the twentieth century school and Church combined in the observance of Empire Day rituals, designed by a variety of Empire Day associations, which were to continue to the 1950s.

Drill had been introduced to the pauper schools as early as the 1850s.[1] The Chartists had drilled illegally as an expression of dissent, but from the 1850s drill was converted into a means of socially disciplining the working class. In the Central London school district there was a school with a mast and four six-pounder guns for training in seaman and gunner duties. In the decade of alarm from the 1850s to the 1860s (the era of wars in South Africa, the Indian Mutiny, and the Crimea, as well as fresh French invasion scares) anxieties about military preparedness led not only to the formation of the Volunteer Force, but also to growing support for school drilling. The great sanitary reformer, Sir Edwin Chadwick, the eminent scientist, T. H. Huxley, and the Society of Arts all pressed for the extension of drilling and offered incentives in the shape of reviews, the competition for colours, and so on. Fear of Prussia aroused a desire to emulate German methods, but drill was also seen — like a patent-medicine panacea — as inculcating industry and discipline, diminishing crime, improving industrial productivity, leading poor children towards the army, and, through methodical order, instilling habits of submission, order, and neatness. The Education Codes of 1871 and 1875 specified military drill for schools, and manuals of teaching methods between the 1870s and the 1890s extolled its efficacy. Towards the end of the century drilling began to disappear, but by then it had been replaced by physical exercises (recommended in the 1895 code). 'Swedish drill' had been introduced in girls' schools in 1887, and by the end of the century the 'English Combined System' had evolved. In 1900 the new Board of Education recognised organised games as a substitute for drill.

The rejection of 40% of volunteers for the Boer War led to the establishment of the Committee on Physical Deterioration in 1904, and the provision of school meals (1906), medical inspection (1907) and grants for medical treatment (1912). It also led to the development of rifle clubs in schools. The justification of these was the frequent observation that Boer children were taught to shoot when young. As we have seen, the Navy League distributed a textbook to schools, intended as a reader to impress on children the historical importance of the navy and the need to maintain a large fleet. Humphries has charted the resistance to these measures among working-class children in Bristol and socialists' attempts to argue for alternative methods of education.[2] But the failure of socialism in this regard was rooted in the 'imperialisation' of significant sectors of the left. H. M. Hyndman's fear of Germany led to his support for the Navy League and for school drilling, because he was convinced that the German working class was in a better physical shape than its British counterpart. 'It is sad to witness,' he wrote, 'the decay of any great nation; it is saddest to witness the deterioration of our own.'[3] It was precisely these patriotic and antiGerman fears which hamstrung the socialist alternative. Hyndman himself castigated the 'imbecile floundering' of the T.U.C. approach to education.

In the public schools, as J. A. Mangan has so ably charted, the same effect was achieved primarily by the ideology of athleticism which developed in most of them in the 1850s, and had become by the 1880s and the succeeding decades a full-blown ideology, complete with its rituals and symbols, its own literature, and its heroic stereotypes.[4] It was consciously used as a means of social control, to destroy the rowdyism evident in the public schools in the earlier part of the century. But the movement went far beyond this initial impulse. It became the prime medium for the development of group and institutional loyalties in the houses (a development of the second half of the century) and the schools as a whole, a means of establishing not just loyalty, but obedience, through a hierarchy of dominance and subordination, controls and disciplines among the boys themselves. Moreover, the courage, 'character', fair play, and self-control developed on the games field were seen as essential to the moulding of a ruling race. Games became the prime means of creating a new Sparta, Seeley's world State. They also became an analogue of war which, with cadet corps and rifle clubs, could prepare the nation's officer class not just for imperial campaigns, but for a global defence against any European rival.

The sports field constituted for most ex-public school boys the idyllic memory of schooldays at home before imperial service abroad. In the schools themselves pupils were assiduously prepared for imperial action, civilian and military. The school magazines became 'unremitting agents of seduction for an imperial dream of noble service and intoxicating adventure',[5] ideological mouthpieces inculcating consciousness of duty, fierce chauvinism, and naive romanticism, and also colonial travel brochures, army advertisements and emigrants' prospectuses. Young warrior-patriots killed in some colonial campaign were eulogised in obituaries. Some became the subject of the 'brief lives' of the period, works redolent of the moral certainties of the age.[6] These young men were exemplars of the certainty of belief in the nobility of imperial enterprise, whose lives, crowned by self-sacrifice, were an inspiration to others, their deeds immortalised on the idealistic path to 'freedom' from 'barbarism' and 'paganism'. They were given monumental form too in heroic statuary and pictorial representation, in memorial tablets in school chapels, cathedrals and parish churches. Through such literary, plastic, pictorial, and monumental art the dead were manipulated into a propaganda for the living.

The public schools were visited by explorers and distinguished old boys returning to be feted and to inspire emulation. At Sedbergh, the boys sat in the chapel beneath a stained glass window in three panels, containing the images of General Gordon, Lord Lawrence, and Bishop Patteson of the South Seas.[7] Lord Lawrence's son-in-law, Henry Hart, was headmaster between 1880 and 1900, and he regaled the boys with lectures on the events of the Indian Mutiny, illustrated by lantern slides. And the propaganda worked. The proportion of public schools boys going into imperial service in one form or another was extraordinarily high.[8] According to Mangan, the imperial ideology of athleticism reached its apogee in the years before the First World War; there was some reaction in the years following it, but in many places the ideology was renewed by the late 1920s and lingered on into the 1950s. For many observers, the sporting philistine remained in the ascendant until at least the latter decade.

The public schools were taken as the model for the rest of the educational system, and for other aspects of juvenile life, like weekly journals and the youth organisations. In State schools, the symbols and rituals of imperial life were no less apparent.[9] There too school loyalties were manipulated for imperial ends, magazines and speech days extolled the activities of old boys in the Empire and in imperial campaigns. Children, as Robert Roberts has described, welcomed the

[230]

flag-waving, the processions, the bands, the uniforms of the soldiers, the group excitements of the royal visit or civic occasion, as a relief from the monotony of routine.[10] The British Empire League provided schools with union jacks, and municipal councils and rich aldermen offered bribes in the shape of chocolates, buns, and mugs to encourage children to discover the full joys of patriotic celebrations. It is certainly possible that children exploited such occasions without imbibing the ideology behind them, and of course no quantitative estimation of the scale of their influence is possible. Nevertheless, the observance of such rituals does seem to have been almost universal, and again its true significance can only be assessed when put together with the overwhelmingly dominant message of so many other media of communication.

Imperial and patriotic school activities were given institutional expression through the Empire Day movements which continued to be active until the 1950s. They too had their rituals of dress, music, and symbolic literature. In Salford before the First World War, Empire Day

> had special significance. We drew union jacks, hung classrooms with flags of the dominions and gazed with pride as they pointed out those massed areas of red on the world map. 'This, and this, and this,' they said, 'belong to us!' When next King George with his queen came on a state visit we were ready, together with 30,000 other children, to ask in song, and then... tell him precisely the 'Meaning of Empire Day'.
> ...Each boy wore a rosette of red, white and blue ribbon and each girl wore a blue sash over a white dress.[11]

The song they sang asked why the flag of Britannia floated o'er fort and bay around the world, why kinsmen gladly hailed 'Our glorious Empire Day'. The answer lay on the 'nation's scroll of glory' with its 'deeds of daring told'... 'of the heroes bold In the days of old'.[12] All this is significant, for at the time Salford children were being encouraged to perform in this way the Empire Day movement had yet to gain official recognition.

The movement owed its origins to the Earl of Meath, a rich, philanthropic aristocrat who was involved in almost all the patriotic, militarist, and imperial organisations of the Edwardian period.[13] In 1890 his attention was drawn to the 'lamentable ignorance of the great mass of our population in regard to Imperial matters', and he addressed the House of Lords on the subject.[14] In 1892 he appealed to the London County Council to introduce into its schools 'the teaching of a sane patriotism'. In 1896 he wrote to *The Times* suggesting that the Queen's birthday, 24 May, should be made a holiday after schools had assembled in the morning to sing the national anthem and salute the flag.

Ontario set aside 24 May as a school holiday in 1897, and it was made a legal holiday throughout Canada (as it still is) by an Act of 1901. In 1898 the *Daily Graphic* suggested that Meath's campaign was achieving some success, since Empire subjects were receiving more attention in the schools, and it published a sketch of pupils in a south London school saluting the flag. In 1899 Meath associated himself closely with the tradition of school drilling by founding the Lads' Drill Association — which he later affiliated to the National Service League — and the following year he campaigned for the reintroduction of drilling in schools. His devotion to military service and to the disciplines of authority, family, and Church were all developed in his adherence to, or leadership of, the Navy League, the National Service League, the Legion of Frontiersmen, the Girls' Patriotic League, the League of Empire, the Boy Scouts, the Church Army, the National Social Purity Crusade, the National Council of Public Morals, the British Empire Union, and the Duty and Discipline Movement, which he founded in 1910.

Meath wrote to Joseph Chamberlain in 1902, attempting to secure acceptance of his Empire Day idea at the colonial conference of that year. In 1903 he founded the organisation to promote Empire Day, and the first public observance was held in 1904. In his opening address in St James's Hall on 24 May 1904, he denied any connection between Empire Day and jingoism. His desire was to create a bond among the 400 million subjects of Edward VII, to celebrate 'the magnificence and power of the Empire', give thanks for the 'blessings of an all-wise and all-knowing Providence' in bestowing 'boundless resources' and 'the unrivalled freedom and liberty' imperial subjects enjoyed.[15] His practical purpose was to prevent the decay of the Empire. He laid out several reasons for the decline and collapse of former empires, and offered his movement as an insurance against a similar fate. In 1905 it was claimed that Empire Day was being observed

> in all the six self-governing Colonies, in 22 Crown Colonies and at home in the schools under the authority of 9 County Councils, of 23 Borough Councils, of 7 Urban District Councils, in 5 training colleges...[16]

In that year 6,000 schools throughout the Empire were said to have participated.

Nevertheless, Meath's movement found it difficult to secure official recognition in Britain. In 1908 the House of Commons rejected a proposal for an official ceremony and holiday, and it was not until 1916, in the patriotic fervour of the war, that it received government support. It had become a statutory holiday in Australia in 1905, in New Zealand

and South Africa (on the formation of the Union) in 1910, and later in India in 1923.

In 1922, when the movement became affiliated with the Royal Colonial Institute, Meath retired and wrote a valedictory article in the *Dominions Yearbook*. In it he stressed his religious concept of the Empire Day movement — its basis was essentially spiritual, and his intention was to inculcate in the British people the same spirit as was taught in Japan through bushido, loyalty, patriotism, sacrifice, Commonwealth, through the watchwords of responsibility, duty, sympathy, self-sacrifice. He regarded it as imperative that the young should read of the downfall of previous empires; Germany's provided a recent lesson in the dangers of subordinating Right to Might. Every school in the Empire was within reach of the movement. The 6,000 that had celebrated Empire Day in 1905 had grown to 80,000. 'Patriotism', he wrote, 'which covers at once a proper pride in ancestral accomplishment, and a determination to hand on the inheritance unsullied, cannot have a better nursery than the school.'[17] Women had a vital role to play as guardian angels, in introducing Empire into the home, and in influencing educational committees, the clergy, and M.P.s.

J. O. Springhall has pointed to the surprising resilience of the Empire Day movement in the post-war period, an era which has so often been depicted as a time of anti-imperialism. 'Curiously enough, as the power of the Empire waned between the two world wars, the strength of public interest in ceremonies like Empire Day seemed to increase.'[18] This seems less surprising when the role of the exhibitions, the cinema, the school texts, and juvenile literature in perpetuating the imperial idea is understood. An estimated 90,000 people attended the Empire Day thanksgiving service at Wembley Stadium in the second year of the Empire Exhibition. During the remaining inter-war years the reports of the movement annually claimed a growth in the incidence of observance, increasing grants and donations, wider circulation of its Empire Day Message and more highly developed propaganda techniques. The 1929 report appealed for funds for an extensive scheme of propaganda among the working classes. Leaflets (prepared by an 'expert publicist') had already been distributed in the great towns. The Rhodes trustees and various City companies annually gave grants, and the influence of new media like radio was noticed. In 1929 the B.B.C. produced a special Empire Day programme, arranged and presented by Sir Henry Newbolt.[19] A vast rally, organised by the *Daily Express*, featuring processions, massed bands and choirs, addressed by the Bishop of Kensington and Stanley Baldwin, was broadcast to the Empire.

Rich patrons were encouraged to supply union jacks to schools, Empire maps and the Empire Marketing Board's poster 'Highways of Empire' for hanging on classroom walls, and to offer prizes for essays on imperial matters. The British Empire Union offered bronze, silver, and gold Empire Day medals. Various leaflets and booklets were produced as 'aids to the celebration of Empire Day'. They included 'King George V: his Life and Reign' (price 3d), 'Pioneers of Empire' (3d), 'An Empire Day Community Song Sheet' (1d each or 6s per 100), 'Some Facts for Empire Day' (1d each), the Empire Day Message, sets of flags, and A. P. Newton's *A Junior History of the British Empire Overseas* (2s). Gramophone records of royal broadcasts (a set of thirteen), samples of Empire products, picture postcards of Empire industries, and the Empire Day Movement badge were all available. Every propaganda technique was now being used to publicise Empire Day, and the movement had been hitched to the spirit of Ottawa and imperial preference. Suggestions for the celebration of Empire Day in 1936 included 'An Exhibition of Empire Products, Posters or Pictures' and 'Observance of the slogan "Empire Meals on Empire Day"', as well as the usual assemblies of 'local dignitaries, Officials, Military, Territorials, Cadet Corps, Boy Scouts, Girl Guides and Schools', lectures illustrated by lantern slides or films, performing an Empire play or pageant, a 'school concert of national songs and dances and the recitation of poems illustrative of heroic duty and of self-sacrifice on behalf of the Nation', listening to Empire Day wireless programmes, hoisting and saluting the union jack, and displaying Empire flags in school playgrounds and on public buildings. In that year, too, a special booklet was issued: *Edward VIII — Inheritor of a Tradition.* The Empire Day broadcasts continued each year, and equivalents were produced in the Dominions. Scout and Guide rallies, Air Days, Empire Shopping Weeks, Empire Day services, and Empire Day concerts (in London, conducted by Sir Walford Davies) were all swept up into the annual observance. Ceremonies were observed at statues of Queen Victoria around the Empire, as well as at the memorial to Lord Meath at Lancaster Gate.

The outbreak of the Second World War produced a fresh outburst of patriotic and imperial fervour. The King became patron of the movement in 1941, and in that year the president, Viscount Bledisloe, marshalled it once again to the protection of Empire.

> It is against the Powers of Darkness that we are fighting, and the fate of the Empire, and with it that of civilisation, are at stake.

> Those who planned the downfall of the British Empire recked not of the unquenchable spirit of the British Race, the staunch loyalty of peoples of

different races and colours owing allegiance to the British Crown and the unshakeable solidarity of the British Empire.

> We have no need to be ashamed of the story of the Empire, but its greatest chapter has yet to be written, and it is for the youth of the Empire, with their boundless opportunities, buoyant hope and unshakeable faith in God to write it, for the benefit of the whole human race.[20]

In that year the motto 'One King, One Flag, one Fleet, one Empire' and the watchwords of the movement, 'Unity, Responsibility, Duty, Sympathy, Self-sacrifice', were prominently displayed as central to the observance of the movement's rituals. Schools and other members were encouraged to make known

> far and wide the fact that Empire Trade is of immense value to the entire population, above all to the working classes; also that Empire is practically self-supporting and that united it is the world's greatest influence for freedom, peace and prosperity.[21]

Now the ceremonies were linked with aspects of war work (in 1941 Empire Day was the culmination of War Weapons Week), and the Home Guard, the civil defence services and 'the newly-formed youth organisations' participated in parades and services.

During the war years the membership and income of the movement increased at an extraordinary rate.[22] At the beginning of the war, subscriptions (as opposed to grants and donations) had barely reached £200. In 1942 they amounted to £3,623 and in 1943 £6,840. The confidence of the movement grew by leaps and bounds. It set up a target of £10,000 annual income, and provided financial support for the Imperial Institute lecture scheme. In 1944 the *Sunday Empire News* paid £750 towards the cost of a massive Festival of Empire at the Royal Albert Hall in the presence of the King and Queen, the two princesses, and an audience of 8,000. So great was the demand that thousands failed to get tickets, but their consolation was that the second half was broadcast to the Empire. Income reached a new peak in 1944 and 1945 (more than 100 companies contributed); a new assistant director was appointed; and the movement decided to sever its links with the Royal Empire Society. Income, new staff, renewed independence allowed it to expand its work into lectures, publications, an Empire correspondence scheme, and a magazine, *New Empire,* which first appeared in 1947 (a pilot *Empire Magazine* had appeared in 1946). The annual Albert Hall occasions continued: in 1946 the *Sunday Empire News* contributed £1,000 and the broadcast was estimated to have reached 20 million people. *New Empire* was distributed to shipping companies and to Imperial Airways, later B.O.A.C., for the use of ocean and air passengers. In 1948 a play with music and ballet, *The Great Endeavour*, by Christopher Hassall, was presented at the Theatre Royal, Drury Lane.

But as suddenly as this extraordinary burgeoning of activity took place, funds and support began to evaporate. Funds declined so rapidly that the posts of director and assistant director had to be amalgamated, and in 1951 the organisation moved back into the Royal Empire Society's building. By that year the festival concert had moved from the Royal Albert Hall to the Kingsway Hall, and the press magnate Lord Kemsley was contributing a mere £50. Nonetheless, school membership continued to rise in the 1950s. Fifty thousand copies of the presidential message were sent out in 1954 (contrasting with a figure of 13,000 in 1935, Jubilee year). Saturday children's cinema clubs presented special Empire programmes (it was claimed that 400 were involved in the scheme), in 1955 John Masefield wrote a poem for Empire Day, and issues of the magazine *New Empire* sold out. But by the time the movement was renamed the Commonwealth Day Movement in December 1958 the annual reports had ceased to be the lavishly illustrated booklets of the post-war years, and had become mere leaflets. From 1955, when the president, the Earl of Gowrie, died, the organisation found increasing difficulty in finding a replacement. Churchill declined to write the Empire Day message in 1959, and the final messages were issued by the last president, Air Marshal Sir Victor Godard and an ex-Governor of Nigeria, Lord Milverton. From the mid-1950s the B.B.C. became increasingly reluctant to feature the E.D.M. message and events in its radio and television news bulletins. In 1962 the movement, faced with growing deficits and recognising the difficulties arising from the existence of several similar organisations, handed over its functions to the Joint Commonwealth Societies Council under the chairmanship of Earl de la Warr, and dissolved itself.

During the last twenty-five years of its existence the movement had faced competition from a rival organisation: the Empire Youth Movement (E.Y.M.), which developed Empire Youth Sunday and Empire Youth Week.[23] This body was founded by a Canadian, Major Frederick J. Ney, who had been inspired by a large imperial youth rally in the Albert Hall on 18 May 1937, which had been addressed by the Duke of Gloucester, Leopold Amery, and Stanley Baldwin, and by special services for Commonwealth youth (attended by 10,000) which took place in Westminster Abbey and Westminster Cathedral the following day, as part of the coronation celebrations of George VI. A committee was formed to maintain the tradition annually, calling the youth of the Empire together into a 'corporate act of worship and self-dedication'.

In one of its publications, the movement suggested that the idea had first developed after the First World War, when

> a group of people in Canada reached the decision that though victory had been won on the world's battlefields, Western Civilisation had yet to win through on the spiritual front. Further, they noted, that unless the unity and influence of the Empire, as we then proudly named it, were maintained, further war and chaos would result, threatening the very existence of world order and wiping out the gains of centuries, spiritual and material.[24]

Ney had organised the fourth triennial Imperial Education Conference in British Columbia in 1929, and had seen to it that considerable emphasis was placed upon the discussion of morals, propaganda, and the use of the cinema in the education of imperial youth. Interestingly the response to his imperial ideas had not been encouraging in the 1920s, but the new patriotic atmosphere created by the jubilee and death of George V and the coronation of George VI presented him and his associates with their opportunity.

The movement, as the above quotation makes clear, was overtly religious, seeking to inculcate what it described as a 'spiritual patriotism'. Its motto was 'First unto God, and then to the King', and it proclaimed itself as adhering to John Buchan's assertion in his memoirs *Memory Hold the Door* that '... in the world as we know it I believe that civilisation must have a Christian basis and must ultimately rest on the Christian Church'.[25] Ney's initial plans were romantically and impractically ambitious. He hoped to establish a trust fund of £10 million, to create an Imperial Order of Chivalry for youth, to build an Empire Youth City in London to accommodate 2,000 students from the Empire, with the chapel of the Order at its heart, to buy a ship or ships for educational travel, and acquire a stately home in England as a training centre. Youth City was announced (and impressive artist's impressions published) by the Earl of Bessborough, the movement's first president, in January 1939. The Earl of Carlisle later offered Naworth Castle in Cumberland as the stately home, but it did not prove acceptable. The movement wished to develop dramatic programmes on important dates in the imperial calendar in order to restore a 'compelling sense of history', 'heightened by the utmost pageantry'.

Although these extravagant ideas were overwhelmed by the Second World War, the movement's observances greatly benefited from the patriotic upsurge of the time. Commonwealth services were held every year in Westminster Abbey, often attended by the royal family and broadcast by the B.B.C. In 1942 a transatlantic service linked the

Abbey to Washington Cathedral, enabling British, American, and Canadian youth to greet each other in a service organised by the Anglican, Episcopal, and Presbyterian Churches in co-operation with the Scout authorities on each side of the Atlantic.[26] The service was broadcast by the B.B.C. and the C.B.C.

The movement developed rapidly in the 1940s. In 1942 Archbishop Temple set aside the Sunday after Ascension as Empire Youth Sunday throughout the Anglican communion, a movable date which was later to cause some confusion. By this time the E.Y.M. was in receipt of funds from all the main clearing banks, a number of companies, including Marks & Spencer, several public schools, as well as contributions from throughout the Empire. It had succeeded in winning over the colonial and home establishments, as well as the Boys' Brigade, the Scouts, Guides, and Sea Cadets. In 1948 it issued a publication entitled *The Great Crusade of Youth,* which proclaimed itself as taking up the challenge issued to the youth of the Empire by Princess Elizabeth at a rally in Cape Town in April 1947, which she had followed with a B.B.C. broadcast on her twenty-first birthday in which she had promised to dedicate her life'... in the service of our great Imperial family'.[27] A series of 'Quests' had already been established just after the war, through which young people from various Commonwealth countries could meet in Britain or the Dominions for a conference. The 'Questors' were expected to take a pledge incorporating the objects of the movement. Clearly influenced by the developing Cold War atmosphere of the later '40s, Ney now dedicated the movement to countering communism, which had 'honeycombed the world with cells of the Cominform'. Hitler had kindled the idealism of youth, and spiritual propaganda should be used to achieve the same end in the British Empire, to withstand the 'oncoming tide' of communism, which threatened 'to overwhelm law and order', 'destroy centuries of human achievement', and turn the world into 'a bloody slave-pen'.

Despite this rhetoric, none of Ney's ambitious plans was any nearer achievement, and the E.Y.M. had to concentrate on the annual observances. Ney's conception of these was that Empire Youth Sunday should be the climax of Empire Youth Week. In 1948 a programme was issued to all secondary and public schools which suggested that assemblies on succeeding days should follow themes such as 'The King and his People', 'Britain, Heart of the Empire', 'The Empire in War', 'The Empire and the World'. Starting in coronation year, 1953, the Queen began to issue a message for Empire Youth Sunday, calling the youth of the Empire to the 'traditions of chivalry and service which created the Empire'. This message was read out, often by governors and governors-general, in thirty-six overseas territories, as well as throughout Britain. All who asked for the message received it in a sealed envelope, which they were to open on the evening before the observance. Each year the movement's report published the Queen's message together with one from the president, Lord Elton, who held office from 1941 to 1962. Like the E.D.M. reports, those of the E.Y.M. proudly displayed lists of observances in Britain and the Empire, together with photographs of parades and services, in which all the uniformed youth organisations were usually conspicuous. In the early '50s photographs showed large crowds watching parades in centres like Cheltenham, Hull, and Edinburgh, while the movement was said to be particularly successful in Vancouver, the Australian state of Victoria, and in Nairobi.

In 1955 an attempt to change the name to Commonwealth Youth Sunday was resisted on the extraordinary grounds that this would appear to link it solely with the Commonwealth of Australia, but the change was effected in 1957. By then the Queen's message was read annually by the Secretary of State for the Colonies in St Paul's Cathedral, and the E.Y.M. was active in distributing films of the Queen's colonial tours to schools. But interest soon declined in Britain, and the observance in the late 1950s became restricted mainly to rural areas and county towns. With decline, funds began to dry up, and the movement became largely dependent on overseas contributions. In 1955 it claimed support in fifty-five territories, but gradually it retreated to fringe areas of the Commonwealth. In 1959 North Borneo sent £64, in 1964 the Cayman Islands £62, and Jamaica £194, by far the largest contributions of those years. By the early '60s it was clear that the celebration of two Commonwealth Days and the issuing of two messages were causing confusion. Colonial governors complained, and indicated that newly independent territories were likely to choose new dates for their own national celebrations. The Joint Commonwealth Societies Council had developed its own observance in the late '50s, had incorporated the E.D.M., and tried to bring the C.Y.M. (as it now was) into the same scheme, a move Lord Elton testily resisted at first.

By 1964, however, the movement accepted the logic of the great wave of Acts of decolonisation and wound itself up. It recognised in its final report that it had become too dependent on the uniformed youth organisations (themselves in decline), too closely identified with the Church in a substantially non-Christian Commonwealth, and with the monarchy at a time when most of the decolonised territories were adopting republican constitutions. In the last few years of its existence the Queen's message, which had had a positive Christian and imperial tone during the middle '50s, became more and more anodine. The Joint

Commonwealth Societies Council duly took over responsibility for Commonwealth Day and the Queen's message from 1965. The ceremonies were moved to March, and from the early '70s experiments were made with multi-faith services.

The late effloresence of the Empire Day and the Empire Youth Movements was a remarkable phenomenon. It can perhaps be attributed to a number of factors. The E.D.M. was dramatically stimulated twice by the patriotic fervour of world war, and the E.Y.M. was able to capitalise on a new burst of royal and imperial feeling in the 1930s just before it too was enormously helped by war. They seemed to satisfy ritualistic needs during periods of economic gloom, and they were adept at converting their propagandist message to the particular needs of the moment, concepts of patriotic duty and imperial defence (linked to the very survival of Christendom and civilisation) in world wars, the economic message carried by the inter-war exhibitions and the Imperial Institute, as well as by school texts, and post-war ideals of a free family of peoples. They succeeded in harnessing the royal family, the armed forces, the Boy Scouts, Girl Guides, and other youth movements, the Church, and a great range of Establishment and capitalist support, as well as utilising every modern technique — pamphlets, badges, gramophone records, films, children's cinema clubs, and above all broadcasting — to their purposes. They were, however, the kinds of body which were unlikely to survive into the television age, and their demise occurred at just the time that the ownership of television sets was growing dramatically.[28]

As we have seen, the uniformed youth organisations were prominent at all Empire Day and Empire Youth Movement services and rituals. They provided the drill, the bands, the standard-bearing, and the variety of uniforms necessary for such public ceremonies. The photographs proudly displayed in the annual reports of the Empire movements right down to the 1950s reveal the active participation of all the youth movements not only in provincial towns and cities, but throughout the Empire. Indeed, the Empire Day rituals provided the youth organisations with one of their best opportunities for public demonstration, the chance to be reviewed by mayors, army officers, senior commissioners of the organisation themselves, and, in the colonies, governors. The presence of uniformed youth in these rituals perfectly reflected the origins and history of such movements in late Victorian and Edwardian times.

The first youth organisations emerged out of a combination of the Volunteer movement and evangelical muscular Christianity. Provision for the raising of cadet corps was made in the Volunteers Act of

1863.[29] In the 1870s public schools like Charterhouse and Dulwich founded corps, and in the late 1880s and 1890s they spread into working-class districts of cities, particularly the East End of London.[30] A Toynbee Hall cadet corps was established in 1886, followed by others in Tower Hamlets, Southwark, and in the 1890s throughout the working-class areas of London. Social reformers like Octavia Hill, Sir Francis Vane, and the journalist Henry Nevinson put their faith in such corps to control the rowdy boys of the working-class youth clubs. City manufacturers, employers, and bankers, recognising their disciplinary value, paid for uniforms and equipment. Springhall has suggested that at first the cadets were drawn from the small crafts, errand boys and warehouse boys, but that by 1899-1901 the skilled trades were declining as the most significant element in their membership, and unskilled participation was increasing.[31] In some places cadet corps were founded to discipline specific concentrated work forces, like the iron foundries in Scotland and the north of England.

The cadet forces served two purposes. They provided an identity for those seeking upward social mobility, a ready means of acquiring a public school ethos, a respectability acceptable to employers. For the unskilled, whose opportunities for employment expanded in the early '90s, only to contract later in the decade, they opened a route into the regular army. The 1st London Battalion sent 1,000 cadets into the armed forces in this period. Once again, war acted as a stimulus. The corps expanded during the Boer War and the First World War, although they experienced vicissitudes in the aftermath, particularly in the 1920s. In 1930 the corps inaugurated a period of revival with the creation of a national body in the British National Cadet Association, and by the later years of the Second World War 40,000 ex-cadets per annum were being fed into the armed forces.

These cadet corps form a useful starting point to any study of the more familiar youth organisations, for the latter all owed something to the Volunteer tradition and to armed forces activism like the National Service League. William Alexander Smith, founder of the Boys' Brigade, developed his idea from a combination of the Volunteers and Christian youth clubs.[32] Smith's father and grandfather had been in the regular army, and he was himself a member of the Glasgow Volunteer Regiment, the 1st Lanarkshire Rifles, of which he later became colonel. He was also involved in young men's clubs, Sunday school Bible classes, and missions to the working-class districts of Glasgow. His ambition was to maintain young people's church adherence through the awkward teenage gap between Sunday school and membership of the Y.M.C.A. and other youth bodies. His first B.B. company was founded in 1883, and its twin religious and military connections were represented in its rules on Sunday school and Bible class attendance, in the uniform evolved for it — pillbox cap, belt, and haversack — and in its concentration on drilling, including the use of dummy rifles. The Boys' Brigade expanded rapidly, and by 1888 Smith was able to become its full-time organiser, his salary paid by Glasgow business interests and Church contributions. In 1889 there were 232 companies in Scotland and eighty-five in England and Wales, but Smith's appointment as full-time activist led to a rapid growth of the movement in England.[33] By 1896 there were 264 companies in Scotland, 435 in England, and the movement soon spread to Canada, New Zealand, Australia, South Africa, the West Indies, India, and Ceylon, as well as the U.S.A. Smith had also proved successful in securing the support of the English ecclesiastical, military, and imperial Establishment. The Archbishops of Canterbury and York, Lords Roberts and Methuen, and G. A. Henty all became vice-presidents.

The Anglican Church Lads' Brigade also had its origins in the Volunteer movement. Its founder, Walter Mallock Gee, was himself a member of the Volunteers, and the movement he started in Fulham in 1891, while sharing the evangelical and temperance objectives of Smith's Boys' Brigade, was much more militarist in form. This caused difficulties within the Church, but the movement received the full support of the military Establishment. By 1897 there were companies in every diocese in England and Wales. The Church Lads' Brigade was, perhaps, more militantly middle-class than the other organisations. It indulged in full-blooded denigration of working-class life and street culture, while consciously seeking to spread public school attitudes to the working class. In 1908 there were 1,300 companies with 70,000 members, but in 1911 the movement secured War Office recognition as a cadet force, an affiliation which it did not drop until 1936, and which, according to Springhall, led to a rapid decline in membership in the 1920s. Throughout this period its executive was almost entirely made up of members of the National Service League and retired senior army officers. Other sectarian brigades similarly sought working-class incorporation into middle-class public school and military values. The Jewish Lads' Brigade, founded in Whitechapel in 1895, was led by Anglo-Jewish upper middle-class officers seeking to secure the rapid integration of Jewish youth in the East End. The Catholic Boys' Brigade, founded in Bermondsey in 1896, attempted to do the same for the immigrant Irish, and was, like the Lads' Brigade, accused of excessive militarism. The Boys' Life Brigade, on the other hand, founded as an organ of the National Sunday School Union in

Nottingham in 1899, attempted to steer Nonconformist youth away from the military preoccupations of the other movements. Yet the Boys' Life Brigade and its female counterpart, the Girls' Life Brigade, still went in for uniforms and drill and pursued the same ideals of patriotic manliness and disciplined duty. Other small brigades, such as the Boys' Rifle Brigade, the London Newsboys' Brigade and the Boys' Naval Brigade, were overtly military in form. The Imperial Lads' Brigade of West Harlepool, dating from 1908, was a drill and rifle club which boasted 250 members in the age group fourteen to twenty-one.

Baden-Powell's movement of the same year, the Boy Scouts, might very well have been called the Imperial Scouts, but he was dissuaded from that title by his publisher, Sir Arthur Pearson.[34] Nevertheless, B.-P.'s movement had much closer imperial connections than the others. His military experience had been in India, in African colonial campaigns against the Matabele and the Ashanti, as well as in the Boer War, where he achieved the fame from which he derived his popularity and influence, and where he first conceived the idea of the Scouts. The uniform was a mixture of Indian and South African elements, and the movement's governing body contained all the leading figures of the conscriptionist and imperial establishment. It was perhaps these colonial connections that gave the Scouts such a different flavour from their urban predecessors. The various brigades were consciously founded as agents of class conciliation, designed to inculcate evangelical values of temperance, self-discipline, obedience, and piety, located in the Church, the church hall, and street parades. From the beginning, the Scouts emphasised things rural, seeking the regeneration of the young through outdoor pursuits. The connections between the Scouts and the national efficiency movement, the Social Darwinian ideas of the Edwardian period, the Tariff Reform League, and the National Service League are well known. All these movements were expressions of an imperial industrial society, but the Scouts also represented a revulsion against urbanisation, an attempt to combine imperial and military values with the woodcraft skills (survival, tracking, observation, hunting, etc.) learned from the white frontiersman spirit as well as from the 'nobler' native peoples of the Empire.

B.-P.'s *Scouting for Boys*, which was based on a military scouting manual he had published in 1899, was written with the encouragement of the Boys' Brigade's founder, William Alexander Smith. It is a strongly imperial, patriotic, and Social Darwinian document, from the outset placing the objective of its subtitle, 'A Handbook for Instruction in Good Citizenship', in an imperial and military context. The opening 'yarn' is about Mafeking and the role of the boys there during the siege.

Its moral is that 'Every boy ought to learn how to shoot and to obey orders, else he is no more good when war breaks out than an old woman'.[35] But the Empire had also been built by peace scouts, frontiersmen, pioneers, explorers, and missionaries, 'the scouts of the nation', to whose exploits the extension of the Empire had been due. The yarn went on to recount the story of Kipling's Kim, a sort of boy scout, who became an ideal intelligence agent in frustrating Russian designs on India (Scout leaders were instructed to point out on a map the respective positions of Russia and Britain). After a section on physical fitness and endurance (which would be seriously impaired by smoking and drinking), Scouts were instructed in patriotism and their duty to maintain the greatness and power of the British Empire and avert the fate of the Roman one (a constant theme of the Earl of Meath). In urging the Scout laws on the adherents of the new movement, B.-P. told them of bushido, the laws of the samurai warriors of Japan, and a noble ideal.

If Scouting was to be about observation, Scouts were to observe their fellow beings as much as natural phenomena. Character, they were told, could be inferred from the way people wore their hair or their hat, the type of shoes they preferred, even the shape of their face. They were asked to divine the personal characteristics of three faces: the first had a quiff, a semitic nose, and a shot-away chin; the second was a Nordic stereotype, fair-haired, with a perfectly proportioned Caucasian face; the third was negroid. After a long central section on camping, observation, chivalry, and the like, Baden-Powell returned to his national theme with extended sections on 'Patriotism', 'How our Empire Grew', 'How the Empire must be Held', 'Stories of Heroism from the Indian Mutiny', and 'The Song of Canada' and 'The Song of Australia'. In 'Our Navy and Army' B.-P. anticipated the theme of the Fletcher and Kipling's 1911 textbook. The armed services must be supplied with good men and money. He went on to contrast 'politicians' and 'statesmen' in the following terms:

There are always members of Parliament who try to make the Army and Navy smaller, so as to save money. They only want to be popular with the voters of England, so that they and the party to which they belong may get into power. These men are called 'politicians'. They do not look to the good of our country. Most of them know and care very little about our Colonies. If they had had their way before, we should by this time have been talking French; and if they are allowed to have their way in the future we may as well learn German or Japanese, for we shall be conquered by these.

But fortunately there are other better men in Parliament, who are called 'statesmen'; these are men who look out for the welfare of the country, and do not mind about being popular or not so long as they keep the country safe.[36]

And then, before going into details of uniforms and medals, he urged all boys to take an interest in the navy, and learn about the fleet by collecting postcards of the ships of His Majesty's navy.

The basis of the Scouts in cadet corps and in the Volunteers is perfectly demonstrated by the first Scout group in Scotland, which also claimed to be one of the first in the world. It was founded in the same district as the Boys' Brigade, Hillhead in Glasgow, and it grew out of the cadet corps of the four schools in the area.[37] Its founder was the adjutant of these combined corps, Captain R. E. Young, who brought four cadet corps patrols together in September 1907. In 1908 this group, under the influence of B.-P.'s *Scouting for Boys*, became the first Scottish Scouts, and Young himself remained the Glasgow Scout commissioner from 1908 to 1940. Like the Boys' Brigade, the Scouts experienced a dramatic initial growth, with over 100,000 members by 1911. *Scouting for Boys* became an international best-seller.

There are three important questions to be asked about these youth organisations. How effective were they in reaching a working-class membership? How significant were the military and patriotic elements? And to what extent is it true that their objectives and ideologies changed fundamentally after the First World War?

There has been a good deal of debate about their social penetration. The Boys' Brigade certainly emerged from a combination of middle-class social conscience and social apprehension, and its early adherents were from skilled manual and white-collar backgrounds. There is some evidence that working-class boys treated it with derision at first, but Smith's desire to proselytise the working class was helped by Glasgow's geographical layout. Hillhead was certainly an area for the middle class and the upwardly mobile lower middle class and aristocracy of labour, but its leading churches established missions in neighbouring working-class areas like Maryhill to the north and Finnieston and the docklands to the south.[38] Boys' Brigade companies were soon created there, and the leisure opportunities they afforded, particularly sports and later the annual camp, were seized upon by large numbers. In Enfield, north London, a company was founded in 1888 and another in 1890.[39] Its middle-class Nonconformist leadership sprang from the puritan radical tradition, but nonetheless it found a following among local schoolboys and errand boys, as well as young Edison & Swan workers, all apparently eager to adopt its aura of respectability. In the same district the Scouts were a spontaneous creation of working-class factory boys in 1908 (no doubt inspired by the appearance of B.-P.'s *Scouting for Boys* as a weekly part-book), who called on the local curate to be their leader. It is true that the initial flood of working-class members was stemmed when many discovered that the 'exciting new "game" invented by the hero of Mafeking' was too expensive. Soon, a variety of Scout troops had settled down into a pattern matching the 'social tone' of the area.[40] There may well be a contrast between the English and Scottish experience in this respect. In Scotland the Boys' Brigade tended to be attached to churches in working-class and skilled manual worker districts. The Scouts emerged in more middle-class suburbs, where parents could afford the accoutrements and where the yearning for, and the opportunity to invade, the rural surroundings were greater.

Michael Blanch has examined the emergence of the youth organisations in central districts of Manchester and Birmingham.[41] In both cities the greatest recruitment to the Boys' Brigade and the Scouts seemed to come from the skilled workers. In Manchester only 5½% of the membership could be described as unskilled. Blanch usefully conflates the figures of involvement in the uniformed youth movements with those of the cadet corps and also the children's clubs, which experienced a dramatic growth in the Edwardian period. In Birmingham, the Street Children's Union was founded in 1904. By 1906 it had eighteen clubs, and by 1913-14 there were forty-three boys' and forty-one girls' clubs with a total membership of 2,500. In Birmingham in 1913 over 30% of the ten-to-eighteen age group in the central wards were involved in organised youth movements of some sort. In Manchester in 1917 the figure for the centre wards was just short of 50%, although it must have been greatly inflated by the war. In Birmingham the figure for the entire city was 15%, in Manchester 33%. In other words, involvement in organised youth movements in working-class central areas was considerably higher than in middle-class suburbs. Wilkinson has estimated that 40% of all males were in the Scouts, the Boys' Brigade, or some other organisation between 1901 and 1920,[42] while Springhall, looking at the twentieth century as a whole, has suggested that three out of five of the population belonged to one of the uniformed youth groups at some time.[43] Thirteen million people, he suggests, passed through the Scouts and Guides; two million through the Boys' Brigade. There can be little doubt that even if the lower reaches of the unskilled were untouched by these movements, the working class as a whole received a considerable infusion of middle-class values through them.

While there was little dispute about the patriotic, good-citizenship, disciplined-and-pious-living aspects of the youth movements, the military elements were without doubt a source of tension in all of them. Smith was clear about the military model the Boys' Brigade set out to emulate, but for him the evangelical purpose predominated. Hence he resisted Haldane's efforts to incorporate the movement into the national cadet force administered by the newly formed Territorials in the period 1909-11. Such an overt adherence to the established military structures would, in his view, have harmed it as a religious organisation.[44] The Church Lads' Brigade did so affiliate, after a period of struggle between its Church connections and its military leadership, and it may be that it later paid the price. Within the Scouts there was a faction, led by Sir Francis Vane, that wished to emphasise the 'peace scouts' part of the Baden-Powell vision (that is, frontiersmanship and Empire-building, not a notably peaceable activity). Baden-Powell succeeded, however, in frustrating this dissident group and they were forced to become an independent splinter movement. The Scouts, like the Boys' Brigade, continued to be ruled by the most notable figures of the imperial and conscriptionist Establishment. That same Establishment was to celebrate the role of the Scouts in the First World War, even providing a separate chapter for them in the official history of the war.[45] The uniformed youth organisations had a much more diverse purpose than the cadet corps. They pursued their religious and citizenship objectives within a framework of military discipline, and they used their military leaders as hero models, but, apart from the Church Lads' Brigade, they avoided becoming simply another type of cadet corps.

Those who have identified a decline in popular imperialism and militarism in the 1920s have cited the youth organisations as evidence. While the Church Lads' Brigade's membership dropped in the 1920s, and cadet corps membership declined from 118,893 in 1920 to 45,510 in 1928, the Scouts proved their resilience by adjusting to the new climate of internationalism. They came to emphasise the League of Nations and developed their membership throughout Europe and the United States, as well as in the British Empire. If the Boys' Brigade (which had accepted cadet recognition by the Territorials between 1917 and 1924, but nonetheless expanded between 1921 and 1937) and the Scouts reduced their direct commitment to militarism, it must be questioned whether it in any way affected their ideological and social objectives. The professed ideals of pre-war Empire were now in fact developed in heightened form in the atmosphere of victorious, and extended, British imperialism. The leaders of the movements saw their role as facilitating a process of incorporation to a particular set of values symbolised by the objectives of public school education, and represented in religious, military, and imperial service. The movements' success meant that the process of incorporation leapt out beyond the domestic working class to embrace not just the white, but also the native subjects of Empire. In this work the youth movements were developing missionary objectives, spreading a disciplined citizenship to the nearest British equivalent of *évolués* or *assimilados* figures. But of course the Boys' Brigade and the Scouts were also taken up in the U.S.A., and throughout Europe, a process which accelerated in the atmosphere of the 1920s. Again, the vision was of youth internationalism through the extension of the objectives and values of the leadership. The fundamental world view was the same. British conceit was, if anything, heightened by the spread of Anglo-Saxon ideals through movements originated among and led by the British.

Nothing better reflects the moderate scale of the adjustment made in the 1920s than the manner in which the rival organisations failed to make an impact. Kibbo Kift, the Woodcraft Folk and other rural, non-military, co-educational, mystical, and quasi-socialist movements remained small, almost secretive bodies. As Wilkinson has put it, these romantic and utopian movements regarded Scouting as authoritarian, Establishment-minded and hidebound.[46] Yet the British Left never offered the full encouragement which might have established the woodcraft movements as serious rivals to the Boys' Brigade and the Scouts. Moreover, Scouting enjoyed the full cachet of royal patronage. The appearance of the royal family, particularly the Prince of Wales (the future Edward VIII) in Scout uniform at jamborees set the final seal of royal and popular approval on it. During royal tours of the Empire, Scout displays were the most common staple of visits to towns and localities throughout the colonies. The *assimilados* were paraded under their white officers, and photographs of such events were used as a source of pride in children's annuals and Scout publications throughout the period. As the princesses Elizabeth and Margaret grew up they began to play an active role in the Brownies and the Guides, appearing in their uniforms at annual displays and national rituals. It so happened that during the Second World War, when the patriotic-imperial ideological cluster was stimulated once more, they had reached a convenient age to play a full part in Empire Day and Empire Youth rituals. In the post-war Empire tours they followed their father and uncle in reviewing Scouts and Guides in colonial territories.

Throughout this period the public school ethos was held up as an ideal for emulation in State schools and youth organisations alike.

Imperial patriotic displays turned the drill and athleticism of schools and the evangelical-military symbiosis of youth organisations and cadet corps into a homogeneous ideology which not only promoted social discipline and 'good citizenship', but also fostered a national conceit, a sense of Social Darwinian superiority, elaborated equally in all juvenile literature, every geography and history text, and the manuals of the uniformed youth organisations. If the First World War led to some reaction against the more starkly military aspects of this ideology, the world view on which it was based continued to flourish. By the 1930s, if not earlier, the patriotic mood was gaining ground once more, assiduously cultivated by youth movements and Empire organisations which harnessed royal patronage to their continuing popularity. The Second World War gave it a new lease of life which was to fade only in the late 1950s. Again the aura of victory and of imperial wartime solidarity, though largely divorced from reality, sanctified the self-satisfactions of a late nineteenth-century ideology of class and racial superiority. That survival was to make the process of disruption and readjustment all the more painful in the ensuing decades.

NOTES

1 J. S. Hurt, 'Drill, discipline, and the elementary school ethos', in Phillip McCann, *Popular Education and Socialisation in the Nineteenth Century*, London, 1977, 167-91.
2 Humphries, '"Hurrah for England": schooling and the working class in Bristol, 1870-1914', *Southern History*, 1, 1979, 171-207.
3 H. M. Hyndman, *Further Reminiscences*, London, 1912, 410-11. See also 126 and 396.
4 J. A. Mangan, *Athleticism in the Victorian and Edwardian Public School*, Cambridge, 1981.
5 J. A. Mangan, 'Images of Empire in the late Victorian public school', *Journal of Educational Administration and History*, XII, 1 (January, 1980), 31.
6 H. John Field, *Toward a Programme of Imperial Life: the British Empire at the Turn of the Century*, Oxford, 1982, 84-8.
7 I am grateful to Lawrence and Mary James for hospitality at Sedbergh, and for information about Sedbergh's imperial connections.
8 Mangan, 'Images of Empire', 37. Mangan, *Athleticism*, 139. Patrick A. Dunae, *Gentlemen Emigrants*, Vancouver, 1981, 99.
9 Humphries, '"Hurrah for England"', 183.
10 Roberts, *Classic Slum*, 142-3 and 182.
11 Roberts, *Classic Slum*, 142. Similar celebrations are described in R. Blythe, *Akenfield*, London, 1972, 146.
12 The song was burlesqued by G. K. Chesterton in 'Geography' from his *Songs of Education*: 'So that Lancashire merchants whenever they like Can water the beer of a man in Klondike Or poison the meat of a man in Bombay; And that is the meaning of Empire Day.'
13 J. O. Springhall, 'Lord Meath, youth, and Empire', *Journal of Contemporary History*, 5, (1970), 97-111.
14 The account of the E.D.M. is based on Springhall, the annual reports of the movement, 'The Importance of Empire Knowledge and the Origins and Purpose of

Empire Day', cyclostyled history in the library of the R.C.S., and on the minute books of the E.D.M. for the period 1950-61 in the archives of the R.C.S.

15 From the programme and text of Meath's 1904 speech, prepared by the Empire Day Movement in 1905.

16 A footnote to the text of Meath's 1904 speech.

17 Earl of Meath, 'The Empire Day Movement', in *The Dominions Year-Book*, 1922, 3-17.

18 Springhall, 'Lord Meath', 107.

19 E.D.M. Annual Report, 1929, 9. This report also recorded the making of the first sound film of an E.D.M. celebration.

20 E.D.M. Annual Report, 1941.

21 This classic piece of economic imperial propaganda appeared in the E.D.M. annual reports throughout the 1930s. For economic and emigration propaganda, see also Howard Drake, 'The British Empire and What it Stands for', E.D.M. pamphlet, 1939 (price 2*d*), 2-3 and 10-11.

22 All the figures in this paragraph come from the annual reports.

23 The account of the E.Y.M. is based on the movement's annual reports and other publications, including 'Commonwealth Youth Movement: Some Notes on the History, Purpose, and Progress of the Movement' issued in connection with its 21st Anniversary in 1958.

24 Foreword to the C.Y.M. '1956 Quest'. Major Ney's activities in the 1929 Education Conference can be found in S. E. Lang, *Education and Leisure*, London, 1930.

25 John Buchan, *Memory Hold the Door*, London, 1940, 292.

26 'The Great Crusade', *Youth Sunday*, 29 April 1942. Forms of service used in broadcasts from Westminster Abbey and Washington Cathedral.

27 'The Great Crusade of Youth', E.Y.M., 1948.

28 Ten per cent of the population had a television set in 1950; 40% in 1955; and 75% in 1959. At the beginning of the decade, politics was banned from the medium, and political and public meetings and rituals continued to be well attended. It was not until 1959 that a general election was fully covered on television.

29 Hugh Cunningham, *The Volunteer Force*, London, 1975.

30 J. O. Springhall, *Youth, Empire, and Society: British Youth Movements, 1883-1940*, London, 1977, chapter 4.

31 Springhall, *Youth*, 75-6.

32 Springhall, *Youth*, chapter 1. Paul Wilkinson, 'English youth movements, 1908-1930', *Journal of Contemporary History*, 4, 2 (1969), 5.

33 Wilkinson, 'English youth', 6.

34 J. O. Springhall, 'The Boy Scouts, class and militarism in relation to British youth movements, 1908-1930', *International Review of Social History*, XVI (1971), 125-58. Victor Bailey, 'Scouting for Empire', *History Today* (July 1982), 5-9.

35 R. S. S. Baden-Powell, *Scouting for Boys*, London, 1908, 3.

36 Baden-Powell, *Scouting*, 253. A surprising amount of the original material survives in recent editions of *Scouting for Boys*. See the 1963 edition, reprinted 1981.

37 H. B. Morton, *A Hillhead Album*, Glasgow, 1973. This book is not paginated, but there are sections on both the Boys' Brigade and the Scouts' origins in the district.

38 The author was brought up in the Hillhead district of Glasgow.

39 Springhall, *Youth*, chapter 5.

40 D. H. Simpson, the historian of the first Scout troop founded in Twickenham in 1908, has pointed out to me the wide variety of objectives and enthusiasms which could go into the foundation of such Scout groups. In Twickenham the founder was a radical curate who later made the care and encouragement of working-class boys in London his special concern.

41 Michael Blanch, 'Imperialism, nationalism, and organised youth', in John Clarke *et al.*, *Working-class Culture*, London, 1979, 103-20.

42 Wilkinson, 'English youth', 3.

43 Springhall, *Youth*, 13.

44 Nevertheless, dummy rifles were not abandoned until 1926. The 16th Highland Light Infantry battalion was formed in Glasgow wholly from members and

ex-members of the Boys' Brigade. Brian Fraser, '"Sure and Stedfast" for a century', *Glasgow Herald*, 2 July 1983. See also Brian Fraser and J. O. Springhall, *Sure and Stedfast: a History of the Boys' Brigade*, Glasgow, 1983, unfortunately published too late to be used in this work.

45 Baden-Powell had an article on the Scouts in Ward Lock's *Wonder Book of Soldiers* in 1919.

46 Wilkinson, 'English youth', 18-23.

CONCLUSION

The imperial world view, with all its attendant belief systems, has frequently been referred to as a 'core ideology'. In *The Dominant Ideology Thesis* Abercrombie, Hill, and Turner attacked the concept of the core ideology, taking as examples three historical periods, medieval feudalism, the years 1790-1850, and the present day.[1] The choice is a strange one. In the case of the last two, it is difficult to argue otherwise than that they were and are times of cultural, intellectual, and social flux, in which old patterns of stability were disrupted. The period between 1850 and 1950-60 is a very different one from those which preceded and followed it. If we are to find confirmation of the dominant ideology thesis, it will be in the late nineteenth, and early twentieth centuries.

In that period an imperial nationalism, compounded of monarchism, militarism, and Social Darwinism, through which the British defined their own unique superiority *vis-à-vis* the rest of the world, was projected by the new visual culture, by advertising, the theatre, the cinema, broadcasting, the Churches, youth organisations, ritual and ceremonial, the educational system, and juvenile literature of all sorts. A whole range of propagandist imperial bodies, conventionally regarded as failures, in fact succeeded in diffusing their patriotic intentions and their world view, if not their specific and sophisticated plans of action, through almost every institution of British life.

We do of course need more precise evidence that such ideas struck home. Bratton suggests that the works of Henty and others may have done no more in 'inspiring imperialism than Gothic melodramas inspired banditry and a belief in ghosts'.[2] Her source is A. J. P. Taylor, who, despite being an avid Henty reader, regarded Henty's imperialism as 'very great nonsense'. This merely demonstrates the intellectual's habit of projecting the powerful beliefs of his formative years back into the past. Henty himself would have been disturbed to think that his ideology had no effect on his readers, but his shade can perhaps be reassured that the left-wing son of a middle-class household was scarcely typical, and Bratton was surely injudicious to regard him as such. In fact such a view seems hard to sustain against the overwhelming concentration of children's and other literature on imperial subjects in every area of publishing, taken together with all the other media surveyed in this book. Again, it is necessary to free ourselves from the case of mistaken identity which has so bedevilled understanding of the period. The imperialism imparted was not of course the imperialism of complex and sophisticated theorising. It was an imperial world view, made up of patriotic, military, and racial ideas only vaguely located in specific imperial contexts, glorifying violence and a sense of national superiority.

The evidence we have from ordinary sources is infinitely more valuable than that of any number of anecdotal historians influenced by the intellectual, but not popular, trends of the 1920s and '30s. Oral evidence compiled by Humphries is particularly precious, and the testimony he secured suggests that imperialism had an especially powerful influence upon his informants in their schooldays and after.[3] Working-class memoirs of the period are strikingly consistent in noting the chauvinism and fascination with royalty, the armed forces, and race. This message emerges strongly from Robert Tressel's classic *The Ragged Trousered Philanthropists*, the descriptions of working-class culture in Swindon and Salford by Alfred Williams and Robert Roberts, and the autobiographies of Harry Pollitt and Willie Gallacher.[4] And, as described in chapter 2, H. M. Hyndman noted the remarkably patriotic fervour of the poorest of the working-class districts of London during the Boer War. The fervent participation of vast crowds in royal ceremonial — indeed, the pressure for more elaborate ritual seemed to come from below at the time of Victoria's greatest reluctance — offers further evidence.[5]

In fact, as Robert Roberts in particular makes clear, the British had created a popular cultural dimension to match their remodelling of the world through economic and political control. That control could be exercised all the more confidently and be better understood by the public at large through the manufacture of cultural images and racial stereotypes. Control — or the illusion of control — was exerted not just by a dominant imperial, military, and settler caste, but was open to all classes contributing to the image-making process. The working class in Britain could participate in the rule of others — and be fed cheaply into the bargain — either indirectly at home or directly in the army or as settlers overseas. They were constantly reminded by missionaries and other agencies of their own good fortune, and their own lot was contrasted by teachers and clerics, school texts and popular literature, with that of peoples in the Empire. The same message was proclaimed by the containers of every beverage they drank, and in a host of advertisements and packagings. Thus through the colonial connection domestic 'under-classes' could become imperial 'over-classes'. They could feel part of a national enterprise on which the majority had been persuaded to agree, an enterprise conducted by the State and great commercial companies, protected by the army and navy, and sanctified by the Church. It was an enterprise tinged with a sense of moral crusade, aided by periodic war, led by charismatic figures, both alive and dead. In its ancestor worship, its ritual, its emphasis on authority, it linked tribal atavisms with cultural self-satisfaction and technical advance.

Nor did these ideas vanish with the First World War. As George Orwell wrote of the Great War in 1940:

> As the war fell back into the past, my particular generation, those who had been 'just too young', became conscious of the vastness of the experience they had missed. You felt yourself a little less than a man because you had missed it. I spent the years 1922-7 mostly among men a little older than myself who had been through the war. They talked about it unceasingly, with horror, of course, but also with a steadily growing nostalgia. You can see this nostalgia perfectly clearly in the English war-books. Besides, the pacifist reaction was only a phase, and even the 'just too young' had all been trained for war. Most of the English middle class are trained for war from the cradle onwards, not technically but morally. The earliest political slogan I can remember is 'We want eight (eight dreadnoughts) and we won't wait'. At seven years old I was a member of the Navy League and wore a sailor suit with H.M.S. *Invincible* on my cap. Even before my public-school O.T.C. I had been in a private school cadet corps. On and off, I have been toting a rifle every since I was ten, in preparation not only for war but for a particular kind of war....[6]

All that had happened, as he noted elsewhere, was that the 'really important fact about so many of the English intelligentsia' in the inter-war years was 'their severance from the common culture of the country'.[7] However much the old late nineteenth-century values might be derided, they continued to be propagated through the most significant popular cultural forms of the day. The jingoistic music hall gave way to the jingoistic cinema. War films proliferated in the 1920s. Social Darwinism and imperial developmental concepts underlay all the expedition, documentary, and newsreel material of the time. The great imperial epics of Alexander Korda and Michael Balcon were among the most popular films of the 1930s, and they were repeatedly reissued during and after the Second World War. The imperial adventure tradition continued to dominate juvenile literature, comics and the annuals which became such a feature of children's publishing. Commercial, religious, and military agencies were no less assiduous in using all the printing and photographic techniques available to them in the inter-war years. Indeed, these materials may have enjoyed an even wider social distribution than before, given the continuing fall in relative costs and the survival and development of collecting manias. It was, for example, the 'golden age' of the cigarette card. A generation brought up on imperial concepts before the First World War matured to propagate them after it. These were the years of the greatest exhibitions of them all, the years of continuing expansion of the youth movements, less militaristic perhaps, but no less imperial and patriotic in their objectives.

Thus it is possible to argue that imperial themes secured greater cultural penetration in the period following the First World War, and indeed prolonged their shelf life until the 1950s. It is true that some internationalist ideas had come to be emphasised in, for example, the youth organisations, but it was an internationalism which continued to be based on an essentially white community: Europe, the United States, and the Dominions. It supplemented rather than cut across the world view created by imperial rule. League of Nations internationalism did not seem in any way incompatible with a sense of racial superiority bred on Social Darwinism or notions of 'development' engendered in imperial propaganda on economic, medical, scientific, and cultural themes. The British Empire, indeed, was often portrayed as a model for the League of Nations. Post-Versailles internationalism merely developed concepts of trusteeship which had emerged from the First World War, ideas that were themselves based upon a vision of a beneficent, idealistic imperialism, an imperialism controlled and made internationally accountable.

That imperial propaganda should have developed along these lines is not particularly surprising. If in the nineteenth and early twentieth centures it was concerned to glorify the combination of military adventure and aggressive expansionist Christian culture, by the end of the First World War it was seeking apologias of two sorts, the economic necessity of Empire to both rulers and ruled, and the international trust involved in that relationship. The first was designed to justify Empire to the British population at home and abroad, at a time when South Africa, Australia, and New Zealand were themselves taking up imperial responsibilities. The second was designed to give the enterprise international respectability. It should be remembered that the inter-war years were the era of classic imperialism in Africa. Only then did administrative consolidation take place after the pre-war 'pacification', and only then did the exploitation of resources like Zambian copper become practicable.

It is perhaps possible to add a third phase to imperial propaganda. If it was strongly militarist before the First World War, and both economic and idealistic after it, by the end of the Second the theme of economic exploitation had ceased to be respectable, despite the Colonial Development and Welfare Acts. The new propaganda was concerned with a variety of cultures united in liberal constitutional advance. The white Dominions had seemed to prove that constitutional developments strengthened moral purpose. Such would be the case in Asia, and, much later, in Africa, if only beneficent education and Christian influences could render Afro-Asian peoples receptive. These three phases of propaganda can be identified in official approaches, in the work of the Imperial Institute, the short-lived Empire Marketing Board, the imperial exhibitions, and were reflected to a certain extent in the concerns of school textbooks. However, the propaganda of popular literature and the cinema was of course much cruder, and more closely related to the simple imperial world view.

All three phases contributed to the complacent habit of superiority which created what might be called 'protected markets of the mind' in Britain, intellectual shells which were only really shattered, like their economic equivalents, in the 1960s. A last generation of schoolchildren was raised on the moral certainties of imperial rule in the 1950s. The sentiments of the old school textbooks still prevailed; much children's literature continued to be pale, updated versions of the late nineteenth-century imperial classics; the cinema, both in feature films and in Saturday morning children's serials, continued to portray adventure in imperial settings, grappling with peoples at best quaint, at worst treacherous, and in both cases requiring a strong hand to lead them in paths designed for their own good. Youth organisations, Empire annuals, and a multitude of children's publications continued to carry an imperial message of missionary, administrative, and commercial endeavour that would lead to the betterment of all.

There is ample evidence of a conscious effort to propagate such ideas. Theatrical, and above all cinema, censorship indicates this, as do education manuals, the avowed aims of the controllers of broadcasting, of many popular writers, of the leaders of youth organisations, the creators of exhibitions, and the publishers of ephemera, as well as the makers of both feature and documentary films. In fact, a generation tutored in the years before and during the First World War came to hold the levers of propaganda of the inter-war period. It was a legacy that proved enduring. Even the spectacle and pageantry of the imperial monarchy survived into another age. Royal weddings, jubilees, and births apparently satisfied a mass emotional need, while television documentaries continued to intone the myths of the thousand-year tradition.[8] Just as the pageantry surrounding Victoria grew as her personal power waned, so national ritual became a nostalgic solace for lost power. The patriotic fervour and orchestrated spectacle of naval and military homecomings after the Anglo-Argentine war revealed the old nineteenth-century magic still at work. The dominant ideology had not entirely lost its grip.

Of all the systems of social discipline applied in the late nineteenth century, it was the imperial core ideology which worked best. Both the Church and controls at the workplace failed. 'Rational recreation' succeeded precisely in those patriotic, xenophobic, imperialist areas which fitted, but greatly developed, an existing tradition. The Empire was remote from everyday experience, yet apparently crucially influencing it for the better. The public had little to set against a patriotic imperialism, and the critics of Empire never really broke through. As the Falklands war demonstrated yet again, criticism of what can too easily be depicted as patriotic endeavour is always politically dangerous. In imperial propaganda, the middle class were able to dress economic benefits in idealistic garb, substituting moral crusade for mercenary motive, romance and adventure for political and military aggression. The values and beliefs of the imperial world view settled like a sediment in the consciousness of the British people, to be stirred again by a brief, renewed challenge in the late twentieth century.

NOTES

1 Abercrombie *et al.*, *The Dominant Ideology Thesis*.
2 Bratton, *Victorian Children's Fiction*, 200.
3 Humphries, *Hooligans or Rebels?* 41-3.
4 R. Tressell, *The Ragged Trousered Philanthropists*, London, 1914. J. Mitchell, *Robert Tressell and the Ragged Trousered Philanthropists*, London, 1969. Alfred Williams, *Life in a Railway Factory*, Newton Abbot, 1969. Roberts, *Classic Slum*. Harry Pollitt, *Serving my Time*, London, 1940. William Gallacher, *Revolt on the Clyde*, London, 1936.
5 Lant, *Insubstantial Pageant*, 31 and *passim*.
6 Orwell, 'My country right or left', 589.
7 Orwell, *Lion and the Unicorn*, 63.
8 B.B.C. TV documentary, 'Nobody minded the rain', thirtieth anniversary of the coronation of Elizabeth II, 2 June 1983. The coronation was portrayed in this as 'the dawn of a new age', the creator of 'new hope for Britain'. In fact it represented the end of an eighty-year tradition, and heralded the 'I'm all right, Jack', 'never had it so good' era of complacency.

SOURCES

PRIMARY

British Library Manuscripts Collection: Lord Chamberlain's Plays.
Grange Museum of Local History, London Borough of Brent: Collections of ephemera and other items on the British Empire Exhibition, Wembley.
Public Record Office, Kew: Records of the Imperial Institute, files P.R.O. 30/76/1-309.
Royal Commonwealth Society Library: Annual Reports and other materials of the Empire Day Movement, 1929-58. Annual Reports and other materials on the Empire Youth Movement, 1938-1958. Collections of ephemera, sheet music, etc. on various imperial and other events.

SECONDARY
Articles

Abbreviations: AJST *Australian Journal of Screen Theory,* BH *Business History,* EHR *English Historical Review,* HJ *Historical Journal,* HJFRTV *Historical Journal of Film, Radio, and Television,* HT *History Today,* HW *History Workshop,* IRSH *International Review of Social History,* JCH *Journal of Contemporary History,* JEAH *Journal of Educational Administration and History,* JICH *Journal of Imperial and Commonwealth History,* JPC *Journal of Popular Culture,* JRSA *Journal of the Royal Society of Arts,* JSH *Journal of Social History,* P&P *Past and Present,* SH *Southern History,* TLS *Times Literary Supplement,* UE *United Empire,* VS *Victorian Studies.*

Anderson, Olive, 'The growth of Christian militarism in mid-Victorian Britain, *EHR,* LXXXVI, 1971, 46-72.
Bailey, Victor, 'Scouting for Empire', *HT,* July 1982, 5-9.
Bartlett, J. Neville, 'Alexander Pirie and Sons of Aberdeen and the expansion of the British paper industry', *BH,* XXII, 1980, 18-34.
Brabazon, Earl of Meath, 'State-directed colonisation', *National Review,* 1887, 525-37.
Bradley, Kenneth, 'The Commonwealth Institute', *Corona,* X, 1958, 222-4.
Bradley, Kenneth, 'The Imperial Institute, *JRSA,* 105, 1956-57, 871-87.
Burroughs, Peter, 'John R. Seeley and British imperial history', *JICH,* 1, 1972-73, 191-211.
Cunningham, Hugh, 'The language of patriotism, 1750/1914', *HW,* 12, 1981, 8-33.
Cunningham, Hugh, 'Jingoism in 1877-78', *VS,* XIV, 1971, 429-53.
Davin, Anna, 'Imperialism and motherhood', *HW,* 5, 1978, 9-65.
Dunae, Patrick A., 'Boys' literature and the idea of Empire, 1870-1914', *VS,* 24, 1980, 105-21.
Dunae, Patrick A., 'Boys' literature and the idea of race', *Wascana Review,* spring 1977, 84-107.
Dunae, Patrick A., 'Making good: the Canadian west in British boys' literature, 1890-1914', *Praire Forum,* 4, 1979, 165-81.
Dunae, Patrick A., 'Penny dreadfuls: late nineteenth-century boys' literature and crime', *VS,* 22, 1979, 133-50.
Falconer, J., 'The photograph collection of the Royal Commonwealth Society', *Photographic Collector,* V, 1981, 34-53.
Fraser, Brian, '"Sure and Stedfast" for a century', *Glasgow Herald,* 2 July 1983.
Green, William A., 'The crest of Empire', *VS,* XVIII, 1975, 345-54.
Greenlee, J. G., 'Imperial studies and the unity of the Empire', *JICH,* VII, 1979, 321-35.
Hammerton, Elizabeth, and Cannadine, David, 'Conflict and consensus on a ceremonial occasion: the Diamond Jubilee in Cambridge in 1897', *HJ,* 24, 1981, 111-46.
Harrison Brian, 'For Church, Queen, and family: the Girls' Friendly Society, 1874-1920', *P&P,* 61, 1973, 107-38.

[259]

Hudson, Rt. Hon, Viscount, 'The future of the Imperial Institute', *UE*, XLVI, 1955, 8-10.

Humphries, S., "Hurrah for England": schooling and the working class in Bristol, 1870-1914', *SH*, 1, 1979, 172.

Hurt, J. S., 'Drill, discipline, and the elementary school ethos', in Phillip McCann (ed.), *Popular Education and Socialisation in the Nineteenth Century*, London, 1977.

James, Louis, 'Tom Brown's imperial sons', *VS*, 17, 1973, 89-99.

Johnson, Douglas H., 'The death of Gordon: a Victorian myth', *JICH*, X, 1982, 285-310.

Jones, Gareth Stedman, 'Class expression versus social control? A critique of recent trends in the social history of leisure', *HW*, 4, 1977, 163.

Jones, Gareth Stedman, 'Working-class culture and working-class politics in London, 1870-1900', *JSH*, 7, 1973, 460-508.

Kiernan, Victor, 'Working class and Nation in Nineteenth-Century Britain' in Maurice Cornforth (ed.) *Rebels and their Causes*, London, 1978, 123-139.

Koss, Stephen, 'Wesleyanism and Empire', *HJ*, XVIII, 1975, 110.

Lavin, Deborah, 'History, morals, and the politics of the Empire: Lionel Curtis and the Round Table', in J. Bossy and P. Jupp (eds.), *Essays presented to Michael Roberts*, Belfast, 1976.

Loring, Arthur H., 'Imperial Federation (Defence) Committee', 1894-1906', *UE*, VI, 1916, 341-6.

Lucas, C.P., 'Imperial studies', *UE*, VI, 1916, 665-9.

MacKenzie, John M., 'By jingo', *The Listener*, 6 January 1983.

MacKenzie, John M., 'Ephemera: reflection or instrument?', *Ephemerist*, 2 June 1983, 4-7.

MacLeod, R., 'The National Service League', *UE*, VI, 1916, 893-901.

Mangan, J. A., 'Images of Empire in the late Victorian public school', *JEAH*, XII, 1980, 31.

Morris, James, 'The popularisation of imperial history', *JICH*, 1, 1973, 113-18.

Murray, C. Freeman, 'The British Empire League', *UE*, VI, 1916, 431-9.

Naidis, Mark, 'G. A. Henty's idea of India'., *VS*, 8, 1964, 49-58.

Norman, A., 'The Imperial Institute: its genesis, history, and possibilities', *Imperial Argus*, 1, January 1902, 393-407.

Pollard, Sir Frederick, 'The League of the Empire', *UE*, VI, 1916, 736-41.

Pronay, Nicholas, 'The newsreels: the illusion of actuality', in Paul Smith (ed.), *The Historian and Film*, Cambridge, 1976.

Reid, Fred, and Washbrook, David, 'Kipling' Kim, and imperialism', *HT*, August 1982, 14-20.

Richards, Jeffrey, 'Spreading the gospel of self-help: G. A. Henty and Samuel Smiles', *JPC*, 16, 1982, 52-65.

Richards, Jeffrey, 'The Smith of Smiths', *Lancaster Comment*, 118, 1982, 14-5.

Richards, Jeffrey, 'Korda's Empire', *AJCT*, 5-6, 1979, 122-37.

Richards, Jeffrey, 'The British Board of Films Censors and content control in the 1930s: images of Britain', *HJFRTV*, 1, 1981, 95-116, and 'Foreign affairs', *HJFRTV*, 2, 1982, 39-48.

Robbins, Keith, 'Sir Edward Grey and the British Empire', *JICH*, 1, 1972-3, 3-21.

Sanders, M. L., 'Wellington House and British propaganda during the First World War', *HJ*, XVIII, 1975, 119-46.

Sargent, E. B., 'The Victoria League', *UE*, VI, 1916, 588-94.

Senelick, Lawrence, 'Politics as entertainment: Victorian music-hall songs', *VS*, XIX, 1975, 149-80.

Springhall, J. O., 'Lord Meath, youth, and Empire', *JCH*, 5, 1970, 97-111.

Springhall, J. O., 'The Boy Scouts, class, and militarism in relation to British youth movements, 1908-1930', *IRSH*, XVI, 1971, 125-58.

Springhall, J. O., 'The rise and fall of Henty's empire', *TLS*, 3 October 1968.

Summers, Anne, 'Militarism in Britain before the Great War', *HW*, 2, 1976, 104-23.

Swann, Paul, 'John Grierson and the G.P.O. Film Unit, 1933-39', *HJFRTV*, 3, 1983, 17-34.

Taylor, John, 'From self-help to glamour: the working-men's club, 1860-1972', *HW* pamphlet, No. 7, 1972.

Walthew, Kenneth, 'The British Empire Exhibition', *HT*, 31, August 1981, 34-9.

SOURCES

Wilkinson Paul, 'English youth movements, 1908-1930', *JCH*, 4, 1969, 3-23

Worsfold, W. Basil, 'The Imperial Federation League, 1884-1893', *UE*, VI, 1916, 263-73.

Books and theses
(School textbooks and popular and juvenile works are not included in this list)

Abercrombie, N., Hill, S., and Turner, Bryan A., *The Dominant Ideology Thesis*, London, 1980.

Aldgate, Anthony, *Cinema and History*, London, 1979.

Allen, Alistair, *A History of Printed Scraps*, London, 1983.

Allwood, John, *The Great Exhibitions*, London, 1977.

Archer, R. L., *The Teaching of History in Elementary Schools*, London, 1916.

Arnold, Guy, *Held Fast for England: G. A. Henty, Imperialist Boys' Writer*, London, 1980.

Attlee, Clement, *Empire into Commonwealth*, London, 1961.

Baden-Powell, R. S. S., *Scouting for Boys*, London, 1908 and 1963.

Baglee, Christopher, and Morley, Andrew, *Street Jewellery*, London, 1978.

Bagnall, Dorothy, *Collecting Cigarette Cards*, London, 1978.

Bailey, Peter, *Leisure and Class in Victorian England: Rational Recreation and the Contest for Control, 1830-85*, London, 1978.

Baker, P. S., 'The Social and Ideological Role of the Monarchy in Late Victorian Britain', Lancaster M. A. thesis, 1978.

Barnicoat, John, *A Concise History of Posters*, London, 1979.

Blanch, M. D. 'Nation, Empire, and the Birmingham Working Class', University of Birmingham Ph.D. thesis, 1975.

Bolt, Christine, *Victorian Attitudes towards Race*, London, 1971.

Bond, Brian, and Roy, Ian, *War and Society: a Yearbook of Military History*, London, 1975.

Booth, Michael, *English Melodrama*, London, 1965.

Booth, Michael, *Victorian Spectacular Theatre, 1850-1910*, London, 1981.

Bradby, David, *et al.* (eds.), *Performance and Politics in Popular Drama*, Cambridge, 1980.

Brandreth, Gyles, *I Scream for Ice Cream: Pearls from the Pantomime*, London, 1974.

Bratton, J. S., *The Victorian Popular Ballad*, London, 1975.

Bratton, J. S., *The Impact of Victorian Children's Fiction*, London, 1981.

Buckland, Gail, *Reality Recorded: Early Documentary Photography*, Newton Abbot, 1974.

Byatt, Anthony, *Picture Postcards and their Publishers*, Malvern, 1978.

Carrington, Charles, *Rudyard Kipling*, London, 1970.

Chancellor, Valerie E., *History for their Masters*, London, 1970.

Clair, Colin, *A History of Printing in Britain*, London, 1965.

Clarke, John *et al.* (eds.), *Working-class Culture*, London, 1979.

Constantine, Stephen, *The Making of British Colonial Development Policy, 1914-40*, London, forthcoming.

Cowham, Joseph H., *A New School Method*, London, 1900.

Crossick, Geoffrey, *The Lower Middle Class in Britain*, London, 1977.

Cunningham, Hugh, *Leisure in the Industrial Revolution*, London, 1980.

Cunningham, Hugh, *The Volunteer Force*, London, 1975.

Curran, James, and Porter, Vincent (eds.), *British Cinema History*, London, 1983.

Denison, George T., *The Struggle for Imperial Unity*, London, 1909.

Dixon, Bob, *Catching Them Young*, 2 vols., Sex, Race, and Class in children's fiction and Political Ideas in children's fiction, London, 1977.

Drummond, Ian M., *British Economic Policy and the Empire, 1919-39*, London, 1972.

Doggett, Frank, *Cigarette Cards and Novelties*, London, 1981.

Dunae, Patrick A., *Gentlemen Emigrants*, Vancouver, 1981.

Durgnat, Raymond, *A Mirror for England*, London, 1970.

Ehrlich, Cyril, *The Piano: a History*, London, 1976.

SOURCES

Eldridge, C. C., *The Imperial Idea in the Age of Gladstone and Disraeli, 1868-1880*, London, 1973.

Erickson, Charlotte, *Emigration from Europe, 1815-1914*, London, 1976.

Faber, Richard, *The Vision and the Need*, London, 1966.

Field, H. John, *Toward a Programme of Imperial Life*, Oxford, 1982.

Findlater, Richard, *Banned! A Review of Theatrical Censorship in Britain*, London, 1967.

Firth, Catherine B., *The Learning of History in Elementary Schools*, London, 1932.

Fleming, Tom, *Voices out of the Air: the Royal Christmas Broadcasts, 1932-81*, London, 1981.

Fletcher, F. A., and Brooks, A. D., *British Exhibitions and their Postcards*, Parts I and II, 1978 and 1979.

Ford, Colin, and Harrison, Brian, *A Hundred Years Ago*, London, 1983.

Franklin, M. J., *British Biscuit Tins*, London, 1979.

Fraser, Brian, and Springhall, J. O., *Sure and Stedfast: a History of the Boys' Brigade*, Glasgow, 1983.

Fraser, W. Hamish, *The Coming of the Mass Market, 1850-1914*, London, 1981.

Girouard, Mark, *The Return to Camelot, Chivalry and the English Gentleman*, New Haven, 1981.

Gibbs-Smith, G. H., *The Great Exhibition of 1851*. London, 1950.

Gloversmith, Frank (ed.), *Class, Culture, and Social Change*, Sussex, 1980.

Goldsworthy, David, *Colonial Issues in British Politics, 1945-6*, Oxford, 1971.

Gray, Robert Q , *The Aristocracy of Labour in Nineteenth-century Britain, c. 1850-1914*, London, 1981.

Green, Martin, *Dreams of Adventure, Deeds of Empire*, London, 1980.

Griffith, David, *Decorative Printed Tins*, London, 1979.

Gunn, Hugh (ed.), *The British Empire*, 12 vols., London, 1924.

Gupta, P. S., *Imperialism and the British Labour Movement, 1914-64*, London, 1975.

Hammerton A. James, *Emigrant Gentlewomen*, London, 1979.

Hannas, Linda, *The Jigsaw Book*, New York, 1981.

Hardie, Frank, *The Political Influence of the British Monarchy*, London, 1970.

Hardy, Forsyth, *John Grierson*, London, 1979.

Hardy, Forsyth, (ed.), *Grierson on Documentary*, London, 1979.

Haste, Cate, *Keep the Home Fires Burning*, London, 1977.

Heider, Karl G., *Ethnographic Film*, Austin, Texas, 1976.

Howlett, Geoffrey, *A History of Wembley*, Brent, 1979.

Hobsbawm, E. J., *Labouring Men*, London, 1964.

Hobsbawm, E. J., *Industry and Empire*, London, 1969.

Hobsbawm, E. J., and Ranger, T. O., *The Invention of Tradition*, Cambridge, 1983.

Hobson, J. A., *The Psychology of Jingoism*, London, 1901.

Holt, Tonie, and Valmai, *Picture Postcards of the Golden Age*, London, 1978.

Howarth, Patrick, *Play up and Play the Game*, London, 1973.

Humphries, Stephen, *Hooligans or Rebels?*, Oxford, 1981.

Hurt, J. S., *Elementary Schooling and the Working Classes, 1860-1918*, London, 1979.

Hyndman, H. M., *Further Reminiscences*, London, 1912.

Jeffrey, Ian, *Photography: a Concise History*, London, 1981.

Lant, Jeffrey L., *Insubstantial Pageant*, London, 1979.

Lorimer, Douglas A., *Colour, Class, and the Victorians*, Leicester, 1978.

Love, Brian, *Play the Game*, London, 1978.

Love, Brian, *Great Board Games*, London, 1979.

Low, Rachael, and Manvell, Roger, *The History of the British Film, 1896-1906*, London, 1948.

Low, Rachael, *The History of the British Film, 1906-1914*, London, 1948.

Low, Rachael, *The History of the British Film, 1914-18*, London, 1950.

Low, Rachael, *The History of the British Film, 1918-29*, London, 1971.

Low, Rachael, *Films of Comment and Persuasion of the 1930s: the History of the British Film, 1929-1939*, London, 1979.

SOURCES

Low, Rachael, *Documentary and Educational Films of the 1930s*, London, 1979.

Lubbock, Mark, *The Complete Book of Light Opera*, London, 1962.

Lucas, C. P., *The British Empire: Six Lectures*, London, 1915.

Macdonald, G., *Camera*, London, 1979.

MacKenzie, J. M., and Dunae, Patrick, (eds.), *Imperialism and Popular Culture*, Manchester, forthcoming.

Mackerness, E. D., *A Social History of English Music*, London, 1964.

Mander, R., and Mitchenson, J., *British Music Hall*, London, 1965.

Mangan, J. A., *Athleticism in the Victorian and Edwardian Public School*, Cambridge, 1981.

Mellor, G. J., *The Northern Music Hall*, Newcastle-upon-Tyne, 1970.

Morris, James, *Farewell the Trumpets*, London, 1979.

Morton, H. B., *A Hillhead Album*, London, 1973.

Newton, A. P., and Ewing, J., *The British Empire since 1783*, London, 1929.

Nimocks, Walter, *Milner's Young Men*, London, 1970.

Noble, Peter, *The Negro in Films*, New York, 1970.

Orwell, George, *The Lion and the Unicorn*, London, 1982.

Orwell, George, *Collected Essays, Journalism, and Letters of George Orwell*, 4 vols., edited by Sonia Orwell and Ian Angus, London, 1970.

Pasold, Eric, *Ladybird, Ladybird*, Manchester, 1977.

Parr, Joy, *Labouring Children*, London, 1980.

Pearsall, Ronald, *Edwardian Popular Music*, Newton Abbot, 1975.

Pearsall, Ronald, *Victorian Popular Music*, Newton Abbot, 1973.

Pearsall, Ronald, *Victorian Sheet Music Covers*, Newton Abbot, 1972.

Pelling, Henry, *Popular Politics and Society in Late Victorian Britain*, London, 1979.

Phillips, Janet and Peter, *Victorians at Home and Away*, London, 1978.

Plumb, J. H., *The Death of the Past*, London, 1969.

Porter, B., *Critics of Empire*, London, 1968.

Price, Richard, *An Imperial War and the British Working Class*, London, 1972.

Pronay, Nicholas, and Spring, D. W. (eds.), *Propaganda, Politics, and Film, 1918-45*, London, 1982.

Quayle, Eric, *Ballantyne the Brave*, London, 1967.

Reese, Trevor R., *The History of the Royal Commonwealth Society*, London, 1968.

Rein, G. A., *Sir John Robert Seeley: a Study of the Historian* (ed. and trans. John L. Herkless), Dover, N.H., 1983.

Richards, Jeffrey, *Visions of Yesterday*, London, 1973.

Richards, Jeffrey, *The Age of the Dream Palace: Cinema and Society in Britain, 1930-39*, London, 1984.

Rickards, Maurice, and Moody, Michael, *The First World War: Ephemera, Mementoes, Documents*, London, 1975.

Robb, J. H., *The Primrose League, 1883-1906*, New York, 1942.

Roberts, Robert, *The Classic Slum*, Manchester, 1971.

Rotha, Paul, *Documentary Film*, London, 1936.

Rotha, Paul, *Documentary Diary*, London, 1973.

Sanders, M. L., and Taylor, Philip M., *British Propaganda during the First World War*, London, 1982.

Sandison, Alan, *The Wheel of Empire*, London, 1967.

Scott, Harold, *The Early Doors: Origins of the Music Hall*, London, 1946.

Semmel, Bernard, *Imperialism and Social Reform*, London, 1960.

Simon, Brian, and Bradley, Ian, (eds.), *The Victorian Public School*, London, 1975.

Skelley, Jeffrey (ed.), *The General Strike, 1926*, London, 1976.

Springhall, J. O., *Youth, Empire, and Society*, London, 1977.

Staff, F., *The Picture Postcard and its Origins*, London, 1979.

Staff, F., *The Picture Postcard and Travel*, London, 1979.

Steinberg, S. H., *Five Hundred Years of Printing*, London, 1955.

Stephens, J. R., *The Censorship of the English Drama, 1824-1901*, Cambridge, 1980.

Storch, Robert D. (ed.), *Popular Culture and Custom in Nineteenth Century England*, London, 1982.

SOURCES

Summerfield, Penny, 'The Imperial Idea and the Music Hall,' University of Sussex B.A. dissertation, 1973.

Sussex, Elizabeth, *The Rise and Fall of British Documentary*, Berkeley, Cal., 1975.

Tallents, S. G., *The Projection of England*, London, 1932.

Taylor, Philip M., *The Projection of Britain: British Overseas Publicity and Propaganda, 1919-39*, Cambridge, 1981.

Thomas, Alan, *The Expanding Eye, London, 1978.*

Thornton, A. P., *For the File on Empire*, London, 1968

Thorpe, Frances, and Pronay, Nicholas, *British Official Films in the Second World War*, Oxford, 1980.

Trewin, J. C., *The Edwardian Theatre*, Oxford, 1976.

Turner, E. S., *Boys will be Boys*, London, 1975.

Wagner, Gillian, *Children of the Empire*, London, 1982.

Warwick, Peter (ed.), *The South African War*, London, 1980.

Welton, James, *Principles and Methods of Teaching*, London, 1924.

Wiener, Martin S., *English Culture and the Decline of the Industrial Spirit, 1850-1980*, Cambridge, 1981.

Willis, Fred, *101 Jubilee Road, London S.E.*, London, 1948.

Yeo, Eileen, and Stephen (eds.), *Popular Culture and Class Conflict, 1590-1914*, Sussex, 1981.

INDEX

INDEX

INDEX

INDEX

Mazawattee, 26
C.W.S., 26
Ty-phoo, 157
Tell England, 81
Temperley, H. W. V., 169
Temple, Archbishop, 238
Tenen, I., 191
Tennyson, Alfred Lord, 4, 101, 102, 125, 186, 192, 215
Territorials, 154, 234, 247
Theatre Royal, Drury Lane, 45, 47, 56, 236
Theatre Royal, Haymarket, 45
Thomas, Lowell, 33, 80
Thomson, D. C., & Co., 219
Tilby, A. Wyatt, 165
The Times, 102, 109, 129, 167, 231
Tit Bits, 203
Tobacco companies
 W. D. & H. O. Wills, 24, 25
 Player, John, 24, 25
 Ogden, 24
 Churchman, 24, 25
 Gallahers, 25
 Lambert & Butler, 25
Toc H, 136
Topreef, Tom, 47, 71
Tournier, Fleury, 115
Toy soldiers, 28
Toynbee, Arnold, 167
Toynbee Hall, 241
Trade, Board of, 128
Trades Union Congress, 229
Travancore, 140
Tressel, Robert, 254
Triple Entente, 117
Triumph, 219
Tupper, Sir Charles, 151
Turner & Newall, 132
Turner, Bryan A., 253
Turner, E. S., 218
Tweedsmuir, Lady, 223
Tweedsmuir, Lord, 141
Tyrrell, Lord, 78
Udaipur, 140
Under the British Flag, 49
Under Two Flags, 89
Union Jack (1880), 203, 210
Union Jack (1894), 204, 219
Union of Students of Black Descent, 110
United Empire, 168, 169, 182
United Empire Trade League, 158
United Radical Club, 61
United States, 69, 77, 84,85, 88, 92, 100, 106 111, 113, 153, 164, 166, 188, 242, 247, 248

Unwin, T. Fisher (publisher), 214
Urban Bioscope Expedition, 73
Urban, Charles, Trading Company, 73
Urban and Paul (film co.), 70
Vane, Sir Francis, 241, 247
Vanier, G. P., 135
Vansittart, Sir Robert, 89
Vereeniging, Peace of, 70
Verne, Jules, 203
Versailles, 43
The Viceroy, 49
Victoria League, 136, 152-3, 163, 165, 169, 170
Victoria, Queen, 4, 5, 8, 20, 21, 27, 43, 53, 72, 79, 122-4, 182, 221, 234, 254
Victoria the Great, 89
Victory Leaders, 81
Vidor, King, 81
Vine, Sir Somers, 126
Volunteer Force, 6, 31, 48, 68, 154, 228, 240, 241, 242
Wagner, Gillian, 160
Wake up, England, 50
Wakefield, Viscount, 131
Wallace, Edgar, 208, 218
The War in Abyssinia, 48
The War in Zululand, 48
War Office, 164, 242; Cinematograph Committee, 75; Topical Committee, 75
War Weapons Week, 235
Ward Lock (publisher), 222, 223
Warne, Frederick (publisher), 213
Warren, Sir Herbert, 169
Waterlow (publisher), 164
Watkin, Sir Edward, 107
Webb, Sidney, 159
Welldon's Illustrated Dressmaker, 26
Wellington, Duke of, 47, 60, 181, 183
Wells, H. G., 10, 202, 217
Welton, James, 177
West Indies, 98, 175, 221, 242
Westerman, Percy, F., 218, 222, 223
West of Zanzibar, 90
Westminster Review, 151
Westminster, Statute of, 188, 217
What we are Fighting for, 75
White City, 101, 103, 105, 108, 112, 115, 152
White, E. S., 174
Wiener, Martin, 8
Wilcox, Herbert, 83, 89, 112
Wild Boys of London, 201
Wilhelm II, 53
Wilkinson, Paul, 246, 248